FORDHAM

The Early Years

FORDHAM
The Early Years

A COMMEMORATION
OF THE JESUITS' ARRIVAL IN 1846

Edited by
Thomas C. Hennessy, S.J.

Foreword by
Joseph A. O'Hare, S.J.

Papers by
Cornelius Michael Buckley, S.J.
Francis X. Curran, S.J.
Allan S. Gilbert and Roger Wines
James Hennesey, S.J.
Thomas C. Hennessy, S.J.
James R. Kelly
John W. Padberg, S.J.
Thomas J. Shelley

SOMETHING MORE PUBLICATIONS

378.747275
F712

This book is being distributed by the Fordham University Press

Library of Congress Catalogue Number 98-61574
ISBN 0-9622889-8-5

Layout, design and cover by George McCauley

This book is dedicated
to the Jesuits at Fordham
whom I have known since 1941,
as an expression of admiration
for their learning
and their educational and religious endeavors,
and in gratitude
for the gracious fraternal assistance
many have given the editor
to make this book a reality.

FOREWORD

The uses of history are many. Stories of our past, particularly of colorful characters like some of those recalled in these essays, can tickle our curiosity and stretch our imaginations. When such stories also nourish the institutional memory of a university, they can help clarify and confirm its institutional identity. Finally, when history recalls great deeds done by great-hearted pioneers, it can offer inspiration and direction to those who might otherwise be intimidated by the uncertainties of the present moment. This volume of essays, which explores the circumstances of the first generation of Jesuits to come to Rose Hill in 1846, contains generous measures of interest, instruction and inspiration for any contemporary reader, whose own life has been engaged at some point with the life of Fordham University, which now spans 156 years.

Many lessons can be drawn from this genial evocation of Fordham's origins, traced from a variety of complementary perspectives, For this reader, three lessons, above all, stand out: the web of relationships that inextricably link Fordham's beginnings to the early challenges confronting the Catholic Church in the United States; the importance of the geographical location of New York City as a defining influence on the development of Fordham as a Jesuit enterprise; and the similarities and differences between that first generation of Jesuits, who came to the new world of North America from the old world of Europe and their successors today, who stand on the threshold of a new millennium.

As these essays demonstrate in compelling fashion, Fordham University was born in response to the needs of an immigrant church that sought to care for its people in a new land, one bright with promise but dominated by a Protestant culture and clouded by anti-Catholic discrimination. Fordham's founder, John Hughes, was a national leader of this new Catholic population. His fierce advocacy of Catholic interests in New York set off national echoes as well. The establishment of St. John's College, along with other Catholic schools and institutions, was only one of the ways in which this first archbishop of New York secured a place for his people in their new land, Another link sealing the origins of the university to those of the church in New York was embodied in the first President of what was to become Fordham University, John McCloskey, who later became the first American Cardinal.

The historic decision of the French Jesuits accepting the invitation of Archbishop Hughes to come to New York and assume responsibility for his new college was not an easy one, nor was it one that the Jesuits working at St. Mary's College in Kentucky welcomed with uniform enthusiasm. Their relationship with Hughes would have its share of rebuffs and 'mutual misunderstanding. But it was a decision that was thoroughly Ignatian in both principle and in process, as the careful analysis of reasons for the move by Father Jean Baptiste Hus, S.J., documents. The driving principle behind the decision was the search for the greater good to be achieved by the commitment of limited Jesuit resources. The conclusion that the geographic location of New York City guaranteed city's future importance led to the choice of the city for the expanded opportunities for Jesuit apostolic activity it promised. Today, when New York City is hailed by Pope John Paul II as the "capital of the world," the wisdom of that original act of Ignatian discernment, made by French Jesuits in a new and bewildering land, is emphatically confirmed.

Finally, the differences between 1846 and 1998 are many and obvious. As we approach a new millennium, it is impossible to predict, much less control, the future that awaits us. We live in a world of ever-accelerating change, and the uncertainties that confront us can be unnerving. But that first generation of Fordham Jesuits, to whose story this book of essays is dedicated, surely faced uncertainties in 1846 at least as intimidating as our own today. The Society of Jesus had only recently been restored, after its suppression in the late 18 th century. There were theological controversies that divided Jesuits in France, as well as the competing interests of bishops who sought to establish their young church on a new and unsettled frontier. Inspired by the Ignatian call to serve the kingdom of God as it is born among us, those first Fordham Jesuits were pioneers and pilgrims with great hearts and generous spirits. They embarked on their journey with the magnanimity of the Spiritual Exercises, free of any illusions of security but full of hope concerning the future to which God called them. The record of what such a spirit allowed them to accomplish is the greatest of their many gifts to their contemporary successors at Fordham and all those who have chosen to continue that journey with us.

The Fordham University community extends around the world and through many generations, past, present and to come. All of us owe a profound debt of gratitude to the Rev. Thomas C. Hennessy, S.J., whose inspiration it was to recover this important chapter of the Fordham story and who enlisted in the completion of the project such distinguished contributors, editors and publishers. While this book was undoubtedly a work of love for Father Hennessy, it also stands as a tribute to the Jesuits of 1846 and a gift to all of us who have followed in their path.

Joseph A. O'Hare, S.J.
President, Fordham University
Oct. 8, 1998

INTRODUCTION

Most editors offer a brief explanation regarding the special nature of the publication that moved them to seek the cooperation of others in the project and express thanks to people who have been particularly helpful on the road to publication. We follow that pattern here.

In 1996 Fordham University commemorated the 150th year of the arrival of the Jesuits at Rose Hill and their assumption of the administration of St. John's College. At the time of the commemoration, those who wished to read about each of the 1846 Jesuit pioneers were disappointed at the limited amount of published material about their lives. Numerous other questions arose, such as: the reasons behind the Jesuits' departing from France; details about their college in Kentucky; the conditions of their lives in Rose Hill; the pre-Jesuit history of St. John's College; reasons for the bishop's calls for help; and, the Jesuits' relations with Archbishop John Hughes. The purpose of this book is to provide answers to such questions, and ultimately to be a source of assistance to later historians who undertake to tell the full Fordham story. To help the reader who has a limited acquaintance with Jesuits, a glossary of Jesuit terminology is provided at the end of the book.

The series of papers begins with James Hennesey's overview of the origins of Fordham that spans Paris, Kentucky and New York and provides highlights of the lives of some of the Fordham pioneer Jesuits (Chapter I). John Padberg reveals the historical background behind the move of many Jesuits out of France when a new regime forced them from their classrooms there (Chapter II). Some of those French emigrants settled in Kentucky, and C. Michael Buckley recounts their early successes and later waning fortunes there from 1831 to 1846 (Chapter III).

Bishop John Hughes began his St. Joseph's Seminary, located "near New York," in the village of Fordham, Westchester County, in 1840, and then on the same grounds founded his St. John's College in the following year. Thomas Shelley takes us back to 1838 when Rose Hill was purchased by the bishop, to the 1841 modest beginning of the college, and then to the summer of 1846 (Chapter IV).

My contribution deals with the individual Jesuits who arrived at Rose Hill in 1846, and provides profiles on thirty-three of them. The profiles summarize what I have learned of their background, personalities, and achievements as shown by their educational and religious activities (Chapter V). Some of the pioneers, such as the administrators and the eight original faculty members, were more important than the student Jesuits for establishing the college and setting its course. The challenge to this generation of both Jesuit and lay historians is to fathom whether the characters, lives and stories of these Fordham pioneers have influenced the later history of the university down to our present day, and whether in future years that influence should be deliberately increased or minimized.

The focus for the time frame of other contributors in this book ranges from 1830 to 1860. Allan S. Gilbert and Roger Wines, on the other hand, have a wider range as they bring us from 1671 when the first patent was issued for the Fordham manor to the present day and beyond for their report on the archeological dig into the Old Manor House. Many readers will appreciate their providing the details of student living at Fordham in the middle and late nineteenth century (Chapter VI).

History has a way of being kind to the memory of most explorers and pioneers. At times, however, it is through learning about the peccadilloes and quarrels of strong personalities that a later generation can get a clearer picture of what was going on at a time when living conditions were so different. The arguments and struggles between the early Fordham Jesuits and Archbishop John Hughes, as recounted by Francis X. Curran, clearly demonstrate the fears and insecurities felt on both sides as they sought the same end through different means (Chapter VII).

James Kelly reflects on some issues that are raised in the various papers, and does so in a way that is meant to stimulate reaction from the reader. He addresses as well one important question raised these days in many Jesuit colleges and universities: in the face of the downturn in religious vocations, can Jesuit institutions retain the educational and religious ideals that their founders and pioneer administrators and faculty members established? He sees signs for a possible affirmative answer to that question (Chapter VIII).

Some readers may be surprised to read of an apparent rigidity and inflexibility in the academic world of our Fordham ancestors with their three Divisions, the seminary regimen, etc. Before passing judgment, however, would it not be fair to learn what was happening at the same time in other residential institutions whose academic goals were similar to Fordham's? Though that task is beyond our present goal, we suggest that other writers attempt such a comparative study.

Apropos of the above mentioned Divisions, I was recently asked by a relative of a Fordham Prep graduate: "When did Fordham Prep begin? Where can I read about *its* early days?" I responded that in the first Fordham years there were three divisions of students, reflecting the typical levels used at other contemporary "colleges." The First Division would clearly be regarded today as college level, and the Third Division as upper elementary (that division was phased out around World War I). Students in the Second Division had a curriculum and activities that resembled those we associate with the Fordham Prep of today. Until 1921, all Fordham students were under the same dean. Then for the first time the Prep had a separate principal, and it was legally separated from the university on June 5, 1970. An excellent book that focuses on the history of the Prep is: *When September Comes: A History of Fordham*

Preparatory School, 1841-1991 by Francis X. Holbrook and August A. Stellwag.

Besides those whose names appear on the title page, thanks are due to many others who contributed information and other kinds of help in the production of this book. Most of them cannot be named but nonetheless they know who they are and have been thanked personally.

Many Jesuit province archivists have been specially cooperative, in particular Patrick Boyle (Upper Canadian Province), Robert Toupin and the late Georges-Émile Giguère (Gallo-Canada Province), Thomas Clancy (New Orleans Province), Robert Bonfils (French Province), and Frederick O'Brien (New York Province). Other archivists have been specially patient and helpful, including Thomas G. Connolly, S.J., (former Fordham University archivist), Patrice Kane (Fordham University archivist), and Vivian Shen (assistant archivist). Jonathan Galente and Eric Larsson provided generous assistance to solve numerous computer problems. Eileen Larsson gave excellent editorial help. Michael S. Connor contributed important artistic work. The layout, design and cover of this book were the careful work of George McCauley, S.J.

I would not feel right about leaving this thank-you section without expressing my gratitude and appreciation for the priests, scholastics, and brothers who were the first Fordham Jesuit pioneers. In reality this whole book is a joyful paean of their praise. As a group those pioneers were notably learned, deeply concerned for their students and for their college, and zealous in seeking to serve the religious needs of their fellow Catholics, many of whom were in dire need of numerous kinds of assistance. I believe that an element of their religious lives that gave them a special esprit de corps and unusual strength flowed from the internal and external discipline that dominated their lives (set times for prayer, a shared understanding of their "ways of proceeding," etc.). That discipline made them happy to accept difficult and challenging apostolic assignments. One such challenge some of them accepted in 1847 when their French-speaking brethren in Montreal asked that English-speaking priests assist in serving plague-stricken Irish immigrants. Answering that call, Fr. Henry DuMerle and Fr. Charles Schianski lost their lives, surely as martyrs of charity; Fr. Michael Driscol and Fr. Martin Férard endured sickness and privation in serving the immigrants. Others spent their equally admirable lives on campus serving long years in the classroom, supervising dining rooms, or laboring on the farm. They, and the pioneer pre-Jesuit diocesan priests, began Fordham well and we who are their heirs owe them all a debt of thanks and appreciation.

History scholars and history buffs will understand that differences in the spelling of names and even variations in dates are due to the variety of source materials used by the several authors. I urge readers who discover such problems and those who have suggestions for a possible later edition of this book, to write to me or to the Fordham University archivist.

Thomas C. Hennessy, S.J.

Table of Contents

Foreword *by Joseph A. O'Hare, S.J.*

Introduction *by Thomas C. Hennessy, S.J.*

Chapter I

The Coming
of the French Jesuits
to Fordham:
An Overview

By James Hennesey, S.J.

A Jesuit presence graced New York City from 1808 to 1814, maintained by Jesuits from Maryland. After that a gap occurred, with no Jesuits in the city until the arrival, in the summer of 1846, of an international group, primarily French, who belonged to the Jesuit province of France — the "Paris" province as it was sometimes called.

The Jesuit order in France had been suppressed by government decree during the course of the years 1762-64 and was reestablished there only in 1814, after the years of the French Revolution and Napoleon. Even so, the Jesuits' situation in France was precarious. The reactionary monarchy of the last of the main Bourbon line, Charles X, brother of the guillotined Louis XVI, was on decidedly shaky ground. The restored Jesuits were seen as the King's allies, but they were an "unauthorized" congregation because they never sought the official license to exist and to run schools in France. When the "July Revolution" of 1830 toppled Charles X and replaced him with his liberal bourgeois cousin Louis Philippe, the Paris Jesuits scattered. Further details about the Jesuits in France at this time are provided by Padberg in the following chapter.

The Jesuits who remained in France were the butt of attacks from the literary left as well as from the remnants of ardent Gallicans and the Jansenists of the Catholic right.[1] At the prestigious College de France, prominent historians Jules Michelet and Edgar Quinet trashed them. They were called "reptiles, birds of prey, insects, chameleons, spiders and wood-lice." It was out of this milieu that Fordham's Jesuit founders came.

Before the nineteenth century was out, classmates of Fordham Jesuits had founded missions and died as martyrs in Lebanon, China and Madagascar. Others faced a firing squad during the uprising of the 1871 Paris Commune. All these interests, as well as those of the contingent in New York, were the concern of a central provincial administration of the Jesuits located in Paris.

COMING TO KENTUCKY

The Paris Jesuits had been invited in 1828 to take over the diocesan St. Joseph's College in Bardstown, Kentucky. But it was not until the events of 1830 at Paris that the French provincial superior saw his way clear to making a positive response. A team headed by Father Pierre Chazelle sailed by way of the West Indies and New Orleans and then made their way up the Mississippi river. On arrival at Bardstown in 1831, they discovered that St. Joseph's had already been given into other hands. The French Jesuits never operated a college in Bardstown, although Missouri Jesuits who came later ran St. Joseph's College there from 1848 to 1868. Chazelle had to settle for a tiny one-man operation, St. Mary's, in Marion county, housed in a former whiskey distillery in the middle of the woods, the creation of an ex-Maryland province Jesuit novice, Father William Byrne.

The Parisian exiles ran St. Mary's until the summer of 1846 and also had a preparatory school called St. Ignatius in Louisville which lasted four years from 1842 to 1846. Near the college they opened a novitiate where several priests and brothers, later part of the Fordham community, began their religious life.

PIERRE CHAZELLE

The architect of this initial phase of what became the Canadian and New York Jesuit provinces and also the founder of revived Jesuit mission work among the indigenous people of Ontario, Pierre Chazelle, was a lyonnais, born with the French Revolution in 1789. Becoming a Jesuit in 1822, he was from 1830 to 1840 superior of the Kentucky mission and rector and president of St. Mary's College. He then returned to France and went to Rome where he was made aware of the "*appel aux Jésuites*" made by Bishop Ignace Bourget of Montreal, a call to the Society of Jesus to resume missionary work among Canada's native peoples, a work begun by martyrs like the seventeenth-century Jean de Brébeuf. Beginning in 1842, Chazelle worked to refound the Ontario missions. Possessed of an enormous energy, he died in 1845 at Green Bay, Wisconsin, where he had gone to explore ancient mission sites.[2]

CLÉMENT BOULANGER

As Chazelle neared death, Clément Boulanger came on the scene. Born in 1790, he entered the Paris novitiate in 1824 and was by 1842 provincial superior of the province of France. He then came to America and was for two years (1845-1846) 'visitor' — an official inspector appointed by the Jesuit superior general and superseding local officials — and then became superior (1846-1855) of the Kentucky mission, which he transferred to New York.[3] There it was joined to the Canada mission founded by Chazelle and known as the New York-Canada mission.

The Kentucky mission had been a losing proposition from the start, as documented by Buckley in Chapter III. Members of the mission were a few lonely Frenchmen directing an English-language college in a poor, out-of-the-way place. Coadjutor Bishop Guy Chabrat of Bardstown was hostile, for reasons unknown. Boulanger quickly made up his mind to accept an offer from Bishop John Hughes of New York. For $40,000 he bought from Hughes the fledgling St. John's College at Fordham, founded in 1841 and floundering. Further details of the college's pre-Jesuit years are provided by Shelley in Chapter IV. The Jesuits also accepted direction of the New York diocesan seminary, recently relocated from Lafargeville in upper New York state to the Fordham property.

The move was made in the summer of 1846. Kentucky was completely abandoned. Twenty-eight Jesuits moved in bands of a half-dozen up the Ohio river by steamer, then by stagecoach and railroad to New York City, and then by the New York and Harlem railroad to Fordham. The New York-Canada mission of the Jesuit province of France, destined to last thirty-three years, until 1879, was begun. Most Jesuit houses in the present-day New York province stem from that jurisdiction.

On that 1846 summer day when he arrived at Rose Hill, Jesuit scholastic Michael Nash was struck by "the splendid appearance of the lawn and the sites of the scattered buildings comprising the college." He wrote, "The view of the railroad winding along the foot of the lawn and the hills west of the road impressed me very favorably."[4] Of the small Jesuit party, only James Graves was American-born, a Kentuckian who later transferred to the French mission of New Orleans at the advent of the Civil War. Cork-born William Stack Murphy came as a Jesuit from France, while the newly ordained priests, Michael Driscol and John Ryan, and the scholastic Michael Nash were pre-famine Irish settled in Kentucky. Nicholas Petit was a Haitian Creole and Frederick William Gockeln and Brother Hennen were Germans. All the rest were French-born.

August Thébaud was the first Jesuit Rector-President. A smallish, rotund Breton, he was possessed of an insatiable curiosity, a philosopher and scientist who had explored Kentucky's Mammoth cave and experimented with hot-air balloons. He was a man with ideas always tumbling over in his head. Before he died he had several books to his credit, analyzing the character of the American and Irish people, and a substantial career as educator and pastor.[5]

A very large — "immensely stout" — and orotund Englishman from Durham, John Larkin, was the first Jesuit dean of the college. He had traveled to India and been a Sulpician priest before joining the Kentucky Jesuits. He was a deliberate and definitive disciplinarian. One of his more memorable actions was in response to a student protest over dining-hall food in March, 1852. In his best English accent he canceled a scheduled St. Patrick's day holiday. He succeeded (1851-54) Thébaud as second Jesuit president of St. John's College.[6]

NEW MEMBERS

There was a rapid buildup of Jesuit personnel. In fifteen years in Kentucky, the French Jesuits had attracted twenty novices. Many of them were French missionary priests. At Fordham, thirty-six novices entered the Society in the first four years,[7] while other Jesuits came from a Europe once again embroiled in a spate of revolutions. Many were aristocratic by birth or inclination. The Paris Jesuit catalogue for 1847 listed at St. John's forty-seven members of the community: professors and administrators, along with Jesuit brothers and scholastics at every stage of their training. Carlos Maldonado, a Spaniard, was later *rector magnificus* at Salamanca. He and Isidore Daubresse, a royalist Frenchman to the core, taught in the seminary, from which Bishop Hughes removed them for their antidemocratic ways. Tiny Thomas Legoüais, "a perfectly proportioned dwarf" less than five feet tall, was professor of scripture, moderator of the Parthenian Sodality, and Master of Novices. His novitiate was initially located in an abandoned frame wash house. Legoüais was a relative of a well-known "philosophe," Count Constantin Volney, and mathematician Simon Fouché was a nephew of Queen Marie Antoinette's confessor. Further details about the first Fordham Jesuits are offered by T. Hennessy in Chapter V.

A half-dozen lay teachers completed the college staff. Fordham bulletins called then "auxiliaries" down to the turn of the century. Among the initial faculty was William Rodrigue from Santo Domingo, the college's architect and brother-in-law of Bishop Hughes. He was a professor of drawing. Other lay professors taught chemistry, history, Spanish and music.

In the Jesuits' first year at Rose Hill there were 110 students. They were not poor boys. John Hughes had designed his college for students whose parents "could afford the costs." Most were local New Yorkers, but there were students from Mexico, the West Indies and South America, as well as from the southern United states, including some who had followed the Jesuits from Kentucky. Michael Nash had problems with students who remained on campus during the summer months. He reported that "a few from Brooklyn and New York were, with exceptions, the worst boys I had ever met. I had met wild and reckless boys in Kentucky, but they were gentlemen. The Brooklyn and New York boys did not possess the remotest instinct of gentlemen."[8]

The Curriculum

President Thébaud and Dean Larkin quickly set about reorganizing what they found to be a "chaotic" curriculum — a system where students changed classrooms every forty-five minutes with resulting confusion and disorder. With help from Maryland Jesuits at Georgetown, they instituted a program based on the Jesuit *Ratio Studiorum*. Thébaud noted that they substituted the term "belles lettres" for "humanities" because of some stupid remarks of the novelist Mrs. [Frances] Trollope [in *The Domestic Manners of the Americans*, 1832], who heartily laughed at "the idea of the Jesuits pretending to 'humanize' the boors of the United States."[9]

Despite his own far-reaching scientific curiosity, Thébaud was no friend of a college science program, "as likely to throw into the shade the all-important classical studies." Even worse in his estimation was the commercial course, "an ugly feature of our institutions." But at Fordham, as in other Jesuit schools, the fathers had ruefully to admit that they badly needed the tuition brought in by the commercial students.

Other Flocks, Other People

Activity soon spread beyond Rose Hill. Jesuits founded parishes in Yonkers, Brewster and Croton Falls, among other places. They undertook chaplaincies in public institutions on the East River islands, at Manhattan's Tombs prison and at Sing Sing. Plans were discussed for an African-American church in New York City. Further afield, Jesuits from the Fordham community went north to Canada, including Chatham, Montreal, and Wikwemikong on Manitoulin Island. At the same time Canadian Jesuits came to New York.

St. John's was until the twentieth century the "country college." In October, 1847, the "big rosy Englishman," John Larkin, was detached from St. John's to found a "city college" and parish in Manhattan. He was given fifty cents, half of which he spent on a train ticket, and sent on his way. He began in the neighborhood of Canal Street, and, after a disastrous fire there, moved to Third Avenue and then to Sixteenth Street. "Holy Name College" eventually became the College of St. Francis Xavier, which lasted until 1912 and continues as Xavier High School.

Other Jesuit foundations in the French era included St. Lawrence O'Toole parish at Park Avenue and 84th Street in Manhattan; St. Peter's parish, college and high school in Jersey City; St. Joseph's parish in Troy, NY; and St. Michael's and St. Ann's parishes in Buffalo. The last two were transferred to the province of Germany in 1868.[10]

Priests from Fordham and Xavier undertook other missions. Carlos Maldonado and the Paris-born Irishman, Charles Hippolyte de Luynes, made successful fund-raising forays among wealthy Latin Americans in Mexico, Chile and Peru. De Luynes was the son of an agent of the "United Irishmen" in France. A ministry which foreshadowed long years of service to Irish immigrants began with the departure of a half-dozen priests for Canada to care for some of the tens of thousands of plague-stricken exiles daily being deposited on the banks of the St. Lawrence. The years 1845 to 1849 were the time of "the Great Hunger" in Ireland, the years of the potato famine when "coffin ships" carrying starving peasants expelled by their landlords were rife with cholera, typhus and smallpox. Father Charles Schianski, far from his native Moravia, and Father Henri du Merle, the college's prefect of Discipline, were among those who lost their lives caring for the sick in Canada. Du Merle was thirty-seven, Schianski forty-five.

The Pioneers and Local and National Issues

Living in their French enclave, the Jesuits seem not to have been involved in the great American debates of the day like abolition. St. John's College does not seem to have been involved when Bishop Hughes let Mayor Harper know that the city would be turned into "another Moscow," burned to the ground, if any Catholic institution were harmed by Nativists in 1846. (The musket that long rested in the Fordham president's office apparently was one of those issued for protection in the 1850s).

Regardless of the Jesuits' apparent noninvolvement in other national issues, three of the Jesuit pioneers volunteered and served in the Civil War as Union chaplains: the Frenchman Peter Tissot with the 37th New York "Irish Rifles," and as a prisoner of war in the notorious Libby prison; Canadian-born Thomas Ouellet with the 69th regiment, New York National Guard, "a small, lithe man with immense energy" and "a perfect martinet in everything that pertained to his sacred duties;" and Irish-born Michael Nash with the 6th U.S. Infantry, "Billy Wilson's Zouaves."

The Archbishop Is Angry

What remains to be told is the tale of the epic battle between the New York-Canada Jesuits and the founder of St. John's College, John Hughes.[11] When he started the college Hughes was coadjutor bishop. He became bishop of the diocese in 1842 and was named archbishop in 1850. He died in 1864. Hughes warmly welcomed the Kentucky Jesuits to Rose Hill in 1846 as "a numerous, learned and pious community of the illustrious Society of Jesus."

6

But problems soon arose. There were the terms of the transfer. Did the Jesuits buy the college for $40,000, as Boulanger thought? Or was it a conditioned gift from the bishop, to be held only so long as the Jesuits operated a college on the property? A reversionary clause in the contract lent some credence to the latter interpretation. Hughes argued that the money he had spent in establishing the college was collected specifically to provide for the education of Catholic young men, and that he was honor-bound to respect the wishes of the donors. What then of the Jesuits' $40,000 payment? The bishop replied that that payment was to clear up the college's outstanding debts. The result, of course, was a clouded title. The Jesuits could neither sell nor mortgage the college property or any part of it. There was the question of "real" versus "legal" ownership.

The Jesuits thought they had bought the property free and clear and were its owners. That was on November 24, 1845. The deed was registered with the papal consul general in New York. But on April 10, 1846, Hughes incorporated the college civilly with a board of directors including four diocesan priests and four laymen, one of them a Protestant. Jesuits were to be added later on, and they were. A further question, which has never been addressed, arose from the papal registration of the deed. Did that indicate that both parties — bishop and Jesuits — considered Fordham to be canonically "ecclesiastical property," requiring the Holy See's approval for "alienation" or sale?

Property lines on Rose Hill were one festering problem. The bishop kept back the Rodrigue cottage, where his sister and her family lived, and also the seminary (now St. John's Hall) and the church, both of which had been built under President James Roosevelt Bayley just before the Jesuits' arrival. An easement allowed parishioners to cross Jesuit property to worship in the church. There was also a complicated agreement about a church for the Jesuits in Manhattan, but that story belongs to the history of Xavier.

No one has ever denied that John Hughes was an autocrat. He had a "high theology" of the episcopacy. When the Jesuits consulted the distinguished attorney, Charles O'Conor, about their legal problems with the bishop, they touched a very raw nerve. Hughes stormed, "This appeal to the laity is a new feature in our ecclesiastical discipline."[12] In another context he had a similar reaction when he discovered that the papal consul general in New York, Louis Binsse, was following Roman orders and sending regular reports on the archbishop to the secretary of state, Cardinal Antonelli.[13] Perhaps he remembered the time when rebellious trustees at St. Peter's church in Barclay Street had threatened to horsewhip him. For Hughes, episcopal authority came from on high, and Catholics "do their duty when they obey their bishop." As he put it during a tiff with the lay philosopher Orestes Brownson, "I will have no one in my diocese whom I cannot control. Either he shall put me down or I shall put him down."[14] One of the bishop's closest lay friends commented that he had known Hughes for thirty or more years, and he had never known him to admit that he was wrong.[15] The Jesuits had a worthy adversary.

Prospects for a solution did not improve when the relatively diplomatic Clément Boulanger in 1855 returned to France. His successor was his former assistant, John B. Hus, a onetime superior of the Jesuit mission in Cayenne, French Guiana, in South America. He was an abrupt and maladroit man who spoke no English. Hughes had no sympathy for him. At one meeting, the bishop began in French, then switched to English, leaving the Jesuit superior completely out of the conversation.

A PEACEFUL SOLUTION

Peace was finally made through the efforts of two Maryland province Jesuits, Charles Stonestreet and John McElroy. Hughes moved his seminary to Troy, New York, and the Jesuits paid another $45,000 for St. John's Hall and the church. Stonestreet and McElroy arranged that the Jesuits apologize in writing and, in person on their knees, to the archbishop.[16] They did not tell Hus of the apology, and he soon returned to France. The battle was over. The full story of that family quarrel and its final, peaceful solution is recounted by Curran in Chapter VII.

Hus's successor in April, 1859, was William Stack Murphy, a charming scion of the Irish gentry who had entered the Jesuits in France.[17] August Thébaud remembered him as "more English than Irish." He had been superior of the Kentucky mission and rector of St. Mary's College from 1840 to 1845 and later was visitor and then vice-provincial of the Missouri province of the Jesuits. When Murphy's health failed, Remi Tellier, a Frenchman remembered in Canada as very pro-New York, succeeded him from November, 1859 to 1866.[18]

FROM MISSION TO PROVINCE

Already the pioneering days of the New York-Canada mission were ending. Some of the younger men wanted an end to the French regime. There was conflict between the Canadian and American branches. Canadians protested that young French Canadian Jesuits were losing their national identity by exposure to New York ways.[19] The binational jurisdiction was awkward. In 1869, the mission was separated from its French mother province. Recruits no longer came from France; scholastics did not go there for studies. Finally, in 1879, the mission was divided, the New York section merging with the existing Maryland province, and Canada being temporarily attached to the English province before becoming independent.[20]

8

THE END OF ONE ERA, THE BEGINNING OF ANOTHER

The French era really came to an end in 1882 with the appointment of Irish-born Patrick J. Dealy as rector-president. Increasing numbers of New York Jesuits were either natives of Ireland or a generation or two removed from it. Dealy had entered the Jesuits from St. John's in 1846 and was later the first English-speaking professor at St. Mary's College, Montreal.[21] With Dealy's return to Rose Hill, the conservatism of the older Jesuits gave way to broader and more modern ideas. The college emerged from its isolation and began to play a larger role in the life of the city. The French coloring of the New York-Canada mission lingered on to the end of the century but a new, and, at least for a time, very Irish-American college was born, sponsored by an equally Irish-American Jesuit province. Memories of the French founders faded quickly, until almost all that was left were the fleurs-de-lis on the college seal.

NOTES

1 Geoffrey Cubitt, *The Jesuit Myth: Conspiracy Theory and Politics in Nineteenth-Century France* (Oxford: Clarendon Press, 1993), quotation on pp. 184-185.

2 *Dictionary of Jesuit Biography: Ministry to English Canada, 1842-1987* (Toronto: Canadian Institute of Jesuit Studies, 1991), 55-58. Henceforth *DJB*.

3 *DJB*, 19-21.

4 Michael Nash, S.J., " Reminiscences of Father Michael Nash," *Woodstock Letters*, 27 (1898), 267. Henceforth *WL*.

5 Augustus J. Thébaud, S.J., *Forty Years in the United States of America (1839-1885)* (New York: The United States Catholic Historical Society, 1904), with a biographical sketch of Father Thébaud, by Thomas J. Campbell, S.J., pp. 9-12; *WL* (1886), 124-125.

6 *DJP*, 181-182. Francis J. Nelligan, S.J., "Father John Larkin, S.J., 1801-1858," *The Canadian Messenger of the Sacred Heart* (January, February, March, 1957), 37-43; 103-110; 181-187. Charles G. Herberman et al., eds., *The College of St. Francis Xavier: A Memorial and Retrospect 1847-1897* (New York: The Meany Printing Company, 1897), 6-23.

7 Robert I. Gannon, S.J., *Up to the Present: The Story of Fordham* (Garden City: Doubleday & Co. 1967), 39.

8 Nash, 267-268.

9 Thébaud, 350.

10 Arthur Weiss, S.J., "Jesuit Mission Years in New York State, 1654 to 1879," *WL* 75 (1946) 129-139.

11 Francis X. Curran, S.J., "Archbishop Hughes and the Jesuits," *WL* 97 (1968) 5-56.

12 Curran, 17.

13 Leo F. Stock, ed., *Consular Relations between the United States and the Papal States: Instructions and Dispatches* (Washington D,C.: American Catholic Historical Association, 1945), 421; 425, n. 46.

14 Curran, 10, n. 13. Richard J. Shaw, *Dagger John: The Unquiet Life and Times of Archbishop John Hughes of New York* (New York: Paulist Press, 1977), 314-315,

15 Curran, 22.

16 Curran, 43.

17 Thébaud, 141.

18 Léon Pouliot, S.J., "Lents et pénibles débuts de la Province du Canada francais: le problème linguistique," *Lettres du Bas-Canada* 22 (1969) 79.

19 Ibid.

20 Weiss, 139.

21 *WL* 21 (1892) 261-262.

CHAPTER II

THE RESTORED SOCIETY OF JESUS IN FRANCE, 1814-1830: WHY FRENCH JESUITS CAME TO AMERICA IN 1831

by John W. Padberg, S.J.

When Fathers Petit, Chazelle and Ladavière and Brother Corne left France for the United States on November 30, 1830, the Society of Jesus had been restored in the universal Church for sixteen years, since August 7, 1814. By the end of the first year of its reestablishment in France it could already count 91 members. In the next fifteen years it grew with extraordinary rapidity, to 432 members at the beginning of 1830: 148 priests, 124 brothers and, boding well for the future, 160 scholastics.

The story of the restored Society in France starts even before its universal restoration. Within a month of Napoleon's abdication at Fontainebleau in April 1814, the superior of the still only partially restored Society, Thaddeus Brzozowski, then resident in Russia, wrote on May 18 to Pierre Clorivière in France and commissioned him to reestablish the Jesuits there. Clorivière was the only fully-trained Jesuit of the pre-suppression Society still alive in France. He was born in 1735 in an old Breton noble family which had ties with the Jesuits (his father had gone to the great Collège Louis-le-Grand in Paris, where he was a classmate of Voltaire). Clorivière entered the Society of Jesus in 1756 and lived and worked in England for some time after the Jesuits were chased from France in 1764. On August 15, 1773 in Brussels, he made solemn profession of his final vows as a Jesuit, on the day before the publication of the papal brief that suppressed the Society.

In 1775 he returned to France as a diocesan priest and worked in Brittany into the years of the Revolution. In 1790 Clorivière founded two religious congregations, the Priests of the Sacred Heart of Jesus and, with Adelaide de Cice, the Daughters of the Heart of Mary, both of which by rule were to have no external marks of religious life. He was a "non-juring" priest, ardently and publicly opposed to the Revolution. Several of his relatives suffered the guillotine. His nephew, Joseph Picot de Limoëlan, who later adopted the Clorivière name[1] was involved in the 1800 plot to assassinate Napoleon. Clorivière himself was in hiding or under police surveillance or in prison for fifteen consecutive years from 1793 to 1809. In 1805, even while in a French prison, he was able to rejoin the Society of Jesus still extant in Russia. Such was the man who at the age of seventy-nine was to bring the Society back to life in France. For five years he worked with extraordinary success at the task until, worn out by his labors, he died in 1820 in a vice-province that had by the time more than doubled in numbers.

MINISTRIES OF THE RESTORED SOCIETY IN FRANCE

Not only in those first five years but during the next ten, too, until 1830, urgent requests inundated the renascent Society to work especially in three fields. The first was the re-evangelization of France through popular mission preaching; the second, the reestablishment of the Marian *Congrégation* (later known as Sodalities and today as Christian Life Communities). The third, increasingly central as an apostolate, was the work of education in newly established colleges that recalled, even in their quite limited number, the 124 such schools that the Society had conducted in France before the government chased the Jesuits out of them in 1764. A fourth field, central to the work of the old Society but external to France itself, was the resumption of foreign missions. But such missionary work could not be started again in an organized way in the midst of all of the difficulties of these first years of the restored Society.

Those first three works met with great success, especially the colleges. The successes, however, were achieved in the midst of difficulties at least as great, both internal and external to the Society. But before such Jesuit works could begin, there had to be Jesuits to do the work.

FATHERS OF THE FAITH

Within a month of Brzozowski's letter to Clorivière, Joseph Varin, the director of the Fathers of the Faith in France, requested admission to the Society. The Fathers of the Faith were the final outcome of two sets of young men who in the 1790s had independently formed groups pledged to a life similar to that of the Jesuits and/or to entering the Society if and when it would be restored. In 1794 Varin joined the first group, founded in Belgium and known as the Society of the Sacred Heart. (He, along with one of the founding members, François-Eleonor de Tournely, was also to be of assistance to Madeleine-Sophie Barat in her founding of the Religious of the Sacred Heart.) Pushed by the French Revolution from one country to another, this group finally settled near Vienna in 1797 where its members elected Varin, then twenty-eight years old, as their superior.

Meanwhile, in Rome during the same 1797, Nicolo Paccanari, a former sergeant in the papal troops, former merchant, former tour guide, quite uneducated but extraordinarily eloquent and persuasive, had with church approval founded the Fathers of the Faith of Jesus as a step to reconstituting the Society of Jesus. In a series of improbabilities and with the encouragement of Pius VI, the two groups got together in 1799 at Vienna and combined forces. The Society of the Sacred Heart was absorbed into the second group, with Paccanari elected general and with the new organization now known simply as the Fathers of the Faith. Within less than a year the new superior began to cause unease in the congregation. He sent its members far and wide (Varin was sent to France), went out of his way to court publicity in Rome, and provided only obscure responses to questions about his plans with regard to the original Society of Jesus.

As the years went on, the unease increased and members in several places broke with Paccanari as stories of a dubious past life circulated. In 1806 the Holy Office sentenced him to ten years in prison. The invading French army opened the prisons in 1809 and Paccanari eventually disappeared, either into Switzerland under an alias or into the Tiber at Rome as a murder victim. Meanwhile Varin had already broken with Paccanari in 1804 and maintained the French Fathers of the Faith until he brought with him to Clorivière and the Jesuit novitiate in 1814 his three companions. They became the first Jesuit novices in France in almost seventy-five years, since the early 1760s. By July 31, 1814, one week before the universal restoration of the Society, five more men joined them and, on that feast day of St. Ignatius, the first ten Jesuits of restoration France gathered at the Convent of the Carmelites where Clorivière then lived and where in 1792 in the September Massacres fourteen former Jesuits had shed their blood.

A LEGAL AND SOCIAL NO MAN'S LAND

Membership in the Society, the rapid increase in such membership, and the works assumed by the newly restored Society all took place in the shadows and interstices in which all non-legally authorized religious orders and congregations operated in the years of the Restoration monarchy. The Society of Jesus had no legal authorization and the existence of the Jesuits was especially open to challenge by the unreconstructed revolutionaries and by the upper bourgeois class infected as it was by Voltairian anticlerical ideas and prejudices.

Brzozowski thought that the Society ought to appeal to Louis XVIII for a formal act of restoration as a legally-recognized religious congregation. The King was not hostile to the Jesuits but he was a realist. When Clorivière informally petitioned for such recognition, Louis replied, according to a report to Rome, "Let the Fathers again take up neither the name nor the garb of the

Society; let them work without making a lot of noise about their affairs and they have nothing to fear."[2] The Jesuits thought that as individuals they could appeal to the *Charte*, the fundamental law of the Restoration monarchy, which guaranteed to every citizen the right "to profess his religion with an equal liberty and obtain for his worship identical protection."[3] But for the Society as a corporate entity, the news was disquieting. That same report to Rome said that "the King is sympathetic to us, most of the members of the royal family are equally so, but [government] ministers are hostile, and our friends are rare."[4] To grant legal authorization to a religious congregation was an act reserved to those legislative bodies. Under the next king, Charles X, the chance of legal recognition was even less likely. The king himself might have been willing to give it, but political opposition to the Ultras, the supporters of the king, saw behind those ardent royalists the hidden and malign power of the Jesuits.

It is true that the French Jesuits of the time were partisans of the monarchy. They saw it as a bulwark against a flood tide of Voltairean impiety. They sang as loudly as the faithful Catholic parishioners to whom they preached their missions, "Vive la France/Vive le Roi/Toujours en France/Les Bourbons et la Foi."[5] At the other end of the spectrum, their opponents sang just as loudly the refrain of one of the popular drinking songs by the poet Pierre-Jean de Béranger, "Hommes noirs, d'où sortez-vous?/Nous sortons de dessous terre./Moité renards, moitié loups/Notre règle est un mystère."[6] In popular myth the Jesuits were crawling up from a tunnel that linked the Tuileries, the royal palace, to the Jesuit novitiate in the Paris suburb of Montrouge where the King, Charles X, regularly went to say Mass and where fifty thousand Jesuits were practicing small arms drill and artillery training.

Not only the taverns but also the university classrooms and the legislature railed against the Jesuits. The philosopher Cousin and the historian Guizot, for example, attacked the Society in their university lectures. The Count de Montlosier, who was an ardent monarchist but also an ardent Gallican, saw the Jesuits as part of "a vast system, . . . a vast conspiracy against religion, against the King, and against society itself. . . ."[7] The author hit a popular nerve; the book rapidly went through eight editions. A patriotic response to such treachery, of course, was to be expected. The house diary of the novitiate at Montrouge records one such effusion:

> Tremble, satellites of Loyola; your last hour is on the way. Vile rabble, filthy corrupter of youth, monsters of treachery, tremble . . . Cursed race, enemies of the fatherland, you will perish! Burdened by your crimes, your name will be held in abhorrence by all future peoples. . . . Forty thousand defenders of our liberties have sworn your destruction. . . Forty more days and Montouge will be no more.[8]

What makes all the sound and fury just that was the fact that the Society of Jesus in the 1820s was in no way a powerful entity. It had all it could do to reconstitute itself again. At the same time, there is no doubt that the Jesuits supported a conservative monarchy. As Joseph Burnichon, the chronicler of the first century of the restored Society in France succinctly put it:

> There is nothing to hide here: they [the Jesuits] were ardently royalist. . . . Certainly the Jesuits were attached by convention to the legitimate royalty which appeared to them as the guarantee of the Christian tradition of France against Voltarian impiety and revolutionary atheism . . . One would have greatly surprised the Jesuits in saying to them that they were engaged in politics because they testified to their loyalty toward the monarchy and the royal family. For them this was simply to act as good Frenchmen, something they considered it their duty to do.[9]

GETTING DOWN TO WORK

Whatever their opinion, the Jesuits had work to do. They began to preach popular missions which, along with their schools, occupied the greater part of the Society of Jesus in France from 1814 to 1830. They took up this work throughout the country as a means of religious renewal. Christian life and practice in much of France had almost been extinguished in the successive upheavals of the revolutionary years. Even the imperial government of Napoleon had been tempted to recognize officially such popular mission preaching. The Restoration climate encouraged it[10] and the early Jesuits entered upon this apostolate with great vigor. A mission included a series of sermons, lectures, prayers, opportunities for reception of the Sacraments, sometimes rather luridly dramatic gestures such as sermons preached in the cemeteries and human skeletons paraded about as evidence of the transience of this life. It all climaxed, to cite numerous examples, in a long and enthusiastic procession of several hundred men led by a military band to the place where an enormous "mission cross" would be planted in the main square of a town in front of the parish church and where prayers would be offered in reparation for the sacrileges of the Revolution and to the memory of the "martyrs," Louis XVI, Louis XVII and Marie Antoinette. The missionaries tried to ensure the continuity of the fervor aroused by organizing associations to carry on works of piety and charity. Such missions attracted those Jesuits who were more inclined to such directly religious works than to those less public, less immediately apostolic tasks such as teaching in the Jesuit schools. And even such week long teaching duties would often be followed by weekend mission preaching.

Father Louis Sellier, a spiritual father at the college of Saint Acheul provides a good example of what such a double apostolate might involve. One of his co-workers described it:

> After hearing the confession of the students [at the college], he would leave on a Sunday evening for some village to begin a three week mission during which he would preach two or three times a day, spend the rest of the time in the confessional and, when he had shaken the tree, four, five or six priests [from parishes in the environs] would come to help and then return to their parishes on Sunday to gather in the harvest. He [Sellier] always went back to Saint Acheul on Thursday or Friday for the students' confession while the [other] priests responded to the needs of the mission until he came back. . . . It was enough to announce that Father Sellier would preach in a village for everyone in the environs to flock there. When there was a crowd, he would be in the confessional until eleven thirty at night, then take time to eat and be back there after midnight, to rise at four in the morning or earlier.[11]

These "missions à l'intérieur," so badly needed throughout France, gained much credit for the Society among the diocesan clergy. As one of the French Jesuits wrote to the General, "The services we provide in missions and retreats have won us the hearts of the bishops. Out of eighty of them, I do not think that there are four who are unfavorable to the Society."[12]

MARIAN CONGREGATIONS

A second apostolate, this time directly involving the laity, was the work of the "Congrégation."[13] In 1801 six Paris students under the guidance of Jean-Baptiste Bourdier-Delpuits, a Jesuit until the Suppression, formed a pious association on the model of the Marian congregation which had been a feature of all the Jesuit schools of the seventeenth and eighteenth centuries. Within five years it numbered almost 200 members.

How unusual any public display of individual piety had become in these years is clear from the astonished reaction of the canons of Notre Dame when during one of the major ceremonies at the cathedral several young men actually received the Eucharist. One of the canons whispered to his confreres, "Where have they come from? Who are they?"[14] Napoleon suppressed the group in 1809, exclaiming, "Enough of this choir boys' plot," when his police discovered some of its members spreading abroad the papal letter excommunicating Napoleon.

One of the first ten restoration Jesuits, Pierre Ronsin, revived the Congrégation. In its revived form it included not only students but also artisans, professional men, members of the clergy, and a significant number of the aristocracy. The first persons admitted under Ronsin can give a concrete example of the range of membership; they were, along with the Duc de Polignac, an artisan in bronze, a shopkeeper and a dentist. The anticlerical press of the "liberal" opposition was convinced or at least proclaimed that the King, Louis XVIII, his brother, the Comte d'Artois, later Charles X, the duc de Bourbon, and other of the royalty were members. This was simply not true.

The group met weekly at the old seminary of the Paris Foreign Mission Society. At first Ronsin did not impress some of the members. "He gives good homilies but that's not what people involved with the world need."[15] But his success was evident, in attracting members, inspiring them publicly to lead convinced Christian lives in the world, and moving them to set up or assist a network of charitable, social and educational organizations. By 1828 the Paris Congrégation had more than 1300 members and some sixty French cities and towns had their own Congrégation. By the mid 1820s the "liberal" press was in full cry against the organization, excoriating it as the preferred means by which the Jesuits would eventually take over the government. Unfortunately this attack became all the easier and seemingly credible because some of the members of the Congrégation were also members of the secret society, the *Chévaliers de la Foi*, which did have as one of its purposes to attain political power.

Ronsin himself became the object of the most public vilification, personally and as emblematic of all that was evil about the Society of Jesus. After the Jesuits in 1828 were prohibited from teaching in their schools in France, the Congrégation's activities and prominence went into eclipse. But some seventeen to twenty years later Ronsin became immortalized, if that is the word for it, in Eugène Sue's famous ten volume serial novel, *Le Juif Errant* (*The Wandering Jew*) that ran issue by issue in the liberal journal, *Le Constitutionnel* from 1845 through 1847. Ronsin, under the name of the villainous Father Rodin, raised theft, deceit, prejudice, lust and betrayal to such fine arts that he was elected General of the Jesuits with hopes of becoming Pope. Virtue triumphed in that his companion in treachery, a certain princess, went mad; he lost his ill-gotten fortune of two hundred million francs, and died from poison in spasms of agony. However melodramatic and nonsensical the novel was, it helped to fix and perpetuate in the minds of many Frenchmen the popular image of the Jesuit.[16] It was no wonder that the Jesuits themselves became almost instinctively more conservative in almost every way and saw in the alliance of "throne and altar" at least some shelter from the attacks of their enemies.

The third major apostolate of the restored Society in France was education. It absorbed the greatest part of its personnel and from the beginning it was the work most desired by French Catholics, both lay and clerical, and the work most bitterly attacked by its opponents. That apostolate took place from 1814 to 1828 in minor seminaries (*petits seminaires*) and, when those schools were closed to Jesuit participation, in exile colleges situated just beyond the French borders.

The Restoration government of Louis XVIII recognized the right of families to choose the education appropriate for their children. This was a theoretical breach in the monopoly that Napoleon had created for the state system of education; in practice the Restoration governments maintained that monopoly, but with one exception, minor seminaries. The bishops requested and a royal statute granted them the right to establish in each civil *département* of France one church school for the preparatory education of prospective students of the major seminaries. These were to be boarding schools with no day students admitted and, of great importance, their students were equally eligible, as students of the state schools, for the government-administered baccalaureate examination and its consequent civilly-recognized degree.

Immediately a wave of requests broke over the renascent Society of Jesus that it take on such seminaries. Bishops tried to press on the Jesuits eighty-seven seminaries or seminaries-to-be in the early years after 1814. Within three months of the revival of the Society in France Clorivière accepted offers from the diocese of Amiens, Bordeaux and Poitiers for seminaries at Saint-Acheul, Bordeaux and Montmorillon. In 1815 Sainte-Anne d'Auray in Vannes and in 1816 Fourcalquier in Digne opened. For five years the provincial in France and the general in Rome held off further foundations, then they took on Aix-en Provence in 1821, Dôle in 1823 and Billom in 1826. That last-named city was where the Jesuits had opened their very first school in France in 1558. For fourteen years these eight schools devoured the attention and the membership of the province. At first, the men therein, many of them still novices who were at the same time studying philosophy or theology, taught full time to the point of exhaustion. By 1828 when things supposedly were better, and the novices no longer were sent into the schools, approximately 300 of the 364 Jesuits of the French province directly worked in those eight institutions.[17]

Four factors especially contributed to this concentration of Jesuit resources in the schools. First, the French bishops, in desperate need of clergy and with almost no hope of getting them from the "royal colleges" of the state, repeatedly importuned the Society. Secondly, the Father General of the Jesuits, Luigi Fortis, wanted the Society, in accord with its post-Suppression traditions, again to undertake the educational apostolate. Third, a great number of Catholic parents were utterly convinced, rightly or wrongly, that the moral and intellectual development of their children would be utterly destroyed by the state schools and that the future of a Christian France lay in a Christian education. Lastly, there were memories. In almost every city of even small size stood the pre-Suppression Jesuit college, a reminder of two hundred years of perhaps the most completely developed educational system that the Jesuits had set up anywhere in the whole Society of Jesus. Could such a system flourish again? Some Jesuits thought so; surely many of their friends did.

But the Jesuits were realists too. They knew that the very existence of these schools depended on the bishops. As Clorivière very early wrote to the General, "Our boarding schools in France are in immediate dependence upon the bishops who entitle them officially 'Minor Seminaries'. . . [and] they have no legal existence except as Seminaries, so our colleges are quite precarious. . ."[18] On the other hand, the bishops were pleased with these schools. "Seminary" was not only a name; they truly did function as feeder schools for the diocesan major seminaries. From St. Acheul alone, for example, thirty and at times up to fifty young men every year entered the major seminary for the diocese of Amiens and for other dioceses too. In truth, however, these seminary-colleges were, above all, colleges, and in accepting students not destined for the ecclesiastical state, the Jesuit schools functioned outside the letter of the law as, indeed, did a good number of other minor seminaries. Everyone knew it — the bishops, the Jesuits, the parents and the government too.

Realism, at times, did not extend to finances. According to the Jesuit Constitutions the schools could not charge tuition.[19] To get started they relied on gifts from families of Jesuits and on loans. Operating expenses depended upon board and lodging fees which the Jesuit Constitutions did not forbid. With no other income and with remissions given to a good percentage of the students, such fees had to be high, a circumstance which narrowed the potential student population.

There was no dearth of students however. In all but one of the schools, the enrollment grew rapidly, often by several hundred percent in the space of two or three years. For example, Ste. Anne d'Auray went from 60 students in 1815 to 200 the next year. Montmorillon opened with 40 or 50 students in 1814 and had more than 300 ten years later. St. Acheul was the largest and the most important of these schools. Starting with 140 students in 1814, it had 900 by 1824, never slipped below that number, and regularly had to turn away annually more than 200 applicants. In prestige, and in influence, it had no peer. Students enrolled there from all over France and from other countries too. Neither did it have a rival in the opposition it brought on. To cite only one example of such opposition from a contemporary source that supposedly gave a glimpse at the interior of St. Acheul and at the education which contemporary Jesuits gave to the youth of France:

Let us draw near and open those iron gates, bolted and reinforced, which keep us from entering these dismal regions. What are those cries which strike our ears? Is it some savage beast which is tearing apart a human victim and slaking its thirst in the blood. No, it is a man, a thousand times more cruel than tigers or leopards who in a cold rage is torturing the hands of a helpless child . . . whose limbs are already bloody from his furious blow.[20]

With all due allowance for the romantic sensibilities of the age, it is still incredible that such lucubrations were taken seriously, but indeed they were.

The *Plan of Studies* used at St. Acheul and adopted elsewhere, written by Nicholas Loriquet, one of the first of the restored French Jesuits, was clear on the purposes of the school. Its aim was "to form the young men who dwell here in knowledge, in morals, and in piety. . . not without order and method."[21] The full course of studies lasted ten years; the youngest students, if they entered the first class, would have been about eight years old. This was a significant change from the presuppression schools, brought about in part by the royal ordinance which required the minor seminaries to instruct "from childhood" the young men who might later become major seminarians. The ability to read and write was the minimum entrance requirement. The major subjects were the grammar and literature of Latin, Greek and French, rhetoric, philosophy, history, geography, mathematics, "gentlemanly accomplishments" (les arts d'agrément) such as drawing, fencing and music, and most importantly, religion. Religion functioned not only as a subject to be taught but as

Collège St. Acheul

a spirit pervasive of the whole school. Latin was at the base of all the learning; rhetoric was the point of convergence of all the studies, rhetoric understood not simply as ease of speaking but as "the art of convincing, of touching, of persuading" by the development of all of a student's imaginative and intellectual talent."[22] Loriquet not only wrote the Plan; he also wrote some of the textbooks, especially some of the first elementary manuals of history for French schools. Even some of the state schools used those books for a while. Latin or Greek history presented no problems but his history of France which was fiercely anti-Revolutionary and anti-Napoleonic helped to arouse much of the anti-Jesuit polemics then and later.[23]

The physical circumstances of the schools were simple, perhaps even austere. The discipline was strict and pervasive. Many of the teachers, former members of the Fathers of the Faith, had lived hard lives during the revolutionary upheavals and they were not going to allow the youthful hope of a future Christian France to turn soft in their hands. "Never are the students left to themselves; the vigilance of the masters extends to every place and to very instant of the day and the night" as the prospectus of the school announced. Infractions of the rules brought disciplinary measures, from confinement to one spot for a period, a special room for extra school work, public reprimands, dining while kneeling, "afflictive manual corrections," dire official warnings and, when all hope for a black sheep was abandoned, expulsion. But the other side of the coin was equally true. Over and over the regulations stressed that really competent teachers or prefects should need no other control then praise or blame and that they were to exhibit "kindness and firmness... [and] a recognized impartiality," that they were to gain "the confidence, the affection and the respect of the students" and that they were "to pray frequently and fervently for the students confided to their care."[24]

Teaching (*enseignement*) was to go hand in hand with training or formation (*éducation*). Religion was to be its most influential part. In addition to classes in religion, an annual spiritual retreat opened the school year. Mass, spiritual reading, and prayers were daily events; the sacrament of confession was always available and obligatory once a month. Communion once a month was usual and for some few students even oftener, a rare occurrence in an era still tinged with the Jansensistic warnings against such an untoward practice. Not everything mirrored an Eden. The records recounted both the good and the bad, and the latter ranged from midnight feasts of cakes and wine in the bell tower "with deplorable results for the digestive system," to the nine-year old corrupter who "gave marks of a perversity as profound as it was precocious."[25] One must wonder at this latter phenomenon! Whatever the problems of lack of personnel and money, and makeshift quarters, and hastily prepared teachers, and what to our eyes would seem excessive rigidity, the schools were immensely popular. The letters of parents and the recollections of alumni provide overwhelming evidence of this. Perhaps the word "patriarchal," with all that it expresses of both affection and severity, best sums up the spirit of these schools.[26]

Of course, not everything was a success. The most lamented problem was the lapse in Catholic practice by many of the students after they left the school. But it surely was not easy in any case for young alumni of sixteen to eighteen years of age to find the external supports in any city, especially Paris, for sustaining the practice of the faith. This was especially the case when they left a highly protective atmosphere of the Jesuit schools to live in the high Restoration society that may have been externally religious but that was often also openly skeptical and equally immoral. On balance, however, their schools were judged a success by the contemporary Jesuits. They educated only a small fraction of French students, but most of them retained a great affection for the Society and many of them went on greatly to influence Catholic life in the next decades. Such alumni provided a link, however thinly stretched at times, between the reputation, great but fading from memory, of presuppression Jesuit schools and the major efflorescence of the schools of the Society when finally they became legal in France in 1850 and Jesuits publicly established and taught in them. As for the success of the seminary aspect of the schools, one example will suffice. From St. Acheul alone in its fourteen years came 70 Jesuits, 550 priests and 8 bishops.

THE BEGINNING OF THE END

All of this crashed to an end in 1828. Throughout the decade of the 1820s, and especially after Charles X succeeded his brother, Louis XVIII, as king in 1824, the seemingly intractable problem was how to reconcile the tradition of the monarchy and its claims to reign by divine right with the popular and at least embryonic democratic spirit that arose in and continued to exist after the Revolution. During Louis XVIII's reign, Charles as Comte d'Artois was identified with the Ultras, the party of the extreme right and reaction. When he became king, three reactionary government ministries impaired whatever popularity he had. Behind the Ultras in much of the popular mind and certainly in that of their opponents lay the Jesuits. During the second and slightly more liberal of those ministries established after the 1827 election victory of the moderate monarchists, the attack on the Jesuits and especially on their schools grew more strident on the part of the political opposition.

To appease the opposition, and to keep the government in power, the king reluctantly but finally signed two *Ordonnances* on June 16, 1828. The second simply emphasized the *seminary* character of the minor seminaries and put limits to their expansion. The first dealt directly with the Jesuits. It made "the eight establishments directed by persons belonging to a non-authorized congregation . . . subject to the regulations of the Université [the national ministry of education]," and it declared that no one could direct or teach in such a school "if he does not affirm in writing that he does not belong to any religious congregation not legally established in France." Much of the episcopate refused at first to accept the regulation but they finally backed down when the Pope, Leo XII, hoping to avoid greater damage to the church, persuaded them to give in. The eight Jesuit schools in France closed. The Society tried to keep a low profile; the Jesuits from those schools took up other work in France or in the missions abroad or in the exile colleges set up almost immediately outside the French borders.

As soon as the schools in France closed, French parents clamored for the Society somehow to provide for religious education of their sons. The first response was an exile college opened in November, 1828, at le Passage near San Sebastian in Spain, a few miles from the French border. It

The Jesuit college residence in Fribourg

lasted for six years until a Liberal ministry of the Spanish government closed it in 1834 and chased the Jesuits out of the country. Some French families sent their sons to already existing Jesuit colleges at Melan and Chambéry in the as yet independent Savoy, and at Brigue, Sion, and Fribourg in Switzerland where some of the Jesuits of the French province went to teach.

But the most famous and important of the exile colleges was at Brugelette in Belgium. Of course, these had been no possibility of starting a Jesuit school in the Belgium ruled by the Protestant king of Holland, William I. But after the Belgian revolt of 1830 brought independence to the land, Belgian Jesuits themselves began their own new schools and delicate negotiations began between the two provinces. Finally in 1835 Brugelette opened as a college of the French Jesuit province. Very rapidly it attracted not only French students but a large number from other lands too, especially after the Spanish school closed and the Protestant victors in the War of the Sonderbund in 1848 sacked and closed Fribourg and exiled the Jesuits from Switzerland. Brugelette itself, only a few miles from the French border, enjoyed a prosperous existence until 1854 by which time the now-legal Jesuit schools in France had drawn off most of its students.

If the Jesuits had to face the external challenges of the world around them, especially in reference to their work in education, they also had an internal challenge in the field of education. This one, however, was internal to the Society itself. It involved positions — philosophical and theological positions — in the education it was giving to its own members. The teachings of what would be called "Mennaisienism" took their origin in the work of Felicité de Lamennais. In the 1820s he was still vigorously propagating and defending an Ultramontane understanding of the papacy, but he was also propagating and defending a novel theory of certitude. According to that theory the content of faith is finally found and guaranteed not so much by individual reason as by a "general reason" that is expressed by everyone in those propositions consented to universally and to which no exception is possible. Popularly this bore the name of the "philosophy of common consent" or *sens commun*. We "must admit as true that which all men believe invincibly. Authority, or the general reason, or common consent is the rule of judgment for the individual man."[27] Obviously, such a simple statement does little or no justice to the whole system that Lamennais elaborated with grace and style and passion. Unfortunately, the subtlety of the system got lost in simplistic oppositions of "faith and reason" and, whether simple or subtle, lines were drawn and positions taken. Lamennais' system had great attraction for Catholics as diverse in personality and viewpoints as Joseph de Maistre, the ardent conservative apologist, and Jean-Baptiste Lacordaire, the great preacher at Notre Dame.

In a supposedly clear contest between a "pure" Cartesian reason and faith, much of the French clergy and other religious circles in France enthusiastically accepted the philosophy of the *sens commun*. Jesuits were no exception. Many of the most prominent first generation French Jesuits, including two provincials, ardently accepted "Mennaisienism." Others ardently opposed it and in almost every Jesuit house divisions arose. The dispute became public in 1823 and the Superior General, Fr. Luigi Fortis, wrote a directive that summarized the doctrine in a series of propositions. Without qualifying them as true or false and without mentioning Lamennais at all, he ordered those propositions not to be taught within the Society. The propositions had been drawn up by one of the General's staff, Fr. Jean Rozaven, himself firmly opposed to "Mennaisienism" while others at the headquarters in Rome favored the doctrine. Indeed, one of the assistants to the General was removed from office for that reason. The quarrel within the Society continued for a good while; some Jesuits asked to be relieved of their vows; Lamennais himself became incensed and justifiably so when, upon inquiry about the General's directive since news of it had become public, the Jesuit provincial told him that it was purely an internal Jesuit matter. The situation became more complicated, of course, after the 1830 revolution when Lamennais' journal *l'Avenir* first appeared with its program of Catholic liberalism. Because that story in detail would take us beyond the scope of this chapter, suffice it to say that the two condemnatory papal encyclicals *Mirari Vos* in 1832 and *Singulari Vos* in 1834, and especially the latter with its prohibition of "that fallacious philosophical system," put an end to open controversy about it in the Society.

MISSIONARIES AT LAST

To turn finally to what was eventually to be one of the great apostolates of the renascent Society, the foreign missions, the French Jesuits, as was true for most of the Society, with rare individual exceptions, only began such work after 1830. The pressures of reestablishment and reorganization of the Society, the lack of trained personnel, the needs of a post-revolutionary Europe, all impeded an earlier sustained missionary endeavor. As an exception, the very first corporately organized foreign mission work of the restored Society began in 1823 with young Belgian Jesuits recruited to work among the native Americans. They arrived that year in Missouri where first they set up at Florissant an Indian school supported in part by the United States government, then took on the school that became St. Louis University, and eventually established the Missouri Province. The Jesuits in France learned very early of that venture. In a letter to all the French Jesuits on October 1, 1826, Nicolas Godinot, the provincial, described this new work:

> At about twenty miles from the poor little town where the bishop of St. Louis lives, thirteen of our brethren live in cabins, four priests, six scholastics and three brothers, working with their hands in the manner of the apostles. To provide food and shelter for themselves and for the twenty-five children whom they have gathered together from various savage tribes, they farm several small pieces of property. Their food is bread when they have it, and potatoes. Despite everything, they carry on a very active apostolate among Catholics and among the Protestants.[28]

The provincial closed his letter in asking his brethren for help for that newborn mission. So, when a year or so later, Benedict Flaget, Bishop of Bardstown in Kentucky, asked for some French Jesuits for his college, the members of the province were well aware of the United States mission, even though the provincial had to turn down the request due to lack of personnel. The July Revolution in 1830 transformed the personnel problem. A good number of the French Jesuits had to seek a refuge and an apostolate outside the houses from which they had been chased. After 1830 and especially after the letter of December 3, 1833, by Father General, Jan Roothaan, that asked the whole Society to take up again the tradition of missionary work in foreign lands, the French province and then the several provinces of France responded to that appeal. They sent their members within a few years not only so far afield as Syria, India, Madagascar, Algeria, Ceylon and China but even to Kentucky and thence to New York.

To return to the last major events in France before the first of those Jesuits came to the United States, if 1828 had been a difficult and discouraging year for the Society in France with their exile from the eight French Jesuit schools, 1830 must have appeared to them at first as a disaster. The July Revolution quickly took on an antireligious and anticlerical and especially anti-Jesuit character. For too long in the Restoration the "throne and altar" had been too closely linked, and the revolution against the monarchy spilled over into violence against the Church. In the very first days of the uprising, the Paris mob pillaged the sacristy of the cathedral of Notre Dame and the archbishop's residence. Later they burned the residence to the ground. The Jesuit residence on the rue de Sèvres and the novitiate at Montrouge were sacked. The destruction spread like wildfire to other French cities. The theaters were full of lowlife burlesques on the Jesuits. A Hungarian diplomat then in France commented on the Jesuits in his memoirs: "The roles of schemers, knaves, scoundrels in the comedies or melodramas are always represented by Jesuits. In addition, the worst insult that you can offer to anyone is to call him a Jesuit."[29] The anti-Jesuit madness persisted beyond the few days of the Revolution itself. The provincial of France described the scene to the General a month after the July Days:

> The streets are hung with inflammatory posters against the Jesuits. They are the ones who. . . gunned down the people . . . I am very worried. It has been a good month now that everything here has been aflame. . . I have very good reason to believe that letters abroad are intercepted and opened. . . .
>
> Our priests, most of them, are disguised, hidden or dispersed. The good Christians beg us not to leave the country. We will not do so as long as the danger does not become clear and open. If that should happen, I do not think it would be your wish that I expose [our members] to certain ruin in helping others in a land that devours its own inhabitants. Already Montrouge has been sacked and ruined. . . . St. Acheul had it the same day . . . . They came to our residence in Paris three times; the fathers are no longer there. Vitry was ransacked the day before yesterday. . . . The populace sacked, stole, ate and drank for almost twenty-four hours. . . .Priests, scho-

lastics, novices, brothers, all would seem happy to suffer for our Lord. They are really reliving the great early days of the Society.[30]

A DIFFERENT COUNTRY

By 1830 the restored Society was on the threshold of living days, both ordinary and great, in a world very different from that of the early Society. Perhaps nowhere was that more true than in that new world of the United States. The first Jesuits to come to this country from the nineteenth-century province of France would find a country where "throne and altar" were not only not linked but officially separated, not in hostility but in mutual respect. The specter of Jesuitry did haunt minds brought up in the rhetoric of English Protestantism but the Society could carry out its work here unhindered by any legal disabilities. The French revolution was at best a faint memory in comparison to the vivid patriotism surrounding the American revolution, and one could hardly imagine a greater contrast in rulers than that between Charles X, by divine right king of the French, and Andrew Jackson, president of the United States

The great popular parish missions of post-Restoration France might summon up analogues in the American Protestant revival meetings and the later Catholic parish missions in the United States would bear a closer resemblance. Certainly there was nothing like the *Congrégation* in the United States. The educational apostolate that the French Jesuits had taken up so rapidly would be matched in the United States but in different circumstances and in different ways. Far from the governmental monopoly of education in France that attempted to impose itself, private and religious primary schools existed in the United States alongside public schools, and by far the greater number of colleges and the few universities here at the time were independent and often explicitly religiously affiliated. Catholic schools were just beginning. The colleges among them were most often of diocesan origin, as was the college in the diocese of Bardstown to which these French Jesuits first went and as was Fordham to which they later moved. As for Jesuit institutions of secondary and higher education, in 1830 only Georgetown and St. Louis existed as such. Both at the time were "colleges" that included in a single curriculum what would today be called secondary and higher education, as was true of other independent institutions. Georgetown traces its foundation as a college to Bishop John Carroll in 1789; St. Louis as a college to Bishop Louis DuBourg to 1818, as Fordham would to Bishop John Hughes in 1841.

Both France and the United States in 1830 were far different from what they are today. But they were also far more different from each other than they are today. To leave a land steeped in history, culture and tradition, a country that the Jesuits certainly regarded as Christian and Catholic, no matter what the temporary calamities of the French Revolution, and come to a land colonized mostly by English Protestants that was still inventing itself in so many ways and was prejudiced if not hostile to Catholics, took imagination and generosity and courage and perseverance on the part of these French Jesuits. Although they may not have recognized it, they surely were among the renascent Jesuits who were "really reliving the great early days of the Society."

NOTES

1. Joseph Picot de Clorivière, as he came to be known, led an adventurous life that mirrored the times from its beginning in Brittany in 1768 to its end in Washington, DC in 1826. He attended the Royal Military School in Paris before the Revolution, resigned his officer's commission in 1791 and became a counterrevolutionary, took an active part in the abortive assassination plot against Napoleon in 1800, escaped to Savannah, Georgia, studied at St. Mary's Seminary in Baltimore, and was ordained in 1812. He first served as a priest at a parish in Charleston, SC, returned to France at the royal restoration, came back to Charleston and engaged in a four year struggle with the lay trustees of the parish who would not accept his appointment. John Carroll and the two subsequent bishops of Baltimore fought the parish to no avail. Finally, to restore peace, Clorivière was appointed chaplain to the Visitation Convent in Georgetown where he was a great support personally and financially. He is regarded as the second founder of the convent and is buried in its chapel.

2. *Archivum Romanum Societatis Jesu* (hereinafter *ARSI)* Franc., Grivel to Fortis, 1820.

3. *Charte*, 1814, article 5.

4. *ARSI*, ibid.

5. "Long live France/ Long live the King/ Forever the Bourbons/ And the faith we sing."

6. "Men in black, whence issue you?/We crawl up from underground./Half-way foxes, half-way wolves/Our way of life is mystery-bound."

7. Montlosier, Francois Dominique, *Memoire à consulter sur un systèm politique tendant à renverser la religion, la société et le trone* (Paris, 1826) as quoted in Joseph Burnichon, S.J., *La Compagnie de Jésus en France: Histoire d'un siècle, 1814-1914* (Paris, 1914-1922), I, 351.

8. *Archivum Provinciae Parisiensis Societatis Jesu* (hereinafter PSJ), D2 1:2422

9. Burnichon, op. cit., I, 289

10. For example, *L' ami de Religion* in 1823 could offer from an anonymous benefactor "100 pistoles" (a thousand francs) to every bishop who could put together a team of priests to give missions; Ibid., 210.

11. *ARSI*, Richardot to Rozaven, August 7, 1821.

12. *ARSI*, Druilhet to Fortis, July 30, 1827.

13. For a fuller account of the "Congrégation," see the excellent work by G. de Bertier de Sauvigny, *Un Type d'ultra-royaliste: Le Comte Ferdinand de Bertier et l'énigrne de la Congrégation* (Paris, 1948).

14. See Adrien Dansette, *Religious History of Modern France*, 2 vols. Translated by John Dingle (New York, 1961); especially vol. 1 for a thoroughly developed description of the religious state of France and the "European church of Napoleon" at the beginning of the nineteenth century.

15. Burnichon, op. cit., I, 127.

16. Sue's book is still in print even at this late date, but it would take great patience to get through it all.

17. See Alexander Vivier, S.J., *Catalogi officiorum et sociorum*, 1819-1836 (Paris, 1894).

18. *ARSI*, Franc., Reg., Clorivière to Brzozowski, August 30, 1816.

19. In 1832 St. Louis University in the United States received from that provision of the Jesuits Constitutions the dispensation upon which all Jesuit schools around the world had to rely until the changes brought about following Vatican II and the thirty-first general congregation of the Society.

20. M. Hyacinthe, *Coup doeil dans l'intérieur de Saint-Acheul, ou de l'Education que donnent les Jésuites modernes à la jeunesse francaise* (Paris, 1826).

21. 'Plan d'Etudes" in *PSJ*, 2220, *Annales*, Introduction. Loriquet produced a hand-written work, of more than 800 pages, the Annales du Petit-Séminaire de Saint-Acheul, which gave in detail, sometimes day by day, the history of the Jesuit community and of the school and rules of procedure for every person and every task in the institution. The other minor seminaries in great part followed the regimen of Saint-Achuel, and after 1828 so did the later exile colleges.

22. Ibid., 815.

23. See Pierre Bliard, *Le Père Loriquet: La Légende et l'Histoire* (Paris, 1922).

24. *Annales*, Rules 16, 22 and 23 for Prefects, 870 ff.

25. Ibid., 175-176; 529-530.

26. One example, among many, of such testimony can be found in Jean-Francois Bellemare, *Le Collège de mon fils* (Paris, 1827).

27. See Felicité de Lamennais, *Défense de l'Essai sur l'indifférence en matière de réligion* (Paris, 1821) 179-180.

28. *PSJ*, Godinot to Province, Oct. 1, 1826.

29. Rodolphe Apponyi, "Autour de la Révolution de 1830," *Revue des Deux Mondes* 71 (October 15, 1912), 798.

30. *ARSJ*, Franc., Druilhet to Roothaan, Aug. 31, 1830.

Chapter III

French Jesuits at St. Mary's College, Marion County, Kentucky 1831-1846

By Cornelius Michael Buckley, S.J.

In 1808, the year Bishop John Carroll of Baltimore was promoted to the rank of archbishop, a French-born Sulpician priest named Benedict Joseph Flaget (1763-1850), former member of the faculty at Georgetown, was nominated first bishop of the area west of the Allegheny and north of the 35th degree latitude. That territory today includes the states of Kentucky, Ohio, Michigan, Indiana, Illinois, Wisconsin, Iowa, Missouri, Tennessee, and half of Arkansas. Bardstown in Kentucky was to be his see. It was where the greatest number of Catholics was concentrated. Seven priests cared for about six thousand Catholics in some thirty parishes and mission stations, only ten of which had churches or chapels. Understandably one of the bishop's first priorities was to recruit priests.

Twenty years later this endeavor was still a priority, and so in 1827 Bishop Flaget dispatched one of his priests, Robert A. Abell (1792-1873), to Billom, France, where he himself had made his seminary training and where the newly established Jesuits of the Province of France had recently opened a college. Flaget proposed that these French Jesuits assume the direction of the combination seminary-college for boys at St. Joseph's in Bardstown, which he had founded in 1819. The Jesuits were as flattered by the bishop's invitation as they were sympathetic with his predicament, but they had neither the men nor the resources to aid him, and really, Kentucky was not a mission field that generated enthusiasm in high-minded spirits. Three years later, the July Revolution erupted, altering inexorably plans for the future of the Province of France. Jesuits were exiled and their colleges closed, leaving many talented men without jobs. The provincial, remembering Flaget's invitation, ordered four of his men to Kentucky: Pierre Chazelle (1789-1845), Nicolas Petit (1789-1855) and Pierre Ladavière (1777-1854) who were priests, and Brother Philippe Corne (1800-1862). Chazelle was designated superior. For this reason he is considered the father of the New York, New England, and the Upper and Lower Canadian provinces, all of which trace their beginnings to this small group.[1]

31

In heavy disguise, the foursome embarked on November 19, 1830 from Pauillac near Bordeaux, and arrived in Guadeloupe on January 5. Chazelle worked there among condemned slaves awaiting execution while Petit and Ladavière conducted missions among the whites. The foursome later sailed on a ship bound for New Orleans. As soon as they disembarked on February 7, they placed themselves at the service of the newly appointed bishop, Leo Raymond De Neckere, C.M. (1800-1833). The bishop had more than enough work for all of them in the parishes, the overcrowded city jails, and the hospitals. Consequently, it was with difficulty that Chazelle tried to explain to the bishop that they were already promised to Flaget. But De Neckere seemed impervious to all logic. At last, a compromise was reached: Chazelle would write a letter to Flaget advising him of the group's arrival and telling him that they were ready to assume direction of his college. At the same time, Chazelle promised De Neckere that until he received an answer to this letter, he and his companions would continue to work in New Orleans.

When Chazelle's letter arrived in Bardstown, it "fell as a thunderbolt on His Lordship, as well as on the priests of his diocese."[2] The reason was that changes had taken place in Kentucky during the three years following the bishop's proffered invitation to the French Jesuits. St. Joseph's seminary was doing very well under the direction of the diocesan clergy, who now, understandably, felt offended and threatened by the incursion of the Jesuits. The local priests wanted the Bishop to reassure them that such was not to be the case. Flaget, however, needed priests in his diocese and — to mix metaphors — while he was willing to smooth feathers, he was loath to look too intently in the mouth of the proverbial gift horse. Under the circumstances, he promised the diocesan clergy that as long as he was bishop the Jesuits would never have anything to do with St. Joseph's.

The Bishop needed time to work himself out of this dilemma. He wrote to Chazelle encouraging the four Frenchmen to come to Kentucky after the thaw, which made river traveling hazardous. He assured Chazelle that there were a few slight details to work out, and, oh yes — the Jesuits would probably not want St. Joseph's, but come, *do* come — "after the thaw." Chazelle read between the lines and was cautious. Now more than ever, he wanted to keep De Neckere's friendship, and so ordered Ladavière and Corne to remain in New Orleans while he and Petit left for Bardstown on April 23. When they arrived on May 14, they were lodged in St. Joseph's, and as the weeks passed, Chazelle became more and more disenchanted with Kentucky. The thaw may have come about on the Mississippi, but the climate was still chilly indeed at St. Joseph's.

Meanwhile, thanks to the letters he was receiving from Ladaviere, he was more inclined to believe that the opportunities for founding a Jesuit college in Louisiana were more auspicious. Toward the end of July, he informed Flaget of his confused feelings about remaining in Kentucky. The Bishop understood, but asked him to grant him one more favor before he and Petit made plans to return to New Orleans. The three men would make a novena to St. Ignatius of Loyola, begging the founder of the Society of Jesus to obtain from the Lord some more definite sign that would dissipate the uncertainty about what the Jesuits should do. Before the nine-day prayer was completed, a sign had indeed been given.

AN ANSWER TO PRAYER

The reader will remember the story, recounted in the Book of Numbers (22:2-24:25), of Balaam, a diviner summoned by the Moabites to curse the invading Israelites. Thanks to the intervention of his talking ass, Balaam ended up blessing rather than cursing the newcomers. In the light of the subsequent history of Fordham, it is amusing to consider that in this case Balaam becomes a magician-bishop who is able to bless the Jesuit newcomers with a gift, and at the same time, assuage the wrath of his Moabite clergy. The talking ass was "an ascetic who seldom smiled and never laughed." His name was William Byrne (1780-1833), a laconic, raw-boned diocesan priest, whose memory was as long as his fuse was short. Byrne had been in the vanguard of the Marion county Moabites — those opposed to any Jesuits coming into the diocese. But apparently Chazelle, who had the grace "to be admired and loved by all those who have the good fortune to know him," had, by charm and piety, deflected Byrne's opposition and won over his admiration.[3] On the last day of the celebrated novena, Flaget received a letter from Byrne offering to deed to the Jesuits the College of St. Mary's.

Geographically, the college was located in Washington — afterwards Marion — County, sixty-two miles south of Louisville, five miles west of Lebanon, and some ten miles from Bardstown. Historically, it was situated in the cradle-land of Catholicism in the old west, on some three-hundred acres of farmland. The only strings attached to the hand-over was that Byrne would keep his saddle-horse and ten dollars, and that Flaget would give him permission to ride to Tennessee where he proposed to found another school in Nashville.

MORE ABOUT REV. WILLIAM BYRNE

Scarred in early life by the bloody aftermath of Vinegar Hill during the Irish Rebellion of 1798, William Byrne emigrated to the United States in 1805. Once the Society was reestablished in Maryland ten years later, he entered its novitiate. Too restless for the sedentary life of a Jesuit novice, he shortly afterwards shook dust from his feet and betook himself to the diocesan seminary at Baltimore where, in December 1818, he was ordained sub-deacon. In the following May, he bolted "without consideration and against the will of his superior," made his way west, and asked Flaget to accept him. With a dearth of priests, Flaget, who hated to say no to anyone, was happy to gamble on the request. Years later the bishop declared that there was no better priest in his diocese.[4]

If Byrne's earlier life had left him handicapped in some respects, it had also provided him with a terrible toughness, a sense of independence and perseverance under adversity. Even though he had left the novitiate with ill feelings for Jesuits, he was certainly in agreement with their ideas about the value of a liberal education for the young men of America. Accordingly, in 1821 he purchased the farm that Kentucky's famous missionary, Father Charles Nerinckx (1761-1824), had bought two years earlier from a certain Mr. Joseph Ray, a man of portly stature weighing more than 500 pounds.

Nerinckx envisioned building a technical school for boys on this site, which he named Mount Mary — an institution patterned after the school he had founded at Loretto for future wives and mothers. But he lacked the cash to do so. In 1820 he left on a fruitless begging tour to Europe to seek aid for his project. During his absence, Byrne persuaded Flaget that what the country needed was not a trade school designed to form better farmers and artisans, but an academic center for young men that would rival the academies in the East. Flaget gave in to the importune requests of his curate and gave him leave to purchase Mount Mary for himself and open his dream school. There was an abandoned moonshine distillery of favorable dimensions located on the premises of what had once been "the fat man's farm." This Byrne remodeled into a makeshift classroom by day and a dormitory by night. He then set about erecting a few more suitable buildings around the old stillhouse where once an elixir that gladden men's hearts was made, and changed the whole conglomerate to St. Mary's Seminary. As providence would have it, this modest a structure of an unused stillhouse was destined to be the embryo from which Fordham University took its present glorious shape.

When Nerinckx returned at the end of 1821, he was shocked to find a school in full operation with boys of various ages learning Latin and history, algebra and trigonometry. (To his credit the old missionary retreated from the scene and devoted his energies to other adventures.) Fire soon destroyed St. Mary's buildings, but phoenix-like they rose again from the ashes, prospered a short time only to succumb once more to a conflagration. Undaunted, Byrne rebuilt what fire had claimed and then, for the third time, the intrepid priest-educator was called to stand in the smoldering ashes to estimate new losses.

Byrne, despite his harsh exterior, was a man of great charity and zeal, and undoubtedly he saw reflected in Chazelle these same qualities. Perhaps that was one of the reasons he was attracted to the Frenchman. Chazelle had a certain disarming simplicity about him; he was not like the Jesuits Byrne had known at Georgetown. But Byrne was no sentimentalist. He was a realist who saw beyond the personal and spiritual qualities of individuals. By temperament and experience, he was more of a frontiersman than a settler, and the crucible of three destructive fires had made him see that the school he began would never last unless a group of dedicated religious men took it on as a project. So, less than a month after his offer to the Jesuits, Chazelle had settled in at St. Mary's.

MANPOWER SCHEDULING

Because the new proprietor was far from having a command of English, and because the ways of American boys were even a greater mystery than the complexities of English syntax, the new superior persuaded the old president, Byrne, to remain on for a year, which was later extended to two. Petit spoke English perfectly, and so the bishop requested that he remain at Bardstown, from where he could make apostolic visits to priests scattered about Kentucky and Indiana. Chazelle then wrote to Lavadière and Corne asking them to join their colleagues in Kentucky. Eventually both made the trip north, but Lavadière remained only a short time. The bishop of New Orleans wanted him back and he was more than willing to go. Chazelle also advised the general in Rome of Byrne's offer and requested permission for the society to take possession officially of St. Mary's. Mail was slow and so it was only in July of the following year, when the school was in full operation as a Jesuit endeavor, that the news of the general's acceptance reached Chazelle.

FIRST JESUIT RECRUITS AND DEATHS IN KENTUCKY

The Province of France in exile assumed responsibility for the college, and the provincial collected three of his men who had been scattered by the Ordinances of 1830 to different parts of Europe — Switzerland, Spain, Italy — and assigned them to the province's newest mission, Kentucky. These newcomer priests were Guy Gilles (1797-1855) and Thomas Legoüais (1793-1876), both French, and a young Irishman named Eugene Maguire (1800-1833). The threesome arrived in the United States via New Orleans, where Brother Corne joined them for the last stage of their journey. This time there was apparently no thaw, and so the party arrived at St. Mary's in time to celebrate Christmas 1832.

Shortly after Chazelle's arrival at Bardstown in April 1831, two French diocesan priests at St. Joseph's College, Simon Fouché (1789-1870) and Evermond Harissart (1792-1859), requested admission to the Society. Chazelle accepted both and sent Harissart, a willowy man, slender and supple, to the novitiate in Maryland. But because Fouché, diminutive in stature and vivacious in action, had committed himself to remain at St. Joseph's for 1831-1832, his novitiate was put off for a year. Meanwhile, the general authorized a novitiate to be established at St. Mary's with Chazelle as the master of novices. This meant that Harissart was recalled to Kentucky to complete his second year novitiate. He arrived there a few days before the appearance of the four newcomers from New Orleans and in time to welcome his friend Simon Fouché, who was now free to begin his first year novitiate. Consequently on New Year's Day, 1833, there were seven Jesuits at St. Mary's. So happy was the superior to welcome them all that he made an exception to one of the community's strictest rules: for an hour they were able to converse with one another in French, rather than in fractured English. On the following day, after rising at four, all the priests were in the classroom under the keen eye of William Byrne. Brother Corne, "a man of rare virtues and still rarer capabilities," took charge of the dormitory and linen room; later he became the director of the college choir.

The 1832 spring term finished nicely, and during the summer, as Byrne was making preparations to make his final adieu and head off to found a new school, he succumbed to the cholera epidemic that was ravishing the countryside. William Maguire and three students suffered the same fate.

ACADEMIC AND FINANCIAL STRUCTURES AT ST. MARY'S

During his twelve year tenure, Byrne had set up a demanding academic curriculum. For this reason, and also because he had the reputation of being a strict disciplinarian, parents from all parts of the country and even as far away as Mexico and Cuba sent their sons to St. Mary's. Chazelle, who had now assumed the function of President and Rector, was determined not merely to carry on the founder's ambitious program, but to expand it. Under Byrne, St. Mary's was an academy; under Chazelle, beginning in 1834, it would become a college with courses in philosophy and theology. The notice on the facing page, which appeared in local newspapers announcing the opening of the 1833 fall term, attests to the variety of classes offered and to the cost of a Jesuit education in the mid-nineteenth century

In France the Jesuits always included the *humaniora*, "the refining arts," in the curriculum, and when the colleges in exile were set up in Switzerland, Spain, and Belgium, music and drama were given a place alongside courses in higher mathematics and classical literature. Chazelle introduced this same tradition to St. Mary's. At the end of the 1834 academic year, he staged an Indian

Latin, Greek, French, English Grammar, Arithmetic, Algebra, Geometry, Surveying, Bookkeeping, Geography with the use of the Globes, and all the common branches of education. To these, at the request of students, are added for next year — 1st Rhetoric, properly so termed, being generally considered the completion of all studies; 2ndly, Hebrew; 3rdly, Spanish.

TERMS

1st. For those who study the high branches during a session, which will consist of five and a half months, Board, Tuition, Washing, &c., (Bed and bedding excepted) in advance — $32.00

2ndly. For those who do not study the high branches, also in advance — $30.00

3rdly. For day scholars or externs a session, from 6 to 12 dollars, according to the number and nature of the classes they attend. This likewise payable in advance.

drama named "Red Hawk," which he had written himself, and which was performed by the students before a sizable audience; in the following year, another play, "Benedict Arnold, the Traitor," was staged. One of the participants later reflected that in this production the final *coup de théâtre* "was the hanging of Major André on stage, so that all could see the ignominious end of a British spy."[5] These productions were enthusiastically received by the country people.[6] The melodramas staged during the commencement exercises of 1838 and 1839 became spectacles that commanded huge audiences. A whole acre of chairs was filled by spectators who clapped, laughed and wept during the performance of such classics as "Winterton Moreton or the Refugee" and "Elphinstone or The Pseudo-Assassin."[7] Meanwhile, Brother Corne trained voices accustomed to calling hogs to sing polyphonic motets and contrapuntal melodies.[8]

INTRODUCING MARTIN J. SPALDING

In addition to being priest, president, carpenter, disciplinarian, mason, prefect, farmer, and treasurer, Byrne had taught most of the courses at the college himself, but in 1826 he hired a lay professor, who was reputed to be a mathematical prodigy. His name was Martin J. Spalding (1810-1872). He was fourteen at the time his name was inscribed on what we might designate today as the tenure track. In his biography, written by his nephew the Bishop of Peoria, John Lancaster Spalding (1840-1916), we learn that people from all over the country "went out of their way to see this wonderful boy-professor," who learned the multiplication-table in a single day when he was eight years old.[9] In 1821, Martin Spalding and his two older brothers were the first to enroll at St.

Mary's. It would not be rash to suggest that Martin holds the record among distinguished 'Fordham' professors for being the youngest faculty member ever hired, at least in the Department of Mathematics. In 1864 he was named Archbishop of Baltimore and, as such, played a pivotal role in giving a particular direction to the Church in the United States. In 1837, there were eight full time lay teachers on the staff.[10]

THE STUDENT BODY

Martin Spalding was also probably younger than most graduates of St. Mary's, although precisely what the average age was is difficult to state. Students could range anywhere between ten and eighteen, with the latter being the normal age of matriculation. The student population at any given time between 1821 and 1846 is likewise difficult to calculate with precision. Archbishop Martin Spalding reported that from 1821 to 1823, that is, during Byrne's tenure, the number of students varied between eighty and one-hundred and twenty.[11] This figure seems inflated when compared to registration figures in Jesuit sources. In February 1834, there were forty-five borders and a dozen day students; by the end of 1836, there were one hundred boarding students. In 1838, there were one hundred and two boarding students out of a total registration of one hundred and twenty-four. In 1841 the total population was down to ninety students and in 1846, the year the Jesuits moved to Fordham, there were seventy-five boarders and three day students.[12]

STUDENTS AND RELIGION

In the 1820s and 1830s, the majority of the students were Protestants; in the 1840s, Catholics were dominant. What would be called a *Mission Statement* at the end of the twentieth century, and was less pretentiously referred to as a college prospectus in the mid-nineteenth century, declared that "without any encroachment on the principles of students of other denominations," the Catholic faith was professed by those who administered the school and by those who taught the students. At the same time, it went on to state, "good order is so indispensable in a large institution that attendance is required at the public exercises of religious worship."[13]

After 1836, lectures on Catholic doctrine were given twice a week in the chapel; all students, including the Protestants, were required to be present. Catholic students made a visit to the Blessed Sacrament each day after breakfast, and it was customary, although not obligatory, for them to attend daily Mass. These and other pious practices, such as those associated with the month of May and with the sodality of the Blessed Virgin, were later brought to

Fordham. Father Thomas Legoüais, was the spiritual father to the students and acted also as chaplain to the girls at Loretto Convent.[14]

Tuition in Money or in Kind

From the very beginning Father Byrne had allowed parents of the local boys to pay tuition in money or in kind: in wheat, corn, vegetables, bacon, cotton. In tallying such staples that could be used as barter, Evremond Harissart cautioned the reader not to forget "the humble tobacco leaf," which also was cultivated in the farmers' gardens: "it is neither the last nor the least of all the plants to which masters and servants, parents and children sometimes address expressions of endearment."[15]

The College Farm: Everybody Works

All the grain needed in the college's storerooms was grown on St. Mary's farm, and the farm also produced the hogs and cattle required to supply enough meat to satisfy so many adolescent appetites. Over the course of years, Father Chazelle bought more pieces of property adjacent to Byrne's original purchase so that by 1846 the farm totaled nine hundred acres. In 1836 Father Chazelle had a treadmill built and from that date on the college could make its own flour, as well as supply a surplus to the neighbors.[16] The college counted among its students sons of state governors, of members of Congress and of federal and state judges, and Byrne exempted none of these from working on the farm one full day each week with the rest of the students. The Jesuits made no changes in this policy until 1837, when the practice was discontinued. The day of physical labor included such tasks as driving teams of oxen and horses, chopping and sawing wood, gathering crops, and making tallow candles for lighting the study hall and dormitory at night.

Another Fire

Zachary Montgomery, who became the Assistant Attorney General in President Cleveland's administration, was the student in charge of these candles. His authority however was not without challenges. For example, on December 20, 1833, when Chazelle "was away on business," a fire broke out in the boys' dormitory, and the next morning "only the walls were standing." Two students, resentful over what they considered an unjust punishment, turned arsonist to obtain revenge. So ended that fall semester; however the fire did not prevent classes from beginning again on schedule for the spring semester.

Dormitory Living

In that new semester "the boarders were housed in a spanking new brick building."[17] This new dormitory was a large room lighted at one end by a floating taper and at the other by a candle in a sconce nailed to the wall. "The bedsteads were long, and separated in the middle by a board to accommodate two occupants, sleeping feet to feet." There was another board on the side designed to prevent the occupant from rolling out at night. There were no curtains and tin wash basins were placed beside the beds.[18] Three years later another building, also made of brick, was constructed providing, at last, the Jesuits with a separate living quarters. By 1841 St. Mary's compound was completed.[19]

Another Jesuit Foursome

In December 1834 the arrival of four new Jesuits, two brothers and two priests, was a further guarantee of the French province's commitment to the American mission. The brothers, Michel Jary (1793-1848) and Philippe Ledoré (1800-1881), were both Bretons. The very day after their arrival, the former went to work on the farm; the latter relieved Brother Corne in the kitchen, enabling him, who had learned English better than the fathers, to spend more time with the students and with his music. The newly arrived priests were William Stack Murphy (1803-1875) and Nicolas Point (1799-1868).

Point, described by his French superiors as "a man for the men in the college," that is, an expert on the theory and practice of Jesuit education, has the distinction of being the first Jesuit formally designated prefect of studies at St. Mary's, even though his English was very limited. During the following twelve months he spent most of his day trying to master the language, an effort that was not crowned by success. The following December he left for Louisiana to found St. Charles College, Grand Coteau, which immediately became a successful competitor with St. Mary's for students from Louisiana. In 1841, Point and Peter De Smet (1801-1873) joined the Bidwell party on the historic journey to the Oregon territory. One of the founding fathers of the Church in Montana, Point also built the first church in Idaho, but he is best known for his paintings and sketches of the Rocky Mountain Indians. During his brief stay at St. Mary's he made several sketches of the college that give today's observer an indication of how far the institution had progressed, even as early as 1835, from the days of the old abandoned distillery.

Murphy was Irish-born and French educated. A polymath, who was perfectly at ease in four languages, he was destined to exert a profound influence on shaping the future of St. Mary's and, indeed, of many Jesuit institutions in the United States.

The buildings in the foreground were built by the St. Mary's Jesuits.

ST. MARY'S FRIENDS IN HIGH PLACES

A few weeks prior to Point's departure from Kentucky, Murphy traveled to the state capital at Frankfort to make an appeal before the legislature for a charter of incorporation for the college. There is something wondrously coincidental in the fact that Murphy's companion on this venture was Father Robert A. Abell, the man who, at the bidding of Bishop Flaget, went to Billom in 1827 or 1828 to invite the Jesuits to come to Kentucky.[20]

The requested charter, empowering St. Mary's to confer the degrees of Bachelor and Master of Arts, was formally granted on January 21, 1837, and signed by Governor James Clark, whose son was a student at the school. Until the 1970s, St. Mary's was the oldest Catholic college in the state in point of continuous existence.[21] The school would never have been able to succeed as it did without the support of a number of politicians, judges and men of influence, most of whom were not Catholics.

Sometimes, in order to keep the fathers at St. Mary's, these benefactors would stretch the law to an extreme. In comparison, their tactics make the methods used by twentieth century politicians appear amateurish. For instance, although Father Byrne had expressed the intention to transfer his property to the Jesuits, he died intestate. His nephew immediately claimed the estate, but despite all of his efforts he was never able to get the requisite three commissioners to draw up the preliminary inventory. Then, his lawyer was somehow persuaded to withdraw his services. Exasperated, the nephew agreed to settle, taking only his uncle's horse as compensation. Later an unexpected discovery of some money left by Father Byrne encouraged the nephew to reopen the case, but his plea was rejected at the local court. He appealed the case to Frankfort and apparently it was rejected there too.[22]

Were Kentucky Boys Gentlemen?

During Point's tenure as prefect of studies, a fight between two students ended in a stabbing with the result that the Jesuits' ancient, honorable ban on students bearing arms was dug up, promulgated and adopted as school policy. The ban was hard to enforce, because two years later Chazelle had to separate rival gangs of armed students intent on doing one another serious damage. Regulations against alcohol were also strictly enforced, at least in theory. Moonshine was always a problem, proving that the Kentucky school authorities could take the stillhouse away from boys, but it was another matter of taking boys away from the stillhouse. In 1836 Chazelle had been threatened by a drunken student brandishing a pistol and in 1838, when several sobered-up students returned to the college from the local jail where they had spent the night, they were summarily expelled.[23] Years later Michael Nash recalled that the Kentucky boys were indeed wild and reckless, but they were also "gentlemen, sons of families of standing in society." They were not at all like the boys from New York and Brooklyn that he had to deal with when, as a scholastic, he came to Fordham. Unlike the boys from "Dark and Bloody Ground," he stated that New York boys, "did not possess the remotest instinct of gentlemen."[24]

Exit Chazelle, Enter Murphy

In the summer of 1839, Chazelle accepted an invitation to preach a retreat to the diocesan priests of Montreal. Although he did not plan it at the time, he would never again make Kentucky his home. While in Canada and later back in France, he explored the possibility of the Jesuits' return to that part of North America which had been made holy by the blood of St. John de Brébeuf and his seventeenth-century French Jesuit companions. These plans were partially effected in 1842 when a Canadian branch of the Kentucky Mission was set up with Chazelle in charge, and they were definitively realized on July 31, 1844, when the general in Rome formally established the Lower and Upper Mission of Canada.

When Chazelle left St. Mary's, he appointed William Murphy acting superior and president. On June 20, 1840, Rome made Murphy's position permanent, adding to his responsibilities the office of superior of all the Jesuits in the Kentucky Mission. St. Mary's had come a long way since the Jesuits assumed control of the college. Michael Nash recorded his impressions of the college

42

when, as a sixteen-year-old student transferring from St. Joseph's College in Bardstown, he saw it for the first time. This was in the late summer of 1841:

> We soon covered the five miles that separates the college from [Lebanon] and brought up at the college gate — a rather pretentious one, flanked by two lodges. The gate opened upon what might be called a vacant park, beyond which stretched spacious play grounds. The college itself instead of being one large and continuous building was composed of some five or six substantial brick structures.

In the absence of the fathers, one of the senior boys volunteered to take Nash and his Bardstown companions on a tour around the campus.

> He first took us out on a magnificent terrace about one hundred and seventy-five feet long by sixty feet wide. On the north side of [the] esplanade, and opening on to it, was a study hall, a neat one story building. On each end, east and west, rose a square building used for classrooms. The chapel, dormitories, infirmary, clothes room, and the fathers' residence were in separate buildings ranged around.

We are indebted to Nash for this description of the college. In those pre-environment-consciousness days, the fact that "the lavatories were in the open air, around a never failing spring," did not seem to affect his sensibilities, but more than fifty years later, he could recall with a shiver how the boys, rising from their warm beds, braved frosty Kentucky mornings and, "half dressed hurried to the spring to make their ablutions and toilet."[25]

Priestly Apostolates

It was not surprising that Michael Nash did not find any of the fathers at home when he visited the college before that fall term of 1841. Both Chazelle and Murphy insisted that the Jesuits make themselves useful to the bishop by serving parishes, giving retreats and missions, and being chaplains to women religious. This same practice was followed when the community moved to Fordham. In Kentucky not even the novices were exempt from apostolic works.

The novitiate was situated about one half mile from the college on one of the two large tracts of land that Chazelle had purchased between 1838 and 1840. In April 1844, Michael Nash became a novice there. By that date, Thomas Legoüais, whom Chazelle named the temporary master of novices in 1836, had long since handed over this office to Nicholas Gilles. Both men were

Jesuits resided here at St. Mary's

highly respected by contemporaries; yet to a modern reader the description of each lends itself to levity. Legoüais was said to have been "a veritable, but well-proportioned dwarf," and Gilles "embalmed the country around the college with the fragrance of his holiness."[26]

Trained under the judicious guidance of these two spiritual directors — dare we say giants? — were a number of men, like Nash, who became prominent in the history of Fordham. For example, there was John Larkin (1801-1858) and Ferdinand Gockeln (1820-1886), two future presidents of the Rose Hill campus. Two others, John Ryan (1810-1861) and Michael Driscoll (1805-1880) left Fordham to become presidents at Xavier College in Manhattan. Others, like Charles de Luynes (1804-1878), William Hennen (1800-1890), John Roy (1819-1877), Henry Hudon (1823-1862), Patrick Crowe (1817-1869), Jeremiah Garvey (1794-1875), and James Graves (1824-1875), also brought to Fordham the Ignatian spirituality they had learned at St. Mary's.

An important "Visitor" is Appointed

William Murphy was in office six years when the newly-named provincial in Paris decided to send a "Visitor" on a fact-finding mission to Canada and Kentucky. He chose one of his most trusted colleagues, Clément Boulanger (1790-1868), for this sensitive position and assigned as his socius or assistant, Jean-Baptiste Hus (1803-1881). Important, far-reaching decisions had to be made about the future of the fast-growing missions in North America, and the provincial, who had no knowledge of that part of the world, wanted to make certain that he would have as much information as possible to steer the future course of American institutions under the jurisdiction of the Province of France.

The provincial probably thought that he could not have chosen a better pair to achieve the purpose of this undertaking. Boulanger had been provincial of France from 1842 to 1845, during the time the Canada Mission was founded and St. Mary's was starting to flourish. He was an experienced administrator, a shrewd judge of character; he found it easy to make difficult decisions. Jean-Baptiste Hus, his enthusiastic companion, had an admiration so intense for everything American that it was almost embarrassing. Later Hus founded the Mission of Guiana, where he served the prisoners on Devil's Island.

DECISIONS AHEAD!

Clément Boulanger and Jean-Baptiste Hus arrived at St. Mary's in June 1845, resolved on four matters of immediate importance that left no room for futher discussion. The Visitor had decided: No, contrary to the bishop's desire, the Jesuits would not be able to take control of St. Joseph's College in Bardstown. Yes, the novitiate that was temporarily closed in 1845 would remain closed. No, the Louisville college, which Fathers Harissart and Larkin had planned in 1842, would not open (the ten Jesuit priests, scholastics, brothers, and novices, who were living in rented quarters there, returned to St. Mary's in mid-February, 1846). And finally, Yes, the rumors that the Jesuits were going to abandon St. Mary's, and indeed all residences in Kentucky, were based on fact.

The reason for the decision to move was that the Visitor and his associate had arranged with Bishop John Hughes of New York to transfer the Mission to Hughes' St. John's College, at Fordham, a short distance from the growing city of New York. For many, the declaration concerning the last item was the hardest to accept. When informed of Boulanger's decision, old Bishop Flaget, who, according to Hus, "was, for the past several years, scarcely able to attend, in the slightest degree, to the administration of the diocese," broke down and wept. Similar expressions of popular regret had already been registered throughout the state.

The Visitor's resolve to pull the Jesuits out of Kentucky, however painful it was to so many, was not made without serious consideration. In his carefully written memo Jean-Baptiste Hus outlined the reasons for the decision, and his arguments for the move to New York follow closely the criteria St. Ignatius gives in the Jesuit Constitutions for accepting a mission.[27]

• First of all, there was no Catholic college in New York, a state that "is so large and so populated," where the bishop needs all the diocesan priests he has to care for the needs of an ever-expanding population.

• Moreover, the proximity of Fordham to the city of New York would offer the fathers many opportunities to preach and hear confessions, and it would also present ample advantages for the scholastics to teach catechism to a larger number of people.

• Graduates of a Jesuit college in New York would also be better placed to bring more good to a greater number of people in the New York area and to the country at large. The more, the greater, the better, such were the considerations that determined the decision.

• Moreover, Hus pointed out that influential Protestant teachers were already headquartered in New York, which meant that unchallenged they were able to do their wonted mischief.

• The city of New York was also near other urban areas with expanding populations, areas from which a greater number of future students could be drawn.

• Also, families in New York were in a better social and financial position to send their sons to college than, presumably, those in Kentucky.

• Another advantage Fordham offered over St. Mary's was the Fathers teaching in Bishop Hughes' seminary would have the opportunity to get to know future New York priests, as well as future priests from four contiguous dioceses who were schooled there. Presumably the consequences would accrue to the advantage of the Society.

• In addition to the college at Rose Hill, the bishop also promised the Jesuits that in the future he would provide them with a residence and church in New York City itself.

• The Bishop further promised the Fathers that he would designate a section of the college building at Fordham for a novitiate.

• There was also, Hus argued, the geographical advantage of New York. The state formed a natural geographical angle between France, the supplier of vocations to the North American missions, and Canada, where the Jesuits were expanding their work among the native peoples. This geographical advantage likewise meant that young Jesuits could be sent with greater facility to France or Rome for their studies, and that formed Jesuits could travel more expeditiously to Europe on annual begging tours.

• Finally, New York counted some 230,000 Catholics who were served by a mere 110 priests, many of whom were of advanced age and in poor health.

By way of summary, Hus argued that in their new home, the Kentucky Mission Jesuits "would be assured of most active support and generous benevo-

46

lence on the part of Bishop Hughes, who was one of the most enlightened, zealous and influential members of the American hierarchy," a man who would encourage rather than hinder vocations to the Society.

Just as there were reasons for resettling in New York, so were there inducements for abandoning Kentucky. Hus pointed out that the inaccessibility of St, Mary's was unfortunate. It was located in a remote area, surrounded by forests. During the summer months the roads to it were difficult; in winter they became impassable. Such judgment confirms the experience of William Murphy, who in 1846, was a prime mover in the transfer of the Jesuits to New York. In the winter of 1836, the well-traveled Murphy confessed that "never in my whole life have I ever seen such a road" as that which brought him and his companions to St. Mary's.[28]

Hus argued that Kentucky's population could not realistically support two Catholic boarding schools. St. Joseph's in Bardstown carried a debt in access of $50,000. The Jesuits would do the diocesan clergy a great favor by refraining from competing for students with St. Joseph's. In the surrounding states there were as many as nine institutions that had been established since 1833, and these schools were struggling to serve the Catholic youth of the extended area. At one time there was a need for a Jesuit boarding school in rural Kentucky, but that need no longer existed.

Hus pointed out that the number of students at the college had declined; the number of non-Catholics was high, and there were even some Know Nothings among the school's population. Hus did not give the relevant statistics to support this point, but such statistics were available to him. Thomas Campbell reported that, from the time Byrne turned over the college to the Jesuits in 1831 until 1846, "only 675 boys had passed under their influence, 361 of whom were not Catholics. Moreover, there was a steady decrease in attendance; for although in 1836 there were 180 students. there were only 30 [boarders] ten years later." (Even when Hus was writing his report, there were only 25 to 30 Catholics boarders at St. Mary's. Hence Campbell's conclusion does not seem unreasonable: "the college was going or had gone to pieces."[29])

Hus' view was that the only place in Kentucky where there was a possibility for the Jesuits to carry on a fruitful apostolate was in the town of Louisville. He noted that the Society had done all in its power to establish a day school there. The land had been purchased, trees had been felled and the ground had been broken in expectation for a large building program, but Hus reported, "the diocese has refused any assistance and has withheld written or even verbal encouragement." The result is that "we remain convinced of the impossibility" of establishing anything in Louisville.[30]

The Louisville diocese at the time was being run by Bishop Guy Chabrat, S.S. (1787-1868), whose resignation from office was made official the following year. In 1835 the aging Flaget, who encouraged the Jesuits to establish a college and seminary in Louisville, had returned to France, leaving his coadjutor Chabrat the administrator of the diocese. Described as having excessive "pride in his accomplishments," Chabrat managed to alienate not only the Jesuits, but most of the diocesan and religious clergy as well.[31] Although later in the letter, Hus insisted that the departure of the Jesuits from Kentucky was in no way connected with Bishop Chabrat's requested resignation; however, rumors equating the two events persisted.[32] In 1839 Flaget had returned to a demoralized diocese, to a situation he did not seem to have the will or ability to rectify. "Sensitive, tenderhearted, nervous, and much too conscientious," Flaget, who was given to fits of depression, was described at this period of his life as an old man "with almost continuous vertigo in the head," and who went about groaning, "Oh, my incompetence!"[33] In 1841 his see was moved from Bardstown to Louisville. The Jesuits had gone to Louisville at his insistence, and Hus seems to accuse him, as well as Chabrat, for the sorry plight they encountered there.

> For three years, five fathers and a brother have been in Louisville giving classes, teaching catechism to children and Negroes, and preaching and hearing confessions whenever they were called upon to do so. And during that time they have been almost totally supported and maintained at our expense. They have had to pay rent out of their own pockets for the house where they live. Because of their shoddy and wretched appearance, children from wealthy families shun them. They planned to build a college and with that purpose in mind, they launched an appeal to the local people. Even though there is no Catholic school in the town, the bishops of Kentucky did not believe that they ought to support this undertaking.[34]

Hus further complained that for the past six or seven years the Society, not the diocese, had been supporting the priests who were responsible for the operation of two diocesan parishes, St. Charles and Rayvuick. Jesuit funds paid for the repairs to the church at St. Charles, and it was the Society which built the church at Rayvuick. Moreover, during the same period of time, the Fathers who worked at the girls' boarding school did so without any remuneration whatsoever from the bishops or the Sisters. The Fathers were the only priests who preached missions throughout the diocese, and they did so without any compensation whatsoever. St. Mary's College and the acreage on which it stood were acquired and supported without any financial assistance from the bishop, and during more than fourteen years, the Jesuits, unaided, paid for clearing, cultivating and improving the land. Recent construction and improvements on the buildings had come to $25,000, "the fruit of our work and our privations," — all of which the society was now turning over gratuitously

48

to the bishop. Hus reported that the diocese of Louisville counted 30,000 Catholics served by forty-five priests, and concluded that "it will not be difficult to replace us."

As if anticipating those who would continue to criticize the move, Hus ended his apologia with a dramatic flourish: "We are answering the invitation extended by His Excellency, the Bishop of New York; we are entering an immense field he opens to our labors; we accept his gracious, generous, active support, etc., etc. Are we to be blamed for this?"[35]

MOVING DAYS

The new rector, August J. Thébaud (1807-1885) and the former rector, William Murphy, were the first to leave St. Mary's. They were followed by the remaining men who left in teams of five or more.[36] These were Fathers Guy Gilles, Simon Fouché, Charles de Luynes, Michael Driscol, Nicholas Petit, Thomas Legoüais, John Larkin, John Ryan, Xavier Maréchal, Peter Lebreton (1809-1849) and Henry du Merle (1815-1851); Messrs. Michael Nash, Henry Hudson, James Graves; and Brothers Patrick Crowe, Jeremiah Garvey, James Roy and William Hennen. By late summer they had settled in at their new home; during the course of the year, others, from different parts of the world, would join them.[37]

WHAT BECAME OF ST. MARY'S CAMPUS?

After the departure of the Jesuits, St. Mary's reverted to the care of the diocesan clergy. In 1869 a visitor praised the beauty of the buildings and was struck by the contents of the library that contained five thousand volumes. The student population that year numbered one hundred and twenty-five. However, the depressed economy following the war and the endemic financial embarrassments of the diocese forced the college to close in 1869. The land was leased to a local farmer and the buildings abandoned. A short time later in 1871 the Fathers of the Congregation of the Resurrection took possession of the property, and in 1872 opened up the repaired buildings for classes.[38] St. Mary's was consolidated with St. Joseph's College of Bardstown in 1893 and thereby became the only Catholic college for men in the Louisville diocese. In 1929 the college was restricted to students studying for the priesthood. By 1971, however, the number of candidates to the clerical state had plummeted making the seminary an anachronism, and since anachronisms are luxury items, the property was put up for sale. The new buyer was a hippy group from San Francisco called The Cornucopias, who themselves quickly became relics of a past era and moved on to Oregon, thereby necessitating a further sale. This time it was purchased (in 1984) by the U.S. Corrections Corporation, a private firm contracted by the State of Kentucky to operate a minimum security prison there, the Marion Adjustment Center. The warden there stated recently by telephone (7/98) that all of the buildings of the Jesuit era have been replaced; a building constructed in 1860 is the oldest one still standing.

Meanwhile, the idea conceived in a fat man's stillhouse by a rebel Irishman and nurtured by French Jesuits continues to flourish in America's largest city, as is demonstrated in the pages that follow.

NOTES

1. The best account of St. Mary's College can be found in "The French Blackrobes Return to America," chapter 3 of Francis X. Curran, S.J., *The Return of the Jesuits: Chapters in the History of the Society of Jesus in Nineteenth-century America* (Chicago: Loyola University Press, 1966), 57-80. Contemporary accounts of the St. Mary's Jesuits can be found in the following: Benjamin J. Webb, *The Centenary of Catholicity in Kentucky* (Louisville: Charles A. Rogers, 1884), 282-87; 385-99; Walter H. Hill, "Some Reminiscences of St. Mary's College, Kentucky," *Woodstock Letters* (henceforth, *WL*), (1891), 25-38; Anon., "An Historical Sketch of the Mission of New York and Canada," *WL*, 2(1873): 109-24; Michael Nash, "Reminiscences of Father Michael Nash," *WL*, 26(1897): 257-83, and Martin J. Spalding. D.D., *Sketches of the Early Catholic Missions of Kentucky from their Commencement in 1787 to the Jubilee of 1826-1827.* (Louisville: B.J. Webb & Brothers, 1844). Two manuscripts on permanent loan in the Gleeson Library at the University of San Francisco are also valuable references to the history of the Kentucky Mission. The first is a four page holograph written by Jean-Baptiste Hus, S.J., April 28, 1846, entitled "Raisons qui ont déterminé les Pères Jésuites à quitter de Kentucky pour l'établir à New-York" (hereafter Hus). The second is the first twenty-five pages of a letter written by Evermond Harissart, S.J. to Jan Roothaan, S.J., St. Mary's Kentucky, December 28, 1843. Unfortunately the last pages have been lost. Another valuable piece for the history of St. Mary's is: Alphonse Lesoucky, "Centenary of St. Mary's College, St. Mary's, Kentucky," *Illinois Catholic Historical Review*, 4 (1921), 154. For additional bibliographical entries on the Jesuits in Kentucky and biographical material on Jesuits mentioned in this chapter, see Cornelius Michael Buckley, S.J., *Nicolas Point, S.J.: His Life and Northwest Indian Chronicles.* (Chicago: Loyola University Press, 1989).93-108; 458-61.

2. "An Historical Sketch of the Mission of New York and Canada," *WL*, 2, (1873):111.

3. Cited in Joseph Herman Schauinger, *Cathedrals in the Wilderness* (Milwaukee: Bruce, 1952), 265.

4. Walter W. Hill, "Some Reminiscences of St. Mary's College, Kentucky," *WL*, 20(1891):26

5. Ibid., 29.

6. Schauinger,. op. cit., 298.

7. Thomas J. Campbell, "Fordham University," *WL*, 45(1916):355.

8.. Hill, op. cit., 32.

9. John L. Spalding, *The Life of the Most Reverend Martin J. Spalding* (New York: Christian Press, n.d.), 24.

10. *Litterae annuae Societatis Jesu in Francia* [1814-1855], 5 vols. (Pictacii: Henrici Oudin) 203.

11. Martin J. Spalding, op. cit., 275.

12. Curran,. op. cit., 64-65.

13. Cited in Thomas J. Campbell, "Fordham University," op. cit., 355.

14. Nash, op. cit., 263; Webb, op. cit., 392-93.

15. Evremond Harissart to Jan Roothaan, St. Mary's, Kentucky. Op. cit, 2.

16. Hill, op. cit., 30,

17. Ibid.

18. Nash, op. cit., 262.

19. Ibid. 2

20. It is very probable that Murphy, who was a scholastic at Billom about this time, met Abell. He implies as much in the account of his journey to St. Mary's. William Murphy, letter January 22, 1836, *Missio Kentukeiensis* (1830-1846), file 3, item 17, p. 2 *Archives of the Society of Jesus*, Rome (hereafter *ASJR*).

21. Lesoucky, op. cit., 154.

22. Curran, op. cit., 87.

23. Campbell, op. cit., 353; *Litterae annuae*, 1836-1837, 196-98; 1838-1839, 104.

24. Nash, op. cit., 262.

25. Ibid.

26. Ibid., 263

27. Hus, 4. St. Ignatius of Loyola, *The Constitutions of the Society of Jesus*, tr. George E. Ganss, S.J. (St Louis: The Institute of Jesuit Sources, 1970), [618], 273; [622-25], 274-78.

28. William Murphy, letter January 22, 1836, ibid.

29. Hus, 2; Campbell, op.cit., 359; *Litterae annuae*, op. cit. 1836-1837, 205; 1837-1838, 302; 1838-1839, 115-31.

30. Hus, 2.

31. Schauinger, op. cit., 197; Webb, op. cit., 253-56.

32. Hus, 3.

33. Schauinger, op. cit., 260, 306.

34. Hus, 2; Hill, op. cit., 31-32.

35. Hus, 3-4.

36. Nash, op. cit., 396.

37. *Catalogus Sociorum et officiorum provinciae Galliae Societatis Jesu, 1846* (n.p.), 39-41. Campbell states that there were fifty-one Jesuits in Kentucky who made the trip to Fordham. About half of the few names he gives came to St. John's College from other places: Arsenius Haveques (1808-1866), Charles Schianski (1807-1852), Edward Doucet (1825-1890), Thomas Ouellet (1819-1894) and Augustin Régnier (1820-1883) came from Canada; the Spaniard, Charles Maldonado (1816-1872) came straightway from Naples; Peter Tissot (1823-1875) and Isidore Daubresse (1810-1895) came directly from France.

38. Lesoucky, op. cit., 165-66.

CHAPTER IV

FORDHAM BEFORE THE JESUITS: BISHOP JOHN HUGHES AND ST. JOHN'S COLLEGE 1838-1846

by Rev. Thomas J. Shelley

Shortly after his appointment as administrator of the diocese of New York in 1839, Bishop John Hughes decided to establish a Catholic college in the suburbs of New York City. In 1841 he achieved his dream with the opening of St. John's College in Rose Hill. The college was a diocesan institution until 1846 when Hughes entrusted it to the Society of Jesus. This article traces the first five years of St. John's College, a period when John Hughes was not only establishing the future Fordham University, but also contending with the problems of lay trusteeism, anti-Catholic bigotry and the poverty of his immigrant Catholic community.

INTRODUCTION

Between 1838 and 1846, during his first eight years in New York, John Hughes became a national figure, one of the best known, if not exactly the best loved Catholic prelates in the United States.

In 1837 Hughes was a young diocesan priest in Philadelphia where he had acquired a certain local prominence because of his sparring with lay trustees and anti-Catholic bigots. In the fall of that year he was appointed coadjutor bishop of New York to assist the aging, French-born bishop of New York, John Dubois. Under ordinary circumstances the new coadjutor would have had only the limited authority delegated to him by Dubois. However, two weeks after Hughes received episcopal ordination on January 7, 1838, in the old St. Patrick's cathedral on Mott Street, Dubois suffered the first of a series of strokes that left him increasingly impaired. Consequently, in August of the following year, Hughes was made the administrator of the diocese and then automatically succeeded Dubois as the fourth bishop of New York upon the latter's death on December 20, 1842. In 1850 Hughes went on to become the first archbishop of New York, a position which he retained until his own death on January 3, 1864.

However, it was during the first eight years of his episcopate in New York that John Hughes acquired the national reputation of a strong and outspoken leader that clung to him for the rest of his life. He won this reputation as a result of his role in three major controversies during that period: lay trusteeism, public education and the Nativist agitation. By 1846 Hughes had become a national hero to most of his largely Irish flock in New York, but he had also become an object of deep suspicion to many non-Catholics throughout the country. During these same eight years Hughes also faced the daunting challenge of giving structure and organization to a diocese that was still in chaotic condition thirty years after it had been established. As he surveyed the scene early in 1838, Hughes admitted to his friend, Bishop John Purcell of Cincinnati, "I feel that I have been appointed in punishment for my sins."[1] The diocese was then ten times the size of the present archdiocese of New York, comprising all of New York state and the northern half of New Jersey, 55,000 square miles, with a Catholic population of almost 200,000 that was increasing rapidly thanks to the growing influx of Irish and German immigrants.

Hughes recalled the situation twenty years later:

> There were then about 46 churches and as many priests for the Catholics scattered over this immense surface. There were no really Catholic schools in existence, except two, kept by Sisters of Charity who had charge of orphan children at the cathedral and at St. Peter's. One or two other churches had schools under a hired male teacher for the instruction of poor boys. There were no religious communities in the diocese — the Sisters of Charity having been obtained from Emmitsburg as missionaries and liable to be recalled at any moment. There was no provision made for the Catholic education of youth or the training of ecclesiastics to meet the increasing wants of the people. The churches were too few and these [were] in debt to an amount greater than they would have brought at public auction. The people were too poor and for a long time the increase of their numbers only added to their poverty as emigrants arrived in our port from Europe penniless and destitute.[2]

There was an urgent need for more churches, rectories, convents, hospitals, orphanages and other charitable institutions, but, from the day that Hughes first set foot in New York in 1838, he made Catholic education his highest priority. "The subject that of all others he had nearest his heart," said John Hassard, his secretary and biographer, "was education." In the thick of Hughes' battle with the Nativists, an admiring newspaper editor commented: "The education of his people is paramount with Bishop Hughes; his object, his glorious object, is to elevate them in the scale of religious and intellectual greatness." Hughes' quarrel with the Public School Society in New York City over elementary education is well known, but, even before he became embroiled in that controversy, he decided to build a college for New York's Catholics.[3]

What he had in mind was an institution similar to his own alma mater, Mount St. Mary's College and Seminary in Emmitsburg, Maryland, a combined liberal arts college and theological seminary. At Mount St. Mary's the tuition of the college students helped to defray the expenses of the seminary and the seminarians subsidized the college by serving as teachers and tutors. Hughes wanted to create a comparable institution in New York. He told Bishop Purcell in February 1838, "The idea that most engages my mind at this moment is the establishment of a seminary for ecclesiastics. There is also a prospect of realizing it now, and in no place at any time was it more wanted." He explained to Purcell that New York required its own seminary to improve the unsatisfactory quality of the local clergy. "Clergymen, some of doubtful character and some of whom there is no doubt have found easy admission into the diocese," he said, "and religion suffers in consequence."[4]

At the same time Hughes saw the need for a liberal arts college for the sons of New York's growing Catholic middle class. Reflecting perhaps on his own experience in Philadelphia where many children of the Catholic elite such as the Careys and Meades had drifted away from the Church, he told some would-be European benefactors that the absence of a Catholic college in New York meant that "the youth of wealthier families are exposed to lose their faith by being educated in dangerous intercourse with Protestantism."[5] Between 1838 and 1846, in the midst of all his other pastoral responsibilities and public controversies, John Hughes never wavered in his determination to provide New York Catholics with their first successful college and seminary.[6]

BROOKLYN AND LAFARGEVILLE

Like Hughes, Bishop Dubois had also hoped to establish a combined college and seminary in New York, which is not surprising since he was the founder of Mount St. Mary's in Emmitsburg. In 1832 Dubois bought a 162-acre farm in Upper Nyack, a beautiful piece of property located directly on the Hudson River about thirty miles north of New York City where the river widens to become the Tappan Zee. On May 29, 1833, he blessed the cornerstone for his new seminary, but he had to suspend construction later that year and again in 1835 when he ran out of money. For a brief period in 1834 the seminary functioned in a farmhouse on the property with five students and two professors, the junior of whom was young Father John McCloskey, later the first president of St. John's College at Rose Hill and later still the second archbishop of New York and the first American Cardinal. Finally in 1837, as the three-story stone building neared completion, it was destroyed by fire. Since anti-Catholic bigotry was rife in New York at the time, and St. Mary's church on Sheriff Street had been burned to the ground only six years earlier, many Catholics suspected arson. The real cause was more prosaic. A careless workman, cooking eggs for his lunch, set fire to some wood shavings and the blaze quickly engulfed the whole building. A hostile crowd gathered to watch the fire and cheered as the roof caved in. Dubois lamented that the fire "swallowed up in two hours $25,000." There was no insurance and he had no money to rebuild the edifice.[7]

Two months after his arrival in New York, Hughes went to inspect the gutted building. "I was at Nyack yesterday," he told a lay friend in Philadelphia, "to witness the ruins of the splendid folly of which I had no conception before .... The whole effect upon my mind has been a conversion to the opinion of Bishop Dubois that the burning of it was providential."[8] The reason for Hughes' optimism was that, by this time, a wealthy layman, Cornelius Heeney, had offered the diocese property in Brooklyn for a college. A week after his visit to Nyack, Hughes told Archbishop Samuel Eccleston of Baltimore: "We are about to commence the college in Brooklyn. I hope to have it under roof by the end of November next. It is to be 120 feet long—50 feet deep and four stories high in a most beautiful location commanding a full view of the bay, the city.... "[9] He warned Father John McCaffrey, rector of Mount St. Mary's, to "look out for your mountain laurels," but then reassured him that "it will be at least two years before it can go into operation, and neither after nor before shall its interests, I hope, be promoted at the expense of yours."[10]

Unfortunately Hughes' hopes were dashed when Heeney withdrew his offer after clashing with Dubois over the legal title to the property. Before that occurred, however, Hughes had already purchased another site in upstate New York, at Lafargeville, in the Thousand Islands, near the Canadian border. For $20,000 he acquired a "plantation" of 460 acres and buildings that he claimed were better than those at Emmitsburg. His original plan was to have a college in Brooklyn and a seminary in Lafargeville. Expenses were so cheap in the north country that Hughes calculated that the tuition of one college student in Brooklyn would support three seminarians in Lafargeville. When the projected college in Brooklyn fell through, Hughes then tried to transform "St. Vincent of Paul" Seminary in Lafargeville into both a college and a seminary, an idea that was doomed to failure from the beginning because of its isolated location.[11]

In recruiting students for Lafargeville, the location was advertised as an asset rather than a liability. The propectus boasted that the college was "removed from noise and bustle of cities — where temptations to pleasure often lure youth away from the acquisition of science — and where frequent interruption arrests the progress of the most studious." The weather was touted as

56

a positive advantage, for Lafargeville was said to be noted for the "salubrity and healthfulness of the climate." One would never have guessed that Lafargeville was in the heart of the snow belt after reading that "the winters are not so severe as in the city of New York." Even the distance from New York City — 300 miles — was brushed aside with the comment that the trip "can easily be performed in two or three days."[12]

Tuition, room and board, and doctor's fees amounted to $112.00 per annum plus an additional $8.00 for washing and mending. The faculty was headed by Father Francis Guth assisted by two other diocesan priests and three lay tutors. Non-Catholics were specifically welcomed but were obliged to attend Catholic religious services. Parents were assured that "corporal chastisements shall not be used except in cases of violent resistance on the part of the pupil," but they were also warned that "unconquerable indolence or insubordination" would lead to dismissal.[13]

Urgent public notices urged prospective students to apply immediately for admission because the limited number of places were fast filling up, but these notices seem to have fooled no one.[14] Few parents were willing to have their sons test the grandiose claims of St. Vincent of Paul Seminary. The college opened on September 20, 1838, with a student body of six young men and two boys. A year later the situation was no better. "Yesterday we commenced our classes again with a handful of children," Guth told Hughes, and he added, "We might be compared to a big stage-coach drawn by four horses and no passengers."[15]

Hughes himself had little confidence in the faculty. He told Father John McCaffrey of Mount St. Mary's: "You can have no idea of the set whom Bishop Dubois sent to Lafargeville, good pious men, if you wish, but utterly incapable of teaching."[16] After two years the student body consisted of nine seminarians and a handful of children. Finally, acting upon repeated requests from Guth, Hughes quietly closed St. Vincent of Paul Seminary in 1840. He could afford to do so because he was now the proud owner of a splendid estate only a few miles north of New York City.[17]

ROSE HILL

On April 29, 1839, John Hughes purchased the Rose Hill estate, approximately 100 acres, located (in the quaint language of the title deed) "in the Manor of Fordham, in the Town and County of Westchester." He bought it for $29,750 from a New York City merchant named Andrew Carrigan.[18] At last he had a suitable site for his college and seminary. At the time he was also basking in the glow from another achievement that brought him far more attention than his real estate transaction. He had just challenged and routed the lay trustees of St. Patrick's cathedral.

For years the cathedral trustees had been a thorn in the side of New York's bishops, first John Connolly (1815-1825), now John Dubois. At issue in 1839 was the status of Father Thomas Levins, a priest whom Dubois had suspended and removed from the rectorship of the cathedral. The trustees thereupon appointed Levins director of the parish school and threatened to cut off Dubois' salary. The conflict turned ugly on Sunday, February 10, 1839, when the trustees authorized Levins to call in the police and remove from the Sunday school a lay catechist appointed by Dubois. Hughes decided to make the incident a test case, for, he said, the civil law invoked by the trustees "gives them the same right to send a constable into the sanctuary to remove a priest from the altar."[19]

After Hughes failed to get an apology from the trustees, two Sundays later, on February 24, he appealed from the trustees to the pew-holders who had elected them. That afternoon a large crowd showed up in the parish school for the meeting he had announced. They included not only all but one of the 200 cathedral pewholders, but also 400 to 500 Catholics from other parishes including a number of trustees. "New York has become a bye-word of reproach to the Catholic name throughout the land," Hughes told them. Getting right to the point, he depicted the issue between Bishop Dubois and the trustees as a matter of divine law versus civil law.

Hughes knew how to sway a crowd of sentimental Irishmen. As he told Archbishop Eccleston the next day, "I recalled to them the glory of their fathers in Ireland battling for three hundred years against the abused civil power of the British government." Pulling out all the stops, he warned them that "the sainted spirits" of their ancestors were looking down upon them from heaven "ready to disavow and disown them if ... they allowed pigmies among themselves to filch away rights of the Church which their glorious ancestors would not yield but with their lives to the persecuting giant of the British Empire." According to Hughes, many in the audience wept like children. "I was not far from it myself," he added.[20]

His words went down like treacle with the pew-holders. "The whole assembly was his," said Hassard, "he could do with it what he wanted." What he wanted and got from them was a resolution disavowing any action that would "hinder or prevent our bishop from the full, free and entire exercise of the rights, powers and duties which God has appointed as inherent in his office."[21]

With the passage of that resolution, the power of the lay trustees in New York was broken, and both the lay trustees and Hughes knew it. He gloated to Archbishop Eccleston: "We killed the trustees, as I told you, but they could not believe that they were dead — it came so sudden. So that now, although they grieve still, they have not strength enough to give even a decent kick." He was so pleased with the outcome that he told Bishop Joseph Rosati of St. Louis: "It is a revolution, and I trust a happy one in its consequences for religion."[22]

Fresh from his triumph over the cathedral trustees, Hughes now turned his attention to his newly acquired property at Rose Hill. The problem was that he had neither the $30,000 to pay for the real estate nor the additional $10,000 that was needed to make the two buildings suitable for a college. "I had not, when I purchased the site of this new college, St. John's, Fordham," he said, "so much as a penny wherewith to commence the payment for it."[23] Hughes devised a two-fold plan. First, he appealed to the Catholics of New York to contribute to a special educational fund-raising drive. He launched the campaign on Sunday, September 1, 1839, speaking at the cathedral and at a different church every evening that week.[24] However, he knew that he could never get $40,000 solely from New York's impoverished Catholics. Therefore, the second part of his plan was to conduct a begging tour of Europe. He left New York on October 16, 1839, and spent the next nine months trying to raise abroad the money that he could not get at home.

The bishop's trip took him to Rome (where he spent three months), England, Ireland, and also to Vienna, Munich and Paris where he visited the headquarters of the Austrian, Bavarian and French missionary aid societies. According to Hassard, in Vienna the Leopoldinen Stiftung made a "liberal donation" to Hughes' college and seminary. There is no indication that he received anything from the Ludwigsmissionverein in Munich where the king, Ludwig I, was increasingly insistent that the Bavarian society's funds should go exclusively to German parishes and institutions in America. However, Hughes had better luck in Paris when he called upon the Society for the Propagation of the Faith. He later told the Society that they had provided the principal financial support for his seminary.[25]

Meanwhile, in America, the fund-raising campaign had gotten off to a good start and then quickly ground to a halt. Two days before Hughes sailed for Europe, he issued a pastoral letter urging generous contributions for the building of the college and seminary. He barely mentioned the college at all, stressing instead the necessity of the seminary in overcoming the shortage of priests. He reminded New York's Catholics how difficult it was for many of them to attend Mass on Sunday or even to find a priest to anoint the dying. Every pastor was told to open a subscription list in his parish and to report every two weeks to a Committee of Accounts and Collection headed by Father John Power, pastor of St. Peter's church and one of New York's two vicars general.[26]

During the first two months the campaign brought in slightly over $7,000, but then contributions slowed to a trickle and only an additional $3,000 was raised during the following seven months. Many who made pledges never came through with the cash. While John Power served as chairman of the campaign,

New York's other vicar general, the Cuban-born Father Felix Varela, pastor of Transfiguration church, kept up a steady drumbeat of appeals in the pages of his newly-founded weekly newspaper, the *New York Catholic Register*. In November he was still sounding an optimistic note, predicting that "the subscriptions thus far augur so favourably as to leave no doubt of ultimate success." By the following February he was not so sanguine, and later that month he was reporting that one-third of the pledges had not yet been paid. In March he raised the possibility that construction at Rose Hill might have to be suspended, and in April he speculated that Bishop Hughes would not be happy when he returned from Europe.[27]

Shortly thereafter New York's Catholics heard directly from Hughes himself. Writing an open letter to Varela from Dublin on June 1, Hughes said that his greatest concern had been the progress of his new college and seminary. "I perceive that but little has been done since I left," he said ominously. However, he added, "This does not discourage me because I think it is owing to causes different from any want of zeal on the part of the Catholics of the city and the diocese. The only effect it will have will be to delay the commencement, for as we have to begin once only, we must wait until we can begin well — and this cannot be before we have the buildings and ground paid for."[28]

Forced to choose between the college and the seminary, Hughes decided to delay the opening of the college for a year so that he could inaugurate the seminary at Rose Hill in the fall of 1840. It was a modest beginning indeed, with about twenty students and apparently a faculty of one person who taught all the subjects, Father Felix Vilanis, a diocesan priest whom Hughes had recruited in Europe.

The Public School Society

Upon his return from Europe to New York on July 18, 1840, Hughes quickly discovered that the biggest concern of the city's Catholics was not the new college or seminary at Rose Hill, but the condition of the public schools. Since 1826 these schools had been under the control of the Public School Society, a private charitable organization designated by the Common Council to be the sole recipient of the educational funds allocated by the state legislature for the city's public schools.

For fourteen years the city's Catholics had chafed under the monopoly enjoyed by the Public School Society, which, according to Hughes, was dominated by Presbyterians. They suffused the schools with a bland, non-denominational kind of Christianity that was quite acceptable to most Protestants, but not to Catholics. Moreover, the atmosphere in the schools was often aggressively anti-Catholic. Hassard commented tartly that "instead of teaching religion without sectarianism, they may almost be said to have taught sectarianism without religion." Catholics objected especially to the mandatory use of the King James version of the Bible and the use of textbooks that ridiculed such Catholic practices as the sacrament of penance. Hughes himself estimated that half of the city's Catholic children received no education at all because their parents would not send them to the public schools and there was no room for them in the overcrowded Catholic schools.[29]

Catholics were not the only New Yorkers who deplored this situation. Governor William H. Seward mentioned it specifically in his annual address to the state legislature on January 7, 1840:

> The children of foreigners, found in great numbers in our cities and towns ... are too often deprived of the advantages of our system of public education in consequence of prejudices arising from differences of language or religion ... I do not hesitate, there-fore, to recommend the establishment of schools in which they may be instructed by teachers speaking the same language and professing the same faith ... [30]

Not unreasonably Catholics interpreted the Governor's remarks as an invi-tation to ask for public funds for their own schools. Bishop Hughes was away in Europe at the time, but Catholics in New York City quickly formed an association to contest the educational monopoly of the Public School Society. The head of the association was Father John Power, and his role in this associa-tion soon overshadowed his other responsibilities as chairman of the fund-raising drive for the new college and seminary. During the spring and summer of 1840 the association held regular meetings every two weeks in the basement of St. James church. One was scheduled for July 20, two days after Hughes' return from Europe. "On my return," said Hughes, "I found my diocese, and especially the city of New York, in a ferment." Hughes showed up at the meeting on July 20 and quickly assumed command of the Catholic forces.[31]

John Hughes' battle with the Public School Society lasted for twenty-one months, from July 1840 to April 1842. It absorbed so much of his time and energy that his friends noticed the toll that it took on his health and even his appearance. More than the fight with the trustees, however, this was the issue that really made Hughes a national figure even though he was still only the coadjutor bishop of New York. "Certainly from 1840 to 1844 he was one of the best abused men in the country," said Hassard. In fact, Hughes became an international figure as news of the controversy spread to England, Ireland, France and Austria.[32]

It is no wonder that Hughes was perceived as a menace by many Protes-tants across the country. His battle with the Public School Society in New York had national implications, threatening the cozy arrangement whereby the "common schools" in many parts of the United States had in fact become non-denominational Protestant public schools. As long as the schools promoted a non-denominational form of Christianity, many Protestants contended that they were non-sectarian and therefore should be acceptable to all members of a still nominally Christian community. The "common" school was nineteenth-century America's closest equivalent to an established Church. By this same reasoning Catholic schools were ipso facto sectarian and undeserving of public funding. When Hughes criticized this double standard, he was pilloried as the Catholic hierarch who wished to drive the Bible from the public schools and to finance his own schools from the public till.

After July 1840 Hughes attended every meeting of the Catholic Association in St. James church and regularly spoke at great length. In August he and a group of laymen issued an "Address of the Roman Catholics to their Fellow Citizens of the City and State of New York." The following month they sent a public petition to the Common Council of the City of New York which set the stage for the most famous incident in this long controversy — Hughes' appearance before the Common Council. On two successive days, October 29 and 30, 1840, Hughes spoke for over three hours presenting the Catholic case to the municipal authorities. When they rejected the Catholic demands in January, 1841, Hughes prepared a petition with 7,000 names for the state legislature which was presented in Albany in February. The state senate passed this hot potato on to the secretary of state, John Spencer, who also happened to be *ex officio* the state superintendent of public schools. Spencer in turn recommended the replacement of the Public School Society with locally elected school boards (which was the practice in the rest of the state).[33]

The proposed bill stalled in the legislature and in the spring the politicians decided to postpone further consideration until after the November elections, thus transforming the elections into a referendum on the future of the Public School Society. Despite his friendship with Governor Seward, Hughes expected strong opposition from the Whigs. They "have often complimented us as the spawn of garrets and cellars," New York's leading Irish Catholic newspaper once noted.[34] However, the bishop was annoyed and angered at the failure of the Democrats to support the proposed legislation. Consequently, four days before the election, Catholics in New York City organized their own political party, the Carroll Hall ticket. They endorsed ten sympathetic Democrats (whose party repudiated the endorsement) and ran five candidates of their own. The Catholic ticket garnered only 2,200 votes, but the Democrats lost New York City by a mere 290 votes. The Catholic vote may not have been decisive, but it was a warning to the Democrats not to take the Catholic vote for granted.

Early in 1842 Spencer's proposed legislation was redrafted by John McClay, a Democratic assemblyman from New York City, and submitted to both houses of the state legislature. The Assembly passed the bill in March by a margin of 65 to 16, but once again the Senate balked. For a second time, therefore, the Catholics organized an ad hoc political party, this time entering candidates in the municipal election scheduled for April 12. On April 9 the Senate passed the McClay bill. On April 11 the Catholic slate withdrew from the municipal elections.

Hughes was consulted on the formulation of the McClay Bill. Its enactment into law was hardly a total victory for him, however, since it expressly forbade public funding of religious schools. Nevertheless, it did replace the Public School Society with elected school boards in New York City, and it was perceived by many as a Catholic victory. In fact, it led to the stoning of Hughes' residence by a crowd of unhappy Protestants. The bishop's stock soared with the members of his own flock. "At this time," said Hassard, "he probably had more influence over the Irish population of New York than any man, in the Church or out of it, ever possessed before or has ever held since."[35]

By the middle of 1841 Hughes' battle over public education in New York City had become — in the words of Henry Browne — "his most absorbing activity." In September of that year, with the crucial state elections only a few weeks away, Bishop Purcell apologized for even writing to him. "You are so constantly engaged in fighting &, of course, winning the battles of Faith, that I scruple intruding a moment longer on yr time."[36] Yet, it was precisely during the hectic summer of 1841 that Hughes also found the time to launch his long-awaited new college at Rose Hill.

ST. JOHN'S COLLEGE

St. John's College finally opened its doors to the first students on June 24, 1841, although presumably classes did not begin until the following September. The college was placed under the protection of St. John the Baptist, but it is not clear whether there was any formal dedication or inaugural ceremony.[37] The total physical plant consisted of the two-story stone manor house to which two wings had been added — the present-day administration building. The seminarians were housed in a separate small stone building somewhere to the west of the manor house. It was intended to be only a temporary arrangement. A permanent seminary building was erected in 1845 (the present-day St. John's Hall) together with a stone chapel which also served as the parish church for the Catholics of the neighborhood.

Hughes pushed ahead with the inauguration of the college despite the desperate state of diocesan finances. At the time there were ten parish churches in New York City whose combined debt amounted to approximately $300,000. The annual interest on this debt was $20,000, "almost enough to build a new church every year," Hassard remarked. The fund-raising drive of the previous year for the college and seminary had raised only about $10,000, or less than half the amount that Hughes had to find every year merely to service the debt on his parish churches. It was a bold gesture to start St. John's College under such circumstances.[38]

Lack of money was not the only problem; Hughes also had to find a suitable president and faculty. In the five short years that the college was in the hands of the New York diocesan clergy, there were no fewer than four presidents. The first incumbent was a young priest in whom John Hughes had great confidence, John McCloskey, quondam professor at Bishop Dubois' ill-starred Nyack seminary eight years earlier and currently pastor of St. Joseph's church in Greenwich Village where he had recently won a long tug-of-war with the lay trustees by dint of his own quiet determination. After leaving Nyack, McCloskey had spent three years studying in Rome and so he was as qualified as any New York diocesan priest to head the institution. He served as president for only one year and appears to have also retained his pastorate of St. Joseph's church.

The vice president was Father Ambrose Manahan, a recent graduate of the Propaganda College in Rome, who also taught Greek and mathematics. He would succeed McCloskey as president in 1842 and prove to be a disaster. The rest of the original faculty consisted of three priests, two lay professors, six tutors, and two seminarians whom Hughes had hurriedly recalled from Mount St. Mary's in Emmitsburg, John Harley and John Conroy. Harley would succeed Manahan as the third president but then die at the age of thirty; he in turn was succeeded by James Roosevelt Bayley, a convert Episcopalian clergyman who later became the first bishop of Newark and archbishop of Baltimore.[39]

Hughes had been particularly eager to add Conroy and Harley to the faculty because they already had teaching experience at Emmitsburg. At the same time he was somewhat embarrassed at raiding the Emmitsburg faculty and he encountered strong resistance from the rector, his old friend, John McCaffrey. A month before the planned opening, he explained to McCaffrey that he was desperate for professors because some of the faculty whom he had recruited in Europe had never arrived. "We must commence next month," he insisted, "and the commencement under the eyes, you may say of this city, must be such as not to fall far short of the anticipations that have been created." At first Hughes asked McCaffrey only for the loan of the two men for six months. "We must in these matters that are undertaken for a common cause be prepared to help one another," he pleaded with McCaffrey, "and he who is most in need has the best claim."[40]

Shortly after the opening of St. John's College, Hughes tried to assuage McCaffrey's wounded feelings. "You know or ought to know," he said, "that I would be the last bishop in the country to do or wish done anything that would materially injure Mount St. Mary's." Again he tried to explain to McCaffrey how hard pressed he was for suitable faculty members in New York.

"You know the abortions that have preceded this effort to get up a house of education in this diocese, and that I am not the one to add to the number, if I can help it. To avoid this, two things are necessary, pupils and teachers. It appears that the pupils will not be wanting, if there are teachers. Am I not bound to provide teachers — otherwise what is the object of the undertaking?"[41]

In launching St. John's College the cruelest blow for Hughes may have been something that he perhaps never anticipated. After begging for money at home and abroad, and scraping together faculty wherever he could find them, he must have been disappointed to discover that St. John's College would begin its first academic year with a grand total of six students.[42]

Catholic colleges, or male literary institutions, as they were frequently called, were still something of a rarity in the United States in 1841. There were only thirteen in the whole country, four of them in the archdiocese of Baltimore, and most were located in isolated rural areas. Significantly neither Boston nor Philadelphia as yet had a full-fledged Catholic college. A few Catholic institutions like Georgetown College were well established, but others were ephemeral schools which did not last, such as St. Philip's University near Detroit, Michigan, or St. Mary's College in Kentucky whose French Jesuit professors would be happy to come to New York in 1846. Admission standards were rudimentary and flexible. The Jesuit-run St. John's Literary Institute near Frederick City, Maryland, advertised: "No scholar received unless he knows how to read and bears a good moral character."[43]

From the beginning St. John's College capitalized on its location combining a healthy country location with easy access to New York City thanks to the recently-completed New York and Harlem Railroad whose right of way ran along the western perimeter of the college. In the bombastic promotional style of the day, parents were assured that "the utmost attention will be paid not only to the intellectual, but also to the *moral* education of the pupils. Their general deportment and manners will be watched over with scrupulous care." With considerable exaggeration, the sole college building was described as "large, elegant and commodious." As to the students' domestic comfort, an 1842 advertisement claimed that "everything which parental affection can desire will be found and supplied in assiduous attentions and skillful management of the Sisters of Charity to whom the charge of this important and highly responsible department is mainly confided."

In fact, the college regulations were hardly different from those of a seminary. Students were forbidden to leave the grounds unless accompanied by a faculty member. Visits to parents in the city were limited to one every three months. All books in the students' possession had first to be approved by the president of the college or the prefect of studies. Pocket money was to be deposited with the treasurer who would dole it out to the students as he saw fit.

The core curriculum consisted of Hebrew, Greek, Latin, English, French, poetry, rhetoric, history, mythology, geography, bookkeeping, arithmetic, algebra, mathematics, and moral and natural philosophy. Instruction in German, Italian and Spanish was available, but at extra cost as was the case with music and drawing. The school year began on the first Monday of September and did not end until July 15. Tuition was $200 per year, the same as at Georgetown College and St. Mary's College in Baltimore. Among the personal items that each student was expected to bring with him were "a silver spoon and silver drinking cup marked with his name."[44]

GROWING PAINS

The first major crisis in the history of the new institution occurred in 1843 after John McCloskey had returned to St. Joseph's church in Greenwich Village and was replaced as rector by Ambrose Manahan. John Harley complained that Manahan was an autocrat who insisted on running everything himself. "What was before the home of harmony and happiness is now the abode of discord and unhappiness," Harley told Hughes in February 1843. "Mr. Manahan has come among us, full to overflowing of wild and useless schemes: schemes that are not at all suited to the character and wants of this institution." As a result, Harley feared that the seminarians might very well leave and seek admission to other dioceses. As for the college students, said Harley, "[They] are almost in a state of rebellion, and nothing but the paucity of their number restrains them from open eruption." In view of the situation, Harley offered Hughes his resignation.[45]

Instead of accepting Harley's resignation, Hughes fired Manahan as president and replaced him with Harley. Harley was only twenty-seven years old, but he was clearly a favorite of Hughes and a very capable man. Under Harley's leadership the students were pacified, good order was restored, and the college surmounted its first crisis. James Roosevelt Bayley credited Harley with devising the academic and disciplinary system that placed the new college on a sound foundation. Unfortunately, in 1845 Harley became seriously ill. Hughes took him to Europe with him to consult physicians in London, Dublin and Paris, but his condition was beyond nineteenth-century medical help. He died at Hughes' residence in New York City on December 8, 1846, at the age of thirty. He seems to have been the most capable and effective of the four diocesan priests who served as presidents of St. John's. Hughes replaced him with James Roosevelt Bayley, who was to be the last diocesan priest to serve as president of the college.[46]

Meanwhile, Hughes found some relief from his personnel problems at Rose Hill when he persuaded the Vincentians to assume the direction of the seminary. However, there was a fatal flaw in the agreement that Hughes made with the Vincentians, for he and they had in mind two different and incompatible models of seminary education. The Vincentians wanted the seminary to be totally separated from the college. Hughes and Harley, however, were still committed to the Emmitsburg system of using the seminarians as tutors in the college. Hughes told Father John Timon, the American superior of the Vincentians: "Everything in my power shall be done to meet your wishes, and, as far as possible, to make things harmonize with the spirit of your Society."[47]

Hughes gave himself an escape clause with the phrase "as far as possible." Harley continued to claim the services of the seminarians who did not pay full tuition (the great majority) much to the annoyance of the seminary rector, Father Anthony Penco, who claimed that Hughes was not living up to his agreement with the Vincentians. Within eighteen months Penco was threatening to resign as seminary rector. He told Timon: "I have already lost almost completely my peace of mind and heart on this account, *viz.*, seeing ... the terms of our agreement altogether forgotten."

Early in 1844 Hughes moved the seminary from Fordham to a house at Fiftieth Street and Fifth Avenue opposite the site of the present cathedral. It was only a temporary move while a permanent seminary building was constructed at Rose Hill. However, only sixteen of the seminarians made the move to New York City; the other twelve remained at Rose Hill, to the consternation of Penco, who said: "I cannot take the idea of being in a seminary, the members of which will be constantly at the disposal of another institution." By the summer of 1844 John Hughes and the Vincentians had come to the parting of the ways. Upon the advice of both Timon and Penco, they terminated their contract with the diocese and gladly relinquished control of the seminary. Once again the faculty was reduced to a single person, a *oiseau de passage* named Rainaidi, apparently an Italian secular priest who came and went without leaving a trace.[48]

While the seminary remained a problem, the college made slow but steady progress. "But what else could we expect?" asked the sycophantic editor of the *Truth Teller* in language worthy of many a future diocesan newspaper editor. "Our highly gifted and energetic bishop is its founder and patron." The curriculum remained basically that of a classical college with a heavy emphasis on Latin and Greek. Interestingly, however, the course offerings were broadened in September 1842 with the addition to the faculty of two businessmen who were to provide practical instruction "for such as only desire a mercantile education." There were as yet, of course, no graduates who had completed the four-year course, but each school year ended with an "exhibition" that included speeches and poems by the students and the distribution of prizes.

A reporter for the *Freeman's Journal*, more than likely the editor, Eugene A. Casserly, witnessed the exhibition of 1843 and noticed that every passing allusion to the grievances of Ireland in the students' orations drew appreciative applause from the crowd. One wonders what to make of the applause that greeted a recital of a Greek Ode in the original language.[49] The anonymous writer was impressed with what he witnessed. He always wondered, he confessed, why a city with so many Catholics should have lacked either a college or seminary. "What was two years ago an experiment," he said, "is now a cheering certainty, and the Diocese of New York has within itself all the means necessary to advance the momentous and kindred interests of education and religion."

In a promotional pitch for the college that the *Freeman's Journal* made at the beginning of the next school year, however, there is a hint that perhaps not all of New York's wealthier Catholics shared the newspaper's enthusiasm for the new college. "We only wish that all would endeavor to avail themselves of its advantages," the paper said and expressed the hope that no Catholic boy would be found at a Protestant college "imbibing with their learning that insidious poison [which results] in the eternal loss of the ill-fated victim of most mischievous parental indiscretion."[50]

NATIVISM

In the 1840's resentment at the ever-increasing flood of immigrants led to the formation of Nativist or Native American political parties in several parts of the country. Nativist sentiment was particularly strong in Philadelphia and New York both of which had large concentrations of poor Irish Catholic immigrants. In New York City the Nativists scored their first major political victory in April 1844 when they elected the first Nativist mayor, James Harper, the candidate of the Native American party.

On election night some twelve hundred Nativists celebrated their victory with a provocative march through Catholic neighborhoods brandishing no-popery banners. Hughes successfully urged restraint on the Irish Catholics, and there was no violence. Writing twenty years later, Hassard claimed that on that election night rumors also circulated that the Nativist marchers intended to attack the cathedral. Therefore, said Hassard, "some three or four thousand Catholics — among whom were the most prominent lay gentlemen of that denomination in the city — assembled in the churchyard armed to the teeth." According to him, the show of force was enough to prevent any damage to the cathedral.[51]

Early in May serious violence erupted in Philadelphia resulting in riots that led to the destruction of two Catholic churches and a dozen deaths. Bishop Francis Kenrick left the city and suspended church services the following Sunday. Nativist leaders in Philadelphia claimed to have rescued an American flag that had been desecrated by Irish Catholics. They made the flag a cause celèbre and announced plans to bring it to New York City in order to rally Native American forces there. Plans were announced for a demonstration in City Hall park to welcome the Nativist delegation from Philadelphia.

The situation was so tense and dangerous that even James Gordon Bennett, the editor of the *New York Herald*, and chronic critic of Hughes, found himself for once on the same side as the bishop in urging a cancellation of the demonstration.[52] Hughes went to City Hall and asked the lame-duck mayor, Robert Morris, to ban the proposed gathering. Under severe public pressure, the Nativist leaders themselves called off the demonstration. Hughes claimed the credit for saving the city from bloodshed in an unsigned editorial in the *Freeman's Journal* that contained few echoes of the Sermon on the Mount:

> If our city has been saved from the bloodshed and infamy that now rest on a sister capital, it is owing exclusively to the forbearance and patience (under insults calculated to make the blood of freemen boil in their veins) of the entire Catholic population of New York. We, of course, as friends of order and peace, feel grateful to them for this extraordinary exercise of patience under insult ... But, at the same time, it is not to be disguised that, if aggression had been carried further than insult, and any act of violence had been committed by the inflamed rabble who made up the train of the "Native American" processions, the carnage that would have ensued is now utterly beyond calculation. There is not a church of the city which was not protected with an average force of one to two thousand men—cool, collected, armed to the teeth, and with a firm determination, after taking as many lives as they could in defence of their property, to give up, if necessary, their own lives for the same cause.[53]

There is no reason to doubt Hassard's assertion that Hughes also said that "if a single Catholic church were burned in New York, the city would become a second Moscow." It is questionable, however, to what extent Hughes' rhetoric matched reality. It is hard to believe that he could have assembled 10,000 to 20,000 armed men without attracting the notice of the civil authorities or the press. James Gordon Bennett never ceased to criticize Hughes for having organized the Carroll Hall political party in 1841; it is hardly likely that he would have let slip an opportunity to depict Hughes as the organizer of his own private militia in 1844.

Hughes' aggressive leadership, whether it was largely bluff or not, helped to prevent bloodshed in New York City in May 1844. Ray Allen Billington, the preeminent historian of American nativism, credits Hughes for "saving New York from a period of mob rule such as that which had racked Philadelphia.[54] Then in June the embattled bishop spilled enormous quantities of ink in the form of four open letters that were widely quoted *in extenso* in the daily newspapers. The first was addressed to Mayor Harper and the latter three to Colonel William L. Stone, editor of the *New York Commercial Advertiser*. However, the main object of the bishop's fury was James Gordon Bennett, a Scottish-born Catholic, whom he blamed for libeling him and the Catholic Church and for bringing the city to the brink of violence.[55]

The first letter filled seven full columns of the *Freeman's Journal* and one reader noted that Hughes used the personal pronoun 361 times.[56] However, newspaper readers were accustomed to verbosity and egotism in public figures; what was extraordinary was the vehemence of Hughes' attack on Bennett, whom he assailed, said Hassard, "with a bitterness of invective almost unparalleled in newspaper controversy." Hughes emerged from the ordeal unscathed and as feisty as ever, perhaps not the most subtle, but certainly one of the most outspoken Catholic opponents of the Nativists. During June 1844, while he was composing his long-winded letters and raking Bennett over the coals as "too contemptible for notice, and yet not sufficiently so to be below the power of mischief," Hughes also found the time to spend three days at Rose Hill giving a retreat on the spiritual life to the students at St. John's College.[57]

THE END OF THE BEGINNING

In 1845 the academic year came to an end at St. John's College on Tuesday, July 15, with the usual "exhibition." It was a hot summer day, but the heat did not prevent thousands of people from descending upon the Rose Hill campus for the ceremonies. The New York and Harlem Railroad laid on special trains which whisked the guests and visitors from the City Hall station to Fordham in one hour, a speed that has hardly been improved upon by public transportation a century and a half later. Eight new classrooms had recently been added to the campus, and the buildings were described as forming a perfect square with interior corridors and neatly finished steeples. A large canvas tent had been erected on the front lawn to shield the participants from the scorching sun. However, the crowd was so large that many people spilled out from the chairs beneath the tent and found places on the lawn.

On the stage were the assembled clerical and academic dignitaries, headed, of course, by Bishop Hughes who presided in his capacity as *praeses emeritus*. On that day at least New York's embattled bishop was among friends, a representative sampling of the Irish Catholics who had cheered him on during the previous five years through all his battles with the lay trustees, the Public School Society, and most recently the Nativists. Amid such surroundings

Hughes could relax for a few hours and savour the victories that he had won among admirers who appreciated them as much as he did.

Not the least of his achievements was the scene that unfolded before him. In the front rows sat 145 students compared with the six with whom he had opened his college only four years earlier. On Hughes' left and right were two New York priests who had just recently been raised to the episcopacy, William Quarter, the first bishop of Chicago, and Andrew Byrne, the first bishop of Little Rock. Present also were Constantine Pise of St. Joseph's parish in Greenwich Village, the only priest ever to serve as chaplain to the U.S. Senate; Felix Varela, who had worked so hard in 1839 and 1840 on behalf of the fundraising campaign for the college and seminary; and the hapless Ambrose Manahan, who no doubt steered clear of John Harley, the college president, who gave an address on the value of Christian education.

Despite the heat, the ceremonies lasted several hours as students delivered prepared speeches and a brass band played such popular Irish-American tunes as "Exile of Erin" and "The Last Rose of Summer." The distribution of "premiums" (a.k.a., prizes) must have been interminable, for the printed list filled two full columns of the *Freeman's Journal* the following week. No one went home unhappy, for virtually every student received several prizes which ran the gamut from proficiency in Latin and Greek to "improvement on bugle." Almost all the names were Irish except for a sprinkling of students from Cuba and Mexico. At the end of the long day Hughes (as usual) had the final word, telling the audience how pleased he was with the progress of the college and emphasizing the dangers of "mixed education," by which he meant the mingling of Catholic and Protestant students in the same institution as in the new Queen's Colleges in Ireland.[58]

Father Harley's deteriorating health forced him to retire as president later that summer. It sealed the fate of St. John's College as a diocesan institution for Hughes had no one to replace him. It also placed an added burden on Hughes himself. "Whilst the college is otherwise prosperous," he told Bishop Purcell at the beginning of the new academic year in September 1845, "[Harley's] associates are all without experience, and the superintendence of the institution with its one hundred sixty boys requires my daily inspection in a quiet and unostentatious way."[59] As usual, Hughes was exaggerating, in this instance because he wanted an excuse to avoid a trip to Cincinnati for the dedication of Purcell's new cathedral. It is as difficult to imagine John Hughes traveling to Fordham everyday by train as it is to imagine him intervening anywhere in "a quiet and unostentatious way." Nonetheless, his comments to Purcell reveal both his own deep commitment to St. John's College and his increasing weariness of trying to maintain the college with the slender resources of his diocesan clergy.

At the commencement exercises the following summer Bishop Hughes was in an especially expansive mood. Those ceremonies, held at Rose Hill on July

15, 1846, were the last conducted under the administration of the diocesan clergy. Once again a large tent had been erected on the lawn with room for 3,000 people. Hughes presided, flanked by his new coadjutor, John McCloskey, and the new college president, James Roosevelt Bayley. One reason for the bishop's good humor was that his new seminary and chapel on the campus were almost completed, and the fund-raising drive had been oversubscribed. He had hoped to raise $12,000 or $13,000, but the campaign brought in almost double that amount, over $24,000.

The ceremonies that year constituted the first real graduation, for in April the state legislature had granted a charter to St. John's College empowering it to confer "such literary honors, degrees and diplomas as are usually granted by any University, College or Seminary of learning in the United States." In his concluding remarks that day, Hughes emphasized that the vote in the legislature had been unanimous, winning the support of even the erstwhile Nativists. He then used that happy development to argue that the anti-Catholic bigotry of recent years had been an aberration and that most Americans harbored no ill feelings toward the Catholic church. In fact, Hughes sounded almost like John Carroll or John England that July afternoon, contrasting the religious freedom that American Catholics enjoyed with the burnt-out ruins of churches and convents in other countries of the world.

One reason for Hughes' high spirits was that he had already made arrangements with French Jesuits in Kentucky to take charge of St. John's College for the following September. He mentioned the impending change at the graduation, comparing it to the voluntary retirement of one dynasty in favor of another and graciously expressing the hope that, under the direction of the Society of Jesus, "the usefulness, the reputation and prosperity of St. John's College may be consolidated and extended in perpetuity."[60]

With the coming of the Jesuits to Rose Hill, Hughes' involvement in St. John's College was drastically curtailed. In later years he expressed disappointment with the Jesuits' management of the institution, claiming that the college had "retrograded.... [and] become comparatively obscure."[61]

Whatever the truth of Hughes' criticism of the Jesuits, there can be little doubt of his own contribution to St. John's College. He purchased the property, raised the funds, hired the faculty, obtained the state charter, and handed over to the Jesuits a flourishing little college whose ownership they were glad to accept. Most remarkably of all, Hughes did all this and established almost single-handedly New York's first permanent Catholic college at the same time that he was coping with the pervasive poverty of a raw new diocese and waging an exhausting battle with lay trustees, public school officials, state and local politicians, and Nativist extremists. It was no mean accomplishment even for John Joseph Hughes.

NOTES

1. *Archives of the University of Notre Dame* (Hereafter, *AUND*), Hughes to Purcell, February 24, 1838.

2. *Archives of the Archdiocese of New York* (Hereafter, *AANY*), A-7, Hughes to Abbot Bernard Smith, July 9, 1858. The letter was edited and published by Henry Browne as "The Archdiocese of New York A Century Ago: A Memoir of Archbishop Hughes, 1838-1858" *Historical Records and Studies* 39-40 (1952), 129-187. *The Catholic Directory* for 1838 lists 38 churches and 12 stations, 50 priests and 50 Sisters of Charity in New York. *The Metropolitan Catholic Almanac and Laity's Directory for the Year of Our Lord* 1838 (Baltimore: Fielding Lucas Jr., 1838), p. 87.

3. John Hassard, *Life of the Most Reverend John Hughes, First Archbishop of New York* (New York: D. Appleton and Company, 1866), p. 189. *Truth Teller*, June 15, 1844.

4. *AUND*, Hughes to Purcell, February 24, 1838.

5. Hughes to the Leopoldine Society, Vienna, April 16, 1840, Lawrence Kehoe, ed., *Complete Works of the Most Rev. John Hughes, D.D.* (New York: Lawrence Kehoe, 1866), II, 463. At the time there were two colleges in New York City: Columbia College which began as King's College in 1754 under Anglican auspices, and New York University, which was chartered in 1831 as a non-sectarian institution. The City College of New York dates from 1847.

6. The Jesuits under Father Anthony Kolhmann had opened New York's first Catholic "college," the New York Literary Institute, in 1808, but they closed it in 1813 in order to concentrate their limited personnel in Georgetown College. See Francis X. Curran, S.J., *The Return of the Jesuits* (Chicago: Loyola University Press, 1966), pp. 10-56.

7. *Archives of the Archdiocese of St. Louis* (Hereafter, *AASTL*), Dubois to Rosati, April 18, 1837. When St. Mary's church was torched, the bell was stuffed so that it could not be used to summon help. *Truth Teller*, November 12, 1831. In an early and unusual example of ecumenism, the First Universalist Church allowed the Catholics of St. Mary's parish to use their church on the corner of Grand and Pitt Streets for three Masses every Sunday morning.

8. Hughes to Frenaye, March 22, 1838, in Hassard, *Hughes*, p. 188.

9. Archives of the Archdiocese of Baltimore (Hereafter, AAB), Hughes to Eccleston, March 30, 1838.

10. Archives of Mount St. Mary's Seminary and College (Hereafter, AMSM), Hughes to McCaffrey, May 4, 1838.

11. Hughes to Frenaye, May 3, 1838, in Hassard, *Hughes*, pp. 190-191.

12. *Truth Teller*, August 11, 1838.

13. Ibid., September 15, 1838.

14. Ibid., September 1, 1838.

15. Guth to Hughes, September 25, 1838; September 1839, in Hassard, *Hughes*, p. 191.

16. *AMSM*, Hughes to McCaffrey, June 2, 1841.

17. The remains of the college, a two-and-a-half story stone building, can still be seen from state route 414 a half-mile west of Lafargeville. Even in the age of interstate highways, Lafargeville is a full day's drive from New York City. It is difficult to imagine how one could have traveled there from New York City in three days in 1838 when there was no direct railroad connection.

18. The indenture identifies Hughes as "Minister of the Gospel." *AANY*, B.

19. Quoted by Hassard, *Hughes*, p. 192.

20. *AAB*, Hughes to Eccleston, February 25, 1839.

21. For details, see Hassard, *Hughes*, pp. 192-196. The financial crisis of 1837 and the following years made many of the trustees happy to get rid of their financial responsibilities. Jay P. Dolan, *The Immigrant Church* (Baltimore: Johns Hopkins University Press, 1975), p. 49.

22. *AAB*, Hughes to Eccleston, March 10, 1839; *AAStL*, Hughes to Rosati, May 7, 1839.

23. Hughes, "Memoir," p. 144.

24. *AANY*, Henry J. Browne, unpublished biography of John Hughes, Chapter VII, p. 2.

25. Hughes to Leopoldine Society, April 16, 1840, in Kehoe, *Works*, II, 463. *AANY*, A-6, Hughes to Society for the Propagation of the Faith, January 22, 1845. Hassard, *Hughes*, p. 212.

26. *New York Catholic Register*, October 24, 1839. Anyone unable to contribute $1.00 was excused as "too straitened in circumstances to contribute at all."

27. Ibid., November 7, 21, 1839; February 13, March 26, April 23, April 30, 1840. The final sums reported in the *New York Catholic Register* were $14,672.55 in pledges of which $9,905.95 had been paid. Ibid., June 10, 1840.

28. Ibid., June 25, 1840.

29. Charles Stuart, deputy superintendent of schools for New York City, reported in 1842 that, of 65,000 children in New York City, 42,000 were enrolled in schools of the Public School Society or in private schools. That left 23,000 children to be accounted for. Stuart estimated that 4,000 of them were in Catholic or other religious schools, and that the remaining 17,000 received no education at all. Stuart also said: "I have also recently visited several of the schools connected with the Catholic churches and found them crowded to overflowing .... In many instance schools were so full that every bench and seat was occupied; the scholars being so closely packed together that they had hardly room to move." *Truth Teller*, July 2, 1842.

30. Quoted in Edward M. Connors, *Church-State Relationships in Education in the State of New York* (Washington: The Catholic University of America Press, 1951), p. 16.

31. Hughes, "Memoir," p. 149.

32. Hassard, *Hughes*, p. 247. Browne, "Hughes," Chapter VI.

33. *Address of the Roman Catholics to their Fellow Citizens of the City and State of New York* (New York: Hugh Cassidy, 1840). The Address used an argument that would be repeated many times in the future by American Catholics. "He [the Catholic citizen] has to pay double taxation for the education of his child, one to the misinterpreted law of the land, and another to his conscience." Ibid., p. 11. The authors of the Address put great stress on the poverty of the average New York Catholic "who sees his child going to [a Catholic] school with perhaps only the fragment of a worn out book, thinly clad, and its feet bare on the frozen pavement," an argument that may seem overdone until one realizes that in 1844 the secretary of St. Patrick's Male Sunday School Society reported that they had distributed 148 pairs of shoes to the approximately 200 poor children attending the Sunday school. *Truth Teller*, February 3, 1844. The text of the petition to the Common Council is in Kehoe, ed., *Works*, I, 102-107.

34. *Truth Teller*, November 2, 1844.

35. Hassard, *Hughes*, pp. 246-247. *Truth Teller*, November 2, 1844.

36. Purcell to Hughes, September 30, 1841, in Browne, "Hughes," Chapter VI, n.83.

37. The author of the fiftieth anniversary history of St. John's College, writing in 1891, could find no trace of any ceremony that occurred on June 24, 1841, but he insisted that "the ceremonies took place." Thomas Gaffney Taaffe, *A History of St. John's College, Fordham, N.Y.* (New York: The Catholic Publication Society, 1891), p. 51.

38. Hassard, *Hughes*, p. 254.

39. James Roosevelt Bayley, *A Brief Sketch of the Early History of the Catholic Church on the Island of New York* (1870), reprint (New York: U.S. Catholic Historical Society, 1973), p. 134. Hassard, *Hughes*, p. 252. Bayley, the fourth president of St. John's College, said that for some time it was more commonly referred to as Rose Hill College.

40. *AMSM*, Hughes to McCaffrey, May 6, 1841. Hughes originally asked for Harley and another New Yorker named John McCloskey. For some reason McCloskey did not come, and in the middle of September, William Starrs, Hughes' secretary, told McCaffrey that it was "absolutely necessary" that Conroy should replace him at Rose Hill. Conroy later became the second bishop of Albany. *AMSM*, Starrs to McCaffrey, September 16, 1841. Harley and Conroy were ordained priests by Hughes on May 21, 1842. *Truth Teller*, June 4, 1842.

41. *AMSM*, Hughes to McCaffrey, October 2, 1841.

42. Hughes, "Memoir," P. 144.

43. *The Metropolitan Catholic Almanac and Laity's Directory for the Year of Our Lord 1841* (Baltimore: Fielding Lucas Jr, 1841), passim.

44. Ibid., 1842, pp. 151-153. In addition to their duties at Rose Hill, the priest members of the faculty also celebrated Sunday Mass at Throg's Point, Saw Pit [Port Chester], Yonkers and Sing Sing [Ossining]. Ibid., p. 149. The rules at St. John's College were similar to those at other Catholic colleges of that era. For a comparison, see the advertisement for the University of Notre Dame in 1847 in John Tracy Ellis, ed., *Documents of American Catholic History* (Wilmington: Michael Glazier, 1987), I, 290-294.

45. *AANY*, A-14, Harley to Hughes, February 28, 1842 [sic], 1843. Manahan had a chequered career. Three years later Hughes sent him a stinging rebuke in ordering him out of the diocese. "Not wishing to have the pain of inflicting any public censure on your character," Hughes wrote, "I advise you to resign, to ask your exeat, in the almost exstinguished hope that on a new scene where your future character will be determined by your future conduct, you may disappoint the melancholy anticipations which the past is too well calculated to inspire." *AANY*, A-5, Hughes to Manahan, September 4, 1845. In 1857 Hughes made Manahan the temporary administrator of St. Stephen's Church in New York City, but Manahan then absconded with the financial records and receipt books of the parish. *AANY*, A-7, Hughes to Manahan, November 4, December 9, 1857. Later in life Manahan described Hughes as "a tyrant, but with feeling." *AANY*, Burtsell Diary, I, July 24, 1865.

46. Bayley, *Brief Sketch*, pp. 134-135. On Harley, see the obituary notice in the *New York Freeman's Journal*, December 12, 1846. Hughes attributed Harley's death to diabetes. *AUND*, Hughes to Purcell, September 23, 1845.

47. *AUND*, Hughes to Timon, August 20, 1842.

48. *Archives of the Curia Generalizia della Missione* (Hereafter, ACGM), Timon to Possou, July 19, 1842. *AUND*, Penco to Timon, January 12, July 18, November 20, December 9, 1843. ACGM, Timon to Etienne, June 1, 1844; Penco to Etienne, June 29, 1844. *AUND*, Penco to Timon, February 1, June 18, July 30, 1844. There is an excellent brief account of the Vincentians and the Rose Hill seminary in John E. Rybolt, C.M., ed., *The American Vincentians: A Popular History of the Congregation of the Mission in the United States* (Brooklyn: New City Press, 1988), pp. 115-117.

49. *Truth Teller*, August 27, 1842; *New York Freeman's Journal*, July 15, 1843.

50. *New York Freeman's Journal*, July 15, August 26, 1843.

51. Hassard, *Hughes*, pp. 274-275. Richard Shaw, *Dagger John: The Unquiet Life and Times of Archbishop John Hughes of New York* (New York: Paulist, 1977) cites Hassard as his only source for the story. Browne treats it with considerable skepticism. Browne, "Hughes,"

Chapter VIII, n.16. A later embellishment of the story has the Ancient Order of Hibernians providing the armed guards for the cathedral.

52. *New York Herald*, May 10, 1844.

53. "Riots in Philadelphia," *New York Freeman's Journal*, May 11, 1844. Hassard identifies Hughes as the author of the editorial. Hassard, *Hughes*, p. 276.

54. Ray Allen Billington, *The Protestant Crusade* (New York: Macmillan, 1938), p. 232. Billington accepts Hughes' claim about posting 1,000 to 2,000 armed guards around each of the city's Catholic churches, but his only source is Hassard.

55. For the text of the letters, see *New York Freeman's Journal*, May 25, June 1, June 15, June 22, 1844. They are reprinted in Kehoe, *Works*, I, 450-500. Perhaps the most significant aspect of these letters is Hughes' firm commitment to the "Americanist" ecclesiology of John Carroll and John England. "I have always contended for the right of conscience, for all men as universally as they are recognized in the American Constitution," he told Mayor Harper. Kehoe, *Works*, I, 458.

56. David Hale, editor of the *New York Journal of Commerce*, was the person who counted Hughes' 361 references to himself.

57. For the vehemence of Hughes' language, see Hassard, *Hughes*, p. 279. On the retreat at St. John's College, see Browne, "Hughes," Chapter VIII, p. 7. Bennett's language was also deliberately inflammatory; the *New York Herald* in some respects was the predecessor of the yellow journalism of the later nineteenth century. Bennett often referred to Hughes as the Bishop of Blarneyopolis, a reference to the fact that as coadjutor Hughes was the titular bishop of Basilopolis in partibus infidelium.

58. *Truth Teller*, August 24, 1844; *New York Freeman's Journal*, July 19, 1845; *Truth Teller*, July 19, 1845.

59. *AUND*, Hughes to Purcell, September 23, 1845.

60. *New York Freeman's Journal*, October 11, November 22, 1845; April 25, July 18, 1846. James Roosevelt Bayley gives the wrong dates for the granting of the charter and the first graduation, March 17 and July 15, 1845, instead of 1846. Bayley, *Brief Sketch*, p. 135.

61. Hughes, "Memoir," p. 145. Hughes also mistakenly places the granting of the charter in 1845. He explained why he offered the college to the Jesuits: "The wants of the mission were so great, and the missionaries so few, that I deemed it expedient to offer it to the Jesuit Fathers; and this I did with the more confidence, as they are supposed to be the best qualified for carrying on such an institution. They have continued it since 1846, but I regret to say, not with anything like the success which until then it had achieved in public estimation .... I regret to say that it has not advanced, but has rather retrograded ever since ... and the institution has become comparatively obscure." Ibid. It should be remembered that Hughes made these disparaging remarks at a time when he was engaged in a running battle with the Jesuits over the management of St. John's College and St. Francis Xavier parish in Manhattan. For details see Francis X. Curran's paper, "Archbishop Hughes and the Jesuits: An Anatomy of their Quarrels" in Chapter VII.

CHAPTER V

THE FIRST JESUITS AT ST. JOHN'S COLLEGE (FORDHAM), 1846

by Thomas C. Hennessy, S.J.

Eighteen forty-six was an eventful year in the history of the United States. The southwest was stirring with the Mexican War which was fought originally over Texas and ended by expanding the nation by 1,193,061 square miles (Arizona, Nevada, California, Utah, and parts of four other states). That same year the northwest area was relieved by the provisions of the Oregon Boundary treaty with Britain, which cleared the nation's title to Oregon, Washington, and parts of Idaho and Montana. In the center of the country 15,000 Mormons trekked from Illinois to Utah. In Washington, DC, the Smithsonian Institution for "the increase and diffusion of knowledge" was founded.

New York City (then limited to Manhattan Island) in 1846 had a population of 314,000 that would increase to 517,000 within four years, as immigrants from all over Europe, particularly from Ireland and Germany, huddled into already crowded tenements. And in that same year Jesuits moved with books and baggage, from various parts of the world, but mostly from St. Mary's College in Marion County, Kentucky, to a little village called Fordham in the town of West Farms in Westchester County, near the nation's metropolis, New York City. There they took over a struggling institution called St. John's College.

The November 24, 1845, agreement between Bishop Hughes and Rev. Clément Boulanger, S.J., to purchase St. John's College included a provision that the Jesuits send two representatives to break the academic ice. So on April 28, 1846, the "advance team" arrived at Rose Hill: the scholar Rev. William Stack Murphy, S.J., who during 1840-45 had been rector-President of St. Mary's College, Kentucky, and the multi-talented Rev. August J. Thébaud, S.J., who was designated the first Jesuit rector-President of the newly acquired institution. They had come to take over the seminary and the college which the indomitable bishop of New York, John Hughes, had founded. St. John's College was started in 1841 and the seminary in the preceding year. An indication of the bishop's difficulties in staffing his college can be gathered from the fact that in the institution's first five years the bishop appointed four different Presidents and several acting Presidents, a kind of record for turnover in college leadership.

By the time that classes began in the fall, Murphy and Thébaud were joined by 45 additional Jesuits. Besides the mission Superior, there were faculty and students in four major sections on the campus: the first section was the college, the second the diocesan seminary, the third section was the Jesuit novitiate (9 novices); the fourth section was the Jesuit seminary (7 studying theology; 3 studying philosophy; 3 studying the humanities).

Those new arrivals at Rose Hill were critically important for the development of a small, struggling institution into an important university. Historians and educators try to learn as much as they can about those responsible for the critically important early days of colleges. They ask: Who were the pioneers? Where did they come from? What did they do in the early days of their institution? How did they spend the rest of their lives? What did their contemporaries think of them? Such questions about the Jesuit pioneers who arrived on the Rose Hill grounds in mid-1846 are the ones that we attempt to explore in the pages that follow.

Besides the Jesuits, there were five lay professors at the college in 1846. They were professors of: Chemistry; History & English Literature; Spanish; Drawing; and Music. We leave to others the task of recounting what is known of those faculty members.

Since the "New York-Canada Mission" was originally staffed by the Province of France whose headquarters were in Paris, it is not surprising that the new Jesuit student theologians at Fordham had earlier been at a seminary in Laval, France, and that the student philosophers had been at the French college-in-exile in Brugelette, Belgium. Some of the Jesuit novices and students of humanities came from Kentucky, and the others from Montreal.

Of the Jesuit employees at St. John's College, 18 had come directly from the Jesuit colleges in Kentucky (St. Mary's and the new, promising Louisville "day" college, the St. Ignatius Literary Institute). Most of the other Jesuits came from France on August 26; the last arrival was Fr. Maldonado who came from Naples on December 14, as noted in the Minister's Diary.

Parts I and II of this paper are devoted to profiles of individual Jesuits who were important for Fordham's early survival and development, most of whom served the college for more than two years. The profiles vary in length depending upon available sources. Part I focuses on the Jesuits who were assigned in 1846 in any capacity to serve at the college; of those, eight worked as full time faculty, four were administrators as well as faculty members, and ten functioned in nonteaching capacities. Part II is devoted to the Jesuits who came to Fordham in 1846 primarily for learning purposes (seminarians or novices); some of these individuals were also part-time teachers.

Some of the original 47 are not profiled for various reasons. One major reason was that some had a limited impact on the development of the college; they were are Fordham for only one or two years. Exceptions were made in the case of DeLuynes and Petit, because of their continuing influence. Another major reason was the unavailability of their records, which is the case of most of those who left the Jesuit order. Yet Ryan, who left the order in 1855, is profiled because of his unusual career as professor and church founder.

In Part III we present some reflections and observations that pertain to the subjects of this paper.

Countries of Origin of the 47 first Jesuits at Fordham[1]

(First names are given for those who are not profiled below; an asterisk indicates a novice or student Jesuit in 1846-1847)

France: (19)
Boulanger, Peter Constance, Corne, Desjacques, Henry duMerle, Férard, Fouché, *Damasus Gauthier, Arsenio Havequez, *Hollinger, Michael Jarry (Breton), Peter Lebreton, Ledoré, (Breton), Legoüais (Breton), *Xavier Maréchal, *Claude Pernot, Séné, Thébaud (Breton), *Tissot

Ireland: (11)
Callaghan, *Crowe, *Dealy, DeLuynes ("nationality Irish"), Driscol, *Jeremiah Garvey, *John Hampston, *Felix McParland, Murphy, *Nash, Ryan

Canada (Quebec): (6)
Doucet, *Hudon, *Ouellet, *Regnier, Roy, *Vachon

Germany: (3)
*Gockeln, Hennen; *Kohler

U.S.A : (3)
*Adams (KY), *Thomas Bidwell (Chautauque, NY), Graves (KY)

Others: (5)
 Belgium: Daubresse; England: Larkin; Spain: Maldonado; Haiti: Petit; Czech:*Charles Sckiansky

Individuals from ten different nations were assembled as an element of fulfilling the bishop's goal to create an outstanding college.

French was the native language of the majority (19 from France; 6 from Quebec; 1 from Haiti). English speakers were the next largest group (11 from Ireland; Larkin; 3 from the U.S.A.). Though all except perhaps nine could speak French, a house rule both at St. Mary's and early Fordham was to use English in all Jesuit conversations, as indicated in Part III of this paper.

PART I

Jesuit Employees, St. John's College, Fordham, 1846[2]

There are three sections in Part I. The first section provides profiles of four administrators (Boulanger, Larkin, Murphy, Thébaud). The second is devoted to the eight full-time faculty members. The third section offers profiles of Jesuit non-faculty college employees.

A. ADMINISTRATORS

Four administrators were especially significant for making policy decisions in the first decade of the college's existence. They were Clément Boulanger, who as the major Superior decided to purchase the college and assigned the college's faculty and staff; John Larkin, who was the first Jesuit dean at Rose Hill and the second Jesuit President and rector; William Stack Murphy, who was Thébaud's predecessor as President of St. Mary's College and who would later become dean and Vice-president at Fordham; and, August Thébaud, who was the first Jesuit President and rector of Fordham. Typically, administrators in those days continued to teach in the classroom.

- FR. CLÉMENT BOULANGER, S.J.
- Lived 78 years
- b. 10/30/1790 at St. Clément, Meurthe, France
- + 6/12/1868, at Issenheim, Upper Rhine, France

Clément Boulanger, son of Pierre Boulanger, a blacksmith (maréchal-ferrant), and Marguerite Receveur,[3] entered the Jesuits as a diocesan priest and a theology professor in 1823. After only one year of noviceship, he made additional theological studies and taught theology at St. Acheul (near Amiens), and at Madrid from 1830 to 1833. From 1833 to 1841 Fr. Boulanger twice held the office of rector, first at the Seminary at LePuy (formerly, Anicensis) and later at the Paris Seminary. He then became Provincial Superior of the Jesuit province of France from February 4, 1842, until March 16, 1845. As the Provincial, he was responsible for making numerous difficult, critical decisions in France and in the New World. One of his decisions was to return the Jesuits to Canada through the on-site leadership of the local mission Superior, Fr. Peter Chazelle. Decisions regarding the Kentucky Jesuits would be made in the following years.

On April 1, 1845, at age 55, shortly after he completed his term as Provincial, Boulanger was appointed official Visitor to the missions in the New World with ample authority to make important decisions on his own. The appointment and the authority to act came from Fr. Jan Roothaan, the Jesuit General. On his way to Kentucky, Boulanger stayed in New York for a few days, and made two courtesy calls on Bishop Hughes. During those visits he must have recalled that when he was the Provincial he had to inform the bishop that he just didn't have the manpower to accept the college at Rose Hill; furthermore, Boulanger was aware of the extensive correspondence beginning in 1839 between Fr. General Roothaan, Fr. De Smet, and others[4] regarding the bishop's hope that the Jesuits have his new college. Yet when the bishop and Boulanger met twice in the spring of 1845, neither made any reference to the college. They were both experienced bargainers. Boulanger wrote to Rome that it would not help his cause to give "the air of wanting it [the college], of looking for it." Likewise when the bishop decided to renew his offer in writing, he did not do it directly to the Visitor but wrote on October 8, 1845, to Fr. Larkin and suggested that he could show the letter to the Visitor.

On June 14, 1845, Fr. Boulanger had arrived as Visitor at St. Mary's, KY, and immediately began an on-site evaluation regarding the future of the college. By June 28 he made the final decision to refuse the oft-repeated offer from the diocese to take over St. Joseph's College in Bardstown. While he was weighing various other options for St. Mary's, a letter arrived from Bishop John Hughes renewing his earlier invitations to the Kentucky Jesuits to move to Rose Hill, near New York City. On November 10 Boulanger left Kentucky for New York to discuss details of the invitation. An agreement was made rapidly because the bishop was leaving shortly for Rome; so, on November 24, 1845, documents to transfer the Rose Hill property were signed by the Visitor and the bishop. In the following decade some Jesuits blamed Boulanger for rushing into the vaguely worded agreement on which he could do little consultation and had no legal advice.

On March 26, 1846, the Jesuit General modified Boulanger's appointment by making him the Superior of the Kentucky and Canada Mission (shortly renamed, the New York-Canada Mission) with headquarters at Fordham. He continued in that assignment until November 17, 1855. The task of a Visitor is temporary; the Mission Superior usually stays in that position for years if his health so warrants.

At Fordham Fr. Boulanger accepted an additional position, that of professor of Moral Theology, an honored teaching post similar to that usually held by college Presidents of his day in American colleges; they usually taught Ethics (Moral Philosophy) courses to seniors.

One of the disappointments of his term of office must have been the increasing tensions between the Jesuits and Archbishop Hughes. Tensions centered around the administration and faculty of the seminary, the seminary grounds, and other issues which escalated to crisis proportions during the term of office of his successor, Rev. John-Baptist Hus, as narrated by F. Curran (see

Chapter VII). On the other hand, Boulanger must have felt a sense of satisfaction at the growth of manpower in the missions: in 1842 the Canada and Kentucky Jesuit personnel totaled 39 but in 1855 the mission numbers mounted to 180.

After completing his term as Mission Superior Boulanger became spiritual father for one year at Collège Ste.-Marie, Montreal. He then returned to France to be Superior of the new Jesuit residence at Nancy, in the diocese where he was born. From 1862 to 1864, he was Rector of the Jesuit College at Laval in France. His final assignment during 1865-68 was again at Nancy, where he was spiritual father.

Fr. Boulanger was a critically important figure in Fordham's history. As official Visitor to the Mission from the Province of France (1845), he rejected other attractive invitations to build colleges in the Midwest, and decided to remove the Jesuits from Kentucky in favor of accepting Bishop Hughes' offer to purchase and staff the struggling college at Rose Hill. Later as Superior of the Mission (1846-1855), he assigned and recruited the founding faculty and administration of the new college.

Better than many of his contemporaries, he recognized that the New York area was an important locale for Jesuit apostolates in both educational and pastoral ministries. During his nine-year term as Mission Superior, in addition to bringing the Jesuits to Fordham, he shared in credit for founding the following institutions: St. Francis Xavier College and parish in New York City (1847), Collège Ste.-Marie in Montreal (1848), and Maison St. Joseph, Sault-au-Récollet in Montreal (1853). In addition, he encouraged renewed missionary and educational activities in numerous sites among the Canadian Indians.

Fr. Boulanger was regarded by most of his contemporaries as an exceptional administrator, though he was later criticized for the details of the Fordham acquisition, as detailed in Chapter VII. He was seen as an affable person, an outstanding counselor, a man well qualified to solve skillfully the difficult problems he faced both in France and in the New World. His solutions to these problems showed his initiative and his vision in entering into new situations and recognizing possibilities for development, and at the same time they demonstrated his zeal to share his Christian and Ignatian worldview with people in the new world. His writings reflect his deep concern for the spiritual progress of his fellow Jesuits and their students, as well as his love for the Church and for the Society of Jesus.

- *FR. JOHN ALOYSIUS LARKIN, S.J.*
- *Lived 57 years*
- *b. 2/2/1801 at Newcastle-upon-Tyne, or Ravensworth, County Durham, England*
- *+ 12/13/1858 at Xavier, NYC*

At age 45, his 1846 assignment was dean (the first Jesuit dean) of St. John's College, Fordham; later he became the second Jesuit President at Fordham, beginning 7/30/1851. He was at Fordham during 1846-47 and 1851-54.

Larkin[5] was born in England of Irish parents (his father, John or Charles, was an inn keeper; Elizabeth Jones was his mother's name). John had three brothers: Charles Fox Larkin (1800-1879), a surgeon who published widely in defense of the Catholic Church; Edward, like John, attended Ushaw College; and, Felix who attended Stonyhurst College and became a distinguished priest in the New York diocese until his death in Astoria (now a part of New York City) on May 20, 1848.

John Larkin's early collegiate education was at Ushaw College (near Durham) where he was a classmate was the future Cardinal Wiseman. After college, Larkin first traveled to the Far East and then joined the Sulpicians at Issy, outside Paris; the Sulpicians are a religious society of priests that is dedicated to the teaching of seminarians. At Issy he studied philosophy for two years and began theological studies. He completed those studies at St. Mary's Seminary in Baltimore, and was ordained there. Next he was assigned to the Grand Séminaire in Montreal where he became a famous orator in both French and English and a celebrated professor of philosophy. But in 1840, leaving behind his honors and achievements in Montreal, he became a Jesuit novice at St. Mary's, Kentucky. During his second year of noviceship, he was made dean and then Superior and President of a small short-lived Jesuit day college, the St. Ignatius Literary Institution in Louisville, KY. In that same city his reputation as a public speaker was widely recognized. Garraghan[6] recounts an event in December, 1843, that spread his renown as a speaker: "On a few hours notice he delivered an eloquent address on 'Genius' before the Mercantile Library Association ... supplying the place of ex-President John Quincy Adams who had been announced as the speaker..." No wonder he was called "the idol in the city of the Falls."[7]

When he was transferred to Rose Hill with the rest of the Kentucky Jesuits in 1846, Larkin became the first Jesuit dean and Vice-president at St. John's

College, Fordham. He stayed at that post for only one year because he was assigned in October, 1847, to found what became the St. Francis Xavier College and parish in Manhattan. His stay there was short because of his unexpected appointment as bishop of Toronto. With the approval of Fr. Boulanger, the Mission Superior, he returned to Europe after he learned that the bishops of Canada were going to petition the Holy Father to order him under his vow of obedience to accept the bishopric. He did escape that honor through the pleas of the Jesuit Fr. General, Jan Roothaan.

However, there was an appointment he could not escape, becoming President/rector of Fordham during 1851-1854. As President he won over the students despite considerable changes in the curriculum and his insistence on better standards of scholarship. Writing almost 40 years later of his presidency, Taaffe claimed: "It is probable that no member of the faculty since the foundation of the college ever acquired such an extraordinary influence on the students ..."[8]

After his term as President he did highly acclaimed retreat and parish work in England during 1854-1855. Upon the completion of those tasks he received a special assignment from the Jesuit General in Rome: "he was appointed [the official] Visitor to the Irish Vice-Province. His colleagues in New York intervened and urgently requested his return because they needed him."[9] So the task in Ireland was transferred to another after Larkin had visited all the Jesuit houses in Ireland and before he made an official report. In early October, 1856, Larkin was back in New York for his last two years of life. He continued giving retreats and preaching throughout the East and made his headquarters at his own St. Francis Xavier parish where he also engaged in the pastoral ministry. He is reported to have had a premonition of his death several months before it occurred as he withdrew from social life and spent much more time than usual in prayerful retirement. He died at St. Francis Xavier's soon after a long session of hearing confessions.

He wrote a Latin grammar which was a textbook at Fordham, Xavier and St. Peter's until the 1870s. He also wrote a very original work on Greek grammar, as reported in Somervogel's Jesuit bibliography.[10]

Biographers said he left a lasting memory on others due to his personal charm and handsome appearance. His physical appearance was impressive; he weighed over 300 pounds and he must also have been tall as a journal description of him mentioned "his commanding form towering above the platform." A later successor in the Fordham presidency, Fr. Laurence McGinley, characterized Fr. Larkin as "impressively round and hearty." When he sought the intercession of the Papal Nuncio in Paris to cancel the episcopal appointment, the Nuncio, struck by his lofty bearing and noble presence, warned him not to appeal in person before the Pope since he was "the very kind of man we wish to wear the miter."

Larkin Hall (the biology building) at Fordham and Larkin Hall at Xavier High School (a classroom building) are memorials to his memory.

The following appreciation of Fr. John Larkin was culled from the various available biographies. He was recalled as "a remarkable man ... a great orator ... a true servant of God," and "esteemed as a profound scholar by the entire clerical body," ... "outstanding in giving St. Ignatius' Spiritual Exercises," "specially devoted to the Holy Spirit ... and to charitable prayer for the souls of the departed." The document that recommended his becoming bishop of Toronto described him briefly and well as "gifted with unusual strength of mind, prudence, and charity."[11]

- *FR. WILLIAM STACK MURPHY, S.J.*
- *Lived 72 years*
- *b. 4/29/1803 at Hyde Park House, Montenotte, Cork, Ireland*
- *+ 10/23/1875 at New Orleans*

At age 43, his 1846 assignment at St. John's College, Fordham, was to teach Greek and Hebrew and be house historian. He was at Fordham from 1846 to 1851 and from 1857 to 1860. He became the second Jesuit dean of Fordham College when he replaced Fr. Larkin in 1847.

William Stack Murphy[12] was born into a prosperous family in Cork; his father, Jeremiah, was a successful attorney, and with his brothers, founder of a flourishing distillery; his mother's name was Mary Stack. There were six children in the family but only three brothers have been identified: Charles, who died in college; Jerry, who was the first Catholic to hold the office of Sheriff since the partial repeal of the penal laws, and in 1829 became the first Catholic Member of Parliament in London, representing Cork; and, Francis Stack Murphy. The latter who lived from 1807 to 1860 had an outstanding career as a barrister and was a Member of Parliament from Cork from 1837 until 1853.

As a child William attracted the attention of his uncle, Bishop John Murphy of Cork, who entertained high hopes and "other plans"[13] for his favorite relative. So he refused to grant the necessary ecclesiastical permission for him to enter the Jesuits. Young Murphy then moved to France where he had been educated at the Jesuit College of St. Acheul, and on August 27, 1823, was accepted into the Society at Paris and made his novitiate at St. Acheul. During his regency, Murphy prefected students and taught at several colleges in France. Then he spent four years in Rome, beginning October, 1830, where he studied theology and was ordained.

After two years of teaching humanities in Spain and volunteering for the American Mission, he was assigned to St. Mary's, Kentucky. He arrived there in early 1836 with the famous Jesuit artist and missionary priest, Nicolas Point, and two Breton Jesuit brothers. Shortly he became the dean of the college. In June, 1840, he was appointed the college rector-President, a position he retained until October, 1845 when he was succeeded in that office by Fr. August Thébaud. Besides being rector and President, Fr. Murphy was also appointed Superior of the mission.

He and Fr. Thébaud were the first of the new Jesuit community to go to Fordham. Thus the new President-rector of the new community (Thébaud) entered the college accompanied by the former President-rector of the former community (Murphy) on April 28, 1846.

When Fr. Murphy arrived at Fordham he was described this way: "His hair was perfectly white, his form was thin and spare, and the deep, thoughtful expression of his intellectual face was heightened by a pair of glasses."[14]   His native talents and travels helped make him multi-lingual as he was able to speak in English, French, Spanish, Irish, and Italian; he taught Greek and was assigned to teach Hebrew. Referring to Fr. Murphy as "more English than Irish," Fr. Thébaud was probably referring to his speech as lacking a "brogue."

After one year of teaching he was assigned to replace Fr. Larkin as Dean and Vice-president. He retained that post for a relatively short time (1847-1851), since the Jesuit General, Fr. Roothaan, honored him by appointing him Visitor to the Missouri vice-province in June, 1851, and named him Vice-Provincial of that vice-province the following August.

With headquarters at St. Louis, Murphy's mandate was to modify and upgrade the educational institutions of the vice-province, to improve training of the young Jesuits according to practices followed in France, and to discourage a premature and exaggerated expansion that threatened the future solid development of that vice-province. The author of Fr. Murphy's obituary in the *Freeman's Journal* (Nov. 20, 1875) noted that "he so enlarged and improved the St. Louis University that he may be regarded as its founder."

Some contemporaries viewed Murphy's efforts as Visitor and his five years as vice-Provincial as a turning point in the work of Midwestern Jesuits, especially in strengthening internal organization. Likewise "his government [was regarded as] spiritual, mild, exact."[15] Several agreed that except for his health he would have been appointed for a successive term as vice-Provincial.[16] He was considered to have provided his brethren with "what circumstances had made it difficult for them previously to enjoy — a manner of government in accordance with Jesuit ideals and demands."[17] His work in higher administration in the Midwest was supported consistently and praised by his Roman Superiors who appreciated his shrewd, penetrating observations on American events and on future opportunities for Jesuits in America.

Upon his return to Fordham from St. Louis, he was made the college Vice-president for several years and professor of rhetoric. Then at the end of John-Baptist Hus' term of office as the Superior General of the New York Mission, Fr. Murphy was appointed to replace him on April 16, 1859. He had been honored with a similar title when in 1840 he was Rector and Mission Superior in Kentucky; but at that time he assumed leadership of 24 Jesuits in one struggling college. By 1859 the numbers involved had increased more than three-fold to 89 Jesuits in two well-established colleges and five parishes, most of them in New York state.

Shortly after this appointment, however, Fr. Murphy's failing health forced him to retire from his new position; according to Taaffe,[18] he was a constant sufferer from dyspepsia. Though he was able to serve as Mission Superior for so short a time (his successor took over on November 7), that appointment must have been a consoling confirmation of higher Superiors' confidence in his talents and judgment.

In 1861 Fr. Murphy's health seemed to have been restored, and he was again recalled to St. Louis and appointed Vice-Provincial of Missouri. The Civil War was raging then and as the Jesuit Superior he had to face numerous conflicts related to that struggle. It is not surprising that under such circumstances his malady returned within the year and he was again relieved of office. He next spent a short time teaching the humanities to young Jesuits in Florissant, Missouri, and finally, for the sake of his health, was transferred to New Orleans where he spent his later years (from 1863 to 1875). He probably expected to feel "at home" in the south and to defend its characteristics. That attitude was indicated earlier by his reaction to a statement by the great Irish Liberator, Daniel O'Connell (1775-1847), who had strongly condemned slavery in the U.S.A. Murphy's reaction was that O'Connell was "out of touch with reality."[19]

At New Orleans he devoted his efforts to the spiritual counseling and direction of religious, and to other kinds of parochial ministry. His counseling was described as understanding, empathic, patient and non-censorious. Thereby he won over many hearts, "but he won them only for his Creator." Though he was not regarded as a great pulpit orator, what he said carried weight and conviction with it.

Fr. Murphy's academic forte was literature; he was a great purist and an enthusiastic admirer of the classics. His teaching methods were not regarded as orthodox, but they were effective.

Some descriptions of him were: "aristocratically and ascetically thin" (Fr. L. McGinley, contrasting him to the more ample Fr. Larkin), "handsome and cheerful," "a man of great executive power and an English scholar of very high attainments," "possessed of ready wit, a wit that was always stingless ... amiable disposition, ... charming in conversation ... [with] a great store of anecdotes." "Never known to speak ill of others." "To his many acquirements ... there was added ... the still nobler gift of true virtue, and also zeal of the good of his neighbor."[20]

In his 1989 life of Nicolas Point, Fr. C. M. Buckley noted[21] that a full life of Fr. W. S. Murphy deserved to be written but had not yet been done. Considerable material for such a biography is available in Garraghan's volumes.

- *FR. AUGUST JULIAN THÉBAUD, S.J.*
- *Lived 78 years*
- *b. 11/20/1807 at Nantes (Brittany)*
- *+ 12/17/1885 at Fordham*

At age 39, Fr. August Thébaud's 1846 assignment at St. John's College, besides being Rector-President, was to be Superior of the Seminary, Prefect of student health and teach French. He was at Fordham during 1846-1852; 1860-63; 1870; 1875. He was President twice (Aug. 15, 1846 to July 2, 1851; Aug. 15, 1860 to July 30, 1863).

Born to a worthy but not wealthy clothing merchant, Louis Clément Thébaud, and a pious mother, Marie Anne Québaud, August Thébaud[22] at an early age attended the local petit séminaire and later the diocesan grand séminaire, was ordained a priest on October 17, 1831 for Nantes in Brittany, and spent three years in parochial duty there in his ruined birthplace. He later decided to become a foreign missionary and was accepted as a Jesuit novice in Rome on November 27, 1835, after a protracted interview with the Jesuit General, Fr. Jan Roothaan.[23] Upon completing his early Jesuit training in the Eternal City, he spent a year studying science under Ampére and other academic celebrities in Paris to prepare for his work in the American missions.

Having landed in New York on December 18, 1838, after three days Thébaud set out for Kentucky with three other French Jesuits. They braved the wintry weather and hazardous vehicles of those days to arrive at St. Mary's on January 14, 1839, almost three months' journey from France. Thébaud first focused on improving his English by attending a class where the elements of English were taught. Later he taught physics, chemistry, and botany before becoming President/rector in 1845; in that capacity he planned the move north and east to Rose Hill and there became the first Jesuit President/rector of St. John's, Fordham.

During his first term as President he presided over the revision of the collegiate curriculum. Too little recognized these days is the fact that Fordham's post-1847 curriculum was based entirely upon Georgetown's curriculum (and that was based in the Jesuits' *Ratio Studiorum*); changes were made only in the titles of some courses, as recounted by Thébaud.[24] He also organized the various sections of the campus endeavors, and built additional classrooms. In the year after his first presidency he served the college as Vice-president.

During his second term as President he planned out the main campus roads, planted trees and improved the overall campus landscape, introduced a university-level graduate philosophy program, and improved relationships between the college and the diocese. During this term he made several purchases: the seminary building, the church and the surrounding eight acres from the diocese for $45,000; the Powell farm to the south of the campus; and several nearby blue-stone quarries for future buildings.

Between his two terms as Fordham President he was pastor of St. Joseph's in Troy, NY, and later did parish work in other areas, such as Montreal, Hudson City, NJ, and St. Francis Xavier, NYC.

He was a recognized writer in publications such as the *Catholic World* and the *Catholic Quarterly Review*. Of his many books, which included several novels, three are regarded as the most important: The *Church and Gentilism*, *The Church and the Moral World*, and *The Irish Race*, the last of which was highly praised by Orestes Brownson, the eminent editor, convert, and columnist, with whom Fr. Thébaud had many public differences. Brownson said that the book made him modify his own philosophy of history and was "a most valuable addition to American literature."[25]

In the years shortly before his death, Fr. Thébaud prepared several volumes of his recollections which were edited and published posthumously in 1904, 1912 and 1913 by Charles Herbermann, the President of the United States Catholic Historical Association.

The full listing of Fr. Thébaud's publications (which does not include his posthumously published books) takes up 1 3/4 columns in Sommervogel's massive 12 volume bibliography of Jesuit publications from 1540 to 1900.

Thébaud wrote a glowing tribute in 1884 to the long-deceased Archbishop John Hughes.[26] In it he noted that others praised Hughes' aggressiveness for Catholic interests. Thébaud did not deny that such was one of the archbishop's traits but claimed that his personality was dominated by an "extraordinary prudence" that was displayed especially in the way he met with his opposition both within and outside the Church. He knew when to push forward and when to be patient, and always displayed charity and good breeding (traits that Thébaud's life also exemplified). His own relations with Hughes were implied when he wrote that they often met "either in his house at the old Cathedral, or in the cottage of the archbishop's sister, Mrs. [Margaret] Rodrigue, at Fordham. He was ever the same affectionate and pleasant companion, ready to enjoy a laugh and to relate an anecdote."[27]

His contemporaries attested to the high esteem they felt for Fr. Thébaud. He was recalled as a cultured Frenchman who warmly embraced all other cultures and peoples. He was a distinguished writer, a recognized scholar, a scientist, and an efficient, prudent organizer.

There were additional tributes written about him after his death and we quote some of them. Webb, who knew him during his years in Kentucky, maintained that: "his admirable writings testify both to his merits as a scholar and to his never tiring zeal as a minister of Christ" and that his writings "are no less full of the fire of intellect than they are pervaded by the spirit of religion."[28]

Charles Herbermann, who knew him well in his middle and later years, and edited his posthumously published volumes, offered perhaps the best over-all tributes to him, describing him in a long footnote as: "a man with his eyes open to all that was good and noble, enthusiastic for all that was charitable, zealous for God, the Church, and his order; a convinced American, who was a warm admirer of the great work of Washington and his friends, and of the people of the United States, and yet not blind to their weaknesses; a good theologian and philosopher, a lover of nature, a student of science, a historical scholar and poet."[29] Herbermann also wrote of him as "an open-minded gentle-man, interested in all that interests the cultured man — science, art, politics, literature, commerce, ... [a man] of sympathy for his fellow men, especially for the humble and the suffering, ...one who appreciates justice, fairness, kindness, charity wherever he meets them."[30]

Fr. Thomas Campbell, who at one time was his Provincial, wrote of him: "He was a quick and eager observer, and his eagerness made him ready to maintain his view of a disputed question without, however, being contentious or disputatious. ... He was a high-souled French gentleman — a short, pudgy man ... of exquisitely tender sensibility, of lofty motives, of large and generous views."[31]

Thébaud Hall on the Bronx campus honors the achievements of Fordham's first President-Rector. It was first called the Science Building and later became by turns the headquarters for the Medical School, the School of Pharmacy and the College of Business Administration. In 1998 it became the center for college admission and related services.

Above we quoted Fr. C.M. Buckley who said that a full life of Fr. William Stack Murphy deserved to be written but had not yet been done. That statement applies equally to Fr. Thébaud who was in many ways a model scholar-priest-writer-administrator from his youth to his old age. And fortunately for a prospective biographer, Fr. Thébaud's many writings contain excellent accounts of his personal experiences and judgments.

B. FULL-TIME JESUIT FACULTY

While there were 25 Jesuit employees at St. John's, Fordham, in 1846, six of them remained there for only one or two years and did not return later. Natural deaths accounted for the short stay of Fr. Lebreton and Br. Jarry, and death from the cholera caught while serving the plague victims in Montreal explains the loss of Fr. DuMerle, and non-faculty member, Fr. Schiansky. The latter two may rightly be considered Fordham's first martyrs of charity. We can only conjecture some reasons (health, language, etc.) for the short stay of Br. Constance and of Br. Corné at Rose Hill. At any rate, those individuals probably had only a minimal influence on the early formation days of the institution and so they are not profiled in the pages below.

We profile only the following eight pioneer full-time Jesuit teachers in this second section: Isidore Daubresse, Edward Doucet, Michael Driscol, Martin Férard, Simon Fouché, Thomas Legoüais, Charles Maldonado, and John Ryan.

- *FR. ISIDORE DAUBRESSE, S.J.*
- *Lived 85 years*
- *b. 4/22/1810 at Werwicq (Nord) on the French-Belgian border; he claimed Belgian nationality*
- *+ 8/17/1895 at Frederick, MD*

At age 36, Fr. Isidore Daubresse's 1846 assignment at St. John's College, Fordham, was to teach theology and philosophy in the diocesan seminary. He was at Fordham from 1846 to 1863.

Before entering the Jesuits young Isidore Daubresse[32] had been a seminarian at Cambrai and was advanced to the subdeaconate. Then in 1832 he entered the Jesuit novitiate at Brieg, Switzerland, and completed his seminary education at Fribourg, Vals, Annecy, and St. Acheul. At the latter institution he was highly honored by doing the "Grand Act,"[33] a kind of public super-doctoral examination which was offered to very few young theologians, even of those marked as specially brilliant.

His first assignment was to teach philosophy at the Jesuit seminary at Brugellete in Belgium, and after that he taught canon law at Vals in France. He came to Fordham as the professor of moral theology in the diocesan seminary;

later he was professor of philosophy in the college. In addition to teaching in the seminary and at the college, for many years he was the Moderator of the New York diocesan priests' Cases of Conscience Conferences (an honored position). However, there seemed to have been a linguistic and cultural gap between him and the seminarians since they criticized him and some other Jesuit professors whose native language was French for their limited English and their ultra-royalist anti-democracy attitudes.[34] He and another Jesuit seminary professor, Fr. Seraphine Schemmel, caused a crisis when they resigned from the faculty of the seminary in 1855 because of their disagreements with the archbishop. Except for a few months in the following year his resignation marked the end of his seminary teaching.

In spite of his resignation from the seminary faculty, Daubresse continued to be held in high esteem by Archbishop Hughes, a judgment based upon his being kept on as Moderator of the diocesan Cases of Conscience Conference, his informal counseling of the Archbishop, and the request that Archbishop Hughes made in 1859 to the Jesuit General Beckx to support his nomination of Daubresse as the future bishop of a new diocese to be cut off from Albany. (Beckx wrote to Sopronis, the Visitor, and said, equivalently, "Request Denied.")

He spent much of the rest of his life in religious activities, such as giving the Spiritual Exercises, usually using the College of St. Francis Xavier as his base of operations. Later, he was made Master of Novices, first in Canada and subsequently in West Park, NY (where he was also the Rector). Campbell wrote of the West Park assignment: "It was a recognition of his strictness of life that, in his old age, he was honored in being appointed the founding rector at the short-lived Jesuit novitiate, [in] West Park, Esopus, NY, from 1876 to 1880."[35]

In his commentary on a picture of the 1859 Fordham faculty, Fr. Campbell[36] maintained that Daubresse was possibly the best known of that group "because of ... the positions of prominence and trust which he held." He was said to be serious yet gentle, dignified, and, to some extent, punctilious. People of all social levels sought his counsel, including Archbishop Hughes. He was confessor to Cardinal McCloskey and to Archbishop Corrigan. The latter's evaluation of him was that he "was a very learned and very holy priest."[37]

In a sketch-obituary, an anonymous author offers some personality and physical characteristics of Fr. Daubresse as seen in his later years. He was recalled as having a "fixed and resolute face, ... locks grizzled a bit with age ... composed and measured pace, ... polished and courteous demeanor, ... serious but amiable manner of speech." The sketch ends with this praise of him and his early associates: "He was one of the last of the founders of the Mission of New York, a generation of learned, refined and courtly French gentlemen who carried their exquisite manners into the priesthood, and who adding human graciousness to a holy life, left a deep impression on the generation that delighted in their ministrations and who will ever be regarded by priests and people alike as rare and most worthy ambassadors of the Son of God."[38]

- *FR. EDWARD DOUCET, S.J.*
- *Lived 65 years*
- *b. 5/12/1825 at Trois Rivières, Quebec*
- *+ 12/9/1890 at Fordham*

At age 21, Edward Doucet's 1846 assignment at St. John's College, Fordham, was to teach youths in Third Division, and prefect in the students' dormitory. He was at Fordham during 1846-52, 1859-65, 1870, 1872, 1874-79, and 1883-90.

Edward Doucet[39] entered the Jesuits on Sept. 7, 1844, in Canada and made most of his novitiate there. Shortly before the end of his period as a novice he came to Rose Hill and on Sept. 8, 1846, pronounced his first vows at Fordham and thereby became the first one of many others to make his Jesuit vows at Fordham; his making his vows is mentioned in the Minister's diary. The next four years at Fordham he spent teaching the youngest students as a scholastic. "Scholastic" here refers to a young Jesuit whose seminary training is deferred for a time to give him a taste of school work or other work and test his likely perseverance as a Jesuit.

After two more years teaching at Xavier he returned to Fordham where he completed his philosophical and theological studies and was ordained. In 1859 he was assigned to Rose Hill as prefect of discipline; in the next year he wore many hats: Vice-president, prefect of studies, of health, and of discipline. In 1861 when the novitiate re-opened at Fordham he became the master of novices.

In 1863 he was appointed President/rector at Fordham. But at the end of the first year of his presidency he went to France for his health, and his duties then devolved on the Vice-president, Fr. Peter Tissot (profiled below). During his recuperation he devoted himself to pastoral work first in Lille and later at the Jesuit college at Amiens where he also became professor of English. In 1868 he returned to Canada and became prefect of studies at St. Mary's College, Montreal.

In 1871 Fr. Doucet was again assigned to Fordham where he spent the remaining years of his life except for short assignments at St. Peter's (Jersey City), Xavier (NYC), and the West Park (NY) novitiate. At the novitiate, where he was also Socius (assistant) to the Master of Novices, the peaceful atmosphere helped him recuperate since his general health and his eyesight had been rapidly failing.

During his term as President he helped draw up the plans for the First Division building. Over the years, besides his work in the classroom he was librarian and moderator of the Fordham College History club. He taught many courses in the philosophy department: metaphysics, ethics, the history of philosophy, logic, and the philosophy of religion.

The author of his *Fordham Monthly* obituary lamented the fact that his ill health and diminishing eyesight in his final years prevented him from putting finishing touches on his voluminous essays on historical subjects. He believed that Fr. Doucet's written reminiscences of Edgar Allan Poe would have been specially appreciated. Perhaps Fr. Doucet's personal shyness and dislike of the limelight had something to do with his not publishing.

He was an excellent musician and an outstanding preacher in both English and French. He was also a close, even an intimate, friend and defender of Edgar Allen Poe, the American poet, storywriter, and critic, who lived nearby and loved to wander about the college grounds and mingle with the Fathers.

Fr. Doucet was sought out as a confessor because he was specially discreet, understanding, kind, and straight-forward. Above all, diocesan clergy found in him a wise counselor and judicious director. He was friend alike of the poor and of the wealthy.

- *FR. MICHAEL DRISCOL, S.J.*
- *Lived 75 years*
- *b. 5/7/1805 at Ennis, Clare, Ireland*
- *+ 3/4/1880 at Fordham*

At age 41, Fr. Michael Driscol's 1846 assignment at St. John's College, Fordham, was to be Director of the Seminary, and to teach mathematics and Latin. He was at Fordham from 1846 to 1847; 1863; 1880.

Born in Ireland, Michael Driscol[40] had been working as a stone mason near Bardstown, KY. In 1834 he visited Fr. de Luynes, who was very impressed by his superior mental and spiritual gifts, as well as by his manner of life. After they became friends, the priest urged Driscol to enter the nearby St. Mary's College. While an undergraduate there he was recognized as a leader of the student body as indicated by his being elected the first prefect of the Parthenian Sodality which was established in 1837 at the college. Sodalities of Our Lady were religious organizations that flourished with special vigor in many Jesuit colleges, including Fordham, and continue today as the Christian Life Communities.

In 1839 he received his degree; a few months later at age 34 he entered the Jesuit novitiate at St. Mary's. His fellow Irish-born St. Mary's alumnus, John Ryan (profiled below), entered the same day. They were among the first scholastic novices in the Kentucky mission. In those pioneer days the period of a Jesuit's course of studies was often quite brief; while doing their own studies, they were usually also recruited to prefect students or to teach in the adjoining college; since Driscol was thus employed while also studying theology, Fr. Thébaud noted that Driscol's theological studies were "elementary" (1904, p. 331).

He was ordained a priest on September 10, 1844, by Bishop Flaget (the first priest ordained in the Louisville cathedral). Later that month, he was appointed dean of St. Mary's College and remained in that post and continued to teach Latin, until the Jesuits left Kentucky for Rose Hill.

At Fordham he taught mathematics and Latin, and was also appointed director of the diocesan seminary by Bishop Hughes; of course in that position he himself was subject to the college President, Fr. Thébaud. But in 1847 Driscol, with Fr. Férard, Fr. Schiansky, and Fr. DuMerle, responded to a request for help from Jesuits in Montreal to assist them in their priestly ministry to Irish immigrants stricken with cholera. Fr. Thébaud observed Driscol's response to the invitation to minister to the plague-stricken: "I found him delighted with the prospect of beginning his labors among his countrymen, at the cost of his life if necessary." He served the immigrants in their emergency sheds, caught the fever, recovered, and then was pastor of the immigrants in St. Patrick's church in Montreal for several years.

On his return to New York, Fr. Driscol taught at the College of St. Francis Xavier, NYC. Then on September 8, 1855, he became Xavier's President/rector and pastor of the church until Aug. 15, 1860. His regime was marked by a 30% increase in the student body, the broadening of the curriculum and an improvement in scholarship. After his term as rector-President, he devoted his life to giving retreats and doing parish work, including being the pastor of St. Joseph's church in Troy, NY, where he also built a nearby new church, appropriated dedicated to St. Michael. Accounts of his work in Montreal and in Yonkers mention the fact that he heard confessions in the Irish language;[41] many Irish immigrants of those days felt more comfortable in confessing in their native Irish language.

Fr. Driscol was "a tall, stately man, with a serious, yet gentle expression of countenance," and an impressive, dignified bearing. He was manly and determined and did not hesitate to urge others to act "calmly and quietly." He was praised for his executive ability in organizing the work of both the parish [St. Francis Xavier] and the college. "A born orator," his warm, sympathetic heart never failed to reach the hearts of his hearers in important pulpits and in private contacts. With qualities such as these it is no wonder that he was considered a likely candidate to be raised to the episcopacy.[42] In summary, he was regarded as one of nature's true noblemen.

- *FR. MARTIN FÉRARD, S.J.*
- *Lived 73 years*
- *b. 9/8/1817 at Tours, France*
- *+ 1/10/1891 at Montreal*

At age 29, Fr. Martin Férard's 1846 tasks at St. John's College, Fordham, were to prefect in the student dormitory and be sub-minister to the Jesuit Community. He was at Fordham from 1846 to 1848 and during 1855.

Like many other Jesuits of his day, Martin Férard[43] transferred from a French diocesan seminary to enter the novitiate on November 2, 1839. He completed his theological studies at Laval, France, and prior to coming to the New World he had taught two years in the Jesuit college in Bruges, Belgium.

He was the first member of the new community to be ordained a priest in the seminary church (now the University church). Bishop John McCloskey ordained him there on February 7, 1847.

As noted above, Fr. Férard was among the Fordham priests who responded generously to the request for help among the cholera-stricken Irish immigrants in Montreal. As reported by Fr. Thébaud, Fr. Férard had been in Canada giving missions when the health crisis among the immigrants became known. Since he could speak English, he was asked to stay on and help the immigrants. He and Father Driscol escaped with their lives from the fevers to which they were exposed during years of ministry among the immigrants.

Later Fr. Férard spent an additional year (1855) at Rose Hill as community minister and professor of French. After leaving Fordham, he continued his apostolate in Canada where he is recalled as a missionary and lexicographer. His missionary labors brought him assignments to Sandwich, Manitoulin Island, Fort William, etc. Much of his work was with the Ojibway Indians whose culture and language he studied. One result of his studies was a three-volume manuscript dictionary of the Ojibway language. He was certainly a worthy successor to the early Jesuit missionary authors of the *Jesuit Relations* whose work was distinguished by zeal, careful observation, and scholarly reporting.

Somervogel's massive bibliography of Jesuit writings mentioned that several of Fr. Férard's letters were published in France. Such letters were a special source of inspiration for others who aspired to serve God and His people in the foreign missions.

- *FR. SIMON WILLIAM FRANCIS FOUCHÉ, S.J.*
- *Lived 81 years*
- *b. 9/1789 at Paris*
- *+ 6/29/1870 at Fordham*

At age 57, Fr. Fouché's 1846 assignments at St. John's College, Fordham, were to teach mathematics and become the first Jesuit treasurer at Fordham. He was at Fordham from 1846 to 1855, and from 1861 to 1863.

Born during the French Revolution, young Simon Fouché[44] was brought up by his priest-uncle, Msgr. E. Maignan, while his mother posed as his uncle's wife to assure the priest's safety. Educated in Paris in an institution later called Le Collège Stanislaus, young Fouché, was ordained a diocesan priest in 1816. After serving for five years as spiritual director in that same institution, in 1821 he moved to New Orleans to join a college faculty in that city. But when that college was destroyed by fire he transferred to St. Joseph's Seminary in Bardstown, KY, and was incardinated into that diocese. However, in 1831, Fr. Peter Chazelle, the Superior General of the Jesuit Kentucky mission gave a retreat at that seminary. After the retreat, Simon Fouché, priest-professor and incoming President of the seminary, as well as another priest there (Evremond Harrisart), decided to become Jesuits.

After his noviceship at St. Mary's College, KY, Fouché joined the Jesuit faculty at that college as professor of philosophy and mathematics. In addition, from 1840 to 1846 he was also spiritual director of the Sisters of Loretto at the Foot of the Cross in their nearby Motherhouse. As spiritual director he was very influential in the revision of the Sisters' rules and constitutions, though the revision process was marked by conflict with some local clergymen.

When he moved to Rose Hill with the rest of the Kentucky community, Fr. Fouché was assigned to teach literature and mathematics. In addition to his work in the classroom he was treasurer or assistant treasurer at Fordham from 1846 to 1855 and from 1861 to 1863. In 1855 he was assigned to St. Francis Xavier College, NYC, where for four years he was spiritual director and librarian. But in 1859 he fell victim to an undiagnosed illness, characterized by progressive deafness, which required him to leave his usual activities. His health needs dictated a year of change which he spent at the Collège Ste.-Marie, Montreal. In 1861 he was back at Fordham as assistant procurator. In 1864 he began his six final years in Xavier at his former posts, librarian and spiritual director of the community.

Fr. Fouché was remembered as diminutive in stature, vivacious in both action and speech, and specially companionable, a man who was very religious, and "the most amiable and gentle of teachers and scholars."

- *FR. THOMAS LEGOÜAIS*
- *Lived 83 years*
- *b. 4/26/1793 at Nantes, France*
- *+ 5/15/1876 at New York*

At age 53, Fr. Thomas Legoüais's 1846 assignments at St. John's College, Fordham, included: be Master of Novices, teach Scripture, be spiritual director and librarian. He served at Fordham for 23 years, from 1846 to 1869 when he was transferred to Xavier College and parish.

Archbishop Corrigan wrote that Thomas Legoüais[45] was "born of a noble family" and an obituary notice said that his father was a "wealthy merchant." He "first saw the light of day in prison at Nantes" during the Reign of Terror. As a young man he studied law in Paris; he received his first law degree in 1815 and the doctorate in laws in 1818. For a short time he practiced law, but surviving documents offer no indication that he directly applied his legal training in his later life.

In 1819 he entered the Sulpicians but two years later on October 31, 1821, he joined the Jesuits, and was ordained in 1825 by Msgr. de Quélen, Archbishop of Paris. His first assignment was to teach theology in France and then in Spain. But in 1832 he was assigned to the Kentucky Mission. At St. Mary's he taught numerous courses: mathematics (1835), chemistry and physics (1836), Spanish (1837-39), chemistry, physics, and Spanish (1840), theology and philosophy (1841-43), mathematics, French and Greek (1844), Latin and French (1845). He was also Novice Master in 1835 and in addition for several years was the house Minister (administrator).

Transferred from St. Mary's in 1846 to St. John's, Fordham, he became the first Jesuit chairman of the theology department and the first Jesuit director of the campus ministry. He had nurtured the Parthenian Sodality at St. Mary's and brought that Sodality to Fordham. At Fordham for ten years he was Novice Master, first for those who planned to become Jesuit priests or Brothers, and later for those who planned to become Brothers. In 1856, in weak health, he was relieved of the responsibility of being Novice Master, and sent home to France to recuperate. Next year he returned to his other duties on Rose Hill.

In his years at Fordham Fr. Legoüais offered spiritual leadership and personal counseling to a wide range of clients, from the college President to the youngest student. In addition, he served for many years as college librarian and as special counselor to the mission Superior.

In the controversy regarding the seminary between Archbishop Hughes and the Jesuits, Shelley reported that "One of the most influential ... Jesuit[s], Thomas Legoüais, S.J., admitted to the Jesuit General ... that many of the complaints about the Jesuits' management of the Fordham seminary had been justified."[46] His calm evaluation of the situation was regarded as a good basis for the solution.

After leaving Fordham in 1869, he was sent to the parish of St. Francis Xavier where people thronged to his confessional hours on end.

Years after his death an admirer wrote: "[His] boy-like proportions [provided a sense] of magnetism for the American boy." Another wrote that he was "an immense favorite both with pupils and with the laity." Everyone who reminisced about Fr. Legoüais mentioned his size: frail, delicate, diminutive, "a pigmy in stature" [his height was a trifle under five feet]; he was said to have been denied entrance into the Jesuits because of his size, "until he obtained the special consent of the [Jesuit] General."[47] He had trouble mounting a horse or re-mounting after falling from it. But Fr. Legoüais was also portrayed as a giant in the vineyard of the Lord. Webb summarized his life as one of quiet, unassuming "self-sacrifice and earnest Christian work."[48] Archbishop Corrigan testified that "for many years he was the favorite spiritual director and confessor of the students at St. Francis Xavier [College] and Fordham."[49]

Details on his funeral were given in the *Freeman's Journal*, May 27, 1876: "The solemn Mass of Requiem was offered ... by [the Rector] Rev. Father Hudon, S.J., ... A large number of the Rev. Clergy were present in the Sanctuary. There was no funeral sermon. The life of the deceased priest speaks for itself. His remains were conveyed to Calvary Cemetery."

- *FR. CHARLES MALDONADO, S.J.*
- *Lived 55 years*
- *b. 9/21/1816 at Quintanar de la Orden, Toledo, or Valentia, Spain*
- *+ 7/24/1872, Woodstock, MD*

At age 30, Fr. Charles Maldonado's 1846 assignment at St. John's College, Fordham, was to teach dogmatic theology. He was at Fordham from 1846 to 1853.

Fr. Maldonado's life was overshadowed by the anti-clerical revolutionary developments in Spain. He entered the Jesuits at age 15, but his early studies were interrupted on July 17, 1834, three years after he entered the seminary. There was a murderous outbreak on the Imperial College, Madrid, where he was studying. So he completed his philosophical and theological studies in Naples, Italy, and spent four years of regency there teaching mathematics.

His first assignment as a priest was to teach dogmatic theology at St. Joseph's Seminary, Fordham, in 1846. His teaching was interrupted by a begging trip with Fr. DeLuynes to Mexico to collect money for the St. Francis Xavier College and church; the trip began in November, 1850, and continued for 14 months. Fr. Maldonado's personal contacts, his great reputation as a theologian and his courtly, exquisite manners produced brilliant financial successes. Later he did the same for Fordham, when he and Fr. DeLuynes went to Mexico, Peru and Chile.

When conditions improved in Spain he returned there in 1853 to teach theology in the College of Loyola for a short time and he did the same in Laval, France. Next, in 1857 he was called to the Seminary of Salamanca, Spain, where for eleven years he occupied the chair of the great Jesuit theologian, Francisco Suarez, and became the rector, a position honored with the title, "Rector Magnificus." Another Spanish revolution again exiled all Jesuits. Around this time a theological faculty was being recruited for Woodstock College, MD, and Fr. Maldonado responded to the call. He taught theology there from 1869 until his death in 1872.

A glowing tribute to him was published in the first volume of *Woodstock Letters*. He was praised as "a real blessing to have had among us" since he was "so perfect a type of the true Jesuit." In addition, L. Frias' history of the Jesuit province of Spain praised him as an excellent professor of theology whose brilliant teaching impressed all his students.[50]

- *FR. JOHN RYAN, S.J.*
- *Lived 51 years*
- *b. 1/24/1810, in Kilchreest, Loughrea, Co.Galway, Ireland*
- *+ 3/22/1861, New York City*

At age 36, Fr. John Ryan's 1846 assignment at St. John's College, Fordham, was to teach Latin and Greek. He was at Rose Hill from 1846 to 1849.

John Ryan[51] was born in Ireland at Kilchreest, Loughrea, County Galway. We do not have his parents' names.

Ryan, like Driscol, had been a workman near Bardstown, KY, who was befriended by Fr. De Luynes, a future Jesuit but then still a diocesan priest. Recognizing his talent, Fr. De Luynes helped Ryan further his education at St. Mary's College, KY. Ryan received his degree there in 1839. A few months later he entered the Jesuits at the same campus. His fellow Irish-born St. Mary's alumnus, Michael Driscol, entered the same day. They were among the first scholastic novices in the Kentucky mission. Ryan was ordained in 1846, and came to Fordham that same year.

While at Fordham he fulfilled his teaching assignments and also administered to the spiritual needs of Catholics scattered along the Hudson River from Spuyten Duyvil to Dobbs Ferry. As a result of that apostolic activity he is credited as the founder of St. Mary's-Immaculate Conception, the first Catholic church in Yonkers.

He was appointed rector of St. Francis Xavier's parish and college on October 25, 1849, after Fr. Larkin had left for Europe. Unlike Larkin, he agreed to Bishop Hughes' limitations on the projected new church and college. The first church and college, called the Holy Name of Jesus, further downtown, had burned down and Bishop Hughes made demands on Larkin regarding the details of the new church and parish, including a change in the name of the church.

Ryan purchased property for the new structures on West 15th St. and built the first St. Francis Xavier church and college there. Having left the Jesuits in 1855, and been incardinated in the New York archdiocese, he was asked by Archbishop Hughes to supervise the building of the Immaculate Conception church (then on East 14th Street between Ave. A and Ave. B, later relocated to 414 E. 14th St.); when he died on March 22, 1861, he was pastor of that church.

Fr. Ryan is rightly regarded as a great church builder: of St. Mary's in Yonkers, St. Francis Xavier, and the Immaculate Conception in Manhattan. He was noted as a zealous pastor with "an unlimited capacity for work, [a man of] intense activity and untiring energy. No obstacles seemed to deter him from the accomplishment of any work he had to perform."[52] Thomas Cornell, an engineer who collaborated with him in the founding of St. Mary's church in Yonkers, wrote of him: "Father Ryan was a spare man, of medium height, with dark hair and complexion and a thin grave face, decidedly Hibernian in speech and appearance, but with the quiet suavity of the Jesuits, and if not courtly, was at least gracious and pleasant in manner. The writer's relations with him ... became so intimate and kindly that he takes pleasure in this mention of him."[53]

C. Non-Teaching Jesuits at St. John's College, 1846

The following pioneers served at the college, not in the classrooms, but in other necessary activities and are profiled in this section: Br. John Callaghan, Br. Patrick Crowe, Fr. Charles Hippolyte de Luynes, Br. Wilhelm Hennen, Br. Philip Ledoré, Fr. Nicolas Petit, Br. John Roy, Br. James Séné, and Br. Francis Vachon. Two of them were priests and the other seven were Brothers. We profile the priests first, and then the brothers.

- *FR. CHARLES HIPPOLYTE de LUYNES,*[54] *S.J.*
- *Lived 72 years*
- *b. 7/29/1805 at Paris ["NATIO: HIBERNIA"]*
- *+ 1/20/1878 at Xavier, NYC*

At age 41, Fr. Charles de Luynes's 1846 assignment was to do parish work, including campus ministry, at St. John's College. He was at Fordham for only 1846-1847.

Father Charles Hippolyte de Luynes regularly described himself as "born in Paris of Irish nationality."[55] In Ireland his father's name was Edward Joseph Lewins and his mother was Mary Anne Brennan. At the time of Charles' birth his Irish parents lived in exile in France. His father was the agent of the United Irishmen who rebelled against England in 1798. That rebellion was largely inspired by Ulster Protestants, but Lewins, a Catholic attorney and father of the future Jesuit, went to Paris as the agent of the mostly Catholic Leinster branch of the United Irishmen. Theobald Wolfe Tone, Lewin's good friend, the main organizer of the United Irishmen and leader of the unsuccessful rebellion, highly praised Lewins' efforts to obtain French aid from Napoleon Bonaparte.

The family name was changed in France to enable the mail from home to arrive through London. The name was first changed to Thomson, then to Luynes; the "de" was added later by Napoleon to honor the fact that Edward improved French methods in manufacturing silk. After the 1798 rebellion of the United Irishmen failed and the father was banished,[56] the family stayed on in Paris and prospered there. The elder brother of the future priest, Laurent, stayed in France and became chief of a division in the French Ministry of Public Instruction; Laurent de Luynes' son was Professor of Chemistry in the Sorbonne.[57]

Young Charles de Luynes was graduated from the University of Paris (College of St. Stanislaus) in 1823, and after a year spent in the study of law, entered the seminary of St. Sulpice, in Paris, and was ordained a diocesan priest by Archbishop de Quélen in June, 1830.

In spite of promises of advancement to the hierarchy of the French church, de Luynes was inspired by the saintly Bishop Flaget to join him as a missionary in Bardstown, KY, and he promised to do so. On the route to America, in 1831, he visited his mother who had returned to Ireland (his father died in 1827). While there, he assisted Bishop James Doyle ("JKL") and was a professor for a brief period in St. Patrick's College, Carlow.[58]

After his arrival at Bardstown, KY, he became successively professor of theology at St. Joseph's Seminary, rector of the cathedral, chaplain of the Motherhouse of the Sisters of Loretto in Nazareth, and editor for several years of *The Catholic Advocate*, the new diocesan paper. He counseled the future Jesuits, Ryan and Driscol, and encouraged them to enter St. Mary's College.

In 1841 he himself entered the Jesuits at St. Mary's where his gifts in languages (English, French, Spanish, and classical languages), in pastoral counseling and in preaching were recognized. Later he looked on his teaching there, mostly the Latin classics, as a time of unusual happiness. He formed many lifelong friendships at St. Mary's.

Though he served at Rose Hill in pastoral ministry for only one year he seemed to have had a strong influence on the other pioneer Jesuits as his name is often mentioned in writings about early Fordham days. In addition, Garraghan reported that he performed a unique service for Fordham in 1855, when he collected money in Chile and Mexico for the struggling college. Hence we profile him here as an exception to the time limitation of "over two years at Fordham" for our profilees.

In 1847 he was assigned to what became the St. Francis Xavier College and church in New York City. Except for two years in St. Joseph's Church in Troy, NY, his headquarters for many years and the focus of his service centered around St. Francis Xavier's parish. Part of that service included travel in 1851-53 to Mexico, especially to the people of Guadalajara, with Fr. Maldonado of Fordham, to beg for assistance for the struggling New York colleges. They returned with $15,000 for Xavier's debt and works of sacred art for both colleges.

The high regard in which de Luynes was held by the clergy can be judged from the fact that the Eighth Provincial Council of Baltimore in 1855 proposed that he became the bishop of Charleston.[59] There was a report[60] that he was in fact appointed bishop of Charleston in 1855. However, in imitation of Larkin's reaction to his appointment as bishop of Toronto, De Luynes left New York and went to Chile before the official document arrived. He remained there until Bishop Lynch was appointed to that office. Thus Fr. De Luynes was able to serve Fordham and the New York missions by seeking benefactions, and at the same time accept sanctuary from the unwelcome appointment.

It is indeed honor enough to be seriously considered and appointed bishop in one diocese. Fr. De Luynes was also strongly suggested by Archbishop A. Blanc in 1855 as a candidate to become his coadjutor bishop of New Orleans.[61]

For his times, de Luynes did an extraordinary amount of traveling (England, Ireland, numerous states in the south and Midwest, Mexico, Peru, Chile, Cuba), and occupied numerous positions, apparently with great success. This writer believes that the routines of college teaching and related functions may have clashed with his strong desires for change and for different experiences.

Contemporaries described him as a courtly man, of comely and impressive appearance (six feet tall and proportionally broad with piercing eyes that a biographer claimed brought discomfort to the wicked), an impressive, earnest and gifted preacher whose powerful bass voice was easily heard in large churches, a learned exegete who loved to expound on St. Paul, and a deep and original thinker. Herbermann, an editor of the first *Catholic Encyclopedia*, and his admirer, said of him: "Like all the old Jesuits of the Kentucky colony that originally settled in Fordham, Father de Luynes became a patriotic American who took the greatest interest in the future of the Republic."[62] Church historian John Gilmary Shea described him as "learned, deeply versed in the Scriptures, of a clear and penetrating mind" and, as a result of those achievements, "he enjoyed universal esteem."[63]

Others wrote of him as "admirable as a pastor, ... known and honored for his benevolence. ... His advice [was] always judicious, ... and the very tones of his voice ... were full of encouragement. ... Loving all in God, he left nothing undone whereby he could possibly render his ministry profitable to the people."[64] He loved the liturgy of the Mass and said the Canon with special solemnity; yet since he was denied musical gifts, when the liturgy called for him to sing he simply read the text in a loud voice.[65]

DeLuynes had friends among the rich, especially among the local Hispanic wealthy class (at one time he was the only Spanish-speaking priest in New York).[66] Those wealthy friends enabled him to show generosity to the poor, many of whom were Irish famine-forced exiles.

- *FR. LOUIS NICOLAS PETIT, S.J.*
- *Lived 65 years*
- *b. 7/8/1789 at St. Michel du-Fond-des-Négres, Haiti*
- *+ 2/1/1855 at Troy, New York*

At age 57, his 1846 assignment at St. John's, Fordham, was to do parish work, including campus ministry at St. John's College. He was at Fordham for only 1846-47. Others who stayed only one or two years at Rose Hill are not included in this account but an exception is made for him and for Fr. De Luynes because of their apparent special impact on the former Kentucky Jesuits. Fr. Petit was probably specially venerated by Community members for his age, his religious experience and prudence (he was a house consultor during most of his Kentucky years) and for his specially virtuous life. The esteem for him which Bishop Simon Bruté expressed and which we quote below was no doubt shared by many of his contemporaries.

He was born in Haiti[67] to a rich Creole planter, Francois-Ignace-Nicolas Petit, originally from Lyons, France, and French mother, Victoire-Marine Le Mau de la Barre. His father was killed in 1793 during an uprising and his mother, fearing the horrors of revolution, brought her children to Baltimore where she taught school.

This move enabled Louis Nicolas to learn English as a child. After nine years in Baltimore, the family moved to the south of France where he was educated by the Fathers of the Faith (many former Jesuits were members of that group) and by the Sulpicians. Upon completing the study of theology he was ordained a diocesan priest. He joined the Jesuits on January 1, 1816, six months after the Society was re-established in France, and was not required to take any further academic work as a Jesuit. His first assignment as a Jesuit was missionary work which aimed at reviving the spirit of faith among Catholics in France.

In 1831 Fr. Petit was assigned to accompany Fr. Peter Chazelle, the mission Superior, to take over a college in Kentucky. Though disappointed regarding their first plan, they finally accepted St. Mary's College, KY. There Fr. Petit combined teaching in the college with a very active pastoral ministry that required him to travel to many parts of the Midwest and the South. The Jesuit province of France's 1834 *Annual Letter,*[68] described some of his successful ministries during Lent and at other times in the diocese of Vincennes, Indiana, Bishop Bruté's diocese.

After spending one year at Rose Hill, doing pastoral work on campus and in nearby New York City, he was assigned to accompany Fr. Larkin in 1847 to begin the institutions that became the college and church of St. Francis Xavier. There he did pastoral work and was a house consultor for two years. After that he was assigned to do pastoral work at St. Joseph's parish in Troy, NY, where he died in 1855.

Bishop Simon Gabriel Bruté, of Vincennes, Indiana, tried several times but in vain to convince the Jesuit General to allow Fr. Petit to become his coadjutor bishop.[69]

Bishop Bruté's appreciation of him is worth reporting: "He excels in piety, learning, eloquence, knowledge of the English and French languages, as also in administrative ability. To all the faithful of ... [the] ... diocese ... he would beyond doubt be highly acceptable."[70] Webb praised Fr. Petit for the following qualities: zeal, faith, piety, fidelity, and efficiency.[71]

BROTHERS IN THE LORD

It is appropirate at this point to indicate the difference between Jesuit priestn and Jesuit brothers. Both priests and brothers feel privileged to serve God in the Jesuit order, priests in works that require ordination, and brothers in other works. Both kinds of labors are needed for success in Jesuit undertakings.

The traditional "other works" of Jesuit brothers meant cooking meals, providing transportation, doing the buying, managing the farm, local housekeeping, working in offices, and similar "temporal" activities.

These days the "other works" have been extended to office and administrative work, which for at least one Jesuit brother, James M. Kenny, meant the financial Vice-Presidency of Fordham University.

Jesuit brothers have used their talents to serve God as artists, musicians, distinguished artisans and missionaries. Several brothers have been declared blessed and saints.

In spite of considerable effort, relatively little has been learned about the personality or even the appearance of most of the 1846 pioneer brothers. We found no picture of any of them. They must have tried to embrace literally St. John the Baptist's saying: "He must increase, I must decrease" (Jn 3:30).

- *BR. JOHN CALLAGHAN, S.J.*
- *Lived 71 years*
- *b. 7/12/1808 at Kilsheelan, County Tipperary, Ireland*
- *+ 8/22/1879, Jersey City*

At age 38, Br. John Callaghan's 1846 assignment at St. John's College, Fordham, was to do gardening and housing. He was at Fordham for 1846-1848, 1862-1864, 1867-1870, and 1878-1879.

Br. Callaghan[72] began his novitiate in 1843 at St. Mary's College, KY. His intelligence was recognized early in his novitiate days and he was given complete charge of a grist mill that belonged to the college. At the mill he produced superior grades of flour and corn meal (much appreciated by the students) by the skillful use of a kiln for parching the grain before passing it through the millstones.

He was at Fordham for its first two Jesuit years when he was employed in gardening and doubtless also in attending to the countless details in setting up a new community.

After he left Fordham he was assigned to various houses in Canada, including Wikwemikong, Ontario, until he finally returned to Fordham. In all those places he performed many necessary tasks: cooking, farming, and building. In Canada he was identified as a miller because of his constructing a small but efficient flour mill in Wikwemikong.[73]

He spent the last years of his life at Fordham. His obituary described his last days: "Broken down with age and labor, he piously breathed forth his soul ... in the Jersey City [St. Francis] Sisters' Hospital, whither he had been sent by the Rector of Fordham College, Father Gockeln."[74]

Br. Callaghan's death certificate was one of the few such documents that we located. It illustrates how little his religious brethren knew about him because of the lack of information it provided. Listed as UNKNOWN were: his father's name, his mother's name, his mother's country of origin; in addition, the cause of his death and the length of his sickness are left blank. The document stated that he was buried at [Manresa] in West Park, Webster County, NY. Since at the time of his death he was a member of the Fordham community, and the Fordham cemetery was operational, we do not know why he was not buried there. Much remains unknown about this good, humble son of Ignatius.

- *BR. PATRICK CROWE , S.J.*
- *Lived 51-52 years*
- *b. 2/28/1817 or 2/18/1818, Carlow, Ireland*
- *+ 12/23/1869, Fordham*

At age 29, Br. Patrick Crowe arrived at Fordham to complete his novitiate but before the year was out he and Br. Vachon, his fellow novice Brother, had taken their vows and continued their earlier assignments for many years. He had entered the Jesuits as a novice at St. Mary's College, KY, on January 10, 1845. Besides his vital statistics[75] (and even here there's some confusion about his date of birth), we know only the title of his longtime assignment, "praes. vill." We did not find an obituary for Br. Crowe. A reason for that fact is that the *Woodstock Letters* (which provided information about many of our other profilees) was not begun until several years after Br. Crowe's death.

His assignment, "Praest villae," meant director or manager of the college farm. He began that assignment in his novitiate days, so his farming skills and experience (doubtless achieved in his family's farm in his native Carlow) was recognized early. Since he kept that position until close to the end of his life, his skills in farming and in directing the work of others at the farm must have been appreciated by his Superiors. Especially in the early days of the college the farm was an important factor in keeping the residential costs of students to a minimum. The large and productive farm extended from the rear of the present Administration Building to the Bronx River (a good section of that farm is now a part of the New York Botanical Garden). Over the years many Jesuit Brothers tended to the farm until it was discontinued many years after Br. Crowe's time.

A hand-written unsigned notebook housed in the Fordham University Archives entitled "Workmen"[76] contains a kind of diary or day book that described work done on the Rose Hill farm and on other Jesuit farms. It reflects a sense of joy and achievement in the daily work on the land and in the farm buildings, attitudes that make it possible to spend one's whole life on the farm, as Brother Crowe did. Though the notebook was not signed, it was most likely written by Br. William Donovan, S.J. (1822-1896). Regardless of authorship, the spirit revealed in the book is the Jesuit perspective of actively seeing God in all things.

- *BR. WILHELM HENNEN, S.J.*
- *Lived 89 years*
- *b. 11/25/1800 at Crombach (Krombach), near Aachen, Rheinland, Germany (now Belgium)*
- *+ 7/4/1890 at Fordham*

At age 46, Br. Hennen's 1846 assignment at St. John's College, Fordham, was to be baker. He continued to do that work there for many years. He was at Fordham from 1846 until the end of his life, an assignment that lasted almost 44 years.

Wilhelm Hennen,[77] the son of Nikolaus Hennen, a laborer, and Margaretha Hilgers, was drafted into the Bavarian army and stayed in that service for ten years. After his release from that service, he began to search for his "place in creation." Attracted to the religious life, he found no satisfaction in the options available to him at home. But he had a strange dream or a revelation in which he saw his "place in creation" embodied in a beautiful house with a Church nearby. This experience has been regarded by some as "mystical." He began to search for the house. He wandered through various countries and cities, such as Belgium, Germany, and France; he came to America and continued his search in New York, Philadelphia and other places, including Bardstown. As he was about to despair of what began to seem a foolhardy adventure, an old man approached him, touched him and said, "I will show you your place in creation." The old man led him to St. Mary's College, explained his mission and then disappeared. Though St. Mary's was not the house William Hennen sought, he stayed and entered the noviceship on November 9, 1839, to become a Jesuit brother. After taking his vows, however, he had a change in status since he was listed in 1841 as a scholastic studying theology along with Driscol and Ryan. But in the following year he was again reported to be a coadjutor brother, doing all kinds of necessary work ("*ad omnia*") in the new St. Ignatius Literary Institution in Louisville, KY. He remained there until 1846 when he and the other Jesuits came to Fordham.

When he first saw Rose Hill with its old mansion and its new and lovely church he recognized it immediately as the "place" of his vision. Brother Hennen could hardly contain himself. He felt happy enough to die. Instead of dying at that time, however, he lived to serve the "place" with utter joy for forty-four years. His service included being baker (he was called the "tutelary genius of the bakeshop"), carpenter, mechanic, etc. An article about him on the occasion of his golden jubilee as a Jesuit (1889) noted that he was no longer able to work. The old chronicle which told this tale concluded by saying that he died in his "place in creation" with beauty and peace, showing the wonder of God in his Saints. His death certificate asserted that he died of "senility" and "heart failure."

- *BR. PHILIP LEDORÉ, S.J.*
- *Lived 81 years*
- *b. 2/13/1800 at Quiberon [Morbihan], France*
- *+ 4/14/1881 at Fordham*

At age 46, Br. Philip Ledoré's 1846 main task at St. John's College, Fordham, centered around his work as gardener at the college. He was at Fordham for 35 years, from 1846 until his death.

Philip Ledoré had spent eight years as a seaman before entering the Jesuits as a coadjutor brother on October 11, 1822. He arrived at St. Mary's, KY, after an eventful journey from France, with Fr. William Stack Murphy, Fr. Nicolas Point, and Br. Jarry.[78] There Br. Ledoré served as cook and gardener from the time of their arrival on January 12, 1836, to the day when the Jesuits made their move to New York. Fr. Thébaud[79] recounted of Br. Ledoré, "a Breton like myself," that the vagaries of the Kentucky weather convinced him to plant vegetables too late in the season for an early crop until he was convinced to use glass-covered beds to control the weather for growing vegetables.

He was transferred in 1846 with other members of the community to Rose Hill, Fordham, where for 34 years he faithfully fulfilled various offices, such as baker, gardener, manager of the clothes room, etc. In many ways his long life at Fordham symbolized the religious dedication, hidden service, self-sacrifice, and generosity of the over 170 Jesuit Brothers who served God at Fordham from 1846 to 1997.

- BR. JOHN ROY, S.J.
- Lived 57 years
- b.11/24/1819 at Vaudreuil, Quebec
- + 7/19/1877 at Fort Hill,[80] NY

At age 26, Br. John Roy's 1846 function at St. John's College was to be cook. He was at Fordham from 1846-1847 and 1848 to 1853.

Jean-Marie Roy, son of Joseph Roy and Josephte Corriveau, entered the Jesuit novitiate in Montreal in October, 1844, and was sent to complete his second year of novitate and to be the cook in the St. Ignatius Literary Institution in Louisville, KY. Before the year was out he moved with his confreres to Rose Hill.

After a year at Fordham, he was transferred in the following year to be cook at the new community that Fr. Larkin began in New York City which later became the St. Francis Xavier College and parish. In 1848 he returned to Fordham as cook until 1853. In his later years he had various duties in the novitiate in Montreal, such as carpenter and gardener. We have not been able to learn more about him.

- BR. JOHN JAMES SÉNÉ, S.J.
- Lived 71 years
- b. 4/14/1793 at
(Somme), France
- + 1/17/1865 at Fordham

At age 53, his 1846 assignment at St. John's College, Fordham, was to be infirmarian. He was at Fordham from 1846 to the time of his death. During his years at Fordham his areas of responsibilities shifted from work in the infirmary to gardening (care of the green house), caring for student housing, and prefecting students.

No obituary of Br. Séné, has been found. Nevertheless, a letter in the *Fordham Monthly*[81] recalled fond memories of him. "A. H. Garland" (the letter was signed thus) wrote that the brother was "a dear soul to me, and one of the best friends I ever had. He was a soldier under Napoleon and ... we used to talk of Napoleon in his hearing as a fraud ... and we had to get away quick. ... For the first few months I was there he would come ... and take me to the infirmary and give me a warm egg-nog, and put me to bed as carefully as a mother could. ... I believe I was then the youngest boy there, and was not very strong or of good health. Precious old soul!" Surely this moving recollection of Br. Séné serves well as an obituary.

- *BR. FRANCIS VACHON, S.J.*
- *Lived 79 years*
- *b. 10/15/1824, St. Hyacinthe, Québec*
- *+ 6/2/1903, Sault-au-Récollet, Canada*

At age 21 in 1846, Br. Vachon came to Fordham from St. Mary's College, Montreal, to complete his novitiate. Son of Augustin Vachon, a sacristan, and Marianne Delande, he had entered the Jesuit novitiate in 1845 in Canada and stayed on at Fordham as tailor for 25 years.

His tailoring skills must have been in general demand since he also functioned as tailor in 1874 when he was transferred to St. Mary's, Montreal, until 1878. At that time he was assigned to St. Joseph's Novitiate, Sault-au-Récollet, near Montreal.

Once more he was assigned as tailor in 1880 at the novitiate in West Park, NY. Then in 1881 he had a real change in assignment when he went to the Gesu parish in Philadelphia to be in charge of the dining room and the clothes room. His final assignment (again back to tailoring) until his death was at St. Joseph's Novitiate, Sault-au-Récollet.

We did not find an obituary for Br. Vachon. But a second obituary written for Br. Hennen[82] very likely may also be applied to Br. Vachon: "He lead a peaceful and exemplary life as a coadjutor brother and died ripe in years and merits."

PART II

Other Jesuits, St. John's College, Fordham, 1846

In Part I we presented brief sketches of the 21 Jesuits (of the original 25) who came in 1846 to serve at St. John's College, Fordham. Besides that group, another 22 Jesuits arrived in that year at the same campus in different capacities. Thus combining the first group of 25 with the additional 22, the number of Jesuits assigned at Rose Hill for 1846-1847 was 47, each of whom is named at the beginning of this paper.[83]

The "other" group consisted of Jesuit seminarians or novices. They contributed to the academic and moral spirit of the college by being informal models of dedicated, conscientious, well-ordered college or graduate students in their contacts with other student groups. In addition, some of them were part-time teachers during their days at Fordham. Their later lives reflected great credit on their Alma Mater.

In the following pages we summarize information about the "other" Jesuits who resided at Rose Hill in 1846-1847 and who persevered in the Order. Some Jesuits who were there that year later left the Order, and we do not profile them, in large part because of lack of information about their later lives. Instead, we focus on the twelve who persevered in their original life plan: Adams, Dealy, Desjacques, Gockeln, Graves, Hollinger, Hudon, Kohler, Nash, Ouellet, Régnier, and Tissot.

- *FR. JOSEPH ADAMS, S.J.*
- *Lived 39 years*
- *b. 12/8 or 12/12/1816, Nelson, KY*
- *+ 8/21/1855, Baton Rouge, LA*

At age 30 and already an ordained diocesan priest, after being educated at St. Mary's, KY, and thus well-known to faculty and students there, Joseph Adams came to Rose Hill on October 31, 1846, to make his novitiate. Though a member of the New Orleans Mission and not a member of the New York-Canada Mission, he was one of the two Jesuits residing in the Mission who were born in the U.S.A. Webb[84] listed him among the dozen priests who were ordained after receiving their theological training at St. Thomas' Seminary which was located in Bardstown.

In 1850 Fr. Adams[85] was assigned to Spring Hill College, a Jesuit college in Mobile, Alabama. His tasks there were prefecting and teaching until 1855 when he was assigned to the Jesuit college in New Orleans. Before the school year started he went to Baton Rouge to prepare a series of missions and consult with his former spiritual director and guide, Rev. Guy Gilles. But at Baton Rouge, sadly, he contracted yellow fever and died.

Walter Hill, S.J., included in his recollections of Kentucky this evaluation of Fr. Adams: he was "reported to be very learned; he was a highly polished preacher. His death brought a great loss on our Society in the South."[86] His apostolate was brief in years but long and full in fruitfulness. In summary praise, Fr. Hill saw Adams as "Alabama's chosen preacher and orator, ... an inspiring teacher and professor and Prefect of Studies."

- *FR. PATRICK FRANCIS DEALY, S.J.*
- *Lived 62 years*
- *b. 4/7/1829, Rathkeale, County Limerick, Ireland;*
- *+ 12/23/1891, NYC*

In 1846 at age 17 Patrick Dealy[87] entered the Jesuit novitiate at Rose Hill. Thereby he became the first Fordham student who became a Jesuit, though he had had no Jesuit teachers and he had not received a Fordham degree.

He was born in Limerick, Ireland, but came as a child with his parents to New York City where he received his elementary education. His parents must have prospered because they were able to enroll him as a lay student at St. John's, Fordham, in 1843. That was in the third year of the college's existence and three years before the Jesuits' arrival.

Dealy entered the Jesuits at Rose Hill on October 31, 1846. Two years later, after he completed his noviceship, he was sent to St. Mary's College, Montreal, where he was the first teacher who spoke English as his first language. When he completed that teaching assignment, he pursued his philosophical and theological studies in various places, first in Canada and thereafter in Belgium (Brugelette), France (Laval) where he was ordained in 1861, Austria (Innsbruck), and finally in Rome. The international flavor in his educational venues is impressive.

His early teaching experiences included four years at St. Mary's College, Montreal, and two years at Fordham. The subjects he taught in his early career were Latin, English, and mathematics. Later he taught English Literature at both Fordham and at Xavier College, NYC. While at Xavier he founded the Xavier Union (later named the Catholic Club) which, with its one thousand members, became a stimulating influence on many leading members of the Catholic laity. For many years he was the spiritual director of this group.

Fr. Dealy was President/rector of St. John's College, Fordham, during 1882-1885. One of his successors in the Fordham presidency, Fr. Robert Gannon, believed that under him "a new era began at Fordham"[88] since older, very conservative views yielded to more modern ideas. During his administration the old seminary building was refitted, the Science Building (Thébaud Hall) was begun, military drill (R.O.T.C.) was introduced, sports (baseball and football) developed, the *Fordham Monthly* was started and the grounds beautified. It also happened that during his presidency the city annexed 26 acres of the campus, the part between Southern Boulevard and the Bronx River, for the New York Botanical Gardens. By 1889 the city paid $93,966.25 for that property, a sum regarded even in an earlier day as "absurdly low."

After Fr. Dealy retired from the presidency, he spent his remaining years in parish ministry at St. Francis Xavier, NYC, and in parishes in Boston, Philadelphia, and finally in St. Lawrence O'Toole (now St. Ignatius Loyola), New York. A characteristic or pattern of his ministry was his sponsorship of the local Sodality of Our Lady. He died of diabetes and pneumonia at St. Lawrence O'Toole parish in New York.

His only writing that has survived is a long article, originally a lecture before a historical association on the struggles and sufferings of the early American missionaries.[89]

Fr. Dealy was distinguished as a professor, pastor and administrator. He was one of the best known priests in New York, due in part to his charming personality and the interest he took in others. An attractive man with polished manners and tact, he won many friends for the college and was sought out by a wide range of people for his prudent and well-informed counsel. In particular, Cardinal McCloskey esteemed him highly, asked him to be his confessor, and regarded him as his best contact among New York Jesuits. The Cardinal also appointed him to lead the first American group pilgrimage to Rome.

His name is well known to Fordham students because an important multi-functioning stone structure in the center of the Bronx campus, Dealy Hall, is named in his honor.

In view of his success as a college President and in his other successful activities, it is interesting to notice an evaluation of his personality that was made on March 12, 1853, probably by his predecessor in the Fordham presidency:[90] his "ingenium" (mental power): mediocre; his judgment: sufficiently right; proficiency in literature: mediocre; his special talent: for teaching youths (in the context and in those times, the latter talent was not a high commendation). Such ratings show how one individual can misjudge another and they demonstrate the need of including several independent judges in evaluating persons.

- *FR. MARINUS DESJACQUES, S.J.*
- *Lived 60 years*
- *b.10/13/1824, Laval (H.-Savoie)*
- *+ 6/17 or 19/1884, Shanghai*

After completing earlier studies in rhetoric and a year of philosophy at Brugelette, Belgium (the French college in exile), Marinus Desjacques[91] at age 22 arrived at Rose Hill as a second year student of philosophy. He spent six years at Fordham, first as a student of philosophy and theology, and after that as a prefect of students. Then Fr. Desjacques joined a large group of French Jesuits who became missionaries in China.

His first post-Fordham assignment in 1856 was at the seminary in Chang-Hai, China, where, in addition to learning the Chinese language, he was Minister, Procurator for the Mission and for the house and French teacher in the seminary. He also did parish work among the Europeans.

He later spent some 38 years serving at St. Ignatius College, in the province of Nanking, near Zi-Ka-Wei. Among his assignments were community Minister and Procurator of the Mission. In addition to those inside "office" kind of assignments he also did missionary and parish work among the Chinese and among Europeans resident in China. For instance, in 1862 his residence was in the city's European section, probably to facilitate his parish work there.

DeBecker-Somervogel's bibliography of Jesuit writings reported that many of Fr. Desjacques' letters written in French about China, the Chinese people, and missions in China, were published from 1870 to 1882.

We do not have more details of his life such as a description of his personality or an appreciation of his activities.

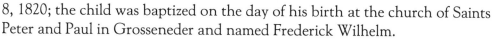

- *FR. WILLIAM GOCKELN, S.J.*
- *Lived 66 years*
- *b.11/8/1820, Grosseneder, near Paderborn, Germany*
- *+ 11/26/1886, Providence, RI*

William Frederick Gockeln[92] at age 26 arrived at Fordham in 1846 to begin his Jesuit philosophical studies and to become a part-time teacher of German.

Farmer Bernard Gockelen (the spelling on his baptismal register)and his wife Anna Maria Müller had a child at 6:00 A.M. on November 8, 1820; the child was baptized on the day of his birth at the church of Saints Peter and Paul in Grosseneder and named Frederick Wilhelm.

When he was thirteen years of age, young Glockeln landed in New York from Germany with his older brother but later went to Canada and after a few years enrolled at the Collège de Montréal. There he became a disciple of his Sulpician teacher, Fr. John Larkin, who had decided to become a Jesuit. Gockeln accompanied Fr. Larkin to St. Mary's, KY, first as a student in the college, and later as a fellow Jesuit novice on the same campus. He began philosophical studies at Fordham and completed those studies in Belgium. He did his theological studies at Laval, France, where he was ordained in 1852. One result of his travels was that his English was without a foreign accent, and his French and German were "elegant."

On his return to the New World in 1853 he began a series of teaching and administrative positions at St. Mary's (Montreal), Fordham, Xavier College, NYC, and later at St. Lawrence's, NYC. His early assignments were summarized thus: he was "at one time ... professor, at another ... prefect of studies, but for the most part ... chief disciplinarian." He was the first Fr. Minister in the new Jesuit scholasticate in Woodstock, MD. He had seven years of missionary life in Guelph and Chatham, Canada.

Fr. Gockeln was President/rector of St. John's College, Fordham, for eight years, 1874-82. His predecessor (Fr. Joseph Shea) had begun a change in students' living: previously they had lived in dormitory style but the new system called for their having private (shared) rooms. The old system required strict discipline. The new system (and Fr. Shea's gentle rule) fostered a collegiate climate that was regarded as too easygoing like that flourishing at many secular colleges. The reputation of the college suffered from the new approach.

Fr. Gockeln reacted to that difficult situation at Fordham by initiating a rigorous regime. Of course, making changes that take away cherished freedoms does not make for popularity. Nevertheless, few students failed to return to the college after the summer vacation. And the reputation of the institution was restored. Yet Fr. Gannon[93] reported that Fr. Gockeln left little special to record. Plans were made but not acted on. It was probably a time of steady but undramatic growth.

After his Fordham presidency, Fr. Gockeln was a dean at Holy Cross College, Worchester MA, in 1883-1884. In 1884-1885, he did parish work at St. Peter's, Jersey City; and then until his death (caused by pneumonia) he was Superior at the Jesuit residence, St. Joseph's, in Providence, Rhode Island.

Gockeln was described by Francis Connolly[94] as "a tall [about six feet two inches], handsome, Prussian." He continued: "Everything about him was large: ... [his height, his weight, his] authority, [his] command and leadership [which] matched his physical proportions."

Fr. Patrick Halpin, who was his associate for many years, wrote about him shortly after his death.[95] He recalled his "urbane and sweet manners and general kindliness of disposition." In making decisions: "His vast experience in college matters rendered him prophetic at times ..." Though not a great orator, he had all the qualities of one: "rich and racy English, ... great rectitude, ... zeal,... 'pectus,' ... knowledge of elocution and [a] kingly presence." "He was loyal and devoted" particularly regarding the Society of Jesus. "His sympathy was boundless." He wrote in summary that he was a "good man, ... pure priest, ... loyal and devoted Jesuit."

- *FR. JAMES MADISON GRAVES, S.J.*
- *Lived 45 years*
- *b. 12/4/1824, Lebanon, KY*
- *+ 8/21/1869, Louisville, KY*

James Graves at age 21 arrived at Rose Hill with the Kentucky Jesuit community to begin his collegiate study of the humanities.

Son of Jesse (for Jessamine) Graves, a farmer, and Elizabeth Gannon,[96] he and Fr. Adams were the only two Jesuits in the Mission who were born

in the U.S.A. He completed his novitiate at St. Mary's, Marion County, KY, and did all his seminary studies at Fordham. While he was a student at Fordham he also taught English part-time, and later during his regency (Jesuits' teaching period between the study of philosophy and theology) taught there full time. Two years after his ordination in 1857 he did parish work at St. Joseph's, Troy, NY, and then in 1862 he was assigned to the same work at St. Francis Xavier, NYC.

In 1864 he was transferred[97] to Spring Hill College, the Jesuit college at Mobile, Alabama. He remained there until 1868 as professor of rhetoric, preacher and consultor. In Mobile he turned the tables triumphantly on the local ministerial clique that had been excoriating Spring Hill College from their pulpits for allegedly proselytizing some Protestant students. In 1868, his health failing, he was transferred first to New Orleans and then to Louisville with the hope that his "native air" would assist his recuperation. But the hope was not fulfilled. He died there and was buried in the cemetery of the Sisters of Nazareth, Kentucky, where his sister was a nun. Garraghan[98] reported that Fr. Graves and eight other Jesuits were buried in that same cemetery.

Historian Fr. C. M. Buckley stated that Fr. Graves was a professional rhetorician, noted for "his masterful elucidation of that subject in the classroom."[99] Buckley also identified the target of his polemical sermons in Mobile as the Episcopalian clergy.

- *ANTHONY HOLLINGER, S.J.*
- *Lived 53 years.*
- *b. 5/29/1814, Ste-Marie-aux-Mines [H-Rhin] [Natio: Gallia];*
- *+ 12/1/1867, Vannes, France*

Having entered the Jesuits on December 15, 1844, and having made his novitiate at St. Acheul's in France, Anthony Hollinger at age 32 came to Fordham in 1846 as a second year student of theology.

Anthony Hollinger had studied medicine for four years.[100] Then he made a dramatic vocational change in entering the Jesuits. But in 1848, instead of being ordained and available for a priestly assignment (as was the case with his classmate, August Kohler), he was still a student. He must have had a major physical or psychological problem because he's not listed at all in the 1849 catalogue, and in the 1850 one, he was reported to be living outside Jesuit houses ("degens extra domos"); in 1852 he was described as ill ("Cur. valetud."). But then in 1853 and 1854 he was a student again at the Seminary at Laval.

In 1855, 1856, 1857 he was at the Jesuit College at Poitiers, and served as community Subminister and also taught English and German there. After a year at Kalksburg (in the Province of Austria), he taught English at the Jesuit College at Poitiers, in 1860, 1861, and 1862. In 1863 until his death he was at the Jesuit College at Vannes, where he taught English and was a college prefect.

He was what was called a "perpetual scholastic," a Jesuit who entered to become a priest but for some reason was never ordained. The reason for his not being promoted to ordination is not publicly known. It could have been connected with his physical health or it could be his unwillingness to accept the responsibilities that go along with the blessings of the priesthood. In any case, his not receiving ordination to the priesthood was most likely a cause of deep frustration and disappointment to Anthony Hollinger and to all his relatives and friends.

The information we report about Anthony Hollinger has been obtained mainly from province catalogues, since no obituary was found.

- *FR. HENRY MARIA HUDON, S.J.*
- *Lived 74 years*
- *b. 9/6/1823, Rivière Ouelle, Quebec*
- *+ 1/26/1897, Montreal*

Henri Hudon,[101] son of Pierre Hudon and Josephte Cassé, entered the Jesuits in Canada. After completing his noviceship there in 1845, he was sent to St. Mary's, KY, to begin the study of humanities. With the rest of the community there he was sent in 1846 to continue those studies at Fordham. His age in 1846 was 23. He completed his studies in philosophy and theology at Rose Hill, and made his regency there teaching Latin and French to youths.

In 1856 he received his first assignment to St. Francis Xavier College, NYC. There he taught Latin until he became Prefect of Studies for three years.

Fr. Hudon's next assignment for two years (1862-1864) was at St. Mary's College, Montreal, where he was community Minister and Prefect of Discipline. Then he returned to Xavier College, NYC, as Vice-president (Prefect of Studies). In 1870 he began an unusually long ten-year term as President-Rector of that institution. During his incumbency the college prospered in numbers and in reputation. In addition, new college structures were added, and the exterior and many sections of the interior of the new church on 16th Street (some have called it an architectural gem) were planned. He let out the contracts for the church which would be completed under his successor.

Fr. Hudon left New York in August, 1880, after completing 20 years of service to Xavier College. He left because he had been honored by being appointed the first Canadian Superior General of what was thereafter known as the Mission of Canada since at that time the Canadian Jesuits were separated from the New York-Maryland province. During his incumbency he built a new scholasticate in Montreal to enable young Canadian Jesuits to complete their studies at home, rather than doing that work elsewhere. He also actively encouraged increased colonization of still unsettled areas of Canada. He remained in the office of Mission Superior General until 1887.

After some years working with Canadian Indians, in 1891 he was appointed rector and procurator of the College of St. Boniface in Calgary in the province of Manitoba. When he was mission Superior he had accepted that college in 1885 for the Jesuits from the bishop. That acceptance was judged by some to be one of the most important events of his Superiorship. The educational leadership he displayed at St. Boniface has been specially praised.

In 1894 he was made Minister at Sault-au-Recollet, the Canadian Jesuit Novitiate. Two years later he was named spiritual father at the Scholasticate of the Immaculate Conception, Montreal, and after a lingering illness he died there.

He was described as leading a saintly life, a man who never forgot his students, a benefactor of youth and a true Jesuit. His leadership style was described as "gentle." An unsigned cyclopedia article described him thus: "He was a strict but very affable prefect of studies; students and professors alike learned to love him, for he had a pleasant word and an encouraging smile for all. He took a fatherly interest in those committed to his charge; ... at the same time, he was very exact in requiring ... a fulfillment of duty."[102]

- *FR. AUGUST KOHLER, S.J.*
- *Lived 51 years*
- *b. 8/10/1821, at Colmar, France*
- *+ 10/15/1871, Georgian Bay, Ontario*

Having made his novitiate during 1842 to 1844 at St. Acheul, France, and completing preliminary studies at Georgetown, August Kohler[103] came to Fordham at age 30 as a second year student of theology. He was ordained by Bishop Hughes in New York City on May 29, 1847.

Later in 1847 he arrived at Manitoulin Island (an 80 mile Canadian island in the Georgian Bay of Lake Huron, the largest freshwater island in the world) to begin a long identification with its Indian inhabitants. His missionary work brought him to Indian and white settlements along the north shore of Lake Superior and elsewhere in Canada. His associates highly esteemed him and regarded him as a perceptive and energetic missionary as can be judged by their recommendation that he succeed Bishop Baraga of the diocese of Marquette, Michigan, when he was "named second for the Vicariate-apostolic of Sault Ste. Marie in northern Michigan."[104]

His involvement with the Indians of Manitoulin Island was such that he took their side when they clashed with the government, went bail for their chief, and later was charged in connection with the death of a fisheries agent. He was completely exonerated by the court of that charge.

In 1865 he went with the Indians from Sault Ste. Marie to their quarters in Garden City, Ontario, and he stayed with them there until 1869. He made a trip back to France in 1869 as he had done in 1853. In 1870 he returned to Canada to resume his missionary work. But in the next year he was drowned when the ship on which he was traveling sank in the Georgian Bay.

Fr. Kohler was a keen observer of Indian customs and environments as well as of the activities of the white traders. He described those observations in letters to Rome. The esteem in which he was held by the Indians was indicated by their name for him which meant "inspiration."

- *FR. MICHAEL NASH, S.J.*
- *Lived 71 years*
- *b. 9/24/1824, Whitechurch, Kilkenny, Ireland*
- *+ 9/6/1895, Troy, NY*

At age 21 in 1846 Michael Nash[105] arrived at Rose Hill with fellow Kentucky Jesuits to complete his collegiate study of humanities. At Fordham he was also a part-time teacher of English.

Son of James Nash and Catherine May, six-year-old Michael Nash and his father left Ireland and came to Kentucky in 1830 to claim a farm that was willed to them. His older brother, Thomas, had originally been scheduled to make the trip, but their mother objected, and Michael was a last-minute substitute to become his

120

father's companion. The father ultimately rejected the inheritance but decided to leave his son in the New World under the care of a Catholic priest.

After completing preparatory education Michael entered St. Mary's College, KY. Upon his graduation he entered the Jesuit novitiate there on April 13, 1844. He made the trip from Kentucky to New York and Fordham in 1846.

After studying the humanities at St. John's College, Fordham, in the 1846 academic year, he was assigned to help Fr. Larkin at his planned new parish and college in New York City (which later became St. Francis Xavier College and parish). In 1852 he returned to St. John's College, Fordham, to continue his studies, but when his health failed, he was sent to Europe. In 1856 he began his theological studies at Laval in France, and completed them in Paderborn, Germany, where he was ordained in 1859.

Fr. Nash volunteered in response to Archbishop Hughes' call for priests to serve in the army and in May, 1861, he was assigned as chaplain to a regiment formed to fight in the Civil War. The *Woodstock Letters*[106] contain eleven letters that record his experiences in that war. Garraghan[107] quoted a letter sent to the Jesuit General Beckx: "Fathers Tissot and Nash ... are praised in the papers for their zeal and disregard of all risks even death itself in the thick of battle ..."

When the term of his enlistment expired in 1863, Fr. Nash was appointed Vice-president of St. John's, Fordham, for the 1863-64 academic year. After that, he had various teaching and parochial assignments in Guelph, Montreal, Troy, St. Francis Xavier, NYC, Canisius College, Buffalo, until 1874. He was then appointed pastor at St. Joseph's, Troy, where he remained for fourteen consecutive years until 1888.

At Troy he taught an evening school for boys, seven of whom afterwards entered the Jesuits. After that he spent three years at the St. Lawrence O'Toole church (now St. Ignatius Loyola), in New York City. Beginning in August, 1892, he spent two years as spiritual father at Holy Cross College, Worcester, MA. He then returned to Troy, where he died.

Fr. Nash's publications, outside of his war letters, include later "Reminiscences" and the translation of several religious books from German and French.

He was described as a master storyteller who could interest his listeners for hours. A fiery temper was one of his characteristics (against which he fought all his life), another was great courage (he was said to have been always ready for a daring expedition), and these qualities endeared him to many who liked his military style. Some retreatants reported that they liked his use of military knowledge when he encouraged them in their fight against temptations. Archbishop Corrigan wrote of him that he "was an exact religious, was much loved by the poor wherever he went, and did not spare himself in laboring for them."[108]

- *FR. THOMAS OUELLET, S.J.*
- *Lived 74 years*
- *b. 12/21/1819, St. Cuthbert, Quebec*
- *+ 11/26/1894, Montreal*

Thomas Ouellet[109] at age 27 came to Fordham as a third year student of theology. Son of Antoine Ouellet and Catherine Michaud, he had first planned to enter the diocesan clergy and for that end he had studied theology and had been ordained a deacon. But he changed his plans and decided to become a Jesuit.

He made his novitiate in Canada, completed his theology at Fordham and was ordained on January 16, 1848. In the 1850's he taught and was prefect in France, Poland, Fordham, and Montreal. And then came the U.S. Civil War!

He responded positively to Archbishop Hughes' call for priests to serve in the army and was appointed chaplain of the New York Irish "Fighting 69th" regiment, one of the six regiments in General Thomas Francis Meagher's Irish Brigade. He was frequently mentioned in fellow-chaplain Corby's memoirs[110] of his priestly activities during the Civil War; William Corby was later President of Notre Dame U., and Superior General of the Holy Cross Fathers. As chaplain, Fr. Ouellet did not hesitate to upbraid those who deserved reprimand, regardless of their position. Once he rebuked an officer who publicly used profanity. The officer dismissed his remarks by telling him he was "only a captain of cavalry, on detached service." At his next Mass, Fr. Ouellet said: "I did not enter the army as a captain of cavalry, but as a soldier of the Savior to preach the doctrine of our holy Church, and I shall, ... as one of the spiritual directors of this command, reprove vice, and preach to you, undefiled, the religion of your fathers."[111] His forthrightness and consistency won the respect of his men.

Conyngham gave sketches of officers in his Irish Brigade and said that Fr. Ouellet was: "... a most zealous and indefatigable priest, universally respected."[112] Physically he was described as: "small of stature, lithe of frame, and immense in energy."[113]

There was an interval in the Civil War when Ouellet was not a military chaplain. Kohl and Richard noted that "After the battle of Fredericksburgh [December, 1862], when the 69th was greatly reduced in numbers, Fr. Ouellet was discharged so that he could enter the hospital service in [Newbern] North

Carolina. However, he returned to the 69th later in the war (February 14, 1864) when the regiment was reorganized and augmented by new recruits."[114]

In ceremonies marking the 25th anniversary of the Battle of Gettysburg, General Denis Burke said: "We have witnessed some scenes which are not recorded by historians, but which ... were as heroic as the charges of the Brigade. I refer to the conduct of our chaplains, Frs. Ouellet [the senior chaplain], Corby and Dillon, in the discharge of their sacred duties."[115] However, if Kohl and Richard (confirmed by a statement in Corby's Memoirs) are correct, Ouellet was not at Gettysburg, though he served at other battles, regarded as among the bloodiest of the war, such as at the battle of Antietam.

After his military chaplaincy, Fr. Ouellet spent the rest of his life in parochial work at many places, such as at St. Peter's, Jersey City, twice at St. Francis Xavier, NYC, at Quebec City, the Gesu, Montreal, and three times at Guelph; in the interval between 1865 and 1879 he was transferred ten times. But his assignment at the Indian mission of Garden River, to which he was very devoted, was a long one. In his parish work he was well known for his special hospitality toward strangers.

He was multi-lingual: besides his native French, he learned English, Polish, and, in his sixties, the Indian Ojibway language, which was spoken at Garden River. He was a much-acclaimed speaker and was invited to be the main preacher on many occasions.

Corby wrote that: "Father Ouellet was ... a very genial companion. ... He was very popular ... and [when he returned to the regiment] his reception was really a cordial one."[116] "He loved his sacred calling, and never neglected its important duties. During Gen. McClellan's famous seven days' retreat before Richmond, he was always to the front, on every occasion ministering to the wounded, and always predicting ...the certainty of final success."[117]

His traits were recalled in his obituary thus: "a perfect martinet in everything that pertained to his sacred duties; full of energy, and possessing in a high degree the positiveness of his race"... "a man of ardent temperament, indomitable of will, inflexible in duty, inexorable in the cause of justice, rich in a store of other fine qualities which go to make up the great servants of God."[118]

- *FR. AUGUST RÉGNIER, S.J.*
- *Lived 63 years*
- *b. 8/22/1820, L'Acadie, Quebec*
- *+ 4/1/1883, Xavier, NYC*

August Régnier[119] at age 26 came to Fordham as a third-year student of theology. Son of Augustin Regnier and Angélique Gagnon, he was the first Canadian-born candidate to join the Society of Jesus. He made his novitiate in Montreal after having begun the study of theology. In fact, he studied theology at four different places: the college of St. Hyacinth in Canada; the Sulpician Seminary in Montreal; Georgetown; and Fordham. Bishop Hughes ordained him in 1847 in the old St. Patrick's cathedral.

During his first years of priesthood (1847-64), he was assigned to various functions in three colleges: Fordham, St. Francis Xavier, NYC, and St. Mary's, Montreal.

He was at Fordham from 1857 to 1864 (except for one year in Montreal). During this period of his life for six years at Fordham he was the college procurator; for two years at Fordham he taught mathematics and gave parochial assistance at Croton Falls; he was community minister for one year; and regularly he provided parish assistance.

The next almost 20 years of his priesthood (1864—) were devoted to parochial ministry in St. Joseph's, Troy, Chatham, Canada, and Blackwell's Island, NYC. Blackwell's Island (later Welfare Island, currently Roosevelt Island) was then a prison and a hospital for contagious diseases. In 1878 he began his final pastoral assignment there, rendering exemplary service to the inmates and staff until he himself fell a victim of disease.

His obituary[120] praised "his generous devotedness ... [and] his tender charity for the poor and the afflicted ..." His affability and courteous manners towards everyone were also recalled in that same account.

- *FR. PETER TISSOT, S.J.*
- *Lived 52 years*
- *b. 10/15/1823, Mégève (diocese: Annecy), Savoy, France*
- *+ 6/19/1875, Xavier, NYC*

Peter Tissot[121] at age 23 arrived at Fordham from France in 1846 as a second year student of philosophy. "Born of pious parents," he had been a student at the Jesuit college in Mélan, and had entered the Society at Avignon for the province of Lyons. While studying philosophy at Brugelette, Belgium, he asked to be sent to America. Assigned to Fordham, he completed his study of philosophy, theology and other disciplines there, and was ordained on October 16, 1853 at St. Joseph's Seminary, Fordham, by Archbishop Bedini, the Papal Nuncio.

For several years after ordination he was the community Minister and procurator at Fordham. He must have been regarded as an expert procurator because for all but about six years he was the college procurator from 1854 to 1872. In his early years at Fordham he also taught French, Spanish, and several scientific subjects. However, his personal hope was to be engaged entirely in pastoral and missionary rather than in collegiate work. Thus he answered Archbishop Hughes' call for priests to volunteer as chaplains for the Army during the U.S. Civil War and his offer was accepted.

Fr. Tissot was chaplain for three years of the 37th Regiment, New York Irish Volunteers, also known as the "Irish Rifles," in the northern Army of the Potomac. Major General Philip Kearny said of Fr. Tissot, as reported by Gen. James O'Beirne,[122] that he was the model army chaplain: when his regiment was in action he was always recognized performing his priestly duties at the front of the line of battle, as illustrated by the fact that three horses were killed under him while in battles. Yet Fr. Tissot himself later wrote that he was convinced that the best place for a chaplain's work in battle was at the hospital station just behind the front lines where he could serve the largest number of individuals in need of his services.

He was captured on June 30, 1862, and imprisoned, first at the cruel Libby Prison, and later with less discomfort in Richmond, VA. During his imprisonment he labored for the salvation of his charges as if he were in church (even conducting the Spiritual Exercises for squad after squad in his tent), though he himself was very ill. General O'Beirne later wrote that he was "saint-like in his uncomplaining endurance of suffering."

We can imagine his surprise during his imprisonment to have a visit from Fr. Louis-Hippolyte Gache, S.J., then a chaplain in the Confederate army.[123] His visitor was one of his former professors at the Jesuit College, Mélan, Savoy. He must have been even more surprised on July 19, 1862, when he was released by the Confederacy with no conditions during a mid-war exchange of prisoners.

The manuscript of his army chaplaincy diary is housed in the Fordham University Archives. Part of that diary has been published.[124] The diary, clearly written in a strong hand, gives a vivid account of the varied religious, social, and personal activities and problems of a Civil War army chaplain.

Shortly after his release from the army and his return to his former position as procurator, he was made vice-rector and acting President of Fordham. He stayed in that role only from January 23 to July 31, 1865, since he protested his unfitness for the unsought honor in daily letters to the local Provincial and to the Jesuit General in Rome. They finally yielded to his protests.

After his brief acting presidency, Fr. Tissot returned to his procurator tasks. However, he was able to combine that work with a great deal of clearly pastoral

FATHER TISSOT
HERO OF THE CIVIL WAR.
WHILE PRESIDENT OF FORDHAM COLLEGE IN NEW YORK CITY WROTE A LETTER OF RESIGNATION EVERY DAY FOR 5 MONTHS —MORE THAN 150 LETTERS— HIS RESIGNATION WAS FINALLY ACCEPTED IN JUNE, 1865

activity. Only in the last few years of his life was he allowed to return full time to the activity that he desired most, giving missions and retreats. That he did all over the country with indefatigable zeal and wonderful success. He was vigorous in spreading devotion to the Sacred Heart, the Blessed Virgin, and the practice of frequent Communion. In addition to all his other activities, he wrote a short book on the Blessed Sacrament, and another on the Scapular of Mount Carmel.

Fr. Thomas Campbell[125] wrote that during this, the final missionary phase of his life, Fr. Tissot "astounded" priests and laity "by the eloquence and fervor of his sermons, and above all by the holiness of his life." During all his apostolic work, unknown to most others, he suffered from numerous infirmities which finally developed into a triple cancer that ultimately obliged him to give up his missionary activities and brought about his early death at the age of fifty-two.

General O'Beirne described him thus: his "darkened olive complexion framed well set eyes that sparkled with merry twinkles of humor. ... scholarly [appearance] ... polished elegance. ... unswerving, unalterable ... moral courage. ... a great soul [with] lofty principles."[126] Historian Fr. C. M. Buckley, S.J., agreed that Fr. Tissot was serious and pious, but regarded him as "decidedly humorless"[127] in spite of General O'Beirne's references to his "merry twinkles of humor," as indicated above. Fr. Campbell[128] wrote that Fr. Tissot gladly accepted his appointment as military chaplain though his quiet, retiring nature was averse to such work. Campbell added that his later missionary work, done mostly alone, ended his life prematurely because of the excessive work it required of him. Most observers recalled him as a shy, refined gentleman whose memory was held in benediction among the clergy and laity.

We have completed the brief profiles of 33 of the Fordham Jesuits who arrived at Rose Hill in 1846. In the next section we offer some reflections that have been stimulated by researching their life histories.

PART III

Observations and Reflections on the Fordham Jesuit Pioneers

Many people have expressed to me their admiration for these pioneer Fordham Jesuits, and often this admiration triggered further questions on their part:

• Why did Jesuits try to avoid being made bishops?

• Does Fordham today have any art works or documents that link it directly with the 1846 Jesuit pioneers and with St. Mary's, KY?

• The pioneer Fordham Jesuits came from many countries and included young and old men. What unified them and made them a community that worked together for the growth of the college?

- How can we characterize the Fordham Jesuit pioneers?
- We summarize in this section our responses to some of these questions.

A. THE EPISCOPACY AND EARLY FORDHAM JESUITS

An important element of Jesuit living is the agreement to avoid external honors, including church honors, unless ordered by the pope under the vow of obedience to accept them. Nevertheless, in the mid-1800s there were four Jesuit bishops in the United States: Benedict Fenwick, second bishop of Boston; James Van de Velde, second bishop of Chicago; John B. Miége, Vicar-apostolic of the Indian Territory east of the Rocky Mountains; and George Carrell, first bishop of Covington, KY. Thus at times in mission places, and in special circumstances, popes in the past have required Jesuits to accept prelacies, and do the same in recent days. Among the fifteen Jesuit priests who came to Fordham in 1846, the following seven are known to have been appointed, nominated or recommended for the episcopacy:

- Larkin, for the diocese of Kingston in Canada, some four years after his ordination, and later, appointed for Toronto;
- Murphy, for the Toronto diocese, second after Larkin on the final list;
- Petit, for Vincennes, Indiana;
- Daubresse, proposed by Bishop Hughes for a new diocese in New York State;
- De Luynes, for Charleston and for New Orleans;
- Kohler, for the Vicariate-apostolic of Sault Ste. Marie in Michigan;
- Driscol, mentioned in Fr. General Beckx' letter on bishop-candidates.

While such recommendations were usually resisted successfully by the Jesuit General in Rome, they give an indication of the esteem in which their peers held the Fordham pioneers. One reason for the Jesuit principle of rejecting honors, including ecclesiastical ones, is that those honors are disruptive of the religious community life and deprive the Society of some of its likely leadership. But there is another basic reason that flows from Jesuits' experiencing the *Spiritual Exercises*. There St. Ignatius, after depicting the poor and humble Jesus as model for our living, asks the exercitant to pray for "poverty with Christ poor, rather than riches; insults with Christ ..., rather than honors." In that same spirit, in Part X of his *Constitutions*, which are the rule for his followers, St. Ignatius wrote that Jesuits should close "the door against seeking, directly or indirectly, any dignity or prelacy ..." Larkin and DeLuynes demon-

Fordham Honors Archbishop Hughes

Though relationships between Archbishop Hughes and Jesuit administrators were sometimes hot and cold, his name is honored on campus in many ways. Here are some of them:

- The impressive stone structure that formerly housed Fordham Prep has been known for years as Hughes Hall.

- The most commanding statue on campus depicts Archbishop Hughes facing the Administration Building (a wag suggested it represents his keeping watch over administrators). The statue itself is eight feet two inches high and is mounted on a ten foot five inch granite pedestal. The college alumni, under its president Judge Morgan J. O'Brien, assumed leadership in a drive to pay the $17,000 needed for it. Its erection highlighted the college's golden anniversary in 1891.

- A new institute at Fordham has been named the Archbishop Hughes Institute on Religion and Culture.

- On a wall in the foyer outside the lecture hall on the first floor of Keating Hall, there is an impressive (somewhat weather-worn) triptych created after his death at the behest of the New York City Common Council. It was meant as a lasting memorial to the Archbishop and his portrait dominates the center panel. Under its depiction of the chapel and St. John's Hall we read the classic statement: "Si quaeris monumentum, circumspice" ("If you're looking for a monument to this man, just take a look around you"). The side panels praise his indomitable perseverance in the cause of truth and justice and his contributions to the causes of religion, education and charity. They describe him as a wise, zealous, and indefatigable advocate, counsellor and guide and make note of the many edifices he erected and dedicated to the service of the living God, the homes for the helpless and dependent orphans he has founded, and the institutions of learning he established.

- On the lighthearted side, the Archbishop is remembered by naming a dining facility in the McGinley Center, Dagger John, a term originally used by some of his opponents.

- A road leading into the campus was formerly called Avenue St. John's because it led to St. John's College (now Fordham University); in 1895 it was renamed Hughes Avenue both to honor of the Archbishop and to avoid confusion with another Ave. St. John in the lower Bronx.

- John McNamara's *History in Asphalt* (p. 19) identifies the name of the drive leading from the university's Third Avenue entrance to the Administration Building and around Martyrs' Court as Archbishop Hughes Circle.

- A recent acquisition, a frame house on the campus fringe on Hughes Avenue, is named Hughes House.

- In addition, for many years the Prep and Fordham College had their own Hughes Debating Society. And Hughes medals such as for Philosophy and for Service have long been awarded at the convocations and graduations of the various schools and colleges.

strated clearly their agreement with St. Ignatius' ideal in this regard by making themselves unavailable through flight from the scene.

B. Current Links to Early Pioneer Jesuits

There are on campus some objects which date back to 1846 or came from St. Mary's, KY, and help link us specially with early Fordham. The university church, the Archives section of the Walsh Memorial
, and, of course, the Jesuit cemetery on campus contain or are objects which can be venerated for their symbolism and for their relative antiquity. Thus:

a. In the *University Church*: the front part of the nave, with its special stained glass windows was built just before the Jesuits' 1846 arrival.

In the sacristy of the University Church: there is a special wooden panel that memorializes the early history of the Parthenian Sodality in St. Mary's College and in St. John's College, Fordham.

b. In the *Walsh Family Library Archives and Special Collections*, the following pertinent items are housed:

1. There is "the St. John's College collection" — some 1,200 pre-1870 books. More than half of the book titles are on religious or theological subjects; most of the books are in French; some are believed to have been brought to Fordham from Kentucky, and some of them from France. They are kept in a separate area because of the fragile condition of their binding.

2. Minutes of the Boards of Trustees of St. Mary's College and of St. John's College and the Fr. Ministers' diaries, and other diaries which pay special attention to the academic and religious activities on campus; some of the early diaries are written in Latin or French.

3. A heavy brass plaque that memorializes the February 2, 1837, beginning of the Parthenian Sodality in St. Mary's, Kentucky; it names the charter members and founder.

4. Many folders, books of minutes, and other items that narrate the history of the Parthenian Sodality and other sodalities in early Fordham.

It is possible that alumni, clergy, and friends of the university may have additional objects (such as religious articles, diaries, books, etc.) that go back to 1846 or to earlier days. The university would welcome a donation of such important links to its early history.

c. Special recognition is due the *Fordham Jesuit Cemetery*, "God's holy acre," which adjoins Faber Hall and is close to the University church. The cemetery contains graves of 125 Jesuits and 17 others. The cemetery was originally located on a hillside of the property that the Botanical Garden obtained from Fordham; until that time the college property extended to the Bronx River. About 26 acres of the campus were condemned by New York City through "eminent domain" in 1885 and the transaction was completed by payment in 1889. From January 21 to 28, 1890, the Fr. Minister's diary recounts the transfer of 77 graves from the old to the new cemetery (the present site); remains of 60 Jesuits, three diocesan seminarians, 12 students, and two workmen were transferred; two bodies for which there were tombstones were not found.

Some transferred graves were those of Fordham early notables: Thébaud, Larkin, Tissot, Dealy; DeLuynes, Doucet, Driscol, and Nash. Eugene Maguire, a promising young Jesuit who died in St. Mary's, Kentucky, is also buried with this group. From January 1890 to January 1909, an additional 65 Jesuits were buried at the new site. Thereafter, locally deceased Jesuits were buried at St. Andrew-on-Hudson, Poughkeepsie, NY, until 1969. A few rows of graves were transferred within the cemetery in preparation for the construction of Faber Hall in 1959.

The *Fordham Monthly* for January, 1890, said of the transfer of the Jesuit graves: "We now have the privilege and honor of once again having our departed saints among us." Would not all the "Fordham Family" be blessed in their endeavors, especially academic and religious ones, if Alumni, Faculty, Students, and friends pray for and to them, and if they venerate the Fordham cemetery as a holy place?

C. WHAT UNIFIED THE JESUIT PIONEERS?

The pioneer Fordham Jesuits came from ten different countries and from many different social and economic conditions; their ages ranged from what was then regarded as old age, 57 (Simon Fouché) to 21 (Edward Doucet). Fortunately they also shared many religious values and devotions and educational achievements. They also faced together the challenges that were endemic to living as immigrants in a new country. Their religious and educational backgrounds as well as their struggles as immigrants all contributed to their developing unity as a religious community focusing on creating a successful college. Some details of the ties that bound them together are summarized as follows:

a. They had undergone a two year novitiate training that introduced them to a new type of living and a new discipline in their lives. The "new discipline" involved learning details of the vows of religion and attending lectures and exercises in prayer, etc.

b. They had all experienced St. Ignatius' Spiritual Exercises that included at least two thirty-day retreats and an annual eight day retreat. This was the bed-rock of the vision that inspired their work for others and for their common unity.

c. Certain religious devotions have been characteristic of Jesuits, such as special dedication to Jesus Christ, to his Blessed Mother, and to St. Ignatius.

Their special dedication to Jesus Christ flowed from the *Spiritual Exercises*. Three of the four "weeks" in those *Exercises* are devoted to the life of Jesus. At one point the retreatant is asked to respond in prayer to these questions: What have I done for Christ? What will I do for Christ? The pioneer Jesuits' zeal to spread the Gospel on and off campus represented their continuing efforts to answer those questions more and more adequately. That dedication was also evident in devotions on and off campus honoring the Sacred Heart of Jesus.

Second, their special devotion to Mary, the virgin Mother of Jesus, was marked by the long history and vigor of the various Sodalities of the Blessed Virgin Mary. An item in the Minister's Diary for August 14, 1846, recalls the first talk given to the Community by Fr. Boulanger, the Regional Superior. He strongly urged one and all to place themselves, their work, and the whole house under the protection of the Blessed Virgin Mary.

Third, they shared with all Jesuits a particular reverence for St. Ignatius Loyola, the founder of the Society. His life of prayer, his dedication to "helping souls" and special concern for his brethren are features that Jesuits admire in him; they eagerly welcome new information and new books about him. His virtues are examined with a view towards imitation, and his personality is studied in an effort to understand him better.

d. The Fordham Jesuit pioneers' education in literature, philosophy and in theology gave them a unifying language and many common interests.

e. Their difficulties and struggles in the new country bound them closer together. For example, the challenge of learning English was a shared experience. There was a strict house rule that Jesuits at St. Mary's and at Fordham were to use only one language, English, in reading at table and in conversing with one another. The house rule was only an application of a general Jesuit rule to "speak in the language of the region in which they reside." Dispensation from that rule was only rarely allowed.

Perhaps an even greater challenge to newcomers lay in the cultural differences between their homelands and the Kentucky countryside. They newly experienced the ways of democracy with political parties debating great issues, like slavery, states' rights, taxation, and problems connected with Indian tribes. How overwhelming the new situation must have been to them, but they must have shared their knowledge, confusion, and anxieties. The experience must have bound them more tightly together.

Fr. Peter Chazelle, the first Jesuit Regional Superior in Kentucky and first college President of St. Mary's College there, wrote several plays for his students. The titles of two of the plays were: *Red Hawk* (an Indian drama), and *Benedict Arnold, the Traitor*, the British spy in the American Revolution. Regardless of their likely literary quality, the very titles of the plays were symbolic of the newly arrived immigrants' desires to learn and communicate about their new country. Likewise, years later, in writing of Fr. De Luynes, Charles Herbermann said that "like all the old Jesuits of the Kentucky colony that originally settled in Fordham, [he] became a patriotic American who took the greatest interest in the future of the republic" (Thébaud, 1904, 134). Two of the Jesuit seminary professors reportedly pined for their old country and for the *ancien regime*. But in view of Herbermann's testimony and in the absence of contemporary or later claims to the contrary, it is likely that the majority of the pioneer Jesuits, after their initial culture shock, tried to reflect on and adopt what seemed acceptable of the mores of the good people they met in Kentucky and New York.

D. HOW CHARACTERIZE THE FORDHAM JESUIT PIONEERS?

Focusing here on the first Jesuit faculty members and administrators, we find it difficult to describe them as a group. There were acknowledged scholars among them (Daubresse, Larkin, Maldonado, Murphy, Thébaud), outstanding speakers (Larkin, DeLuynes, Driscol), and spiritual directors (Fouché, Petit, Legoüais, Murphy). Of the original pioneers only Thébaud wrote books and articles in periodicals.

Were they good teachers? The Jesuits of those days had the reputation of being good teachers. It was the reason why many bishops besieged the Father General in Rome to start or take over a college. It was the reason why many parents, including many who were not Catholic, choose to send their sons to Jesuit colleges.

Perhaps a key to the personal goals of many of the early Jesuits can be seen in their activities or assignments after they left college teaching or administering. Larkin did preaching and confessional work. Murphy's wisdom was recognized in his spiritual direction. Thébaud became pastor and assistant pastor. Doucet, no longer able to teach, became a counselor especially appreciated by priests. Driscol's warm heart and natural eloquence was recognized in retreats and parishes. Férard showed his zeal in work among the Indians in Canada. Fouché was regarded by his peers as "very religious." Legoüais was a man of great religious (if not physical) stature as indicated by his many blessed years in the confessional. Maldonado, the brilliant theologian, was regarded as a special blessing because he was a "perfect type of the true Jesuit." Ryan's zeal was expressed in the three churches he built. DeLuynes loved to expound on St. Paul in sermons and was honored for his judicious counseling. And Petit, on the testimony of Bishop Bruté, excelled in piety, learning, and eloquence. Religious activity capped their works.

The above brief summary of their activities in their "golden years" reveals clearly that their primary desires and goals were to "help souls," as St. Ignatius envisioned it, whether at home or in mission lands, in classrooms or in parishes, always as sons of Ignatius, and followers of their Divine Master. And thus they became and were true Jesuits.

NOTES

1 Vital statistics of the Jesuits profiled in this paper, such as the place and the date of their birth and death, are found in the *Catalogus Defunctorum Societatis Iesu, 1814-1970,* (Henceforth, *CDSI*), Rufo Mendizabal, editor (Rome: Jesuit Curia, 1972).

2 The residences and assignments of Jesuits are published annually in each province's catalogue. For instance, those who were in Rose Hill were listed in the *Catalogus Provinciae Franciae,* 1847. That catalogue, which was published in Paris, gave information about the assignments and residences of the members of the province during the preceding year. The annual catalogues have been used as source material for the assignments of those profiled in this paper.

In addition to the catalogues, diaries kept by the Fr. Minister and by others have been used to determine some dates. Diaries used in this paper are housed in the Fordham University Archives. The diaries in the early years of the college were written in French, then in Latin, and later in English.

3 We sought the names of both parents of our profilees, as a mark of "pietas" towards them. We found those names in only a relatively small number of instances. The names of Fr. Boulanger's parents are provided in his profile in the *Dictionnaire Biographique du Canada,* IX, 1978. His biography is also published in the *Dictionary of Jesuit Biography: Ministry to English Canada,* (Canadian Institute of Jesuit Studies, Toronto, Ontario, 1991), henceforth *DJB.*

4 Gilbert J. Garraghan, "Fordham's Jesuit Beginnings," *Thought,* March, 1941, 17-39.

5 The most complete biography of Fr. John Larkin is found in Francis J. Nelligan, "Father John Larkin, S.J., 1801-1858," *Canadian Messenger of the Sacred Heart,* 1957, 68, 37-43; 102-110; 181-187. In addition, he is profiled in the *Catholic Encyclopedia,* the *Dictionary of American Biography,* Joseph Gillow's *Biographical Dictionary of English Catholics,* (London: Burns Oates, 1885-1902) and *DJB.* A lengthy sketch of his life is also offered in the 1859 *Litterae Annuae of the Province of France.*

6 Gilbert J. Garraghan, *The Jesuits of the Middle United States.* 3 vols. (New York, The America Press, 1938), III, p. 259.

7 Garraghan, op. cit., I, p. 269.

8 Thomas G. Taaffe, *A History of St. John's College, Fordham* (London: Burns & Oates, 1891) p. 90.

9 *DJB,* p. 182.

10 C. Somervogel, *Bibliotheque de la Compagnie de Jesus.* 12 vols. (Bruxelles: O. Schepens, 1890-1932).

11 Nelligan, 106.

12 Garraghan, Op. cit., provides numerous references to Murphy, as does Ben J. Webb, *A Century of Catholicity in Kentucky* (Charles A. Rogers, Louisville, KY, 1884). A long obituary of Fr. Murphy was printed in the *Freeman's Journal,* Nov. 20, 1875. Information about Fr. Murphy's family in Cork can be found in *The Murphy's Story,* by Diarmuid and Donal O Drisceoil, privately published by Murphy Brewery Ltd. Cork, Ireland.

13 His bishop-uncle's "other plans" have not been learned. Yet it is not unlikely that he saw in his nephew an excellent candidate for the priesthood in his diocese, one whom he would be pleased to sponsor for promotion to the hierarchy. The bishop was an

admirer of Peter Kenney, S.J. (1779-1841) who was the first vice-Provincial of the restored Society of Jesus in Ireland, as narrated by Thomas Morrissey, *As One Sent: Peter Kenney, S.J. (1779-1841)* (Catholic University of America Press, Washington, DC, 1996) p. 426.

14 Taaffe, op. cit., p. 77-78.

15 Garraghan, op. cit., p. 562.

16 Garraghan, op. cit., p. 570.

17 Garraghan, op. cit., p. 571.

18 Taaffe, op. cit., p. 79.

19 Morrissey, op. cit., p. 433.

20 Webb, op. cit., p. 393.

21 Cornelius M. Buckley, S.J., *Nicolas Point* (Chicago: Loyola U. Press, 1989) p. 435.

22 Information about August J. Thébaud is found in his three volume reminiscences, all edited posthumously by Charles G. Herbermann, and published by the Unites States Catholic Historical Society in New York. They are: *Forty Years in the United States of America (1839-1885)* (1904); *Three-Quarters of a Century:A Retrospect.* Vol. I, 1912; and Vol. II, 1913). Additional good sources about him are the books by Taaffe and by Webb, cited above. There are articles about him in the *Dictionary of American Biography*, and in the 1910 and 1967 editions of the *Catholic Encyclopedia*.

23 Thébaud, 1913, p. 111.

24 Thébaud, 1904, p. 349-353.

25 *The Works of Orestes A. Brownson*, (Detroit: T. Nourse, 1882) 13, p. 566.

26 Quoted in Thébaud, 1904, p. 282, 294.

27 Thébaud, 1904, p. 290.

28 Webb, p. 394-395.

29 Footnote in Thébaud, 1904, p. 329.

30 Ibid., p. 3.

31 Thomas Campbell, in Thébaud, 1904, p. 9, 10.

32 While there are numerous references to Daubresse in other articles in the *Woodstock Letters* (henceforth *WL*) and in Fordham-related historical publications, the most extensive article about him is the unsigned "Father Isidore Daubresse: A Sketch," *WL*, 26 (1897), 114-117.

33 For details of the "Grand Act," see the unsigned article, "The Grand Act" in *WL*, 21, 87-93. The article describes Fr. De la Motte's defense of 278 theses which were listed in a pamphlet of 67 pages. Eighty guests, including Cardinal Gibbons, provincials, rectors, and professors of various colleges and universities, attended the examination.

34 Thomas J. Shelley, *Dunwoodie: The History of St. Joseph's Seminary* (Westminster, MD: Christian Classics, 1993), p. 22-23.

35 Thomas J. Campbell, "St. John's College, Fordham," *Historical Records and Studies*, III, 1903, 88.

36 Ibid.

37 Rt. Rev. Michael A. Corrigan, "Register of the Clergy Laboring in the Archdiocese of New York from Early Missionary Times to 1885," *Historical Records and Studies*, 3, (1903), 317-318 (henceforth Corrigan). His studies were published in a series of articles over the period 1903-1913.

38 Ibid., 116, 117.

39 Information about Fr. Doucet is found in his obituary in *WL*, 20, 278, and in the *Fordham Monthy*, Dec. 1890, 56 and June, 1891, 86.

40 Sketches of Michael Driscol's life are found in *WL*, 19, 1890, 115-6, and in *The National Cyclopedia of American Biography*, 1921, 4, 115.

41 For his use of the Irish language see "Catholic Beginnings in Yonkers," by Thomas C. Cornell, *Historical Records and Studies*, 36, 76-77.

42 See Finbar Kenneally (Ed.), *United States Documents in the Propaganda Fide Archives* (Washington, DC, Academy of American Franciscan History, 1968), 2, p. 156 (#980).

43 Férard's biography is published in *DJB*, p. 108-109.

44 See Sister M. Lilliana Owens, S.L., "Simon Fouché, S.J.: Missionary, Educator, Spiritual Director," *WL*, 98 (1969), 425-434.

45 Accounts of Fr. Legoüais' life are found in obituary notices, such as in the *Freeman's Journal*, May 27, 1876; and *WL*, 19, 409.

46 Shelley, op. cit., p. 25.

47 From *The College of St. Francis Xavier: A Memorial and a Retrospect*, 1847-1897, p. 127.

48 Webb, op.cit., p. 394.

49 Corrigan, III (1903), 318.

50 Information about Fr. Maldonado is found in *WL*, 1,194; the *Freeman's Journal*, August 24, 1872; Corrigan, op. cit., 3, 319; L. Frias, *La Provincia de España el la Cie. de Jesu*, 1815-1862, Madrid, 1914, p. 134.

51 Finding Ryan's place of birth has been a challenge since most references to his origin simply said he was "Irish-born." However, some unbound loose pages, entitled "Catalogus Primus" were found in the Fordham University Archives. One of those pages listed Ryan's "origin;" though "origin" could mean a long-time residence, in this context it most likely means his place of birth. On the same page a Joseph Ryan, born on Oct. 25, 1815, was listed as a novice Jesuit Brother, whose origin was the same village; he was probably a younger brother of John. Joseph seems to have left the novitiate before taking vows.

52 See John Ryan, *National Cyclopedia of American Biography* (New York, J. T. White, 1891-1921), IV, p. 115.

53 Details of the building of the first church in Yonkers are contained in "Catholic Beginnings in Yonkers," by Thomas C. Cornell, *Historical Records and Studies*, 36, 68-96. Cornell's appreciation of Fr. Ryan is on p. 75 of that article.

54 The family name has been spelled and recorded in numerous variations: Lewin; Lewines; O'Lewins; Luynes; Delouin; DeLuyne; Deluynes.

55 See an excellent biographical sketch, "Reverend Charles Hyppolite De Luynes, S.J.," by Charles G. Herbermann in *Historical Records and Studies*, X (January 1917), 130-151.

56 For a report on the lives of the Irish exiles in Paris, their quarrels and jealousies, see Marianne Elliott, *Partners in Revolution: the United Irishmen and France* (New Haven: Yale, 1982), *passim*. Regarding Lewin's banishment, see "Irish News in the French Press, 1789-98," in David Dickson et al. (Eds.) *The United Irishmen: Republicanism, Radicalism and Rebellion*, p. 267. A post-rebellion Amnesty Bill allowed ninety leaders to return but excluded Napper Tandy, Lewins, and Arthur MacMahon.

57 Corrigan, 1904, 101.

58 Details of his visit to his mother in Ireland are contained in his Jan. 31, 1878, obituary in the *Catholic Advocate* of Cincinnati.

59 Garraghan, II, p. 123.

60 See the editor's note in Thébaud, 1904, p. 208-210.

61 Kenneally, II, p. 149-150 (#944).

62 Herbermann, op. cit., p. 134.

63 John Gilmary Shea, (Ed.), *The Catholic Churches of New York City* (New York: Goulding, 1878), p. 300.

64 Webb, p.397.

65 His practices at Mass were described in Herbermann, op. cit., p. 144.

66 Herbermann, op. cit., p. 146, described his dealing with the rich and the poor.

67 Details of Petit's early life are found in Ben J. Webb, *The Centenary of Catholicity in Kentucky* (Louisville, Charles A. Rogers, 1884), p. 388-389. Webb noted that in Kentucky Fr. Petit was known as Louis, in New York as Nicolas.

68 *Litterae Annuae Provinciae Franciae S.I.*, 1834.

69 See the correspondence of Bishop Bruté with Fr. General Roothaan regarding Fr. Petit's becoming his coadjutor bishop in *WL*, 31, 39-44.

70 Garraghan, II, p. 118n.

71 Webb, p. 389.

72 Brief biographies of Br. Callaghan are given in *DJB*, p. 42, and *WL*, 19, 114.

73 *DJB*, p. 42

74 *WL*, 19, 114.

75 Sources for Br. Crowe's vital statistics and their differing dates for his birth, are: the annual province catalogues (Feb. 28, 1817), the handwritten "Catalogus Primus," (Feb. 15, 1818) and the *CDSI*, 1814-1930 (Feb. 28, 1817); the latter agrees with the catalogues but gives Jan. 1, 1815 as the day when he entered the Society.

76 Fordham University Archives, Diary entitled "Workmen."

77 The main sources of information about Br. Hennen are articles in *WL*, 19, 93 (on his jubilee), and 20, 117 (his obituary).

78 The ocean and overland journey is vividly described in *Nicolas Point, S.J.*, by C. M. Buckley, (Chicago, Loyola University Press, 1989); it also contains details of Br. Ledoré's life that are not readily found elsewhere.

79 Thébaud, 1904, p. 39-40.

80 Fort Hill, NY, was a villa house shared by the Fordham and the Xavier communities. It contained 444 acres and included an active farm. Articles about it are in *WL*, 36, 224, and 75, 136. It was located at Lloyd's Neck, Cold Spring Harbor, on the east side of Oyster Bay, Long Island.

81 *Fordham Monthly*, (henceforth *FM*) Oct., 1891, 62.

82 *FM*, Sept.- Oct., 1890, 33-34 .

83 Using the province Catalogus of 1847, we report 47 as the grand total of Jesuits at Fordham in 1846 (16 priests; 18 scholastics; 13 brothers). However, Fr. T. Campbell, a former Provincial and a former President of Fordham, perhaps using other sources, wrote in 1916 that there were 51 Jesuits at Rose Hill that first year; the different numbers may be accounted for by novices who left the Jesuits or others who were transferred before year's end or publication of the province Catalogus.

84 Webb, op. cit., p. 509.

85 Details of Fr. Adams' life were received from Rev. T. Clancy, S.J., personal communication, and his "Antebellum Jesuits of the New Orleans Province," *Louisiana History*, 34 (1993), 327-343.

86 *WL*, 26, 101.

87 Details of Fr. Dealy's life are found in *WL*, 21, 261; *DJB*, p. 78-79; the *National Cyclopedia of American Biography*, 2, p. 267; and in Corrigan, VI, 1913, 188-189.

88 Robert I. Gannon, *Up to the Present* (Garden City, Doubleday, 1967), p. 80.

89 "Struggles and Sufferings of our First American Missionaries," *WL*, 21, 210-227.

90 *Catalogus Secundus*, 1853, #21.

91 Details of Fr. Desjacques' life were drawn primarily from province catalogues.

92 Details of Fr. Gockeln's life are found in his obituary, *WL*, 16 (1887), 103-105, in *DJB*, p. 124, and in the *National Cyclopedia of American Biography*, 1921, p. 267.

93 Robert I. Gannon, op. cit., p. 77.

94 Francis X. Connolly, "Fordham History," *The Centurian*, 1941 Fordham University Yearbook, p. 141.

95 Patrick A. Halpin, Letter, *FM*, Jan. 1887, 52-53.

96 The names of Fr. Graves' parents were learned through a telephone conversation with James Graves, a descendant of Fr. Graves' brother.

97 According to Corrigan, V (1904), 193, "Fr. Graves was so ardent a Southerner that his Superiors thought it advisable to send him to the South" at the time the Civil War was still being fought.

98 Garraghan, III, p. 282.

99 *Louis-Hypollyte Gache: A Frenchman, A Chaplain, A Rebel: Wartime Letters*, Translated by Cornelius M. Buckley (Chicago: Loyola University Press, 1981), p. 168.

100 Noted in the "Catalogus Primus, 1847," Hollinger.

101 Sources of information about Fr. Hudon are: the *National Cyclopedia of American Biography*; Corrigan, IV (1904), 105-6; and an obituary in the *Montreal Star*, Feb. 27, 1897.

102 *The National Cyclopedia of American Biography*, 1921, p 268.

103 Details of Fr. Kohler's life are found in *DJB*, P. 172-173.

104 Garraghan, Op. cit., II, p. 121.

105 Information about Fr. Nash is available from his obituary in the *WL*, 26, 334-336; his own "Reminiscences" in the *WL*, 26, 257-283; Corrigan, VI (1913), 193-195. Information about Fr. Nash's parentage was provided through the kindness of Mary Flood, Administrator of the Kilkenny Archaeological Society.

106 *WL*, 14 to 19.

107 Garraghan, II, p. 155.

108 Corrigan, VI, 194-195.

109 Details of Fr. Ouelette's life are found in *DJB*, p. 276; and, in the *WL*, 24, 375-378.

110 *William Corby, Memoirs of Chaplain Life: Three Years with the Irish Brigade in the Army of the Potomac*, Lawrence F. Kohl, Ed. (New York, Fordham University Press, 1992).

111 Corby, p. 301.

112 David Conyngham, *The Irish Brigade and its Campaigns* (New York, W. McSorley, 1867), p. 320.

113 *DJB*, p. 276.

114 Lawrence F. Kohl with Margaret C. Richard (Eds.), *Irish Green and Union Blue: the Civil War Letters of Peter Welsh* (New York, Fordham University Press, 1986), p. 36.

115 *WL*, 17, 320.

116 Corby, p. 216.

117 Corby, op. cit., p. 302

118 *WL*, 24, 378.

119 Information about Fr. Régnier is found in *DJB*, p. 302.

120 *WL*, 12, 200-201.

121 Information about Fr. Tissot is found in *WL* 19, 408; Corrigan, V, 182; Thomas G. Taaffe, "Rev. Peter Tissot, S.J." *Historical Records and Studies*, III, Part 1, 1903, 38-41; his own article, "A Year with the Army of the Potomac," *Historical Records and Studies*, III, 1904, 42-87; and Gache, *Letters*, Translated by C.M. Buckley.

122 James R. O'Beirne, "Reminiscences: In War Times," *FM*, June, 1916, 52-53.

123 Gache, op. cit., p. 121.

124 *Historical Records and Studies*, III, Part I, 42-88.

125 Thomas J. Campbell, Menology, MS in Fordham Community Library, August 15, Father Tissot, Army Chaplain.

126 O'Beirne, op. cit., 52-53.

127 Gache, op. cit., p. 124.

128 Campbell, *Historical Records and Studies*, III, 1903, 90.

CHAPTER VI

FROM EARLIEST TO LATEST FORDHAM: BACKGROUND HISTORY AND ONGOING ARCHAEOLOGY

By Allan S. Gilbert and Roger Wines

I. INTRODUCTION

The name Rose Hill made its first appearance in what is now the central Bronx when one of New York's elite families established a country estate on an aging Dutch farm just after the Revolution. This was nearly 60 years before the arrival of the Jesuits in 1846. Older still is the Fordham name, which emerged with the granting of colonial New York's first manorial patent in 1671, 170 years before the inauguration of St. John's College. Archbishop John Hughes's fledgling school marks the beginning of a Catholic tradition at Rose Hill, but it also caps a long history of prior settlement, begun by pioneering Dutch farmers as early as 1694.

A substantial documentary record chronicles many of the personalities and events of these earliest Fordham years, but new perspectives on the already familiar can often be gained by looking beyond the written word and examining the physical evidence. The modern Bronx campus of Fordham University, where the principal events took place, can be read like a large chart, annotated in a language of landscape and architecture. Venerable edifices, many of which have earned landmark status, bear silent witness to a former era in many elements of their construction and design, while old plans, pictures, and descriptions permit us to plot the changes in layout and land use for the property as a whole. These "snapshots" in time, when arranged in sequence, map out the evolution of the place not only in its visual appearance but also in its ideology and sense of self.

History is also hidden in the archaeological deposits under foot. These unintentional gifts to posterity have the power to illuminate dark corners of the historical narrative, disclosing details forgotten or unrecorded. For over 12 years, the authors have been granted the privilege of exploring early Fordham through the excavation of its most celebrated relic, the old Rose Hill Manor.

Vestiges of Fordham's colonial and early American origins are there in the broken implements and fragmentary walls. These remains have also had much to say about the style and tempo of everyday life at St. John's College.

The St. John's College campus of 1846 provides the starting point for this excursion into Fordham's past. After touring the school and its grounds, the narrative retraces the ownership of the Rose Hill estate since the colonial chartering of Fordham Manor. Finally, selected archaeological finds that relate to the early college are discussed.

II. THE EARLY CAMPUS OF ST. JOHN'S COLLEGE

As he described it, Michael Nash arrived by train at St. John's College in August, 1846, to find an idyllic, rural retreat at the outskirts of a great port city.[1] The college proper consisted of a small cluster of buildings surrounded by expansive lawns, farmland, rustic lanes, and patches of forest and glade only a short trip from New York City on the New York and Harlem steam train. Here, in the pure country air of Westchester County, the Jesuit fathers could inspire their charges without the distractions of urban vice and commerce, at least until the place was engulfed by the city at the end of the nineteenth century.

St. John's College was established by Rev. John Hughes on the 106-acre Rose Hill estate in the small village of Fordham. In 1848, Robert Bolton described Fordham as having "three taverns, two stores, a Dutch Reformed Church and thirty or forty homes" scattered about its hilly terrain.[2] Two principal roads intersected near the entrance to the college. The first led southeast from the old Kingsbridge crossing over Spuyten Duyvil Creek at the northern tip of Manhattan and continued as far as West Farms. Today, the line of this former thoroughfare is taken by Kingsbridge Road in the north, but to the south, it is interrupted by the street pattern of East Tremont. The second road departed from Fordham Landing on the Harlem River and proceeded eastward, terminating near the college. The present Fordham Road runs beyond the old terminus, bordering the university on the south. No road existed here in the 1840s.

In October of 1841, just three months after the college inauguration, the rail line reached Rose Hill, and a grey stone depot was built adjacent to the campus that would make Fordham accessible to travelers from 26th Street in Manhattan.[3] To allow the tracks to advance northward to White Plains, Hughes later shaved a right-of-way off the western edge of the college property and ceded it to the railroad in exchange for one dollar and two tickets per year in perpetuity for the college president. His action was less a gesture of magnanimity than a means of insuring that the tracks would not be laid according to company plans straight through the campus. Yet, it would pass close enough to facilitate access for the rest of the world to Rose Hill's doorstep. In this way, an active rail link has formed a campus boundary for very nearly the entire history of the school.

From the train station, Nash walked east toward the entrance to St. John's. Before him, a long, stone wall extended into the distance marking the southern boundary of the school grounds. South of this wall, the Episcopal Reverend Dr. Powell had run a boarding school for boys on what, in colonial times, had been the Union Hill farm of the Delancey family. In the early years of the college, Powell's apple orchard could still be seen above the stones. Nash turned left onto a narrow path lined by cherry trees and a northward extension of the wall. The path merged shortly into the great oval drive that led around a broad lawn into the core of the early campus.

The panoramic view that opened before him has been preserved in a drawing by William Rodrigue, brother-in-law of Archbishop Hughes (Figure 1; this and figures 2, 4,5 and 14 are from theFordham University archives). Rodrigue and his family had accompanied Hughes from Philadelphia to New York when Hughes was named coadjutor of the New York Diocese. He served the early college as professor of drawing, penmanship, and civil engineering, while designing and building the new Seminary of St. Joseph and Church of Our Lady of Mercy (now St. John's Hall and the University Church) in 1845-46. Rodrigue's drawing must have been completed shortly after the new buildings were standing. The effort was probably a first attempt at public relations in the service of student admissions, for though the original is lost, one surviving copy is attached to a Spanish language advertisement for St. John's College. Human

Figure 1

COLLEGE IN 1846
Nº 1 COLLEGE 2 INFIRMARY. 3 SEMINARY

interest was provided by a strolling Jesuit father and several other figures on the oval drive, and beyond on the grass, a few boys playing cricket and two others playing soldier. This perspective of St. John's College at its inception is unique in being the only one produced by an eyewitness. Richard S. Treacy (Class of 1869) donated a copy of the drawing to the college, where it hung for many years in the Fathers' Library.[4] Rodrigue's drawing was later copied in an etching by Weldon McKeon, and this rendering has been widely reproduced in most Fordham-related publications[5] as well as in Figure 1.

From the foot of the oval drive, most of the central buildings of the campus were visible. As depicted by Rodrigue, the first edifice on the right was the wide, sprawling mansion of Dr. Horatio Shepheard Moat, an English-born

Figure 2

physician and herbalist of Brooklyn.[6] Moat had owned the Rose Hill estate briefly between 1836 and 1838. His three-story stone house faced west, and on the north and south sides, he had added long, one-story wings, classically-inspired with columns and a triangular pediment, as seen in this 1863 photograph (Figure 2; college-related buildings had been added to the rear of his house by this time). In 1846, the story was current that Moat had intended to use the southern wing as a greenhouse. One of the deeds of sale in 1839 indicated that, indeed, it had been a conservatory.[7]

When Hughes acquired the property, the mansion was "an unfinished house in the field." He completed it and added several brick extensions in the rear. Fr. August Thébaud, the first Jesuit president of the college, expanded and altered these appendages, giving the mansion something of the character of a huge letter E in bird's-eye view (see plan in Figure 3).[8] In this form, the main building of the college persisted for two decades until the late 1860s.

The original white marble front portico and fieldstone facade of the central portion still survive today. Once inside the entrance, one entered a central hallway with a staircase to the upper floors. To the north was the parlor, where visitors were greeted by faculty and students. To the south was a small chapel. The second floor was originally divided into classrooms for science courses and a small library, but later the Sodality Chapel would be built there. The third floor was occupied as a dormitory by Jesuit brothers, and on the roof was a

Figure 3

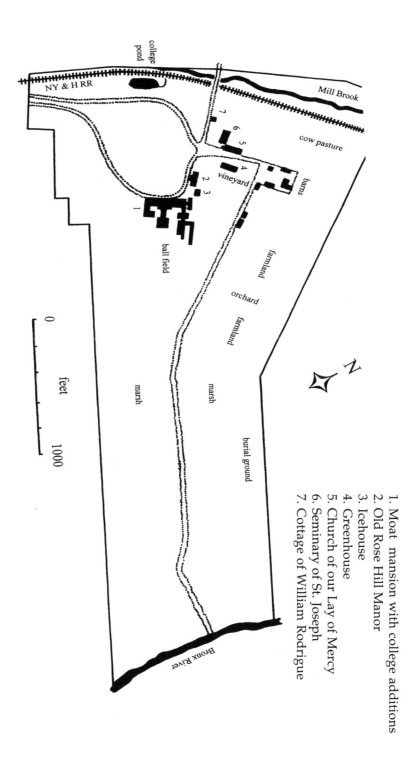

college pond

NY & H RR

Mill Brook

cow pasture

barns

vineyard

ball field

farmland

orchard

farmland

marsh

marsh

burial ground

Bronx River

0

feet

1000

N

1. Moat mansion with college additions
2. Old Rose Hill Manor
3. Icehouse
4. Greenhouse
5. Church of our Lay of Mercy
6. Seminary of St. Joseph
7. Cottage of William Rodrigue

white octagonal cupola used as an astronomical observatory.[9] Moat's original northern wing was used as the student refectory, while that on the south became a study hall, and then, in the 1850s, a student chapel. The one-story wings with their columns and triangular pediments were eventually replaced in 1869 by the present two-story brick wings.

Of the three wings built by the college to the east, only the southernmost can be clearly seen in Rodrigue's famous drawing. Attached to the end of Moat's southern wing, it was a one story brick building used for classrooms, and it terminated in a square three-story brick structure nicknamed "The Castle." Here, the first Jesuits set up a music room, a reading room, and an office for the first prefect. At various times, the Castle contained classrooms and offices, and it was the birthplace of the *Fordham Monthly*, the college newspaper and literary magazine established in 1882. The basement held a boiler.[10]

The wing on the opposite northern side of the mansion was a mixture of brick and wooden structures that ultimately assumed a two-pronged arrangement. The three-story square brick structure at its core was used after 1855 as the Third Division, so that the youngest boys could be segregated from the others. The first floor was their playroom, the second their classroom, and the third their dormitory. Connecting the Third Division to the refectory wing was a one-story wooden structure that served as a study hall for the day students (commuters). After 1846, Fr. Thébaud built a wood frame structure, just north of the refectory wing, to serve as a dispensary and pantry, and on its second floor a refectory for the fathers. In 1854, Fr. John Larkin added an ice house a few yards to the west, very close to the old Rose Hill Manor. During Fr. Thébaud's second term as college president (1860-63), another wood frame structure was erected with a hip roof and dormers for the young boys of the Third Division. A series of low sheds housing service functions, bakery, pie shop, wardrobe, and washrooms surrounded these buildings and extended eastward to the edge of the playing fields, which were located in the area now occupied by the greensward known as Edwards Parade.[11]

The central wing originally consisted of a low wooden shed connecting to a three-story brick building that housed the college students. Fr. Thébaud expanded the brick structure to serve both the First Division college students on the southern side and the Second Division secondary school students on the northern side (Figure 4). The building was divided internally by a broad center hall, to the rear of which, facing the playing fields to the east, were the separate wash rooms, one for each division. A pump stood adjacent to the fields a short distance away, and servants would bring pails of cold water each morning so that students could wash. Thébaud also replaced Bishop Hughes's low wooden shed with a substantial three-story brick structure, which contained on its first

Figure 4

floor a music room and wardrobe, on its second a student library, and on its third a library for the community.[12]

The oval drive was tree-lined. Fr. Thébaud had planted elms along its length, and extant photographs taken in the 1860s (see Figure 2) do show that some trees were young at the time.[13] Others, however, were tall and dignified, probable veterans of post-Revolutionary landscaping. One great willow that stood opposite Moat's stone mansion was a spot favored by the college fathers for shady repose on warm summer days.[14] From its vantage point, an admirable view could be had of the campus and much of the surrounding countryside.

To the left of the main building was the old Rose Hill Manor (Figure 5). A white, clap-boarded, wood frame farmhouse, it had been built most likely by a Dutchman, Reyer Michielsen, in 1694. No details of the original house are known, but comparative studies of 17th century Dutch farmhouses show that many were built as one large, multi-purpose room with a chimney and fireplace erected at one end but inside the wall.[15] Modifications over many years had, by 1846, given it the form of a squarish center hall of two stories with one and one-half story wings on the east and west.[16] From the very beginning of the college, the manor was used by some Sisters of Charity who handled domestic affairs, including laundry and care of the young and sick boys. With the arrival of the Jesuits, it became a novitiate, but the eastern wing continued to serve until 1891 as an infirmary.[17] The building was often referred to throughout the rest of the century as the Old Infirmary. In 1856, the manor was refurbished to accommodate the Jesuit theology stu-

Figure 5

dents who had been withdrawn from the seminary (see discussion below), and a cellar was dug beneath the center hall. Subsequently, it housed some of the Jesuit brothers. In the early 1890s, it held workmen's quarters, workshops, and a dairy.[18] Finally demolished in 1896, the manor has been the focus of archaeological excavations at Fordham University since 1985.

West of the manor and set back from the oval drive, was the Church of Our Lady of Mercy and, adjoining it, the Seminary of St. Joseph. Both of Rodrigue's buildings were brand new in 1846. The seminary cornerstone had been laid on April 3 of the previous year,[19] and construction had just been completed earlier in 1846.[20] To obtain stone for the facades, Rodrigue had opened a quarry on the property.[21] According to a sketch included within a book of hand-drawn plans of the early campus compiled by the Father Minister, Rev. Joseph Zwinge, S.J.,[22] the quarry was located somewhere in the vicinity of present Freeman Hall.[23]

In 1860, after Hughes removed the seminary, the Jesuits made the building headquarters for the Superior of the Mission and a retreat house. In the 1870s, Fr. Thomas Freeman, S.J., converted its rooms into science classes, and after major renovation in 1885 by Fr. Patrick Dealy, S.J., it became dormitory and classrooms for the Third Division.[24]

The church appears to have been built soon after the seminary building.[25] In Rodrigue's day, the church was small, just a nave with a pointed steeple. The interior was richly painted, and six stained glass windows had been installed, gifts to Bishop Hughes from the French King Louis Philippe. Fabricated in St. Omer during the early revival of stained glass art in France, the windows had proved unsuitable in their intended destination, old St. Patrick's Cathedral on Mott Street, and so were transferred to Rose Hill.[26] When the seminary left for Troy, the Jesuits took charge of the parish until Sunday, December 4, 1893, when, after the 9:00 Mass, the congregation moved to new quarters on Webster Avenue.[27] Only occasionally did the early students of St. John's College use the church, as the college chapel was located in the southern wing of Moat's mansion. The front lawn of the church, shaded by a stand of enormous elms planted by the Watts family, was the site of the College commencements in the 1850s.[28] By the late 19th century, photographs show that the steeple had been replaced by a stubby tower.[29]

Although it does not appear on his drawing, the small cottage of William Rodrigue stood near the western end of the drive, where it served as home for Hughes's sister and her family (Figure 6). Constructed of fieldstone in 1840, it originally had four rooms on each of its two floors, a hall, and a staircase.[30] Rodrigue held his appointment on the college faculty until the 1855-56 academic year, when his name disappears from the annual catalogue. His departure may have been spurred by the schism that occurred between the Archbishop and the Jesuits of St. John's at that time. Rodrigue may have stayed at

Figure 6

Rose Hill until the seminary was closed in 1859 and its land purchased by the college a year later. After 1860, when the Jesuits took over, the house became the residence of the parish priest. Later, it functioned as a classroom.[31]

Rodrigue may have omitted his own, seemingly insignificant, house from his drawing in Figure 1 and drastically shortened the slope to its west in order to fit in the New York and Harlem train, seen in the lower left corner steaming southbound from Williamsbridge along the corridor "donated" by Hughes. Just west of the rail line — well off the edge of Rodrigue's drawing — was the Mill Brook, a small south-flowing stream that presently runs through the sewers beneath Webster Avenue. The college pond was a small body of water at the foot of the lawn east of the tracks that flowed into the Mill Brook. From the brook's opposite bank rose a massive ridge, on the slope of which was the farm belonging to Jacob Berrian.

On the northern portion of the campus, beyond the buildings that circled the oval drive, was the major part of the Rose Hill farm. Here stood the barns and related outbuildings, including residences for the field laborers, carpentry shops, and storage sheds. The farm was maintained throughout the nineteenth century to help feed the students and faculty of the college, and only in the early years of the present century was agriculture abandoned.[32] A pasture with 30-40 cows was located on the tract presently occupied by the field of Fordham Prep. East of the barns, lay the plowed fields, and an orchard stood on the spot where today's Gymnasium now stands. Apples, pears, and cherries were grown. Just behind the Rose Hill Manor was a small truck garden for vegetables, such as tomatoes, potatoes, and corn. In the area of the present college cemetery was a vineyard that produced grapes for the table and for wine that was used in the church and the father's refectory. Two or three barrels could be counted on in a good year. The cornucopia that emerged from these fields and gardens underwrote the cost of running the college, and it allowed tuition to remain stable for decades. The whole endeavor was managed by Jesuit brothers, who cultivated the crops and supervised the workmen.[33]

Bordering the campus on the north was the farm belonging to Andrew Corsa, an illustrious figure in Westchester history, and one possessing an intimate association with Rose Hill. His family had owned the college property in the eighteenth century, and in his youth, the old Rose Hill Manor had been his home up until the close of the Revolution.

Leading eastward from the college barns was a small lane overhung with old trees. On the right, it passed a hedged garden, then the playing fields, and a little wooded hill where Keating Hall now stands. In the area of the present parking lots, the lane bisected a low-lying marsh, which was flooded before each winter and used for skating and ice production. Continuing eastward, the lane entered the woods that, in the 1880s, was incorporated into Bronx Park, eventually to become part of the New York Botanical Garden. The Jesuit cemetery lay to the left nestled between rocky outcrops and probably surrounded by a stone wall. It was used over the next four decades, and provided final repose for numerous Fordham notables, including Fathers August Thébaud, Thomas Legoüais, Edward Doucet, and Peter Tissot. Their repose there was not quite final, however, as the city takeover obliged the Jesuit community to move their remains onto the main campus. Fr. Zwinge supervised the exhumations and reburial in the present plot adjacent to the church in 1890.[34]

Beyond the old cemetery, the lane passed through a wooded area until it opened onto the eastern border of the Rose Hill estate, the Bronx River. Students used this stream as a swimming hole from April to October. The splashing and dunking could be heard just downriver from the well-known snuff mill of the Lorillard family.

III. HISTORY OF THE ROSE HILL FARM

The farm on which the St. John's College campus was built was one of the oldest in the Bronx. Earlier histories of Fordham University by Thomas Gaffney Taaffe,[35] Rev. Thomas J. Campbell, S.J.,[36] and Rev. Robert I. Gannon, S.J.,[37] include incomplete and erroneous details of its colonial foundations. Both Campbell's and Gannon's accounts are based on Taaffe, who was a young St. John's alumnus (Class of 1890) and former editor of the *Fordham Monthly* in his senior year. His narrative, written in a mere seven weeks for the fiftieth anniversary in 1891, was gathered mostly from internal sources by Fr. Zwinge, who served at the time as the College Librarian as well as Father Minister. In the early years of the present century, Rev. Patrick J. Cormican, S.J. compiled extensive amounts of information about the college from older Jesuits, providing additional details upon which this project depended.[38] The present authors have attempted to condense much of the previous narrative, revising inaccuracies based upon fresh research into the original deeds, wills, and other records, all conducted in connection with the archaeological investigation of the manor.[39]

COLONIAL BEGINNINGS, 1671-1783

The Rose Hill campus was originally part of the Manor of Fordham, a tract of about 3,900 acres extending from the Bronx River to the Harlem River in today's central Bronx.[40] The Manor was assembled by John Archer from smaller parcels of land during the 1660s. In 1671, Archer secured a patent from then Governor Francis Lovelace that established Fordham as the first manorial holding in provincial New York.[41] Later strapped for cash, Archer sold several farms from his Manor in 1678 with the approval of his mortgage holder, Cornelius Steenwyck. One of these farms was a 102-acre parcel on "the great plain by the Bronx River," which referred to the broad, flat terrain extending south from the New York Botanical Garden toward West Farms. This farm was purchased by Roger Barton, a resident of the neighboring Town of Westchester. Barton's deed made no mention of a house or improvements, in contrast to the one issued the same day to Thomas Statham for a nearby farm, which lay to the north on "the little plain by the Bronx River." Barton apparently built his home soon thereafter, for it is mentioned as "his now dwelling place on west bank of Brunxis River" in the Town of Westchester records in 1682.[42]

After Archer died in 1684, Fordham Manor passed to Steenwyck, his creditor. Upon Steenwyck's death shortly thereafter, the land became the property of his widow, Margareta, who deeded it as an endowment to the Reformed Dutch Church. A long legal battle then ensued between the Church and the Town of Westchester, which had laid claim to a portion of the Manor lands.[43] Barton took a prominent role in this conflict, advocating for the Town. When the Church finally triumphed in the case, Barton subdivided his property and, in 1694, sold the southern half to Reyer Michielsen, a Dutch farmer who had been a tenant elsewhere on the Manor.[44] Barton's house was probably located in the northern half, near the eastern end of Bedford Park Boulevard. He finally sold this half to William Davenport, Sr., in 1704/5, and left.[45] The southern half, occupied by the Michielsen family, eventually became the Rose Hill farm, and Michielsen was almost certainly the first to build a home on the property. He raised his family there, died there in 1733, and his mortal remains still lie there, interred near the university church.

On a map of Fordham Manor, surveyed in 1717 by Peter Berrian for the Dutch Church, Michielsen's farm is clearly marked as a 51 acre rectangle (Figure 7).[46] It ran from the area of Keating Hall (excluding the marshy ground beyond) westward across the Mill Brook and up the hill to the back yard line of present Marion Avenue. Berrian labeled the stream 'Reyer Michielsen's Brook'

Figure 7

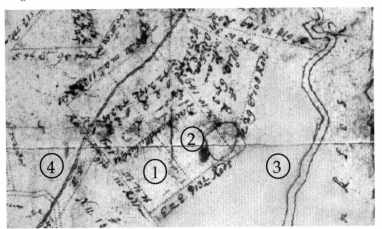

(1) Michielson Farm; (2) Davenport Farm; (3) Bronx River; (4) Reyer Michielson's Brook. From H. Melick's The Manor of Fordham.

on the map and indicated that access into the farm from the Kingsbridge-Westchester road was a narrow strip flanking the east bank of the brook.

It was in 1718 that Michielsen's daughter Jannetje married Benjamin Fletcher Corsa,[47] a young Dutchman who had been born in New York in 1692 and baptized at the Fort with Governor Fletcher as godfather. The couple may have lived at the Fordham farm, but their residence is not known with certainty. Reyer Michielsen's will of 1733 provided that his farm should be sold three years after his death and the proceeds divided among the heirs.[48] Corsa purchased the shares of his relatives and assumed control of the property in 1736. While he raised a family and farmed his land, Corsa rented additional parcels from the Dutch Church. In 1764, after the Church had decided to sell off the Manor lands and convert its holdings into a money endowment, Corsa bought a substantial amount of property, apparently extending from the marshy ground eastward to the Bronx River. To finance the purchase, he secured a loan of 155£ from Robert Watts, a young attorney and merchant in New York City.[49]

When Benjamin Corsa died in 1770, his son Isaac succeeded him.[50] In a few years, Isaac was caught up in the violence and uncertainty of the Revolution, America's first civil war. Particularly in New York, which was taken by the British early in the conflict and held until the end, the Revolution pitted family members against one another based upon their political leanings. Isaac Corsa opted for loyalty to the King, a safe gesture considering the proximity of British forces on the heights above his farm. His young son Andrew, however, sympathized with the American rebels.

War came to the Corsa farm in October of 1776, shortly after the British invasion and seizure of New York City. Washington's army was posted in lower Westchester County, and a detachment of the Continental Army occupied the flat by Corsa's orchard.[51] The General may have visited the troops camped among the trees, and perhaps it was this tenuous inference that led to the 19th century legend designating the old Rose Hill Manor as "Washington's Headquarters." After British advance drove the Americans north to White Plains, lower Westchester became the Neutral Zone within which raiders from both sides pillaged the farms and stole horses, cattle, and anything else that could be lifted for the war effort.[52] Isaac Corsa became a captain in the Loyalist militia units commanded by Major Bearmore and Colonel James Delancey. He was, on one occasion, captured by a French and American raiding party and detained as a prisoner for 15 months until an exchange was arranged.

Young Andrew Corsa worked for the other side, most notably as the youngest of the Westchester Guides. His moment of fame came on July 22, 1781, when Generals Washington and Rochambeau led a joint Grand Reconnaissance of the British defenses along the Harlem River. Andrew recalled in later years how aides had roused him from bed and summoned him to guide the rebel forces along the roads and ridges, chasing Loyalist militiamen and coming under fire from the forts. After the day's explorations, the generals and their army camped somewhere behind the Corsa farm.[53]

Figure 8

With American victory in 1783, the British commander of New York, Sir Guy Carleton, began the process of evacuation. Many loyalists had fled behind British lines, some to avoid prosecution for treason, others to join loyalist regiments. Col. James Delancey was attainted for treason by the New York Legislature and condemned to death.[54] Isaac Corsa was accosted and beaten by returning patriots and was eventually indicted.[55] He fled to Nova Scotia with Delancey and thousands of other American loyalists, while Andrew, seen here in his old age (Figure 8), was left in charge of the farm.[56]

Andrew did not retain his legacy for long. Robert Watts now pressed for collection of Benjamin Corsa's old debt, and sued.[57] The property was sold at auction and purchased by John Watts, Jr., a prominent young attorney, and Robert's brother . Corsa eventually married and took over an adjacent farm — essentially the same land that Roger Barton had sold to William Davenport — and he lived beside his old homestead until his death in 1852 at the age of 90.

THE EARLY AMERICAN COUNTRY ESTATE, 1783-1839

The Watts family had come originally from Scotland, and their ancestral home near Edinburgh had been called "Rose Hill." Several generations of Watts family members had given their country estates the same name in familial respect. John Watts, Sr., John's and Robert's father, had been a successful

New York merchant and member of the Governor's Council, who built his country home, also called Rose Hill, on Manhattan's east side, just north of the Stuyvesant estate. Forced to flee New York in 1775 as hostilities increased, he lived the rest of his life in England. His lands in America were confiscated.[58]

John, Jr., and Robert bought them back from the New York State Commissioners of Forfeiture after the war. Robert sold to John half of their father's property in Manhattan together with the old house, and John sold to Robert the Corsa farm, which he had purchased at auction.[59] Robert then enlarged the front lawn by purchasing part of the adjacent Union Hill farm and assumed residence, christening his new home "Rose Hill" in accordance with Watts family tradition.

Assuming ownership in 1787, Robert Watts managed his properties and farmed Rose Hill, dividing his time between Fordham and his city home on Pearl Street. His wife since 1775 was Lady Mary Alexander, daughter of the Revolutionary War General Lord Stirling.[60] During the war, Robert and Mary had lived in British-occupied New York City, but they moved finally in 1780 to Westchester where they rented first the estate of Mrs. Richard Montgomery, widow of the American General killed in the invasion of Canada, and then the Union Hill farm, prior to buying Rose Hill.[61]

Their son, Robert, Jr., and his wife Matilda Ridley, were installed next door at Union Hill in deference to his son's wishes to become a gentleman farmer, and the young couple renamed their farm 'Sherborne', a family name from Matilda's side. Robert, Sr., left Rose Hill to Robert, Jr., in his will of 1814,[62] and upon his death in that year, the young couple moved in with their first son, and rented out Sherborne. The earliest known rendering of Rose Hill

Figure 9

is a watercolor by that name painted by the Scottish artist Archibald Robertson in 1815.[63] In a detail from it (Figure 9), the house is seen from across the lawn; it is very likely the happy young couple depicted in front of their manor .

When Robert, Jr. decided to leave the neighborhood in 1823, he sold his Westchester properties to his brother-in-law, Henry Barclay, to repay outstanding debts.[64] Barclay had the Rose Hill estate surveyed and divided by a line that ran just to the east of the Mill Brook. The eastern part, consisting of 106 acres and the house, was sold to Warren Delancey in 1827. After disposing of Sherborne, Barclay returned the remaining western part of Rose Hill to Robert Watts, who in turn sold it to Jacob Berrian in 1828. This property extended from the Mill Brook up the hill to today's Marion Avenue.

The Rose Hill farm now became the object of active speculation, and over the next 12 years, it passed through eight successive owners — including Dr. Moat — before it was finally sold to John Hughes in 1839 as the site for his proposed Catholic college and seminary.[65]

EARLY ST. JOHN'S COLLEGE, 1839-1866

When Hughes acquired Rose Hill in 1839, aside from some undescribed farm buildings, the only structures were the old wooden Rose Hill Manor and the unfinished stone mansion built by Moat with its two single-story wings. The Bishop spent $30,000 for the property and immediately invested another $10,000 for improvements, including the Rodrigue cottage (1840), the seminary and church (1845-46), and the major wood and brick extensions to the rear of the mansion (1840-45). After Fr. Thébaud's alterations and additions, the resulting facilities remained nearly unchanged until the eastern wing of Dealy Hall was completed in 1867. The small cluster of buildings around an oval drive became the setting for the College of the first Jesuits, and the stage upon which their students performed.[66]

A college manuscript entitled "Rules and Customs Book for St. John's College, Fordham" provides details of the daily schedule. Though no date is given, a reference to 1865 in the text indicates that it must be coeval or later than that year. [70]

A.M.
5:30 Rise, wash
6:00 Daily prayers & Mass
6:30 Study hall
7:30 Breakfast
8:00 Class
10:00 Recreation
10:15 Study hall
P.M.
12:15 Dinner
12:45 Recreation
2:00 Study hall
3:00 Class
5:00 Recreation
5:30 Study hall
7:30 Supper
7:45 Recreation
8:15 Prayers & bed

The college of 1846 to 1866 was a secluded world tied together by rules, order, and custom. There were rules for everyone — the Jesuit Community, the students, and the workmen. Everything was regulated, from the order of the day to the annual cycle of religious and civic celebrations. There was a Rector for the Jesuit Community, and Prefects of Studies and Prefects of Discipline for the students. Occasionally, a free-spirited youth might rebel, and he would be disciplined or expelled, or he would persuade his parents to send him elsewhere for his education. Some alumni, writing for the *Fordham Monthly* years after graduating, recalled with great fondness their boyhood in the strict confines of a French boarding college. Above all, it was a world in which all efforts and achievements, however praiseworthy in themselves, were also done "A.M.D.G. — for the greater glory of God."[67]

St. John's was a small place. From 1846 to 1866, it averaged a total of about 200 students a year, and in the late 1850s, the rosters were more limited still.[68] Only 164 student attended the school in 1855. Most students were in the Third and Second Divisions — the elementary and high school levels, respectively. The First Division college level was generally the least populous. In 1858, there were 59 undergraduates and 100 pupils in the other divisions.[69]

Students from the three divisions lived quite separate lives, each division having its own prefects, dormitory, study halls, play rooms, and play grounds. Students were instructed not to speak with those of another division, and even brothers had to get special permission to converse with an older or younger sibling. Day students, or commuters, were also separated to some degree from the boarders. Under the supervision of their prefects, students marched quietly to prayers, study hall, and refectory. During most meals, they sat in assigned places on wooden benches and ate in silence, while an older student read excerpts from works of history or literature. Except when making excursions with their classes, or with rarely given individual permission, they were forbidden to leave the college or to go to New York City. On Thursday and Sunday afternoons, no classes were held, and the students could relax. These were the days for parental visits.[71] This routine extended throughout the academic year, which began on September 1 and lasted to the end of July.[72]

Sports gave the energetic young spirits of the students an outlet from all the restrictions. In the earlier years of the college, they played various ball games. After 1859, baseball came to be an essential element in college life.[73] The ball field had been created immediately to the east of the main college building by Hughes, who had cleared away a hill of stone, some of which had been used in the construction of the seminary and church.[74] In the summer, students would set out in groups of 15 with a Jesuit prefect to hike through the countryside, perhaps to swim in the Harlem River. More frequently, they went to the college swimming hole on the Bronx River. In winter, snowballing and ice skating were popular. The two marshy areas in the rear of the college were flooded, and the Third Division utilized the northern pond, while the First and Second took the one to the south. After the Civil War, military drill and other highly organized sports came to replace the less formal recreation of the early days.

St. John's students slept in large open dormitories under the watchful surveillance of their Jesuit prefects. The rule of silence was kept in the dormitories. No boy could disturb another or touch his bed. When a boy was ill, he was sent to the infirmary, which occupied the eastern side of the old Rose Hill Manor. Here, Jesuit brothers dispensed medication or hospitalized the boys for serious diseases.[75]

Studies were carefully organized in the basic scheme devised by Fr. Thébaud in 1846. He adapted the traditional Jesuit *Ratio Studiorum* to 19th century American conditions, modeling his system on that of Georgetown.[76] The course of study extended ideally over seven or eight years, starting at about age 10. It was heavily weighted with the classics, culminating in philosophy. Some history, modern languages, mathematics, and other subjects were also taught.

The Third Division was an elementary school that taught basic reading, writing, and arithmetic — to prepare pupils to study classics. After 1850, the Second Division comprised three years of grammar in ascending degrees of difficulty, Latin, Greek, French, and English. History and mathematics were also taught. First Division was divided into four year-long programs: Classics, Belles Lettres, Rhetoric, and Philosophy. Students came to read works of literature in their original languages while learning to analyze them critically. In Rhetoric, they were taught to express their thoughts effectively in writing and in speech, and the close study of philosophy would occupy their last year at college. On completion of the four years, they were awarded their A.B. A postgraduate course offered students another year of study in philosophy, after which they would be awarded a Master's degree.

Most classes were taught by a single teacher for all the liberal arts subjects. He came to know their individual strengths and weaknesses, and he could work to improve their learning on a more personal basis.[77] Such teachers had their students for an entire year, sometimes two. Frequent study halls, often lit by dim oil lamps, helped to support an intensive and competitive scholarly atmosphere. Fr. Thébaud, a Jesuit with wide experience in American and European educational institutions, considered the high standards of the Jesuit colleges to be superior to those of the more progressive American schools, such as Harvard.[78]

The Jesuit system, in place from 1846, lasted relatively unchanged until 1879, when the older generation of French-trained Jesuits began to yield to the influence of younger leaders under the aegis of the New York-Maryland Province.[79] Slowly, the Jesuits accepted more and more of the mainstream American educational practices. By 1907, the old continental "gymnasium" had been formally separated into a four year high school and a four year college.[80] Fordham became a modern urban university in that year, already dominated by day scholars. The little world of St. John's was submerged beneath the inexorable waves of change. It exists now only in the remnant papers saved from the trash and archived as historic manuscripts, catalogues, publications, and pictures, and it survives as the still unstudied remains that lie beneath the modern campus lawns awaiting the archaeologist.

IV. ARCHAEOLOGY AT ROSE HILL MANOR

When excavations began at the site of the old Rose Hill manor in September of 1985, little was known about the extent or degree of preservation of the remains. Expectation held that archaeology would likely yield some new information while providing a hands-on educational exercise for Fordham College students. Digging was anticipated to last no longer than a few seasons, giving those undergraduates who enrolled each year in the fieldwork course an introduction to archaeological fundamentals on the grounds of their own school. The project continued far longer than could have been imagined, however, and is still ongoing largely because the richness and detail of the buried ruins could be safely retrieved only at a slow and measured pace commensurate with the skills of a perennially inexperienced crew.[81]

With the encouragement of Fordham president Rev. Joseph A. O'Hare, S.J., and university support for a ground-penetrating radar survey of the site to help locate the building's outlines,[82] the project began its first field season in a manner that has been repeated over the last dozen years. Students registered for coursework or internships in excavation techniques have learned by "doing" and "observing" as well as the familiar pedagogical routines of "listening" and "reading" that characterize most other college courses. Unlike a science laboratory, however, field situations are unpredictable and study assignments designed to help interpret the finds inevitably plunge one into strange and arcane areas of knowledge. When laboriously researched term papers produce, as they so often do, very modest gains in understanding, students quickly come to appreciate the challenges involved in obtaining new historical information and the hard-won battles of scholarship that lie behind the battles described in history books.

Digging continues to be conducted during fall semesters and over summer recess. In the fall, when only a few hours per week can be claimed from students' hectic schedules for the tedious process of excavation, field sessions are tightly organized to minimize inefficiency and maximize worktime on the site. Summer provides greater opportunity for those with the freedom and desire to recover the bits and pieces of old Fordham. This research effort, pursued over the years by so many enthusiastic supporters, places Fordham among a limited number of universities that has engaged in the archaeology of itself. The project has been sponsored jointly by the university and the Bronx County Historical Society, but in addition, deeply heart-felt thanks are due to Fordham alumnus R.B. Marrin (FC '67, LAW '70) for a generous five-year grant that has made it possible to process the numerous finds, cover the costs of technical analysis, and continue to build and maintain an ever-growing framework of lumber and tarpaulins to protect the site from the elements.

After the manor's demolition in 1896, its foundations lay shallowly buried until construction began on Collins Auditorium in 1902. The basement of the new building destroyed much of the rear of the old manor, while the monumental stone steps leading up to the front door entombed the manor's western half, including much of its center hall (Figure 10). In the east, however, the manor suffered only a few disturbances by intrusive utility lines. Foundation walls of the center hall were submerged beneath a landscaped embankment,

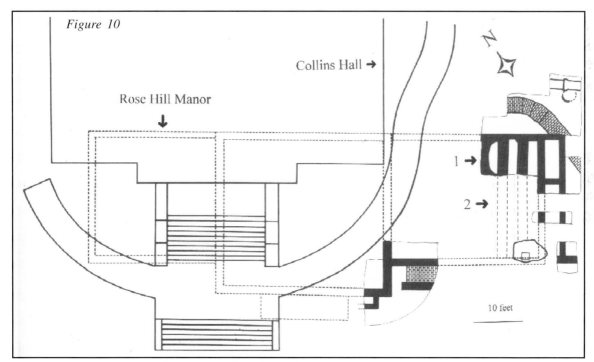

and beyond, remnants of the wing slumbered only 15 inches beneath the surface of the modern lawn. Matters of preservation and accessibility thus determined that digging would start in the east.

THE RENOVATIONS OF 1856

Among the events of major consequence for young St. John's College that also had an impact on the manor was the developing discord between

Archbishop Hughes and the Jesuits. Hughes had retained ownership of the Seminary of St. Joseph after deeding the college to the Jesuits on July 15, 1846, but he gave the new arrivals a large share in the seminary's care, including its administration and the provision of faculty to give instruction. Though Hughes still held a parcel of about eight acres, the boundary between the two institutions was merely recorded and not physically plotted. In actuality, it skirted closely around the seminary and church on the east and north. The Jesuits passed back and forth over the border each time they crossed a seminary threshold, holding managerial responsibility, if not proprietary status, on either side. In the summer of 1855, mounting disagreements led to the withdrawal of the Jesuits from further service at St. Joseph's. Later that fall, Hughes ordered a proper survey of his property, the results of which he disputed. To make matters worse, William Rodrigue had built his small cottage in 1840 on Hughes's side of the property line, oriented with its south-facing front door flush against the frontier. Whenever Mrs. Rodrigue stepped off her stoop, she trespassed on the grounds of the Jesuit school.[83]

It fell to Rev. Remigius Tellier, S.J., rector of St. John's at the time, to find accommodations for the Jesuit scholastics who left the seminary with the professors. Cormican wrote that "about 1856" the old Rose Hill manor was outfitted so that the refugees could take up residence in the house. He described these modifications simply as an "extension" onto the old infirmary and added that a cellar was excavated — presumably beneath the center hall — to serve as a theologate.[84] These vague remarks are perhaps corroborated by the terse records made in the college treasurer's ledger on several dates between February 6 and September 26, 1856.[85] No mention of the infirmary is made, but purchases of lumber for the collective sum of $199.48, roofing for $55.00, and possibly as many as 4,000 bricks for $14.63 suggest major expenditures for renovation of a wooden structure. In addition to the above, a few old images of the house gave some indication of the above-ground changes, while archaeology provided further insights into how the manor was prepared for its added functions.

By themselves, the old 19th century views of the house provided revealing information if only it could be connected with certainty to Fr Tellier's dormitory shortage. Rodrigue's drawing (Figure 1), the earliest representation of the manor after its incorporation into St. John's College, is in substantial agreement with the watercolor image of Robert Watts Jr.'s home (Figure 9). Both comprised a two story, side-gabled center hall with projecting eastern and western wings of one-and-a-half stories each.

Only three photographs of the manor taken later in the century, perhaps between 1880 and 1896, have been preserved in the university archives. These images (e.g., Figure 5) reveal, among other things, a single dormer window emerging from the front roof slope of both wings, illuminating the garrets and presumably rendering them habitable. If the extensive lumber purchases of 1856 reflect this construction episode, then the date of the dormers can be fixed at the time of the Jesuit departure from the seminary.

Excavations at the site of the manor have uncovered parts of the center hall and east wing foundations, and examination of these walls has revealed numerous modifications. One major remodeling campaign, which made extensive changes to the east wing, must have occurred very close in time to 1856 according to the archaeological evidence.

The end of the east wing was dismantled to replace an old cistern that lay below. This pre-existing water tank, probably inherited from the years of the Watts occupation, was constructed of fieldstone rubble with a thick plaster facing. (Figure 10:1) College workmen broke up the stone cistern, leaving only its western end intact, and then built over it a new, trough cistern of brick that ran across the entire width of the wing (Figure 10:2; Figure 11). When filled to capacity, the new brick cistern would have held about 1,000 gallons of water. Small brick pillars were spaced about four feet apart on the bottom of the trough. Such pillars probably supported outtake pipes intended to draw water up to manual pumps on the first floor. The pillars elevated the pipes above the sludge that invariably collected on the trough bottom so that a reasonably clear liquid would spew from the spigots above.

Figure 11

In a curious way, the trough cistern provided its own dating. Its bricks displayed brands, or letters in raised relief, that were impressed during the molding process. Three additional bricks, similarly branded, were mortared onto a cornerstone of the rebuilt foundation after the cistern installation was completed. Brick makers in the New York area began this practice of labeling their output around 1850 as competition in the urban building materials market grew. The cistern brand spelled out the name REID followed by a five-pointed star.

The brickyard of Mr. Reid was traced to the area of Haverstraw on the Hudson River by comparing the chemical composition of the cistern bricks to others from the metropolitan region.[86] According to the federal census of 1850, only one person named Reid lived in Rockland County at the time. He was a 24-year-old Irish immigrant named Patrick Reid, who was registered as a laborer on a brickyard in the town of Haverstraw. Reid's name is absent from Haverstraw in the state census of 1855 as well as later federal counts, and thus his residence and brick producing in Haverstraw must be at least as early as 1850 and no later than 1855. Some of his output, perhaps as many as 4,000 if the treasurer's records reflect this purchase, arrived at Rose Hill for use in the new cistern. The bricks themselves show no signs of reuse — such as breaks or old mortar — and therefore betray no prior service within a previous building. Allowing a limited delay for transport downriver to New York and distribution by middlemen, the bricks seem eminently well dated for purchase by St. John's College and incorporation into the massive manor renovation ordered by Fr. Tellier in 1856.

Nothing in the evidence from below ground confirms that the dormers were added to the wing garrets at the same time as the cistern upgrade, but it is a logical assumption given the other evidence. The provision of domicile space may have increased the demand for water beyond what could be provided by the old Watts cistern, especially considering that the same tank had to supply the college infirmary, which occupied the eastern half of the manor.[87]

OBJECTS OF DAILY LIFE AT ST. JOHN'S COLLEGE

Artifacts unearthed at the Rose Hill manor site are mostly fragmentary and minimally restorable. Shards of shattered window glass and lumps of mortar and stucco head the list of finds, with more limited quantities of other items, including ceramic, glassware, animal bone, clam and oyster shell. Many of the personal articles were likely lost, broken, or casually discarded since they emerge typically from buried layers that were at one time surface soils. Archaeological deposition is frequently haphazard, illuminating curious, and often unexpected, aspects of the past. Thus the recovered material does not reflect all aspects of life in and around the manor. Stratigraphic study and detailed artifact analysis will eventually permit more subtle distinctions to be made in dating, use, and significance of the objects from St. John's.

Construction of two new university dormitories, Alumni Court North and South, beginning in June, 1986, brought about the discovery of several trash dumps located in the northwestern corner of the campus, behind the church and seminary building. Archaeologists excavating at the manor that summer were able to shift their attention to the dump sites to remove objects from the bulldozer's path of destruction. In this way, a larger and more informative collection of college-related material was acquired than the manor site would have yielded by itself.

1. Dinnerware and Foodways

Most abundant among the finds in the trash dumps were broken but mendable plates, saucers, bowls, cups, and platters fashioned in the mid-19th century utilitarian earthenware known as white granite or ironstone. White opaque pottery was extremely popular in the U.S. and Canada from the 1840s to the end of the century, and English manufacturers virtually controlled the market with cheaper and better made wares until American firms began to compete effectively after 1870. All pieces bearing a maker's mark on their underside were produced by firms of the renowned Staffordshire pottery district of England, e.g., Davenport, T. & R. Boote, Elsmore & Forster, Thomas Goodfellow, and James Edwards. Most pieces revealed worn surfaces and chipped edges suggesting that old dishes were being scrapped at the end of their useful service in the college refectories.

Only one registry mark was preserved on the fragmentary base of an octagonal vessel (Figure 12). Between 1842 and 1883, these registry marks were stamped onto ceramics before glazing to signal the issue of a design patent that prohibited pattern infringement for three years. The diamond-shaped graphic reveals in its corner codes the initial production date for the design, which in this case was August 26, 1847.[88] Other dishes in the trash were likely produced throughout the following decades, but detailed analysis of the styles of the maker's marks may eventually provide greater chronological control.

Among the recovered ironstone vessels, shapes were mostly plain, the color uniformly white, and the character almost without exception thick and durable (Figure 13). Plates were 9 3/4 inches in diameter and possessed no molded borders. Soup plates were similar in size with shallow wells and wide surrounds, and 6 inch tea saucers curved slightly upward from their base. Only handleless cups were found. They predominated in the trade prior to 1870 because they could be made more easily and were less prone to damage during shipment.[89] Cup profiles varied greatly, suggesting that these items were commonly broken in daily use and replaced with whatever new forms could be found. One of the profiles was somewhat bell-shaped, while others showed different curvatures. In a photograph from the university archives taken of the students' dining hall decorated for Christmas dinner in 1921 (Figure 14), the festive table settings bear an uncanny resemblance in virtually every detail to the articles unearthed from the dumps, including the familiar bell-shaped cups. The archaeological pieces must predate the photograph by at least 34 years, but if they are indeed remnants of the earliest tablewares used by St. John's College, then the holiday remembrance documents a conservatism in culinary furnishings at least three-quarters of a century old.

Almost the entire pottery assemblage revealed patterns of stark austerity. Only several serving bowls deviated from the unadorned simplicity in their

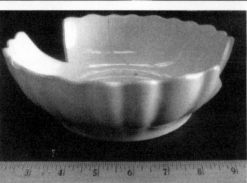

Top: Figures 14, 12
Middle: Figures 15, 16
Bottom: Figure 13

thick, vertical ribbing (or gadrooning) and scalloped rims (Figure 15). White pitchers were set at intervals on the long tables in the 1921 photograph; a poorly preserved example made of enameled metal was pulled from the trash. Also according to the photograph, cold beverages were served in clear glass tumblers. Fragments of paneled tumblers in the same material were the most frequently encountered drinking vessels within the manor site. Flatware finds were rare. One silver-plated copper spoon and a knife were among the few removed from the middens. In the college catalogue of 1854-55, each student

162

was instructed to bring with him one silver spoon, one silver fork, and one silver drinking cup marked with his name.[90]

Archaeological evidence of food consumption is limited to the most durable residues. The majority of the recovered bones reflect a dependence upon pork and beef, and both pigs and cattle were raised on the Rose Hill farm. A full study of the faunal remains is yet to be done. Pieces of clam and oyster shell are common throughout the layers of the manor site, and much evidence exists in the Father Minister's diary of the provisioning of oysters for the college. One entry page in the 1889-1900 volume outlines standard menus to be served to the Community, the boys, and the workmen. Oysters appear occasionally in ordinary meals for the boys, but for the workmen, an addendum stated, "N.B. Oysters never"![91] Other menu listings suggest that shellfish were part of celebratory meals, served together with various meats, including ham, mutton, chicken, squab, and tongue.[92] A number of white, cylindrical ceramic jars from the dumps might have contained jelly, mustard, or other condiments.

A number of beer, wine, and soda bottles were recovered from the trash dumps, and fragments of thick, dark bottle glass have been common in the sediments surrounding the manor. The wine, much of which was produced from the fruits of the Rose Hill vineyard, was most likely intended for the tables of the Jesuit community. Beer was often handed out at meals to the workmen, but occasionally it was served to the college seniors. The young boys drank the soda, which was mostly ginger ale and sarsaparilla (or "sass" as it was called). Soda was also sold at the Second Division pie shop. Bottles produced by two soda companies were recovered from the ground (Figure 16). A tall bottle of clear glass with rectangular panels contained sarsaparilla, which, according to its molded identification, was produced by Ayers of Lowell, Massachusetts. Other pieces of thick, light green glass came from cylindrical bottles with rounded ends that contained an early carbonated beverage — perhaps ginger ale — and bore the molded inscription "CANTRELL & COCHRANE / BELFAST & DUBLIN." Such containers were sealed with a cork, and their transport horizontally in cases kept the cork moist, thereby preventing its shrinkage and unwanted escape of the pressurized gas inside. Though the modern beverage company now known as C & C Cola, Inc., started business in 1865, the Rose Hill soda bottles are not necessarily among the earliest produced. Yet, they testify to the embryonic development of the American soft drink industry, whose colas today go to war for world domination.

Aspects of the mealtime routine were set down in a published account of 1895.[93] Though the dining facilities had by that time been moved to Dealy Hall, the anonymous narrator was an 1883 graduate reminiscing about the late 1870s when the refectory still occupied the new brick north wing of Moat's mansion. Just as it heralded other rites of the day, the college bell called students of all three divisions to breakfast, dinner, and supper together. Activities ceased at its peals. The long rectangular room with lofty ceiling into which everyone converged was lit by windows on the east, looking out on the Second Division ball field, and west, which offered a view across the front lawn. Student tables were long and narrow, with eight boys seated upon a portable bench on one side only, the spacing thereby insuring free and speedy movement of the waiters who served the "hungry horde." First Division students sat along the western windows, facing east, and their peculiar orientation likened them to "Mussulmen," as they bowed thrice daily toward Mecca. The central part of the room was taken up by the Second Division, which faced west, and the Third Division followed just behind with their backs to the eastern windows.

In 1845, college enrollment was 78, but it increased to 128 when the Jesuits arrived in 1846. From 1849 to 1862, enrollment averaged 188, with the number topping 200 three times during the interval. In 1863, 1865, and 1866 college enrollment was over 300, but it dropped in the succeeding decade, bottoming out at 166 in 1877, then rising to 200 by 1881.[94] Prior to 1869, as many as 40 and as few as 16 tables filled the refectory, furnishing the demographic needs of dining during the college's first 20 years.

Students attended mess under the watchful eye of the Prefect, who sat at a table bedecked in a white cloth at the north end of the room. On Sundays, holidays, and during schoolday supper, open conversation was permitted at meals, but at breakfast and dinner when classes were in session, dining took place in silence while an upperclassman engaged the assembled college with a reading from literature or history. The high reading desk was situated among the First Division tables, and the reader took pains beforehand to review his work and perfect his pronunciation in order to avoid the embarrassment of correction by the Prefect. Some of the readers, it was noted, had so mastered the art of reading aloud that ideas and style were freed from the distractions of word and speech, allowing full appreciation of the subtle beauty and intellectual depth of the text. It was also mentioned that a number of selections may have been aimed too high for the younger boys, whose minds were more likely riveted on baseball.

The *Rules and Customs Book* for the college provides additional information about mealtime manners.[95] There were 14 "Rules for the Refectory." Rule #1 was that each division must enter the refectory in absolute silence. Rules #2 and #3 ordered that each boy stand at his place and not touch anything until grace was said. Rule #5 demanded that no sound be made during eating that could distract from the reading, since every boy was "to listen so as to be able to give an account of what is read, if called upon." Rules #12, #13, and #14 governed the close of meals. When the bell signaled the end, students were to stop eating and remain silent. When the Prefect rose, all were to stand, face him, answer the prayer, make the sign of the cross, then turn to leave in single file with folded arms and without speaking until they had reached their destination.

Father Minister reported that tablecloths were red for breakfast, white for dinner and supper, but only white on feast days.[96] An added note mentioned that boys furnished their own napkins.

2. Aspects of Learning, Personal Care, and Amusements

Brief mention should be made of a number of finds, which bear upon the character of life at St. John's College. Few of these items has received more than preliminary study, so that detailed discussion and interpretive conclusions would be premature, however, both the manor and dump sites yielded items of interest that relate to school, health, grooming, and play.

A number of pencils have been retrieved including both the small extruded rods of metallic lead that were designed to write on slate (Figure 17) as well as the graphite strands encased in wood (now largely rotted away) and capped with a brass band, or ferrule, that held an eraser end. The patent for such eraser ends was obtained by the American Hyman Lipman in 1858. Some of the fragments of slate found in the manor ruins may be pieces of former writing slates.

Figure 17

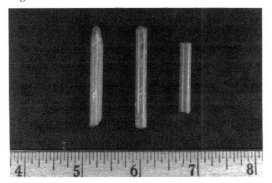

In England, goose quill pens were replaced after 1828 by the steel nib invented by John Mitchell, and two years later, James Perry created a larger, more efficient reservoir by punching a hole in the slit for greater ink retention. Excavations have recovered several nibs, quite plain without identifying markings, and bearing both straight slits as well as one with a reservoir. Ink bottles in various shapes were also removed from the dumps.

A fine foot-long measuring rule of 3/8 inch wide strip copper was found with two rivets allowing it to be folded down to one third its complete length.

Until the very end of the 19th century, the college infirmary was within the old Rose Hill manor. For this reason, it seems pertinent to mention one aspect of the medical evidence upon which archaeology has shed some light. Several glass bottles that contained patent medicines were retrieved from the trash dumps. The containers were molded with the name of the pharmaceutical manufacturer, and these entrepreneurs are well-known as a result of the avid interest of amateur bottle collectors. Among the medically-related bottles recovered were the following: Dr. McMunn's Elixir of Opium, Ely Bros. Cream

Balm, Dr. August Koenig's Hamburger Troepfen, and Dr. Kilmer's Swamp Root Remedy (Figure 18).

Other items included a squat jar of clear glass (Figure 18: center, front row) bearing the embossed identification "CHESEBROUGH MFG CO / VASELINE." Robert Chesebrough's petroleum jelly was marketed under this name from 1880.[97] Two ceramic lids from shaving cream containers were recovered, one from the dump, and another from a load of fill dumped into the manor site upon demolition. Both lids had underglaze inscriptions identifying the products as those of Xavier Bazin, a widely-known cosmetics merchant and importer of fancy goods in Philadelphia. Bazin opened his business in 1850 and quickly won recognition at the World's Fair of 1851 in London. One of his jar lids prominently advertised this accomplishment: "NINE HIGHEST PREMIUMS AWARDED." The other lid bore the modest declaration: "UNRIVALLED / PREMIUM / SHAVING CREAM / Gold & Silver Medals awarded / by the Institutes of New York / Philadelphia & Boston." Though Bazin's name was respected years after his passing, the finds must predate 1877, when he left business. Toothbrushes, several of which were found, were fashioned from bone at the time; the bristles, none of which remain, were natural (Figure 19). In very fragile condition, and mostly fragmentary are the several examples of fine-tooth combs, also made from bone.

Figure 18

Most of the games recalled by St. John's students in their later reminiscences were vigorous ones played on the fields. In the early years of the college, rounders and cricket were common. After 1859, it was baseball, then from the 1880s, football. Various forms of running games also existed, while seasonal exercise could be gotten at swimming in the Bronx River and skating on the winter ice over the marshes. A single skate blade of steel was recovered from the brick debris of the main building's middle wing when it was disturbed in 1997 during preparations for landscaped gardens.

Excavations have also uncovered evidence of quieter recreation in the form of marbles, dominoes, and a single die. The marbles were fashioned of marble, clay, and glass, while the dominoes and die were cut from pieces of animal bone (Figure 19). Perhaps, these pastimes were rainy day or after supper activities for the Third and Second Divisions. Also pictured in Figure 19 are several of the fairly abundant buttons, most made of bone and china, that may have popped off students' clothing while at play.

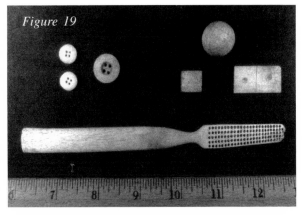

Figure 19

3. Religious Life

Students at St. John's College during its early years lived an academic life with a strong religious orientation, which aimed not merely to impart knowledge but also to build character and save souls. The strict schedule included mandatory prayer and attendance at Mass, and prefects kept close watch over spiritual as well as scholarly growth.

Attendance was required at morning prayers and mass — which was at 6:00 AM in the early years, 7:00 AM later on. Breakfast followed these devotions. Grace accompanied every meal, and evening prayers were said before retiring in the dormitories. Students went to confession once each month, and they were invited to receive communion. Further, the yearly cycle was punctuated by the major religious feasts, solemnly celebrated with High Masses, singing, and processions. An annual retreat was also provided for all students. In general, private devotions, prayer, reading of spiritual books, and counseling by spiritual advisors were encouraged.

Boys displaying high academic records and exemplary character were recommended for induction into the college sodalities,[98] the most prominent of which was older than the college. The Parthenian Sodality had been organized by the Jesuits at St. Mary's College in Kentucky on February 2, 1837, and it had moved with the fathers when they departed for St. John's.[99] The record books for the Sodality, preserved within the Fordham University archives, show the transition from Kentucky to New York without hiatus. The Parthenian Sodality was affiliated with the Prima Primaria, the original Jesuit student sodality in Rome. Its members met separately for Mass, communion, sermons, and prayers, and they were expected to lead a pious lifestyle as an example to their peers. The western side of the second story of Moat's mansion was renovated as a Sodality Chapel. The plaque listing the founding members presently rests in the university archives, but the stained glass windows installed in the western wall of the Chapel still illuminate the space where once the Sodality prayed.

In 1847, a discrete Sodality of the Holy Angels was established for the Second Division students, and a third, the Sodality of St. Stanislaus, was set up in 1856 for those of the Third Division.[100]

Devotion to the Blessed Virgin was a central part of sodality activities, including saying the rosary and the carrying of religious medals. The sodalities especially celebrated the major feasts associated with Mary: the Immaculate Conception, the Annunciation, the Purification, the Marian Month of May, and the Assumption.[101]

One other monument to the 19th century student sodality tradition post-dates the period considered here but deserves mention as it is still extant. A statue of the Blessed Virgin was dedicated on February 2, 1887, the fiftieth anniversary of the Parthenian Sodality.[102] Initially, it stood in the quadrangle formed by the southern and middle wings in the rear of the main building, but it now graces the front of the new Fordham Prep building.

In the earliest days of St. John's, a small student chapel was located on the first floor in the southern part of the mansion. A larger chapel was later built within the one-story southern wing. In 1869, when the wings were replaced, the chapel remained on the ground floor. Finally, in 1891, the chapel was moved to the north wing of the new Faculty Building — presently the western part of Dealy Hall — where the oversize windows may still be seen. The seminary church of Our Lady of Mercy was used principally as a local parish church, but it sometimes served for gatherings of the entire student body.

Given the dedication to religious practice at St. John's College, it is curious to note that few items recovered from the manor site and dumps have given any hint that the institution maintained so strong a spiritual orientation. Not surprisingly, articles of devotion are not normally discarded in the trash. Several finds, doubtless unintentionally lost, underscore the evidence of historical sources. Three religious medals have been recovered from various places within the site, and though they are still being cleaned and studied, brief mention may be made here.

One is a small copper miraculous medal. In general description, it appears to be one of the millions stamped out in response to the vision of the Virgin that appeared to Sister Catherine Labouré, during her novitiate at the Sisters of Charity motherhouse in Paris on November 27, 1830.[103] The Rose Hill medal bears the signature of the original engraver, Adrien Maximilien Vachette of Paris, so it is likely to be an early specimen. The obverse shows the Virgin standing in the center, Her hands lowered with palms facing out, and from Her fingers rays of light emanate downward. She stands upon a rounded eminence meant to represent the globe. Around the perimeter in two lines of upper case letters reads the inscription: "O MARIE CONCUE SANS PECHE PRIEZ POUR NOUS / QUI AVONS RECOURS A VOUS" (O Mary, conceived without sin, pray for us who have recourse to Thee). At the very bottom is a date, poorly preserved, but almost certainly "1830," the year of the vision. The reverse bears in the center the curious symbol of a cross surmounting a horizontal bar, which is interwoven between the legs of a large letter M. Below are two hearts, the one on the right with a thorny crown symbolizing Christ, the one on the left with an embedded sword symbolizing the Virgin. Around the perimeter are 12 five-pointed stars, and at the bottom is the name of the engraver.

From 1841 to 1846, the old Rose Hill manor was staffed by Sisters of Charity from Emmitsburg, Maryland, who managed the housekeeping, laundry, and care for the sick. As the order was first to receive miraculous medals from France (in 1835),[104] the sisters may have played a part in bringing them to Fordham. Research continues into the precise dating of the Rose Hill medal, as information bearing upon when it was made might suggest how it came to St. John's College.

Another medal is a small, round copper pendant with the side-view bust of Pope Pius IX on the obverse and another image of the Virgin on the reverse. Mary is posed in the manner of the miraculous medal on a background of what appear to be stylized fleurs-de-lis. Two inscriptions appear within a scroll-like border around the medal margins, reading on the obverse, "PIE IX PONT MAX," and on the reverse the familiar, "O MARIE CONCUE SANS PECHE PRIEZ POUR NOUS."

A still uncleaned medal appears to be for St. Philomena.

V. CONCLUSION

Excavations at the Rose Hill manor are still in progress, and upon completion of fieldwork, evaluation of the finds must follow before a full report can be written. The information offered here represents some of the gains in knowledge so far obtained through the analysis of historic records and the recovery of the tangible remnants of St. John's College interred within the ruins of the old manor. The house witnessed the passing of several eras, and in its final period of use, it served a small, isolated, and tightly-knit community of scholars and students, who were sheltered from the rigors of urban life but subject to the rigors of a highly disciplined pedagogy. The manor ceased to exist at the close of the last century, but younger generations of Fordham students, living and learning in one of America's great universities, are currently bringing its memory back to life through archaeology as the present century draws to a close.

NOTES

1 Anonymous [Rev. Michael Nash, S.J.], "Fordham College and the way from New York City to it in the year 1846," *The Fordham Monthly* (henceforth, FM) IX, no. 4 (January/February, 1891), pp. 70-71.

2 Robert Bolton, *History of Westchester County from Its First Settlement to the Present Time*, Vol. I, p. 330. (Alexander S. Gould, New York, 1848).

3 Charles L. Ballard, "Reflections on the New York and Harlem," *National Railway Bulletin* 56, no. 6 (1991):4-20.

4 Rev. Patrick J. Cormican, S.J., "A Sketch of St. John's College, Fordham, N. Y." Unpublished typescript, *Fordham University Archives* (henceforth FUA), 1904, p. 105.

5 McKeon's reproduction included a legend in the center foreground reading "College in 1846," and the principal buildings were identified by number. The date of this oft published rendering is uncertain, though it must be at least as early as its appearance in the college bulletin of 1876-77. Two additional engravings by McKeon were also published in the college catalogue. They portrayed the front and rear of the main building. The latter, showing the salient eastern wings, is reproduced here in Figure 4.

6 Dr. Moat's name shows substantial variations in spelling. His middle name is most variable, appearing as Shepard, Shepherd, and Shepheard, while Moatt and Moet are also attested.

7 Thomas Gaffney Taaffe, *A History of St. John's College, Fordham, N. Y.* (The Catholic Publication Society Co., New York, 1891), p. 28; Cormican, op. cit., pp. 103-105; Anonymous [Nash], op. cit., p. 71; see deed of Alexander Watson to Andrew Carrigan, July 18, 1839 (note 65).

8 Taaffe, op. cit., pp. 10-11; Cormican, op. cit., pp. 103-105; Arthur J. Scanlan, *St. Joseph's Seminary, Dunwoodie, New York, 1896-1921, With an Account of the Other Seminaries of New York* (United States Catholic Historical Society, New York, 1922), p. 19.

9 Taaffe, op. cit., pp. 8-9; John Homer French, *Historical and Statistical Gazetteer of the State of New York* (Heart of the Lakes Publishing, Interlaken, New York, 1980 [originally published 1860], p. 707.

10 Taaffe, op. cit., pp. 56-57; Cormican, op. cit., pp. 103-105; see also Thomas Gaffney Taaffe, "Some history and a few memories," FM XV, no. 4 (January, 1897):67.

11 Anonymous [Nash], op. cit., p. 72.

12 Taaffe, op. cit., pp. 8-9; Cormican, op. cit., p. 103.

13 Taaffe, op. cit., p. 7; Cormican, op. cit., p. 22.

14 William Seton, "Memories of an old boy," FM XIV, no. 2 (Nov., 1895), p. 19.

15 David S. Cohen, *The Dutch American Farm* (New York University Press, New York & London, 1992), pp. 49-50.

16 Cohen (ibid.) adds that 18th century renovations of earlier houses frequently subdivided the interior into the familiar English arrangement of central hallway with two rooms on either side.

17 Thomas Gaffney Taaffe, "The old manor house," FM XV, no. 1 (October, 1896):10-11.

18 Cormican, op. cit., pp. 102-103; Anonymous [Nash], op. cit., pp. 71-72; Anonymous [One of the Old Boys], "More about the good old days," FM XVIII, no. 3 (December, 1899):153.

19 Rev. Henry Gabriels, *Historical Sketch of St. Joseph's Provincial Seminary, Troy, N. Y.* (United States Catholic Historical Society, New York, 1905), p. 24; Rev. Thomas J. Shelley, *Dunwoodie: The History of St. Joseph's Seminary, Yonkers, New York* (Christian Classics, Westminster, Maryland 1993).

20 "New Roman Catholic College," *The Northern Standard* [Clarksville, Texas] January 21, 1846, p.1.

21 Taaffe, op. cit., p. 56; Rev. Thomas J. Campbell, S. J., "Fordham University," FM XXXIV, no. 9 (June, 1916):30-32.

22 Rev. Joseph Zwinge, S.J., "Maps of Property of St. John's College since the beginning by Father Minister," map labeled "Plan of College Before 1890." FUA, 1893-94.

23 The stone removed from this spot was a calcite marble schist, light in overall color with fine layering. It was offset by brownstone trim of a rich maroon hue that glittered from numerous micaceous inclusions. The building stones were probably quite impressive when fresh, but Rodrigue could not have foreseen the problems wrought by the passage of time. The brownstone trim eventually cracked and spalled to the point where their crumbled exterior edges had to be sealed beneath a coating of cement stained to imitate the original. Acid precipitation eroded the surface of the marble schist, and oxidation of the (unfortunately plentiful) iron sulfide minerals created a rusty cast. In recent years, weathering, especially on the buttresses, so weakened the fabric of the schist that load stresses created numerous vertical fissures which had to be stabilized during a major restoration in 1994-96: Pamela S. Jerome, Norman R. Weiss, Allan S. Gilbert, & John A. Scott, "Ethyl silicate as a treatment for marble: conservation of St. John's Hall, Fordham University," *Bulletin, Association for Preservation Technology* XXIX, no. 1 (1998):19-26. Campus buildings constructed after 1860 employed the sturdier Manhattan schist, which was removed from pits opened by Fr. Thébaud in the woods farther to the east on land now within the New York Botanical Garden. The Gate House was built near the train depot in 1862 to test this new black stone, and its success convinced the fathers to use the darker material in all building activity conducted until the end of the century.

24 Taaffe, op. cit., pp. 13-14; Cormican, op. cit., p. 105; Campbell, op. cit. (note 22), pp. 30-32.

25 *The Northern Standard*, op. cit.

26 Cormican, op. cit., p. 106; Robert Bolton, op. cit., p. 350.

27 Cormican, op. cit., p. 45; Rev. Robert I. Gannon, S.J., *Up to the Present: The Story of Fordham* (Doubleday & Co., Garden City, 1967), p. 113. The Archdiocese assigned a second priest, Fr. Rigney, in December 1892, a year before the parish moved.

28 Taaffe, op. cit., p. 13; Anonymous [Nash], op. cit., p. 71; Seton, op. cit., p. 20; Anonymous [One of the Old Boys], op. cit., p. 153.

29 Gannon, op. cit., p. 36; Photograph Collection, "Old Buildings," FUA.

30 "More improvements at Fordham," *Fordham Alumni Magazine* II, no. 1 (October, 1931), p. 1.

31 Cormican, op. cit., p. 106.

32 The newspaper reported the destruction of the horse barns by fire on March 2, 1912: "Fordham boys fight fire," *New York Times* (March 3, 1912) pt 2, p. 6, c. 4.

33 A late description of the farm by Harry Adams (Class of 1903) appears in "As Fordham village appeared to a small boy 50 years ago," *Fordham Alumni Magazine* VIII, no. 3 (April, 1941):2-3; Anonymous [Morituri te Salutant], "Souvenirs of Fordham, 1888," *Fordham Alumni Magazine* VII, no. 2 (June, 1939):6. Fr. Ministers' diaries in the university archives have occasional entries about the farm, e.g., April 14, 1890 and February, 1, 1894. In 1856, there were 20 priests, 16 scholastics, and 28 coadjutor Jesuit brothers: St. John's College, "Catalogus Primus Collegii Scti. Johannes, Neo-Eborac.," July 1, 1856. MS., FUA. Many of the brothers were farm or garden workers, or they maintained the physical facilities. In addition, numerous workmen had their houses near the barns. In 1899, they totaled 23, most with mechanical or agricultural jobs: St. John's College, "Father Minister's diary," volume for 1889-1900, "Christmas list, 1899." FUA.

34 St. John's College, "Father Minister's diary," volume for 1889-1900, entry for January 1890. FUA; Nicholas Falco, "The old cemetery in Fordham University," *Bronx County Historical Society Journal* 8, no. 1 (1971):20-25; Betsy Kearns & Cece Saunders, "The business of archaeology: cultural resource management in the Bronx," in *Archaeology in the Bronx*, edited by Allan S. Gilbert (The Bronx County Historical Society, Bronx, New York, in press).

35 Taaffe, op. cit., pp. 22-29.

36 Campbell, op. cit., pp. 10-11.

37 Gannon, op. cit., pp. 46-47.

38 Cormican, op. cit.

39 Valued assistance in matters of institutional research was provided by three generations of university archivists: Rev. Edward Dunn, S.J., Rev. Gerard Connolly, S.J., and Patrice Kane. A special debt is owed to Mr. Frank Licameli, who conducted extensive research in municipal, county, and state archives, church records, and other sources. Many of the historical documents bearing upon the early history of Fordham were found as a result of his extraordinary persistence and ingenuity.

40 Harry C. W. Melick, *The Manor of Fordham and Its Founder* (Fordham University Press, New York, 1950), pp. 46, 60, 70; Lloyd Ultan, *The Bronx in the Frontier Era: From the Beginning to 1696*. Written in collaboration with the Bronx County Historical Society (Kendall/Hunt, Dubuque, 1993), pp. 71 ff.; Jerrold Seymann, *Colonial Charters, Patents, and Grants to the Communities Comprising the City of New York* (Board of Statutory Consolidation of the City of New York, New York, 1939), pp. 425-431: Elias Doughty to John Archer, March 1, 1666 and September 10, 1667; Indian deed to John Archer, September 28, 1669; Royal Patent for Fordham, November 13, 1671.

41 Perhaps the most plausible of several explanations for the origin of the name Fordham comes from its use to describe the original settlement of Fordham Manor. It was located in the Bronx neighborhood of Kingsbridge, adjacent to the wading place across marshy ground for travelers leaving the northern tip of Manhattan for the mainland. "Ford-" referred to the crossing point, and "-ham" indicated a manor. Thus, the name signified "Manor by the Ford."

42 For the Barton and Statham deeds, see Melick, op. cit., pp. 92-93; John Archer to Roger Barton, November 20, 1678. Westchester County Clerk Deeds, Liber C, p. 68; Town of Westchester to Roger Barton, July 4, 1682. Westchester Town Records, Vol. 53, p. 105.

43 Ultan, op. cit., pp. 128-133, 137, 141, 150-154; Harry C. W. Melick, "The Fordham ryott of July 16, 1688," *New York Historical Society Quarterly* XXXVI (April, 1952):214-217.

44 Roger Barton & Bridget Barton to Reyer Michielsen, June 9, 1694. Westchester Town Records, Liber 56, p. 206; see also Melick, op. cit., 113, 118.

45 Roger Barton & Bridget Barton to William Davenport, Sr., February 26, 1704/5. Westchester County Clerk Deeds, Liber D, pp. 27-29.

46 "Map of the survey made by Peter Berrien, June 13, 1717." From the archives of the Collegiate Church of the City of New York; the map is reproduced in Melick, op. cit., opposite p. 120; in Campbell, op. cit., p. 33. The Corsa farm is also indicated on a later map: "A Map of the Country Adjacent to Kingsbridge, Surveyed by Order of His Excellency Sir Henry Clinton, K.B. Commander in Chief of His Majesty's Forces &c &c &c, 1781." Clinton Papers MS. map no. 152. William M. Clements Library, University of Michigan, Ann Arbor.

47 Benjamin Corsa of New York married Jannetje Reyers of the Manor of Fordham in the Dutch Reformed Church, April 17, 1718: *New York Genealogical and Biographical Record* XII (1884), p. 194; see the Corsa family genealogy in Alvah P. French, *History of Westchester County, New York*, Vol. V, pp. 90-95. Lewis Historical Publishing Co., New York, 1925.

48 Reyer Michielsen's will of July 7, 1733 is in William Smith Pelletreau, *Early Wills of Westchester County, New York, from 1664-1784* (F.P. Harper, New York, 1898), p. 67.

49 The Dutch Reformed Church to Benjamin Corsa, July 18, 1764, for the sum of 157 £ 7d 4 1/2p: *Ecclesiastical Records of the State of New York* VI (1905):3941. Corsa borrowed 155 £ . from Robert Watts of New York City on November 8, 1766: Robert Watts vs. Isaac Corson & al., June 4, 1786. MSS. Chancery Court Records, J0065-W62 (back of p. 62), New York State Archives, Albany.

50 Benjamin Corsa's will of October 1, 1770 is in Pelletreau, op. cit., p. 241.

51 Continental Army, "MS Orderly Book of the Continental Army," records for Kingsbridge, NY, August 22, 1776. Yale University Library, New Haven, Misc. MS. 40, GP no. 352, Series XIV, Box 68, Folder 1488, p. 10.

52 Continental Army, ibid., p. 53 for September 7, 1776. For a description of the events of the American Revolution in the area, see: Otto Hufeland, *Westchester County During the American Revolution, 1775-1783*, [White Plains, 1926], 2nd edition (Harbor Hill Books, Harrison, New York, 1974); Robert Bolton, *The History of the Several Towns, Manors, and Patents of the County of Westchester*, 2 Vols. (C. F. Roper, New York, 1881); Catherine S. Crary, "Guerilla activities of James Delancey's cowboys in Westchester County: conventional warfare or self-interested freebooting," in *The Loyalist Americans, A Focus on Greater New York*, edited by Robert Ernst & Jacob Judd, pp. 14-24 (Sleepy Hollow Restorations, Tarrytown, New York, 1975).

53 The remarkable oral interviews conducted by John McLean McDonald preserve the best descriptions of the local war in Westchester. See Andrew Corsa's four transcripted narratives in John McLean McDonald, "The McDonald Interviews." MSS., Thomas Paine-Huguenot Historical Society Library, New Rochelle, New York. For critical evaluation, see Stuart D. Golding, "The McDonald interviews," *History Today* XXIX (July, 1979):429-440.

54 Thomas Jones, *History of New York in the Revolutionary War*, 2 Vols. (New-York Historical Society, New York, 1879).

55 "Statement of Isaac Corsa," September 3, 1783, "Loyalist Transcripts—Royal Institution Transcripts," MSS., VI, no. 21, 1783, New York Public Library; "Indictment of Isaac Corsa," August 23, 1783, New York Court of Oyer and Terminer, MSS. Records of the Supreme Court of the State of New York, New York City Hall of Records.

56 Isaac Corsa of Annapolis, Nova Scotia, "New Claims at Halifax," Public Archives of Nova Scotia, Halifax, N.S., A/0 13, Halifax Loyalist Claims no. 162. For copies of Corsa's claim to the Crown for wartime losses (amounting to 2171 lbs.) in crops and livestock on his Westchester farm, see Westchester Historical Society, "Andrew Corsa," *Quarterly Bulletin of the Westchester County Historical Society* 8, no. 2 (April, 1932):55-58. Figure 8 is also taken from there.

57 Robert Watts vs. Isaac Corson, op. cit..

58 Harriet Mott Stryker-Rodda, *Watts, Ancestry and Descendants of Ridley Watts* (Polyanthos, New Orleans, 1975), pp. 22ff.; Clifton James Taylor, "John Watts in Colonial and Revolutionary New York." Unpublished Ph.D. dissertation, University of Tennessee, Knoxville, 1981; John Watts DePeyster, *Local Memorials Relating to the DePeyster and Watts, and Affiliated Families Connected with Red Hook Township, Dutchess Co., S. N. Y.* (C.H. Ludwig, New York, 1881), pp. 1-6, 19-32.

59 John Watts to Robert Watts, May 11, 1787, Westchester County Clerk Deeds, Liber W, p. 330; Robert Watts to John Watts, Jr., February 19/20, 1786, Watts Papers, MSS. New-York Historical Society. John Watts, Jr., had asked his father for the Rose Hill estate in New York, and his father had asked Robert to give it to him: Stryker-Rodda, op. cit., pp. 15-17.

60 Kenneth Scott, compiler, *Rivington's New York Newspaper: Excerpts from a Loyalist Press 1773-1783* (New-York Historical Society, New York, 1973), p. 103.

61 Stryker-Rodda, op. cit. , pp. 23-25; Jones, op. cit., Vol. II, p. 324; Alan Valentine, *Lord Stirling* (Oxford University Press, New York, 1969), pp. 235-236.

62 Will of Robert Watts, Sr., January 24, 1814. Westchester County Clerk Wills, Liber D, p. 156.

63 The "Rose Hill" watercolor is in the collection of Mr. & Mrs. Stuart P. Feld, New York, and presently in the Princeton Art Museum, Princeton University.

64 Robert Watts, Jr. to Henry Barclay, November 17, 1824. Westchester County Clerk Deeds, Liber 26, p. 306.

65 Transactions involving the Rose Hill property after Henry Barclay are recorded as follows (Westchester County Clerk Deeds):

September 1, 1826	Henry Barclay to James Ponsford (Sherborne/Union Hill) Liber 28, p. 80
May 1, 1826	Henry Barclay to Warren Delancey (Rose Hill) Liber 31, p. 344
April 27, 1827	Henry Barclay to Robert Watts, Jr. (west end of Rose Hill) Liber 32, p. 71
March 25, 1828	Robert Watts, Jr., to Jacob Berrian (west end of Rose Hill) Liber 32, p. 240

Successive owners of the 106-acre Rose Hill estate after Warren Delancey are as follows (Westchester County Clerk Deeds):

November 22, 1827	Warren Delancey to Samuel Fickett	Liber 29, p. 327
August 6, 1828	Samuel Fickett to Charles J. Hubbs	Liber 33, p. 157
December 29, 1829	Charles J. Hubbs to Henry Packard	Liber 39, p. 276
September 26, 1834	Henry Packard to Elias Brevoort	Liber 56, p. 189
April 1, 1836	Elias Brevoort to Horatio S. Moat	Liber 71, p. 102
May 11, 1838	Horatio S. Moat to Alexander Watson	Liber 81, p. 478
July 18, 1839	Alexander Watson to Andrew Carrigan	Liber 86, p. 115
July 23, 1839	Alexander Watson to Andrew Carrigan	Liber 86, p. 120
July 24, 1839	Horatio S. Moat to Andrew Carrigan	Liber 86, p. 124
August 29, 1839	Andrew Carrigan to John Hughes	Liber 92, p. 125
July 15, 1846	John Hughes to St. John's College	Liber 120, p. 489
December 1, 1854	John Hughes to the NY & Harlem RR Co.	Liber 334, p. 279
July 16, 1860	John Hughes to St. John's College	Liber 439, p. 347

66 A discussion of the social uses of space at St. John's College appears in Christa R. Klein, "The Jesuits and Catholic Boyhood in Nineteenth-Century New York City: A Study of St. John's College and the College of St. Francis Xavier, 1846-1912." Unpublished Ph.D. dissertation, University of Pennsylvania, Philadelphia, 1976, pp. 291-95.

67 For a discussion of the significance of rules and patterns of authority at Jesuit colleges, see Klein, ibid., pp. 81-103, and for details on student discipline, see pp. 286-87.

68 St. John's College, "Notanda Collegii, 1846-1904." MSS., FUA, p. 13. The 1850 U.S. Census for Westchester County, New York, and the college student record file of the university archives were analyzed by Gregory A. Katsas for the archaeology project: "The Early Character of St. John's College." MS., Fordham Archaeology Project, 1988. Katsas found the following distribution of student origins for 1850:

Number	Percent	Origin
89	46	New York State
8	4.5	New Jersey, Pennsylvania, New England
31	16	Born in Ireland
25	10	U.S. southern states

174

| 13 | 7 | Latin America |
| 20 | 10 | Caribbean |

69 French, op. cit., p. 707.

70 St. John's College, "Rules and Customs Book for St. John's College, Fordham, New York" [c. 1865 with addenda and sections crossed out]. MS., FUA.

71 Ibid.

72 Klein, op. cit., pp. 222, 227-29.

73 Taaffe, op. cit., p. 97, discusses the first intercollegiate baseball game: Fordham's "Rosehill's" vs. Xavier, November 3, 1859. Previously, cricket and rounders were played. See also William Seton's account prior to 1850: Seton, op. cit., pp. 19-20.

74 Taaffe, op. cit., p. 56.

75 St. John's College, "Rules and Customs Book," op. cit.

76 Rev. August J. Thébaud, S.J., *Forty Years in the United States of America* (The United States Catholic Historical Society, New York, 1904), pp. 349-53; Taaffe, op. cit., p. 73. Descriptions of the curriculum can be found in the annual college catalogues, 1847-1867, FUA. The description used here is from the 1865-66 catalogue.

77 Thébaud, op. cit.; Klein, op. cit., p. 143.

78 Thébaud, op. cit., pp. 340ff.

79 Klein, op. cit., p. 153.

80 Ibid. See *Catalogue of St. John's College* for the 1907-08 academic year for a clear separation of the college and high school.

81 The authors wish to thank Fordham University president Rev. Joseph A. O'Hare, S.J. for the opportunity to conduct the archaeological project, and the Bronx County Historical Society for its share in sponsoring the project over the years. Thanks are also due to Dr. Joseph R. Cammarosano, Dr. Brian J. Byrne, and their facilities personnel charged with maintaining the university grounds. Their cooperation in working with an active excavation has been most appreciated. During the past 12 years, nearly 150 students have worked at the site as a course of instruction, and dozens more have volunteered their time to the endeavor. The success of the project is due to the efforts of all these participants. For further description of results, see Allan S. Gilbert and Roger Wines, "Twelve years of excavations at Rose Hill manor, Fordham University," in *Archaeology in the Bronx*, edited by Allan S. Gilbert (The Bronx County Historical Society, Bronx, New York, in press).

82 The radar survey was performed by geophysicist Dr. Bruce V. Bevan of Geosight, Inc., Pitman, New Jersey (now relocated to Weems, Virginia).

83 Shelley, op. cit., pp. 22-25; Rev. Francis X. Curran, S.J., "Archbishop Hughes and the Jesuits, Fordham's prologue" [reprinted in this volume].

84 Cormican, op. cit., p. 102.

85 St. John's College, "Cash Book, February 6 to September 26, 1856." FUA.

86 Independent of the Rose Hill manor excavations, Fordham's archaeology program has become involved in the chemical sourcing of ceramic objects. This research is designed to ascertain the origin of clay items, such as bricks or pottery, by comparing their compositional profile to those obtained from other specimens of known provenience. Over several years, and with the initial assistance of a faculty research grant from Fordham University, a substantial archive of chemical data has been created, including the results of over 400 bricks representing manufacturers who supplied metropolitan New York builders during the 19th century. See Allan S. Gilbert, Richard B. Marrin, Jr., Roger A. Wines, & Garman Harbottle, "The New Netherland/New York brick archive at Fordham University," *The Bronx County Historical Society Journal* 29 (1992):51-67; and Allan S. Gilbert, Garman Harbottle, & Daniel deNoyelles, "A ceramic chemistry archive for New Netherland/New York," *Historical Archaeology* 27, no. 2 (1993):14-53.

87 Anonymous [Nash], op. cit., p. 70.

88 Jean Wetherbee, *White Ironstone: A Collector's Guide* (Antique Trader Books, Dubuque, Iowa), 1996, pp. 14-15; Geoffrey A. Godden, *Encyclopaedia of British Pottery and Porcelain Marks* (Barrie & Jenkins, London, 1991), pp. 526-528.

89 Wetherbee, op. cit., p. 25.

90 St. John's College, *Catalogue of St. John's College* for 1854-55. *FUA.*

91 St. John's College, "Father Minister's diary," volume for 1889-1900. *FUA.*

92 Ibid., entries for April 6, 1890, and April 23, 1891.

93 Anonymous [(Class of) '83], "The refectory," FM XIII, no. 6 (March, 1895):1-5.

94 Gannon, op. cit., p. 71.

95 St. John's College, "Rules and Customs Book," op. cit.

96 "Father Minister's diary," volume for 1889-1900, op. cit.

97 Richard E. Fike, *The Bottle Book; A Comprehensive Guide to Historic, Embossed Medicine Bottles* (Peregrine Smith Books, Salt Lake City, 1987), p. 56.

98 Cormican, op. cit., p. 87.

99 Taaffe, op. cit., p. 130.

100 Ibid., p. 132.

101 "The Parthenian Sodality Recordbook, 1837-1884." *FUA*; Taaffe, op. cit., pp. 65, 129-32; Klein, op. cit., pp. 230-34.

102 Taaffe, op. cit., p. 37.

103 Rev. Joseph I. Dirvin, C.M., *Saint Catherine Labouré, of the Miraculous Medal.* (Farrar, Straus and Cudahy, New York, 1958); R. Laurentin & Rev. P. Roche, C.M., *Catherine Labouré, et La Médaille Miraculeuse; documents authentiques, 1830-1876.* (Congrégation de la Mission, Filles de la Charité, Dessain et Tolra, Paris, 1976).

104 Communication from Sister Betty Ann McNeil, D.C., Mission Services, Emmitsburg, MD.

CHAPTER VII

ARCHBISHOP HUGHES
AND THE JESUITS:
AN ANATOMY OF THEIR QUARRELS

*By Francis X. Curran, S.J.**

In 1845, the Provice of France agreed to transfer its Kentucky mission to New York City. At the same time, it agreed to take control of (the then) St. John's College, the present Forham University. A formal agreement was drawn up, but serious differences developed over what such "control" meant both concerning St. John's and various parishes in New York City. This article deals with the ownership of Fordham University and the corresponding autonomy of the parishes.

On January 6, 1856, Fr. John Baptist Hus wrote to inform the Jesuit General, Peter Beckx, that he had arrived in New York City, and taken up his office as Regional Superior of the New York-Canada Mission.[1] Hus had been in New York before. When Clement Boulanger, his predecessor as Regional Superior, had come to the United States as Visitor to the North American missions of the Province of France in 1845, Hus had accompanied him as his socius. He had been present at the meetings during which Boulanger and John Hughes, then Bishop of New York, had negotiated the terms of the transfer of the Kentucky Mission of the Jesuits to the diocese of New York.[2] This time Hus had been summoned to his new post from the superiorship of the Jesuit mission of Cayenne in South America.[3]

When he arrived in New York, Hus found that the Jesuits were embroiled in a conflict with Archbishop Hughes. This dispute was to persist throughout Hus' period in office. The main sources of Jesuit discontent were mentioned in Hus' letter to the General. Apparently he had entered office with instructions to do what he could to remove these sources of irritation.[4]

---

* The original title of this paper in the *Woodstock Letters* was "Archbishop Hughes and the Jesuits: Prologue to Fordham." Three changes were made to the original article: the footnotes have been placed at the end of the article; the title "Superior General" of the mission has been replaced by the current usage, "Regional Superior;" and, in the main text, translations have been added to the foreign language quotations.

The first problem was embedded in the convention signed November 24, 1845, between Bishop Hughes and Boulanger. According to the ninth and final clause of that contract, it was agreed that if the Jesuits withdrew from the diocese they were to restore the title of St. John's College at Fordham to the Bishop of New York.[5] Over the course of the ensuing years, the Jesuits found this provision for reversion a cramping clause. While the clause was not mentioned in the deed of sale of St. John's College, and while the Jesuits were convinced that the proviso, absolutely without legal effect, also had no moral effect, they wanted the clause either revoked or given an interpretation by the Archbishop which would permit them freely to develop the college and, if advisable, sell or mortgage part of its lands.

The second point of contention was the ownership of the Church of St. Francis Xavier on 16th Street in New York City. Before construction of that church had begun in 1850, Archbishop Hughes had demanded and received its legal title from the Jesuits. The Fathers were dissatisfied by this development and continually sought to have the title restored to the Society of Jesus. The third major source of Jesuit discontent was their belief that the Archbishop had failed to implement the sixth clause of the contract of 1845.[6] The Archbishop had promised to give the Jesuits a church and residence in New York City. He had, according to the Jesuit viewpoint, never carried out his obligation.

PROPERTY AT FORDHAM

The incident which set off the long and bitter dispute was occasioned by the property at Fordham. When, in 1846, the Jesuits took over St. John's College, they also assumed the direction of the diocesan seminary of St. Joseph's. Both these institutions were located on the land Bishop Hughes had purchased in 1839 in the village of Fordham. By the deed of sale of St. John's College of July 15, 1846, between eight and nine acres of the original purchase were reserved as the property of the seminary: the boundaries of this seminary land were written into the deed. But the boundary lines were not marked.

In the summer of 1855, Archbishop Hughes removed the Jesuits from the seminary and substituted his own secular clergy. Shortly thereafter, the boundary between the seminary and college land was surveyed.[7] The results were a bit surprising. Indeed, the boundary line cut immediately in front of the house on the seminary grounds occupied by the Archbishop's sister and her Husband. If Mrs. Rodrigue stepped out on her front stoop, she trespassed on the property of St. John's College. According to the rector of St. John's College, the Archbishop heard the news with extreme bitterness and at once declared that the deed of 1846 was in error. The Jesuits had no desire to deprive Mrs. Rodrigue of her stoop. They decided to rectify the boundary lines.[8] The Regional Superior, Boulanger, called upon the Archbishop and informed him that the matter would be arranged to his complete satisfaction.[9]

But the Archbishop did not wait for the Jesuits to act. On November 14, 1855, the Board of Trustees of St. John's college convened for a regular meeting. When the college had been incorporated before the arrival of the Jesuits, its Board of Trustees was composed of five secular clerics and four laymen. It was planned that these trustees should gradually resign and be replaced by Jesuits. In 1855, four non-Jesuits still remained on the Board. They were Fr. William Starrs, vicar general of the Archdiocese, Mr. Thomas James Glover, the Archbishop's lawyer, Mr. Terence Donnelly and Mr. Peter Hargous, president of the Board.

At the meeting, Glover, declaring that he was acting at the request of the Archbishop, proposed the following resolution:

> That a committee be appointed with the power to appoint a surveyor in concert with the Most Rev. Archbishop to survey the property described in the deed from the Archbishop to St. John's College and to ascertain & agree upon the true description thereof according to the intentions of the parties and that the president and Secretary be authorized to affix the Corporate Seal to such document as shall be agreed upon between the Archbishop and said Committee.[10]

A committee was appointed, consisting of Fr. John Blettner and Messrs. Hargous and Donnelly.

The Jesuits were greatly disquieted by this demarche of the Archbishop. They believed that Hughes should have applied for a rectification of the boundary line not to the Board of Trustees, created and maintained to satisfy the laws of incorporation, but to the Society of Jesus, the real owner of the property. By this move, it would appear that the Archbishop was calling into question the Jesuit ownership of the College of St. John's.

A memorandum dated December 30, 1855 shows Jesuit thought at that time on the problem of their relations with the Archbishop.[11] It noted that the Archbishop had failed to implement the sixth clause of the convention of 1845. He had indeed offered a church, but never a house. And the church was so burdened with debts that it had been refused. This offer, in the opinion of the writer of the memorandum, could not be considered the offer of a gift. Instead of giving the Jesuits a church, the Archbishop had deprived them of the title of their own Church of St. Francis Xavier.

The memorandum recalled Bishop Hughes' pastoral letter of February 10, 1847. That letter stated that the Jesuits had received St. John's College as a gift and that they had assumed the debts of the college, which amounted to $40,000.

It went on to declare that, if the Jesuits did not carry out the terms of the gift, the property could be reclaimed by the Bishop of New York. The memorandum reflected the unceasing Jesuit uneasiness about that last statement. It maintained the constant Jesuit contention that the Society had not received the college as a gift, but had purchased it. And the writer declared:

> Now, to my knowledge, (and, I believe, I am well informed about the matter) no mention was ever made of accepting the debts of the College; we never accepted them nor were ever applied to by any creditors of the former owners. We simply consented to pay $40,000, and we paid of that sum 14,000d., to the Bishop himself, and to no one else.

First attempts at a settlement

In the Spring of 1856, Hus, about to leave to inspect the Jesuit houses in Canada, paid a call on Archbishop Hughes.[12] At the meeting, Archbishop Hughes advanced the idea that the difficulty at Fordham could be settled if the Jesuits purchased the seminary buildings. Tellier, the rector of St. John's, who reported this meeting declared that the Archbishop has shown at the meeting his obvious disgust with the Jesuits. He passed on to the Jesuit General Mr. Hargous' advice that the best thing for the Jesuits to do was to give the Archbishop a year's notice and clear out of the diocese. Tellier declared that the conflict in New York was due but to two causes; all the other reasons advanced to explain the trouble were simply pretexts. Archbishop Hughes badly needed more priests. While many vocations came from the Jesuit colleges, the Fathers would not, to the great displeasure of Hughes, turn their colleges into minor seminaries. And the Archbishop has "*un esprit extraordinaire de domination; il a besoin de dominer*" (his character is overbearing; he needs to dominate.)[13] He was enraged by the fact that the Jesuits had a majority on the St. John's Board of Trustees and could tHus curb his autocratic rule over that institution.

Soon after Hus had departed for Canada, Archbishop Hughes made a new demarche. His lawyer sent a letter to the rector of St. John's delineating the boundaries desired by the Archbishop and requesting the Jesuits' approval.[14] Tellier immediately informed the Regional Superior in Montreal. In response, Hus instructed Tellier to inform Glover that the Jesuits would willingly make a gift of the desired land to the Archbishop.[15] He further offered to give the prelate a strip of land, suitable for a road across the college property to the land of the seminary.

Before Hughes had transferred the Fordham property to the Jesuits, he had given to the New York and Harlem Rail Road a right of way along the western boundary of the property. This right of way, comprising about eight acres, had isolated a few strips of property to the west of the railroad; it had further cut off access to the seminary from the west. The seminary lands, in the northwestern comer of the original purchase, could then be approached only from the south, and that meant over the college lands. No easement permitting access to the seminary over the college property was written into the deed of sale of 1846; but the practice was allowed to the seminarians and their professors. Several years after the Jesuits took possession of St. John's, the Archbishop had made the chapel of St. Joseph's Seminary a parish church. Consequently, the college lands were now used, not by a handful of seminarians, but by hundreds of parishioners. To get rid of this annoyance, Hus offered to the Archbishop a strip of land twenty-five feet broad immediately to the east of the railroad. He asked, in exchange, that the prelate pay half the cost of a fence to separate the college lands from the proposed road.

But when Tellier received these instructions, he hesitated to pass them on. Instead, he called together his consultors and discussed the letter with them.[16] They agreed that to offer the Archbishop as a gift what he demanded as his right would only anger Hughes the more. But if the Archbishop could be inflexible, so could the Regional Superior. He instructed Tellier to reassemble the consultors, read them the rebuke in his new letter, and then carry out the instructions in his first letter.[17] Soon after, Tellier reported to Hus that his directions were fulfilled.[18]

There the matter hung in abeyance for several months. As the regular meeting of the St. John's Board of Trustees approached, Hus drew up his instructions to the Jesuit members of the Board.[19] The Fathers were not to consent to a new deed of sale to replace the deed of July 15, 1846. Instead, they were to propose that a codicil be added to the original deed, and that the codicil should state that the Archbishop had requested more land and that the Jesuits had consented. If the Archbishop objected to receiving the land as a gift, the Fathers were to propose that an exchange be made. Part of the college lands was used as a farm, connected with the college buildings by a road that ran over the southeast comer of the seminary property. The Jesuit trustees were to propose that the land occupied by this road be exchanged for the land the Archbishop wished to add to the southern boundary of the seminary lands. And the Jesuit trustees were to raise another point. According to the deed of sale of 1846, the Archbishop had transferred to the Jesuits the lands lying west of the railroad. The Archbishop claimed these strips of land. The trustees were to advance the Jesuit claims.

The Board of Trustees met on September 11, 1856. The minutes inform us:

> On motion of Thos. J. Glover, the committee appointed in the last meeting were called upon to give their report. But the committee

from various circumstances, not being prepared to give a report, and not being in number for further action, two new members were proposed, Wm. S. Murphy, as trustee and as member of the committee, in lieu of John Blettner, resigned; and Terence Donnelly as member of the committee in lieu of Thos. Legoüais, absent.[20]

The effort of the Archbishop to attain his ends through the Board of Trustees had met a setback. Glover tried to retrieve the situation by a motion that the Board should reconvene within a month. The motion was seconded by Fr. William Gockeln and passed unanimously.[21]

But according to the minute-book of the Board, that meeting was not held. The Board did not meet again until November 7, 1857 when "it was decided by majority of votes that the Committee, who have not yet (been) enabled to report on the matter of the Survey, be declared a standing committee."[22] Glover was conspicuous at this meeting by his absence. He never again appeared, though duly notified each year, at the meetings of the Board. Finally, in 1863, his seat was declared vacant and a successor elected.[23]

DISPLEASURE

The Archbishop was not pleased at this repulse. He angrily told one of the Fordham Fathers that the Jesuits were trying to cut off his access to his own seminary, and that he was not going to stand for it; if he had to take the Jesuits into every court in the United States.[24]

Towards the end of 1856, Hus called together his consultors to review the situation and to see what could be done to put an end to the dispute.[25] The Fathers consulted were not inconsiderable men: Remigius Tellier, William Stack Murphy, John Larkin and Isidore Daubresse. They agreed that an approach to the Archbishop should be made by the Regional Superior. The approach should not be made by letter; past experience had taught them that a letter would probably only anger the Archbishop the more, and would remain unanswered. In a personal interview, the superior should bring up the question of the sixth article of the convention of 1845, and note that the Jesuits, through the failure to implement this article, had lost an income that over a decade would have mounted to an appreciable sum. If the Archbishop expressed himself as not bound by the sixth article, he should be asked to agree with the Jesuit contention that they were not bound by the ninth clause.[26]

But if the interview was ever had, it was without success. In the early Spring of 1857, Hus reported to the Jesuit General that the fathers in New York were under heavy pressure.[27] The Jesuit offer to the Archbishop to make him a present of the land he desired or to exchange it for a portion of the seminary land had been met by an angry rejection. *"C'est un caractère inabordable!*

Il faut que tous plie sous ses voluntés suprêmes" (It's impossible to argue with him. All must bend under his unflinching will). So desperate did the situation appear that Hus thought it necessary to prepare a statement of the case and send it on to the general, so that it might be presented, if necessity demanded, to the Roman Congregation of the Propaganda, or to the Pope himself.[28]

Since Hus informed the general that the statement had the approval of his consultors, it may be accepted as an official Jesuit view of the controversy. The document declares that Bishop Hughes had purchased the land at Fordham in 1839 for $29,000, and had spent another $10,000 in preparing the buildings there for use as a college. Of the 106 acres, Hughes had disposed of eight, worth $5,000, to the railroad, and had reserved another nine, worth $6,000, for his seminary. The Jesuits had paid him $40,000 for what had cost him $28,000 — and Archbishop Hughes had retained the free disposal of the money be had collected for the college.

Jesuit assumption of the burden of the college had brought the prelate a number of advantages, which the document lists.

1. Archbishop Hughes has the title of the founder of the College of St. John's.

2. He has full and free use of the money given for the purpose of assisting the college.

3. He has made a net profit of $12,000.

4. He has an annual income of $2,000—the 5% interest on the mortgage of $40,000 assumed by the Jesuits to pay for the college.

5. He has acquired the benefits of a Catholic college, and none of the worries.

6. He is freed of the tasks of administering the college and recruiting a faculty.

7. He has obtained a substantial number of Jesuit priests to assist in the works of his diocese.

8. The secular priests who constituted the college faculty have been released for service in the diocese.

9. He had secured a trained faculty for his seminary.

10. Other bishops would gladly underwrite the expenses of establishing a Jesuit college in their dioceses. Archbishop Hughes secured the services of the Jesuits without cost to himself, — indeed, at a large profit.

11. And the Archbishop has all these advantages guaranteed, or he recovers full possession of his college, developed and enriched.

The statement then looked on the other side of the coin. It found that the Society of Jesus had not profited from the removal of its Kentucky Mission to New York.

1. The Jesuits had, in the service of the archdiocese of New York, used up the financial resources they had brought to New York.

2. They had not been able, during their eleven years in New York, substantially to reduce their debts.

3. They found their work at St. John's College crippled by the cramping clause.

The statement noted that Archbishop Hughes had not carried out his obligation to make the Jesuits a gift of a church and residence in New York City. On the contrary, when the Fathers were planning their church on 16th Street, the Archbishop, as a sine qua non for his permission to take up a collection in the diocese, had demanded the title to the church and the land on which it stood. The Jesuits felt constrained to agree. Consequently, the Archbishop now had title to a church worth over $60,000, which had cost him only a permission to take up a collection.

In the Spring of 1857, the Archbishop made another move. In reporting the action to the general, Hus noted that these demarches occurred only when the Regional Superior was out of New York City.[29] It had happened under Boulanger. Now, when Hus was in Canada on his regular visitation of the Jesuit houses there, Hughes had sent Glover, his lawyer, to the Rector of Fordham with a new deed, *"avec sommation de l'accepter tel quel"* (with a demand to accept it just as it is.) By letter, Hus had instructed Tellier to reply that he could do nothing in the absence of the Jesuit Regional Superior. On Hus' return to New York, he arranged a meeting with Glover on neutral ground. After keeping Hus waiting an hour, Glover finally appeared, only to put forth the Archbishop's demands *"en termes d'un absolutisme ridicule"* (in terms that were ridiculously absolute.) To Hus' representations, Glover answered with disdainful expressions; a dozen times he declared that the Jesuit knew nothing about the management of affairs and that he did not want to discuss the matter with him. Finally, Hus proposed that the Jesuits delegate their lawyer to negotiate with him. Glover agreed *"d'un air triomphant"* (triumphantly.)

The Jesuits' lawyer was Charles O'Conor, one of the outstanding members of the American bar. He made a careful examination of all the documents and had several conferences with the Archbishop's lawyer. At a conference with O'Conor and Glover, Hus asked O'Conor, who was a personal friend of the Archbishop, to seek means of conciliation and to make suggestions to end the strife. Hus proposed that, if the Archbishop agreed, both parties would accept O'Conor's proposals. Glover expressed the opinion that Archbishop Hughes would accept O'Conor's arbitration.

O'Conor thereupon drew up a statement of the case and appended his suggestions for an amicable and just solution.[30] He found that in the deed of sale of July 15, 1846, the Archbishop had reserved, from his original purchase of 106 acres, only the eight or nine acres for the seminary. No mention had been made of the grant of eight acres to the railroad, nor had the bishop reserved, as he claimed, the strips of land west of the railroad, nor had a right of way over the college lands to the seminary been stipulated. Now it was claimed that there were several errors in the deed, due either to the surveyor or the scribe. The southern boundary of the seminary land should have been drawn forty links (twenty-five feet) further south; the land west of the railroad and a right of way over the college lands should have been reserved.

O'Conor's opinion was that, if the matter were taken to the civil courts, the decision would give the Archbishop the additional forty links and the right of way, but would confirm the Jesuits' title to the land west of the railroad. O'Conor proposed that, since a public road had recently been constructed west of the railroad, an access to the seminary over the railroad be constructed, and the Archbishop surrender the claim to a right of way over the college lands. He further proposed that the Jesuits deed over to the prelate the additional forty links south of the seminary and the lands of the railroad, while they received from the Archbishop that portion of the seminary land occupied by their farm road.

TWO RESERVATIONS

Hus, once more in Canada, expressed his willingness to accept O'Conor's solution.[31] He made but two reservations: he would prefer to have the changes effected, not by a new deed, but by a codicil to the original deed; and he would like something done about the fancy-fence which the railroad, in exchange for its right of way, had agreed to build, but had failed to do so.

O'Conor had not sent a copy of his proposals to the Archbishop or his lawyer. As he informed Tellier, he had not been established as umpire, nor was he Hughes' legal adviser.[32] He had received a request from Glover for a copy of his statement, and he wanted Tellier's instructions in the matter. The rector of St. John's told O'Conor he might send a copy to the Archbishop's lawyer, with the notation that, since the prelate had not agreed to be bound by O'Conor's decision, neither were the Jesuits.[33] O'Conor sent the desired copy to Glover.

The upshot was an uproar. Archbishop Hughes sent a letter to Tellier stating:

> I have understood that the Jesuits in my diocese have been making appeals to some of our lay-Catholics in the way of seeking redress or securing sympathy on account of real or imaginary grievances which your Society have had to suffer at my hands. This appeal to the laity is a new feature in our ecclesiastical discipline."[34]

The letter went on to charge that the Jesuits "have selected umpires without my knowledge or consent," and that these umpires have not heard the prelate's side of the case but only "your very absurd and unfounded charges." As a consequence, the lay Catholics must now consider their Archbishop "as a prelate deficient in honor, in veracity, in honesty and in candor." The letter ended with a demand that the Jesuits submit a list of their charges to the Archbishop that he might know of what be was accused and be able to defend himself.

The rector of Xavier also received a letter, requiring him, if the practice were not being followed, to keep separate accounts of all the income and expenditures of the parish church on 16th Street.[35] The Archbishop also demanded a written account of all monies received and disbursed since the date when the church was first planned.

Tellier acknowledged receipt of the Archbishop's letter, and informed him that it had been forwarded to the Regional Superior.[36] The rector of St. John's expressed his grief at the accusations of the Archbishop and declared that he did not know of any basis for the charges. If laymen had been introduced into the dispute, they were first introduced by the Archbishop himself, through the proposal made to the Board of Trustees in November, 1855. When the committee demanded by the Archbishop had been selected by the Board, Glover refused to serve on it, alleging that he was Hughes' legal adviser:

> That a Trustee of our Board could be at the same time the counsel that might be called upon to uphold interests at variance with our claims appeared again very strange to Father Hus and to us all. . . It is then, and then only, that for the first time we applied to another counsel than to Mr. Glover.

NO FREEDOM TO LIE

While this matter was still hanging fire, a delegation of Jesuits from Fordham waited on Hughes to extend the customary annual invitation to preside at the commencement of St. John's College. Judging by the report of a member of the delegation, the interview was stormy.[37] The Archbishop declared that he would accept no more Jesuit invitations. "How *dare* you," he continued, "assert that I had sold the land to the railroad, and pocketed the money?" He castigated the impudence of Hus "to tell me in my own house that he could cut off all access to my seminary." He said that the Jesuits' freedom of speech did not extend to freedom to lie. He demanded that the Jesuits call together their Board of Trustees, "If I do not succeed [in] convincing you of the injury you have done me, all the world shall know it. You have done your best to *degrade* me."

A few days after this meeting, the Archbishop once more demanded that the Jesuits send him a list of their accusations against him, and summon their Trustees to a meeting at which the Jesuits' lawyer was to be present.[38] "Things cannot remain long in their present position, and the sooner I know the worst that has been said of me by the Jesuits in regard to the relation between them and me the better." Tellier's answer opened with a declaration of sorrow that the Archbishop had been put to the trouble of a second communication.[39] He informed the prelate that Fr. Hus was still absent, but would take care of the matter on his return in the near future. The letter ended with a repetition of the invitation to preside at the college commencement.

But the Archbishop was not willing to wait. He demanded that Hargous, the lay president of the Board of Trustees, call an immediate meeting, and request Charles O'Conor to be present.[40] Undoubtedly, Hargous felt compelled to comply with the Archbishop's demand, and the trustees were notified by letter — at least, some of them. The rector of St. John's was surprised that of the three Jesuit trustees at the college, only William Murphy received a notification; neither he nor William Gockeln received summonses to the meeting. From the silence of the minute book of the Board of Trustees, it appears that this meeting was not held.[41] Again frustrated in his attempt to obtain his desires through the Board of Trustees, the Archbishop again tried a step that had previously failed. Once more, through his lawyer, he sent to the Jesuits a new deed of transfer of St. John's to replace the original deed of 1846.[42]

A day or two after this last move of the Archbishop, the Regional Superior returned to New York. Immediately he assembled his consultors to consider the situation.[43] Since the Archbishop's demand for a list of the complaints against him could no longer be ignored in the face of his repeated demands, it was decided to send him such a list. Several drafts were made before agreement among the consultors was reached.[44] Nor was unanimity reached. Legoüais refused to approve the draft which was sent to the Archbishop; he agreed with every statement of fact, but insisted that words used were too strong.[45]

HUS SUMS UP HIS CASE

On August 17, 1857, the Regional Superior sent a letter to the Archbishop embodying the Jesuits' complaints.[46] Hus denied that the Jesuits had introduced innovations into ecclesiastical discipline, and noted that they had consulted a lawyer, professionally bound to secrecy, only after the Archbishop had given them the example. He then listed the complaints:

1. Without any forewarning, the Archbishop had had introduced at a meeting of the St. John's Board of Trustees a motion to deprive the true owners of the land of some of their property, a motion that the Board was incompetent, in point of honor or of conscience, to act upon.

2. Ten years after the Archbishop had sold St. John's College on his own terms, he now wanted to nullify his own deed of sale.

3. The Archbishop now advances, as his rights, intentions he kept secret when he sold the college to the Jesuits.

4. The Archbishop wants arbitrarily to deprive the Society of its own property.

5. When St. John's was sold at its full price, it was with the understanding that the Archbishop would see to it that the railroad would fulfill its obligation to construct a fancy-fence between its right way and the college property. This obligation has not been carried out.

6. The Jesuits purchased the land free of servitudes. It was understood that the seminarians would have right of passage over college lands. Since then, the college chapel has been made a parish church, and hundreds of people trespass on the college lands.

7. The Jesuits have been unable to get possession of the strips of land they own west of the railroad. The Jesuits protest again the bishop's pastoral letter of February 10, 1847, in which their title of ownership of the college is called into question.

8. The Archbishop has never fulfilled his solemn promise to give the Society the gift of a church and a house in New York City. To serve the prelate and his people, the Jesuits moved here at their own expense. At their own expense, they have trained their men and paid their way from Europe. The Jesuits have carried out the part of the convention of November 24, 1845; the Archbishop has not. To serve the Church of New York, the Jesuits have spent more than $60,000. Though these disbursements were made to serve the Archdiocese of New York, the Archbishop has not borne any of the financial burden.

9. Against all law and equity, the Archbishop exacted from the Jesuits title to possession of the Church of St. Francis Xavier which had been built at Jesuit expense

10 The Archbishop has restricted the spiritual ministry of the Society by ordering the fathers not to hear the confessions of men save in the regular confessionals in their church, which are always besieged by women.

11. Finally the Archbishop has ordered the Jesuits to convoke their Board of Trustees and have their lawyer present. Nor has he given any reason for this unusual proceeding.[47] Apparently the Jesuits were justified in their belief that it was useless to write letters to the Archbishop. Though be must have received it a day or so after it was dispatched on August 17, the Jesuits had received no answer in October[48] or even by the middle of November.[49]

COUNTER CHARGES

But the Archbishop did answer in November, not by writing to the Jesuits but by sending counter-charges in a letter to be read before the St. John's Board of Trustees.[50] He asserted that misunderstandings have grown out of "an irregular course adopted by the Jesuits themselves, in appealing to third parties." The Archbishop had desired to present his side of the case to the Board, but his request for such an opportunity "has been steadily denied and disregarded." The prelate expressed his opinion that the Jesuits did not deliberately intend to degrade him, but the effects of their actions have been to do just that:

> They had charged him with attempting to abbridge [sic] them of rights which were theirs, and by a process substantially equivalent to fraud. They had charged him with having denied them advantages which he had promised them on their coming to the Diocese. They have dogged his transactions in matters which had occurred before their coming to the diocese in order to find out in what particular they had been defrauded, in reference to many transactions with which they never had, have not now, and never shall have any right whatever to interfere.
>
> On all these points, the undersigned wished to show them, in a private and friendly way, how mistaken and erroneous were the views which they took up and calumniously circulated, more or less, among the Clergy and laity of this Diocese, whilst they carefully concealed from him the process of investigations in which they were engaged.

The Archbishop declared that he did not bring these accusations against all the Jesuits in his diocese, but against their officials and superiors:

The undersigned is prepared to prove that the Jesuits are unwarranted by truth, unwarranted by justice, unwarranted by right, whether by positive agreement or otherwise, in every calumnious charge they have made against the Archbishop.

The Archbishop then requested the Board of Trustees to appoint some of their members to study the prelate's case, not as judges of his conduct but as witnesses to the truth of his charges. He finished by declaring:

The Jesuits have placed themselves with regard to these matters, in such a position, that the Archbishop need only publish the truth to create a profound scandal among their best friends.

No mention of this letter is made in the minutes of the meeting of the Board of Trustees on November 10, 1857.[51] The letter, however, was read to the Board by its president, Peter Hargous.[52] After the Board adjourned, Hargous sought an interview with the Jesuit Regional Superior. He informed Hus that, during the twenty-nine years he had known the Archbishop, he had never heard—nor, ever expected to hear—Hughes admit he was in the wrong. He declared that the only way the Jesuits could get their rights was by an appeal to the Pope. Hus informed the General that he, too, believed that an appeal should be made, for be was convinced that the Archbishop would obey no instructions save those of the supreme pontiff. He went on to report that the Archbishop was speaking angrily about the Jesuits to anyone who would listen and stating that he was thinking about taking the title of St. John's College away from them.

A few days after the Board adjourned, some of its members held an unofficial meeting to explore avenues of possible reconciliations.[53] Hus and Murphy represented the Jesuits; Fr. Starrs, Hughes' vicar general, and Peter Hargous were the other persons present. The meeting, however, produced no results. It strengthened Hus' opinion that the only recourse left to the Jesuits was an appeal to the Pope. He declared that, save for the scandal that would result, he and a number of his consultors would like to move out of the archdiocese.

The Archbishop's letter to the Board could not be ignored. Hus called his consultors together to discuss what measures should be taken. It was decided that an answer should be made, and addressed to the president of the Board.[54] Hus forwarded a copy of this letter to Rome.[55] It followed the pattern of Hus' letter to the Archbishop of August 17, 1857. Once again, Hus insisted that the Jesuits had bought St. John's, not received it as a gift. Once again, he listed the advantages accruing to the Archbishop through the coming of the Jesuits to his

190

diocese. Hus went on to compile another list of the Jesuit efforts for the Church in New York.

1. In leaving Kentucky, they had sacrificed large properties there.

2. They had spent $60,000 of their own money in New York.

3. They had further incurred debts of more than that amount.

4. At their own expense, they had devoted to the service of the Archdiocese of New York, for over ten years, twenty priests, thirty brothers, and ten scholastics.

5. At their own expense, they had trained, for the service of New York, large numbers of scholastics — eighteen in France, ten at Fordham and fifteen in Canada.

6. They had served the glory of God in New York.

7. They had worked and saved to pay the interest on the debts on the College of St. John's and the Church and College of St. Francis Xavier.

To this letter, the Regional Superior appended another list of the steps to be taken to restore peace between the Jesuits and the Archbishop.

1. Let the Archbishop be content with the seminary property as it is.

2. Let the Jesuits have peaceful possession of the rest of the land at Fordham.

3. Let the Archbishop see to it that the fence between the railroad and the college lands be constructed.

4. Let the Archbishop give the Jesuits the promised church and residence in New York City, and further indemnify them for the dozen years of revenue they had lost through failure to implement the promise.

5. Let the Archbishop restore to the Jesuits the title of their Church of St. Francis Xavier. If he desires, the Jesuits will turn over to him the $6,116 they had received from the collection taken up throughout the diocese to help defray the cost of construction of the church.

6. Let the Archbishop turn over to St. John's College the legacy left to it in the will of Mrs. Eliza McCarthy.[56]

7. Let the Archbishop cease his criticism of the Jesuit methods of education.[57]

8. Let the Archbishop not consider the ninth clause of the convention of 1845 as giving him the right to preempt the College of St. John's.

9. Let the Jesuits be free to mortgage their property at Fordham, or sell part of it, to get the necessary financial resources for further construction.

10. Let the Fordham College be freed of the annoyance caused by the trespassing of hundreds of people on their way to the parish church, formerly the seminary chapel.

Hargous later reported to Hus that he had passed on the letter to Starrs, and told the vicar general that, if he thought it advisable, he might show it to the Archbishop.[58]

The Jesuit General intervenes

From Rome, Hus received the information that the Jesuit general had decided that the dispute would have to be brought to the attention of the Congregation of the Propaganda.[59] The Regional Superior declared that the New York fathers approved of that step. But he suggested that the general might first intervene by a direct letter to the Archbishop.

The general may have been more inclined to follow Hus' suggestion after he read a long review of the situation from the pen of Thomas Legoüais, one of the consultors of the New York-Canada Mission.[60] Legoüais noted that the enrollment of St. John's College in 1858 was about 130, a notable drop from the high of 180 in 1856. He attributed the falling off to the hostility shown the school by the Archbishop and the secular clergy. How to handle the Archbishop, Legoüais frankly confessed he did not know. Every attempt that had been made to mitigate his wrath had only made him still more angry and less inclined to conciliation. For some time, things had been fairly quiet, but the fathers apprehensively judged that it was the quiet before the storm. "*A longo tempore silet, quasi meditans. CC [consultors] non dubitant quin se paret ad fulmen subito feriendum*" (He's silent for a long time, as though he's meditating. The consultors do not doubt that he is preparing to drop a bolt of lightening (on us) all of a sudden.) They believed it possible that the prelate would accuse the Jesuits in Rome, and more than probable that he would attempt to eject them from Fordham, for he had frequently expressed his regret that he had given the college to the Jesuits.

Though giving Hus full marks for good intentions, Legoüais questioned his ability to settle the dispute. The problem of the seminary boundaries had been practically settled by Boulanger. But when Hus took office, he reopened the question and added conditions which would never be granted by Hughes. Instead of one bone of contention, Hus had dug up four or five. In the

Archbishop's circle, it was asserted that the Jesuits were being difficult due to their anger at being expelled from the diocesan seminary. Legoüais regretted the fact that Hus had brought forth the sixth clause of the convention of 1845 and, on that basis, had advanced a claim for a church and a house and a further demand for $50,000-60,000 in lost revenue. These claims could not but anger the Archbishop the more. Since they had been brought forth, he had refused to have any communication with the Regional Superior. Although Legoüais had opposed these claims from the beginning, most of the consultors, he noted, approved Hus' stand.

But the thunderbolt apprehensively expected by the Jesuits did not fall. Although the Regional Superior reported that the Archbishop was announcing that he had never promised the Jesuits the gift of a church and a house, [61] and was accusing Hus of discussing private matters with laymen,[62] Hughes made no move.

Then the Jesuit general, adopting the suggestion of Hus, intervened by a personal letter to the Archbishop.[63] He expressed his regret over the dispute, the more regrettable in that it concerned only temporal affairs. If his subjects had carried frankness or their demands too far, the General asked the Archbishop's pardon. The New York fathers found the present state of tension unbearable. But the General was reluctant to appeal to Propaganda. He asked the Archbishop for any suggestions of measures to restore peace.

In his response, the Archbishop charged the Jesuits in New York of "calumnies secretly and stealthily uttered by them against me."[64] He accused them of having "traduced me to laymen, without giving me an opportunity of explaining." He requested that a conference be arranged in which he would confront the New York Jesuits and prove the falseness of their charges. He asked that the general appoint two of his subjects to attend the conference in the capacity of witnesses. These witnesses should not be members of the New York-Canada Mission. Hughes suggested two members of the Maryland Province, Charles Stonestreet, a former provincial of Maryland, and John McElroy, an intimate friend of the Archbishop and one of the outstanding Jesuits in America.

Both parties in New York were quite ready to accept the intervention of the General. Before the general's response to the Archbishop's letter had reached America, the consultors of the New York-Canada Mission had decided that no one in America could restore peace and that the General should intervene.[65] And the General's initiative notably changed the attitude of the Archbishop. Although he had refused the invitation to preside over the commencement of St. John's, he unexpectedly appeared at Fordham on commencement day.[66] From the pulpit of the seminary chapel, he announced that he never intended the chapel should be used permanently as a parish church, and offered the parish a site west of the railroad for their future church. Then the Archbishop attended the commencement exercises, addressed the audience, and afterwards inspected the college buildings.

BEGINNINGS OF ARBITRATION

No doubt the general wondered how the conference the Archbishop wanted solely to justify himself could advance the cause of peace. But since Hughes obviously thought his proposal of importance, the General acceded to the request. Stonestreet and McElroy were instructed to attend the conference and report their impressions to Jesuit headquarters.[67] The New York Jesuits were told to attend and to bring their complaints as the Archbishop required.[68]

Since it was the Archbishop who wanted the confrontation, the arrangement of details was left in his hands. He called the meeting for 10 A.M. on September 21, in the sacristy of the Cathedral.[69] Eight persons were to be present—the Archbishop, his vicar general, — two secretaries whom the Archbishop would appoint, two New York Jesuits, and the two Maryland Jesuits as witnesses. The sole purpose of the meeting the Archbishop underlined in a letter to the Regional Superior:[70]

> You are aware that imputations have been put more or less into circulation by the Society of Jesus in this Diocese (for I will not speak of individuals), well calculated to degrade me, both in my own estimation and in the estimation of others, if they were true. The examination of their truth will be the object of our meeting. If true, I shall have nothing more to say — if not true, I will expect that these imputations shall be frankly and fully retracted in writing.
>
> The form of the proceeding will be framed exclusively with the view to test the truth of what has been alleged against me by your Society.

As he informed the General, Hus wrote to the Archbishop to request some changes.[71] He asked that the Jesuits be allowed to name one of the secretaries; that before the prelate declare that the Jesuits spread calumnies, he prove that they uttered any; that he inform the fathers in advance, at least summarily, what the calumnies were, who said them, where and before whom; and, finally, that the conference be broadened to cover all the points of disagreement between the Jesuits and the Archbishop. Hus went on to report that McElroy, after he had visited Hughes, had expressed the opinion that if the Archbishop did not get everything he demanded, he would appeal to Rome— a fact which neither Hus nor any of his consultors would be inclined to doubt. He also reported an incident as indicative of the Archbishop's frame of mind. A Jesuit priest, Claude Pernot, had requested his discharge from the Society. Without waiting for his dismissal letters, he had left the Jesuit community and gone to New York. Although the Archbishop could not know whether or not Pernot was an apostate from religion, he at once appointed him pastor of one of the city churches. *"N'importe, il se separe de la Compagnie, donc il est digne de toutes faveurs"* (No matter. He's out of the Society, and hence he's worthy of all favors.)

Fr. William Murphy carried Hus' letter to the Archbishop, who seemed quite pleased with it.[72] Hughes agreed that the Jesuits should appoint their own secretary. He promised to send the Jesuits the list of his complaints and requested that they send him theirs. He found the other points suggested by the Regional Superior were also acceptable. The Archbishop notified Murphy that, since McElroy could not be present in New York on September 20, the "date of the conference had been shifted to September 28. He told Murphy that he had no legal right to the land west of the railroad or south of the seminary property. But he wanted that land, and in exchange he would give the Jesuits the seminary land occupied by the Jesuits' road to their farm. Murphy's hopes for some substantial good from the conference were raised by the Archbishop's declaration that "the talk among priests and laity about our dispute had happily died away"; "that occasionally carried away by his feelings and under a sense of indignity done to him as a man and as a prelate, he had expressed himself somewhat harshly."

In the interval before the confrontation, the Jesuits busied themselves in drawing up the list of grievances to be presented to the Archbishop. Before they were satisfied, they considered a number of drafts.[73] The drafts, however, agreed on essentials. The Jesuits denied they had spread calumnies against the Archbishop. They had discussed their difficulties with only two laymen—one the president of the Board of Trustees, who could not help but know of the dispute and the other their lawyer, a man of the highest reputation and professionally bound to secrecy, whom they had consulted only after the Archbishop had given them the example. Both men had been consulted in confidence, and neither had violated the Jesuits' trust. All the drafts contained special mention of the three major Jesuits' complaints — the cramping clause, the title of the Church on 16th Street, the unfulfilled promise of a church and a house. A number of minor complaints were considered, but not mentioned in the draft to be presented to the Archbishop.

The Archbishop, too, had drawn up the list of his grievances. They were presented to the Jesuits in a document entitled "Mode of proceeding in the investigation of topics controverted between the Society of Jesus in this diocese, and the Archbishop.[74] Hughes proposed to open the meeting by expounding a simple history of the facts, which would be open to correction or emendation by the Jesuits. Then the Jesuits should be called upon to prove or to retract:

1st. They have said that the Archbishop wished to deprive them of property on the west side of the railroad which was theirs ...

2nd. That he must have received pecuniary compensation from the Harlem Rail Road Co. for the right of way through their ground and that this compensation properly belonged to them ...

3rd. That they are entitled to a bequest made by the late Mrs. Eliza McCarthy, several years before they came to the diocese, and which the Archbishop withheld.

4th. That in a survey of the ground, the Archbishop has attempted to claim more than belongs to him.

These four charges were the sum total of the grievances that the Archbishop complained of.[75] If the Jesuits did not prove these charges at the conference, the Archbishop expected to receive a written apology.

PLAN OF RECONCILIATION

Apparently encouraged by the progress Murphy had made in his interview with the Archbishop of September 8, the Regional Superior decided to see if some further progress could not be registered in another interview. On September 22, 1858, Hus, accompanied by Murphy, called at the Archbishop's residence with what he considered a plan of reconciliation. While the plan made no mention of any Jesuit concession to the Archbishop, it requested that Hughes revoke the cramping clause, give the Jesuits the title of the Church on 16th Street, make a free gift to the Jesuits of a church and house in New York City, and further indemnify the Jesuits for the loss of revenue they had sustained through the failure to implement the promise over a period of twelve years. Since the Archbishop was absent at Saratoga, Hus sent his plan with a covering letter informing the Archbishop that he would wait on him on his return to New York.[76]

The results of this communication could have been foreseen. The Regional Superior received no answer to his letter.[77] Nevertheless, on September 27, the day before the conference, Hus, again accompanied by Murphy, called on the Archbishop. After keeping the Jesuits waiting for an hour and a half, the Archbishop appeared in the parlor, blasted Hus in French for demanding "his pound of flesh," declared he would have nothing more to do with him, and then made a point of speaking in English, which Hus did not understand, to Murphy.[78]

HUGHES' VERSION OF THE CONTROVERSY

The conference was held as scheduled on the morning of September 28 in the Cathedral sacristy.[79] Archbishop Hughes was present with his vicar general and Fr. McNerny, the secretary he had chosen. McElroy and Stonestreet were there. For the New York Jesuits appeared Murphy and Larkin, with Legoüais as their secretary.[80]

The Archbishop opened the meeting by reading a long document he entitled "Statement of the facts connected with the introduction of the Jesuit Fathers into the diocese of New York."[81] This statement contained a survey of the early history of St. John's College — how Hughes purchased the land, collected the necessary funds, engaged a faculty. In 1844-45 the bishop had applied for a charter from the Regents of the University of the State of New York; at that time, he had collected evidence that the property at Fordham was worth $129,000. When the Archbishop decided to turn the college over to a religious order, the Regional Superior of the French Jesuits and he had quickly reached agreement. Before that event, the prelate had given the Harlem Rail Road a right of way over the college land in exchange for a free pass on the trains for the college and some other trifling conditions.

The Archbishop managed, before the Jesuits took over the college to get a charter, not from the Regents but from the State Legislature. When the Board of Trustees was constituted, it was with the understanding that the trustees would resign, one after the other, until the Jesuits had a majority of the Board. When the Archbishop was ready to transfer the college property, he and the Regional Superior decided that there should be two documents, the first a deed of conveyance, "as if the property had been sold in fee simple, and paid for," the second, not intended for public record, which specified the uses and purposes for which the property was transferred. Unfortunately, the prelate went on, several mistakes had been made in the deed of conveyance, whence the present conflict arose.

The Jesuits, the Archbishop insisted, had assumed the debts of the college, which amounted, he believed at the time, to $40,000. After the Jesuits had taken over, another $6,000 in debts were discovered and paid off by the prelate. Since the Jesuits declared they could not raise the $40,000, Hughes "agreed to stand between them and those depositors for a certain time, until they could pay it off by degrees." The unspecified depositors were to receive 5% interest on their money, and the Jesuits agreed to pay these charges. Since Boulanger believed it might be difficult to raise the 5%, the Archbishop proposed that the fathers staff his seminary and use their salaries to work off the interest, at least in part. The Archbishop noted that, to the present, the Jesuits had paid off only $17,000 of their debt, while on the other hand, to support the seminary, "I have paid them about $50,000."

197

He then turned to other topics. It was mutually understood that the Jesuits had come to New York "exclusively for the purposes of Catholic education, that is, they were not invited for the purpose of missionary duties." To encourage them to open schools in New York City, Hughes had offered them a church, "the only one then at his disposal." The superior agreed, but when the Archbishop later made the actual offer of the church, the Jesuits declined the proffered gift, on the plea that the church was in debt.

When the Regional Superior later approached the Archbishop with the proposition that the Jesuits buy or build a church, the prelate readily gave his permission. The fathers did buy a church. Although it was agreed that "in this diocese the Jesuit Fathers should never claim the privilege of a mendicant order — should never make a collection or appeal to the faithful for alms-except with the previous knowledge and consent of the Ordinary," the Jesuits, in violation of the agreement, did take up a collection for their church. The Archbishop knew of this violation, but said nothing.

Permission to Rebuild

Subsequently, the church was destroyed by fire. The Jesuits then asked the Archbishop for permission to take up a collection to rebuild, which permission they received. Had the prelate known the methods the Jesuits would use, he would have refused. For they solicited "almost from door to door through both cities (New York and Brooklyn), at least, and especially, in the city of New York." And in a sermon soliciting for the collection, a father declared that the Jesuits had purchased St. John's College for a price. When the Archbishop told the Jesuits that they must terminate their collection on a specific date, they approached him "with very polite threats and menaces, not indeed frankly expressed." "The Archbishop understood these menaces and treated them as they deserved."

Although the Jesuits had collected on the plea of rebuilding their church, they never rebuilt. Many subscribers later complained with bitterness that the fathers had obtained money under false pretenses. After some time had passed, the Jesuits collected the insurance money, sold the site of their church and moved their school to another section of the city. They neither accounted for the money they had collected, nor used it for the purpose for which it was given. Later, the Jesuits approached the Archbishop about building a new church. The results of these negotiations is the Church on 16th Street. That church now has an annual income, as reported by the pastor, of $10,000-$12,000, "whilst the only credit given for collections to build the church is scarcely equal to the amount which the organ cost, say $7,000."

Boulanger and Hughes had agreed that, if any dispute arose between the Archbishop and the Jesuits, it should be settled quietly by the prelate and the

Regional Superior. When the Jesuit church went up in flames, the Superior asked the Archbishop that the priests serving the church be assigned to rectories about the city. The Archbishop at once agreed. But he soon heard reports that the Jesuits were working only with the most pious members of the parishes to which they had been assigned, "as if those required to be converted anew," and among the pious, only with the richest. For the poor, the fathers had no time. Further, "it became whispered all about that the Jesuits received nothing for their ministerial toil." Other reports reached the Archbishop: a Jesuit was seen in a public theatre, another at the opera during Holy Week. The prelate requested the Regional Superior either to exercise direct supervision over these men, or place them under the authority of the bishop, who would take upon himself to see that at least they should not attend theatres or opera." The result of the prelate's representations was that the superior withdrew the offenders from the city. Within a few days, the laity were "in a state of fermentation against the Archbishop," who was accused of expelling the fathers from the city. The prelate summoned the Superior and rebuked him for violating "the secret and sacred understanding" to keep any differences quiet. While the superior only shrugged his shoulders, his companion declared that the Archbishop had separated penitents from their confessors, and declared that St. Ignatius had predicted that the Society would never lack persecutors, even among popes and bishops. "From that period to the present," Hughes concluded, "the Archbishop has not known any one member of the Society of Jesus in the diocese of New York with whom, although he has made repeated efforts, he could hold official communication."

The reading of the "Statement of the facts" occupied the better part of an hour. It was followed by discussion which lasted for another several hours.[82] Murphy noted that the man best to speak for the Jesuit side, the Regional Superior, was not present at the conference.

GOOD AND USEFUL JESUITS

The Archbishop declared that he was favorably disposed towards the Jesuits. They were good and useful men, and he did not want them to leave his diocese. Since they wanted a church, he would see what he could do to satisfy them. By offering them a church in 1847, he had fulfilled his obligation under the sixth clause of the convention of 1845. He went on to assert that the word "house" was not in that document; he had never intended to make the Jesuits the gift of a house.

To the Archbishop's claim that the Jesuits had profited from the destruction of their original church, Larkin, who had been rector of the church at the time of the fire, was able to enter a rebuttal. He pointed out that the church had been heavily in debt. The money obtained from the fire insurance, the sale of the property and the collection in the diocese had been raised to pay off the debt. But $1,600 remained, which was used in the construction of the Church on 16th Street, which was owned by the Archbishop. Larkin went on to declare that the bishop's offer of a church burdened with very heavy debts could scarcely be considered the offer of a gift.

On the question of the title of the Church of St. Francis Xavier, the Archbishop brought out and read the correspondence be had had with Boulanger about the matter. He conceded that be had perhaps spoken too strongly when he wrote the Superior General that the Jesuits were doing almost nothing for education. Although he did not care a farthing for the title of the church, that was the arrangement between the Regional Superior and himself. The argument was adduced that, since Boulanger at that time had not brought up the sixth clause, this was a renunciation of that clause by the Jesuit Regional Superior.

Towards the end of the meeting, Legoüais broke his silence as secretary to propose the major Jesuit demands. The Jesuits would transfer to the Archbishop what land he wanted at Fordham. Since Hughes did not at all care about the title of the Xavier church, let him give that title to the Jesuits. Let the Archbishop either annul the cramping clause, or so interpret it that the Jesuits might be free to develop the college. In response, the prelate once more denied that he had sold St. John's. He declared the fathers had full rights to mortgage its property, and that he would discuss the revocation of the cramping clause in some future conversation. Thereupon the conference came to an end.

McElroy and Stonestreet at once drew up their report of the conference for Fr. Beckx.[83] In their opinion, Hughes had completely answered all the complaints that were alleged against him. "In fine the A. B. [Archbishop] convinced us perfectly that our FF [fathers] were in fault ..." "We are convinced that the A. B. is by no means unfriendly to the Society; that we regret to be obliged to say — that our FF have not acted as they should have done to Episcopal authority and the respect due to it."

Later, McElroy sent a fuller individual report to the Jesuit General when he put at the root of all the trouble the cramping clause and the title to the church at Xavier. When the bad effects of these agreements appeared, the Jesuits turned hostile to the Archbishop. Boulanger should never have agreed to these sources of troubles. He was a bad manager of affairs; the same is to be said of Hus, who should be replaced. McElroy and Stonestreet were of the opinion that an apology should be made to the Archbishop. At the conference of September 28, Hughes proved that he had carried out all his obligations under the convention of 1845. To his explanations, the New York Jesuits had nothing to say. In McElroy's judgment, the conference had been a humiliation for the Society of Jesus.

REACTION OF THE NEW YORK JESUITS

The reaction of the New York Jesuits was quite different from that of McElroy and Stonestreet. They believed that the confrontation was quite unfair, that the Archbishop had stacked the cards against the Jesuits.[85] Hus was the Regional Superior of the New York Canada Mission; he had been present at the negotiations of the convention of 1845; he was the best informed Jesuit on the problems to be discussed. But Hus was not allowed to attend the conference.[86] Not only had the Archbishop excluded Hus, but he prevented the two official representatives of the New York Jesuits from consulting one another during the conference by assigning them seats at different sides of the conference table.[87]

As to the "Statement of facts," Larkin characterized it as *"summa arte scripta — factis enumerandis, colorandis, exaggerandis"* (written with the highest skill in listing facts, in interpreting them, [and] exaggerating them), as a *"veram calumniam"* (a true calumny) of the Society of Jesus.[88] The Archbishop had notified the Jesuits he would bring four accusation against them. These charges were the very basis of the meeting. But the Archbishop made no attempt to prove them; indeed, be did not even so much as mention them.[89] Instead, he brought up all sorts of matters from the past. The fathers had received no forewarning, and were consequently unprepared to answer. As a result, they could speak only at random.[90] And the fathers balked at accepting several contentions of the Archbishop — that the convention he had signed and to which he had affixed his seal in 1845 was merely a simple declaration of the views of the two parties, that the words promising the Jesuits a house had not been in the contract he signed but had been inserted later.[91]

The Archbishop's "Statement of facts" was not available to the Jesuits till the prelate presented a copy for the General a year after the conference. The Regional Superior did, however, have the impressions of the Jesuits who had been present and the notes of Legoüais. Hus consequently wrote several letters to Rome to refute some of the prelate's major contentions. He rejected the Archbishop's views on the promised church and house, and on the title of the Xavier church.[92] He went to some length to show that the debts of the College of St. John could not, on the evidence at hand, been $40,000 in 1846.[93] He cited evidence against the Archbishop's contention that St. John's made a net profit each year of the prelate's administration of $10,000-$12,000.[94] And he rejected the valuation of $129,000 put on the college by Hughes.[95]

Shortly after the eventful conference, Thomas Legoüais sent another thoughtful survey of the situation to the Jesuit General.[96] He would find neither side in the dispute free of fault. Shortly after the Jesuits had arrived in New York, an antipathy had developed between Bishop Hughes and Boulanger, who had sometimes spoken and acted imprudently. And the mode of action of the fathers during their first years in the city did more to alienate than to please the Archbishop. The poor administration of the diocesan seminary by the Jesuits further alienated the bishop and his clergy. On the seminary question, Legoüais declared that the chief faults were attributable to the Jesuits.

All the major problems were in being before Hus arrived in New York, but they were dormant till be came. The new Regional Superior quite rightly thought that the cramping clause should be removed and the title of the Xavier church restored to the Jesuits. He declared that he had been instructed to attain those ends, and he set out to do so.[97] The position of Boulanger towards the bishop had been, in Legoüais' opinion, weak, undignified and humiliating for the fathers. It was true that Hus changed that, and inspirited the fathers; but *"il vint ici, la tête montée, et elle ne s'est calmée depuis"* (he came here, his head held high and it hasn't come down since.) Within a few months, Hus had made the Archbishop much more hostile to him than he had ever been to Boulanger. The Jesuits had had two major problems with the prelate. Hus had multiplied them. He had, for example, brought up the sixth clause, and in a most abrupt and maladroit manner. Hus had begun his campaign over the miserable question of the seminary boundaries. He informed his consultors that he intended to take a strong position on this very minor question, merely to show the Archbishop that he could not intimidate the Jesuits. He hoped tHus to force the prelate to be accommodating on more important matters; he only succeeded in enraging him. Legoüais believed that nothing could be gained by an appeal to Propaganda. He urged the General to send a special emissary to conciliate Hughes, and then seek the major Jesuit demands. To attain those points, be suggested the sixth clause as a bargaining weapon.

Hus meanwhile sent to Rome reports of other incidents which showed, in his opinion, the Archbishop's unfair treatment of the Jesuits.[98] The fathers had begun, in New York, work among the neglected Negro Catholics, which Hughes had terminated by refusing a special church for the colored people. The Fordham Jesuits had built up a parish in Yonkers, which Hughes saw for the first time when he came to bless the church. A few weeks later, be ejected the Jesuits from the parish. For years, the fathers had been working in the prisons, without a word of appreciation or a penny of financial assistance from the diocese.

BECKX WORKS FOR A SETTLEMENT

With the evidence now at hand, the Jesuit authorities in Rome were considering the steps to be taken. Boulanger, now the superior of the Jesuit house in Nancy, was asked to clarify a number of points and submit his suggestions. The former Regional Superior believed that the Jesuits should accede to Hughes' demands for more land at Fordham, and expressed his strong opposition to Hus' demand for a indemnity from the Archbishop for failure to implement the sixth clause.[99] He confirmed Hus' statement that Hughes had not requested the troublesome ninth clause, but that the Regional Superior himself had proposed it.[100] He had never believed the prelate would make a gift, in the strict sense, of a church and a house to the Jesuits. But since the bishop had not put these buildings at the disposal of the Jesuits until they could establish themselves in the city, Boulanger believed the fathers would be justified in demanding that the bishop reimburse them for the expenses to which they had been put. One step was quite clear to the Jesuit headquarters. Hus would have to be replaced. He himself had requested it,[101] and the fathers in New York were sure that he was not the man to end the conflict.[102]

In November 1858, the General communicated his decisions to the Regional Superior.[103] An appeal to Propaganda was ruled out. Any accusations made against the propriety of the Archbishop's actions were to be retracted. The claim for the gift of a church and house was not to be pressed, nor was a claim to the legacy of Mrs. McCarthy to be made. Beckx informed Hus that a negotiated settlement must be made. He proposed to send an emissary who was not a member of the New York-Canada Mission, and asked Hus' opinion on McElroy and Stonestreet for the office of peacemaker. He informed the Regional Superior that when the settlement had been effected be would be relieved of his office.

That the General's decisions would receive ready acceptance among the New York Jesuits was indicated by a letter from Tellier which reached Rome after the General's missive had been dispatched.[104] The rector of St. John's lamented the fact that the enrollment of the college had dropped to 124 students, due to the hostility of the Archbishop and his clergy. He believed his retention of his office was displeasing to Hughes, and he reported it to be the common rumor that the Archbishop demanded, as the price of peace, the official heads of himself and of Hus. He declared that, with the possible exception of Murphy, no New York Jesuit could negotiate peace and called for a Visitor to accomplish that end.

Hus himself accepted the General's decision without demur.[105] But he found hard to bear the vision of the Archbishop's rejoicing over his triumph and the removal of the Regional Superior. Despondently he predicted that the fathers who brought Hughes the news would get a warm welcome — but nothing for the Society.

Hus called together the consultors of the Mission and read them the General's letter.[106] There was unanimous approval of the decision that no appeal should be made to Propaganda and that a negotiated settlement should be made.[107] The consultors agreed that the best man to attempt reconciliation was John McElroy. But there was some opposition to his appointment as an official Visitor, for fear of the effect on some of the younger men of the Mission who wanted to end what they termed the "French regime."[108] Hus ended his report to the general with the intimation that he expected Murphy, who was well liked by the Archbishop, as his replacement, and with the suggestion that a special superior — he recommended Stonestreet — be appointed for the New York half of the Mission. He vented his disappointment and resentment of Hughes, whom he accused of a long list of deceits, in a separate letter to the French Assistant.[109]

MCELROY'S MISSION

On receiving the reactions to his decisions, the General immediately set about the arrangements for the negotiations. McElroy was informed of his special office and endowed with all necessary authority as the General's alter ego to settle the quarrel.[110] He was instructed to accomplish three things—to placate the Archbishop, to obtain the title of the Church on 16th Street, to end the cramping clause. These three objectives secured, McElroy was empowered to renounce every other Jesuit claim on the Archbishop and to give him whatever he desired at Fordham. Hughes was to be informed that Hus would soon be replaced. If the prelate demanded a retractation, it should be made; but McElroy was to avoid, if possible, a retraction in writing. The general also addressed a letter to the Archbishop, informing him of McElroy's functions.[111] Both these letters he sent to Hus, with instructions to forward them to McElroy. They were received in New York at the end of January, 1859[112] and forwarded to McElroy.[113]

On February 22, 1859, McElroy came to New York to accomplish his task.[114] He met Hus and his consultors at Fordham and informed them of the General's instructions. He had several conferences with the Archbishop and was briefed by both sides.[115] On February 26, McElroy, at a meeting with Hus and his consultors, proposed that the Jesuits apologize to the Archbishop, who demanded it, for any injury to the prelate's honor and veracity. But the Regional Superior, declaring that in conscience he could not apologize, refused.[116]

Indeed, Hus' actions seemed designed to hinder McElroy's mission. He protested his actions, even objecting to the fact that McElroy, probably to emphasize his impartiality, chose to stop, not at a Jesuit house, but with a private family.[117] He declared to the general that McElroy refused to tell the New York fathers just what power he had been granted.[118] When Hus declared his readiness to make some excuses, but no apology, since he had spoken only the truth to the Archbishop, McElroy had claimed, but would not show Hus, authorization from the general to impose this obligation on the Regional Superior.[119]

McElroy decided that the apology should be made without the Regional Superior, and that the Archbishop should not be informed of Hus' refusal.[120] On February 27, accompanied by Legoüais and Murphy, McElroy went to the

Archbishop's residence. The Archbishop had the satisfaction of seeing the three Jesuits kneeling before him while McElroy apologized for their faults. At his demand, McElroy later wrote and presented a signed copy to the prelate.[121]

The written apology covers the background of the quarrel and then goes on to declare:

> First, that every statement made against the Archbishop, as if he had been wanting in veracity, in candor, in honor, or in honesty, in his dealing with the Jesuit Fathers, has proved to be unfounded in fact, and to have resulted from misconception or misinformation on the part of the Fathers.
>
> Second, that the Fathers were by an original agreement with their Superior, bound to make known, in the first instance exclusively to the Archbishop, the subject of their real or imaginary grievance in every case, so that he might explain, or, if possible, remedy the grievance complained of.
>
> Third, that imprudently, instead of adhering to this agreement, the Fathers or some of them made their complaints to laymen, contrary to the usage and discipline of this diocese.
>
> Fourth, that if these statements had been true, they would be calculated to degrade the character of the Archbishop in the estimation of the laymen to whom the complaints were made known.
>
> Fifth & finally. . . . no statement derogatory to the character of the Archbishop has been or can be proved . . .
>
> Every such complaint, therefore, made to laymen against the Archbishop is hereby revoked and regretted. The undersigned regrets especially the pain which these events must have given to the Archbishop of New York, and he trusts that this declaration will be accepted as a sufficient apology and reparation for the past, hoping at the same time that for the future nothing of the kind shall occur; and trusting as he has reason to do, that the Most Rev. Archbishop will forgive and forget whatever may have been said unjustly or injuriously to his prejudice, through the misconception or misinformation under which the Fathers labored.

Whether or not the statements of the apology can be justified, the apology did accomplish the desired effect of placating the Archbishop. A few days later, the prelate attended a lecture at St. John's College and, together with many other clergy and laity, remained for dinner with the Jesuits.[122] As the party was taking its leave, McElroy requested Murphy, Legoüais and Tellier to come to a consultation at the college on 16th Street the following morning,

According to Hus, McElroy instructed the fathers not to inform the Regional Superior, but they believed it their duty to notify him.[123]

CONSULTATION AT XAVIER

A consultation was held by McElroy on March 3, 1859 at the College of St. Francis Xavier to discuss the settlement of outstanding problems with the Archbishop.[124] The fathers unanimously agreed to give the Archbishop whatever land he wanted at Fordham. McElroy informed them that Hughes regretted that the Jesuits had not applied for the title to the Xavier church before the law on church tenure was passed by the New York State Legislature in 1853, for "he would have then most willingly complied with our wishes." "The FF [fathers] could and did not say anything to the contrary," but they urged McElroy to secure a written declaration of the Archbishop's expressed intention to give the church back to the Jesuits as soon as the law allowed.

On the problem of the cramping clause, the fathers pointed out that at the conference of September 28, 1858 the Archbishop had declared that the Jesuits had the right to mortgage their land at Fordham. But the prelate would not say that the Jesuits had the right to sell part of the land, nor would he put his declaration in writing. McElroy stated he had raised this question with Hughes. He too had failed to get a written statement. But he announced that the Archbishop was willing to raise the sum of money he would repay the Jesuits, if they left the diocese, beyond the $40,000 stipulated in the convention of 1845. The fathers expressed their preference to see the ninth clause revoked.

At the consultation, the fathers from Fordham presented to McElroy a letter from the Regional Superior. It was a protest which, as Hus informed the General, he believed he should enter.[125] Another copy was sent to the Archbishop by messenger. Hus told Beckx that if the Jesuit General disapproved his action, he would submit. But be considered his protest a politic move, inasmuch as it would lay the basis for a future appeal to Propaganda and could be used to put off ratification of McElroy's settlement.

The "Protest and Appeal" asserted that the Jesuit General, in appointing McElroy, acted on insufficient and incorrect information; that McElroy had excluded the Regional Superior of the Mission from his councils; that McElroy had not stated, though summoned to do so, the powers he had received; that new documents, unknown to the Jesuit General, had been discovered. Consequently, the Regional Superior entered his protest against any settlement made between the Archbishop, who had not answered Hus' letter of August 17, 1857, and the delegate of the Jesuit General.[126]

This demarche of Hus had no effect on developments. He learned that McElroy believed it was not worth paying attention to.[127] Nevertheless, McElroy, fearing the effect of the protest on the Archbishop, had hurried to visit him. To his relief, he found the Archbishop undisturbed by the protest and quite willing to go on with the settlement.[128] And the protest tried also the patience of the consultors of the Mission; they expressed to McElroy their regret that the General's delegate had not the power to remove the Regional Superior from office. But though no one in New York paid attention to his protest, Hus did his best, by a number of letters, to make sure that attention was paid to it in Rome.[129] In this attempt he failed, since the Jesuit General also repudiated the appeal.[130]

With good relations with the Archbishop reestablished, McElroy went on to negotiate the other objectives set him by Fr. Beckx. The seminary boundaries were rearranged to Hughes' satisfaction. On this point, McElroy declared "I found the Archbishop perfectly correct and just in all be required, and that Ours were in error and had misconstrued His Grace's intentions."[131] The Archbishop was quite ready to give the Jesuits the deed of the Church on 16th Street, but the law of 1853 forbade it:

> The Archbishop has done all he could in this affair, and looks upon the church as ours, without any restriction whatever, save the formality of rendering an account annually . . . This affair I look upon as settled to the satisfaction of all parties.

On the complaint of the fathers that their ministry in the church on 16th Street was curtailed, McElroy wrote:

> On the subject of the confessional, His Grace informed me that his Clergy in the City were a little jealous of their penitents going to St. Fr. Xaviers, and to conciliate and appease them he made the rule of three confessors, which he presumed were quite sufficient, but he says they have only to let him know at any time if more are necessary and he will willingly grant it.

When the discussion moved around to Fordham, McElroy announced to the General that he had made the discovery that St. John's College belonged to the Jesuits:

> ... which the Archbishop was not aware of until I found it out from the Lawyers. The reason of the Archbishop's error was that be thought the private arrangement made between him and Fr. Boulanger had been placed on Record (archives publiques) with the original deed . . . As this was omitted, this private arrangement has no force in law.

On the Archbishop hearing this from the lawyer, he wrote me a note in which I find these words "I have discovered that the qualifying clause [i.e., the ninth clause of reversion] has not been put on record, and that the Fathers can legally sell or mortgage the whole property." Still, the Archbishop thinks himself bound in conscience to secure as far as be can the property of St. John's for the education of Cath: youth, as the means collected for its purchase were given with that understanding, and having sent a copy of this agreement to the Cardinal Prefect.

But the Archbishop now agreed that, if the Jesuits left the diocese, they should recover not only the $40,000 they had paid for St. John's, but the additional money they expended on the improvement and construction of the college:

This was looked upon by Ours as the greatest grievance the[y] had to complain of, and this clause in now inserted in a supplement to the said private agreement; so that our Fathers can build and improve as far as they have means to do so. This vexed question has been concluded satisfactorily, in my humble opinion, both to the interests of our Soc[iety] and to the approbation, and I may add, gratification of His Grace.

Only on one point did McElroy believe he had failed to carry to a successful conclusion the General's instructions:

One thing only I could not obtain from his Grace, that is, not to commit the apology we made to writing. His Grace insisted that his honor, veracity and even integrity had been impeached in the Board of Trustees at their meetings, and that he wanted to vindicate himself before the three laymen members of the board of Trustees, and to no others would he ever show it.

The prelate had informed McElroy, to the latter's edification, that he had mentioned his dispute with the Jesuits to no one, save his vicar general. "This I admire very much, as he had great provocation, particularly since the appointment of Fr. Hus." McElroy concluded his long report with praise of the Archbishop:

I must say that his Grace is truly just, honorable, zealous and disinterested, seeking nothing, but the good of our Holy religion. . . . I may add that our Fathers were invariably in fault by forming conjectures in their own mind, from want of correct information, from misrepresentation of others or of ignorance of the real state of affairs between them and His Grace.

Before McElroy despatched his report to the Jesuit General, be received a letter from the Archbishop, congratulating him on the success of his mission.[132] The prelate requested McElroy to inform the General that no public scandal had resulted from the misunderstanding. Hughes himself had told no one save his vicar General, and "the laymen to whom the Fathers appealed have with great prudence and charity kept the matter to themselves." The Archbishop expressed the hope that the settlement would be as satisfactory to the Jesuits as it was to him. For McElroy, he had words of praise:

> I confess that if it had not been for the very patience and prudence exercised by yourself, in conducting the affair, I might have been tempted to exact more in the way of repairing the past that I have done.

In acknowledging the receipt of McElroy's report, Beckx thanked him for his good work in restoring peace in New York.[133] He made no mention of the instructions which McElroy had failed to carry through.

When the details of the settlement had been agreed on, but not yet implemented, McElroy left New York. Peace had been achieved between the Archbishop and the Jesuits. Murphy wrote to express his relief that the long contest was over.[134] He noted, however, that the cramping clause still remained, and the Archbishop's promise to turn the Xavier church over to the Jesuits was still only a vocal, not a written, one.

In the meanwhile Hus, too, left New York to go to the Jesuit houses in Canada. By a letter of April 6, 1859, the provincial of the Province of France, acting under the instructions of Beckx, recalled Hus to France and appointed Remigius Tellier as vice-superior.[135] The appointment was only temporary. By a letter of April 16, 1859. William Murphy was appointed Regional Superior of the New York-Canada Mission by the Jesuit General.[136] Murphy, however, was a sick man, and before the end of the year Tellier was once again appointed to the office of Regional Superior of the mission.[137]

During the few months Murphy remained in the office of Regional Superior, things were at a standstill. A report written at the end of November 1859 declared that the situation in New York was exactly as it had been at the beginning of March.[138] It noted that since McElroy had left New York early in March, he had written only once. "It is all we have heard of him and of the affair in these last nine months." But in the interval there had been blessed peace.

During the interval there was brought to maturity at Jesuit headquarters a plan to appoint an official Visitor for all the Jesuit missions and provinces in the United States and Canada. By *Litterae Patentes* (letters patent) of September 20, 1859, the Jesuit General appointed as Visitor one of the outstanding Italian Jesuits, Fr. Felix Sopranis.[139] The new appointee spoke English, and had spent some time in the United States.

A FINAL SETTLEMENT

The Visitor received instructions to put a definite end to the controversy with Archbishop Hughes.[140] The terms of the peace treaty were to be put down in writing. The boundary lines at Fordham were to be drawn so that the trespassing on the college lands would be stopped. The cramping clause was to be revoked. If the Archbishop refused to renounce that clause, Sopranis was to get Hughes' written permission for the Fordham Jesuits to mortgage their property and the prelate's written guarantee that the Jesuits would, if they left Fordham, recover the full amount of the money they invested in St. John's College. The Visitor was further instructed to obtain, in writing, the Archbishop's promise to turn the title of Xavier church over the Jesuits when the law allowed. And he was to see that the Fathers used every means to cultivate good relations with the Archbishop.

Sopranis arrived in New York on October 25, 1859, but went immediately to the Maryland Province, where be began his visitation.[141] Towards the end of November, he interrupted this visitation to return to New York. There, in company with McElroy, he paid a call on Archbishop Hughes. In the interview, the Archbishop proposed that the boundary difficulty at Fordham receive a definite ending through the purchase of the seminary and its lands by the Jesuits.[142]

A few days later, Archbishop Hughes wrote to McElroy to express his pleasure at meeting Sopranis and to renew the offer of the sale of the seminary.[143] He enclosed in the letter the copy of his "Statement of the facts" which he had promised to send to the General, and asked McElroy to forward it to Beckx, together with a covering letter. In his letter to the general, Hughes thanked him for the conference of September 28, 1858, and for his appointment of McElroy to negotiate peace. He declared the settlement was

> satisfactory to me, and, I trust, not humiliating to the Fathers at Fordham. Their mistakes — their erroneous impressions — their hasty measures to vindicate themselves in the estimation of laymen, have all been acknowledged and apologized for.[144]

The Archbishop explained his tardiness in sending the "Statement of the facts" by his unwillingness to send what he knew would be unpleasant reading to the Jesuit General. To Beckx, Hughes repeated his offer to sell the seminary property at Fordham. He declared "it should be an absolute sale, without any conditions whatever. At the same time, with regard to the property already conceded to the Fathers, the conditions might be modified."

To negotiate the sale, the Archbishop proposed McElroy and Sopranis.[145] Apparently the Archbishop had no doubts that the Jesuits would be interested. The implication that through the purchase of the seminary the cramping clause might be canceled could not but stir the fathers. Nor was the Archbishop mistaken. As soon as he received the letter, the Jesuit general sent instructions to the Visitor to negotiate, with the assistance of McElroy, the proposed sale.[146] The fathers in New York were more than ready to make the purchase; as early as 1856, they had decided that, if the Archbishop made such an offer, they would close with it.[147]

At the end of March 1860, Sopranis reported to the General that he had discussed the matter with the Archbishop. It had been agreed that the Jesuits should purchase the property; only the price remained to be settled.[148] A future meeting had been arranged at which the Archbishop, the Visitor and McElroy would agree on the price to be paid. At this first interview, Sopranis wrote the General, the Archbishop had told him in the greatest secrecy, with the understanding that be would pass on the information to the general, two things: First, that the Archbishop was somewhat displeased that the General did not send direct answers to his letters. This *delicatus admodum homo* (very sensitive man), Sopranis noted, thought the general might have adopted this practice, since the Archbishop had sent his letters to Jesuit headquarters through intermediaries. The Visitor believed that the Archbishop would be pacified if the general sent him a pleasant note. The second secret was that the prelate wanted Isidore Daubresse to be the first bishop of a new diocese to be created in New York State, and he did not want the General to oppose the nomination of his subject.

To this letter of Sopranis, Beckx wrote that he had sent a letter to the Archbishop; in the letter, however, be had informed Hughes that he would do everything in his power to prevent the nomination of a Jesuit to a bishopric.[149]

Early in April 1860, Sopranis completed his visitation of the Maryland Province, and came to New York to begin the visitation of the New York-Canada Mission.[150] About the middle of the month, accompanied by McElroy, he met with the Archbishop and agreed to purchase the seminary lands for the price of $45,000. The Archbishop, at long last, agreed to revoke the cramping clause.

The consultors of the New York-Canada Mission agreed to the purchase, although they considered the price rather high.[151] In France, Hus raised his voice against the purchase, declaring that the Archbishop was unloading a white elephant, which had been to him "a mountain of expense and an abyss of shame".[152] The Jesuit general forwarded a copy of Hus' letter to the Visitor, with a notation that not too much weight should be given to Hus' opinion.[153] Beckx himself approved the purchase at the agreed price and the concomitant cancellation of the cramping clause.[154] As required by law, the St. John's Board of Trustees sanctioned the purchase.[155] At its meeting, one of the Jesuit trustees moved a resolution, unanimously passed the following :

> That this Board cannot separate without placing on record some expression of the strong sense of gratitude which they entertain towards the Most Reverend the Archbishop of New York in return for the fatherly interest which he has ever manifested for the welfare of St. John's College — of which warm interest His Grace has given still further proof in a recent transaction.

The actual transfer of the seminary property to the Jesuits was a rather long and protracted affair.[156] The fathers still had a large portion of their original debt to the Archbishop still unpaid, and the prelate wanted a down payment of $20,000 on the seminary property. A mortgage of $30,000 with private individuals was at length arranged. Finally, the matter was done. The cramping clause was canceled. The Archbishop received title to the strips of land west of the railroad.[157] And on July 16, 1860, the prelate signed the deed making over the seminary property to the College of St. John.[158] The long conflict over the tenure of the land at Fordham was finished.

In Rome, the General waited impatiently for the news that the matter had been accomplished.[159] At long last, Sopranis was able to inform him that the business was finished.[160] He noted, however, that the Archbishop would not reduce to writing his promise to turn the title of the Church of St. Francis Xavier over to the Jesuits. He urged that the General intercede by a personal letter. Beckx expressed his pleasure that the business had been brought to a successful conclusion.[161] To avoid any recurrence of questioning of the Jesuit rights to Fordham, he urged Sopranis to secure from the Archbishop any documents that might be the basis for future claims and to destroy them. This request was put to the Archbishop. In September 1860, the prelate did, in fact, turn over a number of documents to Tellier with a request that they be destroyed.[162] On hearing this news, the General expressed his relief; he felt that now the problem was forever ended.[163]

TITLE OF ST. FRANCIS XAVIER CHURCH

The question of the title of the Church of St. Francis Xavier still remained. Sopranis, however, declared that both he and McElroy were confident that the Archbishop would turn over the deed to the church before the end of 1861.[164] To the Visitor's suggestion that the general write to request the title from the Archbishop, Beckx answered that he would wait and see what Hughes' reactions were to the letter he had sent him to express his gratification at the advent of peace and the settlement of the problem of Fordham.[165]

It would appear that the general did not, at that time, request the title from the Archbishop. But in the summer of 1861, the question was discussed by Hughes and McElroy. In answer to a request from the Archbishop, McElroy listed his reason why the prelate should turn the title to the 16th Street Church over to the Jesuits.[166] The Jesuits feared that one of Hughes' successors as Archbishop of New York might replace them by secular priests; all the other Jesuit churches in America, as far as McElroy's information went, were possessions of the Society; the grant of the church's deed would increase Jesuit devotion to Hughes' service, and would be a recognition by the Archbishop of past services. Finally, McElroy requested the transfer of the title as a personal favor to himself, and as a consolation to the Jesuit general. He urged that if the title could not now be legally transferred, the Archbishop would give a written promise to the Jesuits to the effect that he would give them the title as soon as he could.

The prelate answered that the Jesuits already had a solemn document guaranteeing their rights in the 16th Street Church.[167] He further stated:

> I never had occasion to require the title to the Church of St. Francis Xavier. It was mine before the Jesuits moved to that neighborhood. It was not by their consent, but by their agreement and at their request, so far as the pastorship is concerned.

Nor could Hughes see his way clear to make a written promise of a future transfer. He ended by warning the Jesuits, "if they were wise they would be, for the present at least, quiet on this topic." The Archbishop's warning was heeded. Although in the Spring of 1862, Sopranis once more urged the Jesuit general to write to Hughes a request for a transfer of the title,[168] the suggestion was not followed.

In the course of the years following the reestablishment of peace with the Archbishop, relations between the prelate and the Jesuits became cordial. Hughes once more visited the Jesuit schools and presided at the St. John's commencements. In the Spring of 1863, for example, be was present at an academic exhibition at the College of St. Francis Xavier, and in an address to the audience expressed warm appreciation of the Jesuit school, regretting there were not another ten such colleges in his city.[169]

In the autumn of 1863, Father Beckx decided the time had come to send his request to the Archbishop for the title of Xavier church. Hughes was, at the time, on what proved to be his deathbed. Among the priests who came to pay their respects to the sick prelate were Pierre De Smet, the famous Jesuit missionary to the Indians, Felix Sopranis and John McElroy. To the general, Sopranis reported that the Archbishop had mentioned the general's request for the title of the 16th Street Church both to himself and to De Smet.[170] But to neither had the prelate given his decision. McElroy, however, reported that the Archbishop

> said not a word to Fr. Sopranis who called, nor to the other Fathers on the subject. When I called, he told me at once and that be would make a Deed of the property &c., and that I might write to that effect to Rev. Fr. General, which I did.[171]

Though the Archbishop died before be could carry his resolution into effect, his successor, John McCloskey, was aware of Hughes' desire, and as soon as he was possessed of the see of New York, he transferred the title of the church to the Jesuits.[172]

And so, as the great Archbishop awaited his end, he sealed the peace between the Jesuits and himself by the grant of the last outstanding claim of the fathers. It was with regret that the Jesuits heard of the passing of their quondam antagonist.[173]

So good men fought

It cannot be said that the history of the conflict between the Archbishop and the Jesuits is an edifying tale, or shows its chief characters in a flattering light. It was a struggle, not of principles, but of personalities. And the key to the struggle was the character of the great Archbishop of New York.

John Hughes towers above all other men in the history of the American Church in the mid 19th century. The Church then needed, above all things, a dominant leader, strong willed, resolute, inflexible. There came a man, sent from God, whose name was John. The times called for a great man, and a great man appeared. Hughes was not a man to take half-measures. Bishop Dubois was ailing and feeble; Hughes shelved him without ceremony. Trustees needed to be curbed; Hughes smashed them. Nativists threatened to attack his churches; Hughes promised that if a church was destroyed, New York, as a second Moscow, would go up in flames. It is the measure of the man that no one even suggested that he was bluffing. "I will suffer no man in my diocese that I cannot control. I will either put him down, or he shall put me down." Orestes Brownson did not question Hughes' claim. And the Jesuits, to their sorrow, learned its truth. Strong, self-confident, autocratic, Hughes had the defects of a dominant personality. He could not admit he had made a mistake. He could not brook opposition. He could not tolerate a dissenting opinion. If documentary evidence contradicted his statements, the documents were in error. His view was truth, and it must prevail. Prevail it did.

Before such a man, the actions, or rather the evasions, of the first Jesuit Regional Superior in New York are understandable. In the first years in New York, Boulanger tested the temper of the Archbishop. Thereafter, he avoided conflict with Hughes. His fellow Jesuits considered him weak; he was more probably wise. Prudence is still the better part of valor.

But Hus strode into the arena, panoplied for war. He did not wait to measure his opponent, nor consider well the ground he chose to fight on. His maladroit raising of dead issues made impossible, considering the character of the Archbishop, a conciliatory settlement of the problems the Jesuits had. His rigidity in pressing the Jesuit claims was met by an equal inflexibility, Hughes being what he was, on the part of the Archbishop. The results should have been foreseen. Battered and bruised, the Regional Superior was forced to retire. His cause may have been just, but he was not the equal of the great Archbishop.

Even the peacemaker does not show up well in the story. McElroy is one of the greatest priests America has had. He used the only method possible to placate the Archbishop — complete and abject surrender. It would be understandable if McElroy had adopted that course as a matter of policy. But be believed it was a matter of justice. Blindly, be accepted the word of his friend, and rejected the testimony of his brothers. His dependence, almost sycophantic, on Hughes does McElroy no credit.

So good men fought. It was a bitter struggle. But when peace came, the contestants, as good men, renewed friendship. The fight left no permanent scars — a testimony to the soundness of both sides. Hughes was always a redoubtable opponent, but always a good bishop and a good friend. In peace, the Jesuits secured what they had failed to obtain through war. And the Archbishop and the Jesuits, having made peace with one another, went like brothers to offer their sacrifice at the altar of the Lord.

NOTES

1 Archivum Romanum Societatis Jesu (hereafter ArchRSJ), Hus to Beckx, Jan. 6, 1856. Hus' appointment to office dated from Nov. 28, 1855; *Catalogus Provinciae Franciae*, 1856, p. 81. He had been in New York at least since Dec. 20, 1855, when he first assembled

his consultors; Archives of the New York Province (hereafter NYPA), Acta consultationum Superioris Missionis Neo-Eboracensis-Canadensis, Dec. 20, 1855.

2 See the present writer's "The Jesuits in Kentucky, 1831-1846", *MidAmerica* 35 (1953) , 242-243.

3 He had held this post since 1852; *Catalogus Provinciae Franciae*, 1855, p. 83.

4 ArchRSJ, Legoüais to Beckx, Oct. 13, 1858. Thomas Legoüais, S.J., had been with the Jesuit mission in Kentucky and later in New York from the earliest days. Before the end of his term of office, Boulanger had received similar instructions; NYPA, Acta consult., Sept. 9, 1855.

5 The original of this contract is in NYPA. The ninth clause is as follows: "Dans le cas ou les Pères Jesuites quitteront l'etablissement de New-York par le fait de leur propre volonté, la propriété, reviendroit à Monseigneur l'Évêque, qui devroit rendre aux Pĉres les sommes dejà payées sur leur dette de quarante mille dollars."

6 The sixth clause is as follows: "Monseigneur a bien voulu promettre qu'il donnera à la Compagnie une église avec une maison dans New-York aussitôt que les Pères voudront y exercet le St ministère. Cette église ne sera point paroisse et les Pères n'auront point la charge de Curé. Ils n'y célébreront pas les mariages, enterremens, baptêmes . . . Mais ils prècheront, feront le catéchisme, confesseront, donneront la bénédiction du St Sacrament &c ... recevront le produit de la location des bancs." The dots do not mark elisions; they are in the original.

7 ArchRSJ, Remigius Tellier, S.J., to Beckx, April 29, 1856. Tellier was Rector of St. John's College,, 1854-1860.

8 NYPA, Acta consult., Nov. 15, 1855.

9 NYPA, Tellier to Hus, April 24, 1856.

10 Archives of Fordham University (hereafter FUA), Minutes of the Board of Trustees of St. John's College, Nov. 14, 1855.

11 NYPA, Questions concerning the property at Fordham, Dec. 30, 1855. The author of the memorandum was probably Thomas Legoüais.

12 ArchRSJ, Tellier to Beckx, April 29, 1856.

13 It would appear that Tellier's view was just. According to Orestes Brownson, the Archbishop declared: "I will suffer no man in my diocese that I cannot control. I will either put him down, or he shall put me down." And Brownson believed the Archbishop. "The Most Rev.. John Hughes, D.D.," *Brownson's Quarterly Review*, Last Series 2 (1874) 84, cited in Henry J. Browne, "Archbishop Hughes and Western Colonization," *Catholic Historical Review*, 36 (1950) 284.

14 NYPA, Clover to the "Rev. Gent. of St. John's College," March 30, 1856.

15 NYPA, Hus to Tellier, April 19, 1856.

16 NYPA, Tellier, to Hus, April 24, 1856.

17 NYPA, Hus to Tellier, April 20, 1856.

18 NYPA, Tellier to Hus, May 13, 1856.

19 NYPA, Hus, Directions to Jesuit Trustees, Sept. 7, 1856; another draft, dated Sept. 10, 1856, gives the same instructions.

20 FUA, Minutes of Board, Sept. 11, 1856.

21 Ibid.

22 Ibid., Nov. 7, 1857.

23 Ibid., Dec. 10, 1863.

24 NYPA, Hus to Tellier, Oct. 29, 1856. The priest to whom the Archbishop spoke was John Larkin, S.J.

25 ArchRSJ, Hus to Beckx, Dec. 3, 1856.

26 NYPA, Acta consult., Dec. 4, 1856.

27 ArchRSJ, Hus to Beckx, March 7, 1857.

28 ArchRSJ, Hus, *Situation materielle des deux Etablissements de la Cie de Jésus à New York, March 5, 1857.*

29 ArchRSJ, Hus to Beckx, Aug. 4, 1857.

30 NYPA, O'Connor, Statement of case, May 7, 1857.

31 NYPA, Hus to Tellier, May 15, 1857.

32 NYPA, O'Conor to Tellier, June 1, 1857.

33 NYPA, Tellier to O'Conor, June 3, 1857.

34 NYPA, Hughes to Tellier, June 24, 1857.

35 NYPA, Hughes to Michael Driscol, S.J., June 24, 1857.

36 NYPA, Tellier to Hughes, June 25, 1857.

37 NYPA, Murphy, Account of the Archbishop's reception of the Jesuits, July 9, 1857.

38 NYPA, Hughes to Tellier, July 12, 1857.

39 NYPA, Tellier to Hughes, July 13, 1857.

40 NYPA, Tellier to Hus, July 21, 1857.

41 FUA, Minutes of Board. The Board did not meet until November 10, 1857

42 NYPA, Glover to Tellier (?), August 11, 1857.

43 NYPA, Acta consult., Aug. 13, 1857.

44 NYPA, Acta consult. Aug. 20, Aug. 26, 1857.

45 ArchRSJ, Hus to Beckx, Aug. 20, 1857.

46 ArchRSJ, Hus to Hughes, Aug. 17, 1857. This was the copy Hus sent to the Jesuit general.

47 This final complaint is disingenuous. Although in his letter to Tellier and, apparently, to Hargous, the Archbishop did not mention the reason why he wanted the Board to meet, it is clear that he intended to appear at the meeting and have the Board listen to his refutation of the charges allegedly brought against him by the Jesuits.

48 NYPA, Acta consult., Oct. 4, 1857.

49 ArchRSJ, Hus to Ambrose Rubillon, S.J., Nov. 17, 1857. Rubillon was the French assistant to the Jesuit general.

50 NYPA, Hughes to Board of Trustees, Nov. 9, 1857.

51 FUA, Minutes of Board, Nov. 10, 1857. Glover, the Archbishop's lawyer, was absent from this and subsequent meetings of the Board.

52 ArchRSJ, Hus to Rubillon, Nov. 17, 1857.

53 ArchRSJ, Hus to Rubillon, Dec. 5, 1857. This meeting took place on Nov. 23, 1857 .

54 NYPA, Acta consult., Nov. 13; Nov. 26, 1857.

55 ArchRSJ, Hus to Hargous, Nov. 26, 1857.

56 When Bishop Hughes was preparing to open the College of St. John he had made an appeal for the college throughout his diocese. The Mrs. McCarthy in question had then made a will which included a legacy of $10,000 for St. John's College. Though she died shortly after, the will was not probated until 1855. The fathers had not received the money by the end of 1857; ArchRSJ, Hus to Rubillon, Nov. 17, 1857. The lawyer in charge of the probate informed the fathers that since the will stipulated that the money was to be turned over to Bishop Hughes for the College of St. John's, the money had been delivered to the Archbishop. Fr. Starrs informed the Jesuits that the Archbishop was using the money, stipulated for the College of St. John, to pay the expenses of the students in the Seminary of St. Joseph; ArchRSJ, Hus to Rubillon, Jan. 20, 1858.

57 The import of this complaint may refer to a number of incidents. Later the Archbishop was to admit that he spoke too strongly when he wrote to Boulanger asserting that the Jesuits in his diocese had done nothing to advance the work of education; ArchRSJ, Legoüais, Procès-verbal, Sept. 28, 1858. It may also refer to the criticism of Jesuit

education, as favoring the growth of infidelity and as inimical to the republican institutions of the United States which had appeared in the *Freeman's Journal* in 1849-1850. Since the *Freeman's Journal* very frequently reflected Hughes' opinions, and since the prelate did nothing to prevent the publications of these strictures nor did he publicly reprehend them, the Jesuits were very much perturbed; ArchRSJ, Ignatius Brocard, S.J., to John Roothaan, S.J., Oct. 6, Dec. 15, 1849, Jan. 6, 1850. Brocard was then provincial of the Maryland Province, and Roothaan was the Jesuit General. As a result of these attacks, the fathers at St. John's College decided to cease the publication of the college prospectus in the *Freeman's Journal*; FUA, Acta consultationum Collegii Sti. Joannis, May 17, 1850.

58 ArchRSJ, Hus to Rubillon, Jan. 20, 1858.

59 ArchRSJ, Hus to Rubillon, Feb. 1, 1858.

60 ArchRSJ, Legoüais to Beckx, Feb. 12, 1858.

61 ArchRSJ, Hus to Rubillon, March 9, 1858.

62 ArchRSJ, Hus to Rubillon, April 8, 1858.

63 NYPA, Beckx to Hughes, May 8, 1858.

64 ArchRSJ, Hughes to Beckx, June 3, 1858.

65 NYPA, Acta consult., Aug. 26, 1858.

66 ArchRSJ, Legoüais to Rubillon, Sept. 17, 1858.

67 NYPA, Beckx to McElroy, Aug. 14, 1858.

68 NYPA, Hus to Tellier (?), Aug. 15, 1858.

69 NYPA, Hughes to McElroy, Sept. 4, 1858.

70 NYPA, Hughes to Hus, Sept. 4, 1858.

71 ArchRSJ, Hus to Beckx, Sept. 10, 1858.

72 NYPA, Murphy to Hus, Sept. 9, Sept. 10, 1858.

73 ArchRSJ, Plaintes des Pères de la Compagnie de Jésus contre Msgr. John Hughes, Archevêque de New York, undated; 2e Project d'Exposé, de nos griefs, Sept. 10, 1858. NYPA, Draft of difficulties . . . , Sept. 12 (?), 1858.

74 NYPA, Hughes, "Mode of proceeding . . . . " Sept. 14, 1858.

75 It may be noted that the present writer has seen no Jesuit document which gives any basis for the Archbishop's second grievance. The other three complaints are based on claims which the Jesuits did make.

76 NYPA, Hus to Hughes, Sept. 22, 1858.

77 ArchRSJ, Hus to Rubillon, Oct. 6, 1858.

78 ArchRSJ, Legoüais, 3e note sur les affaires de N.Y., Oct. 4, 1858; Hus to Rubillon, Oct. 6, 1858.

79 ArchRSJ, Legoüais, Procès-verbal de la Conférence du 28 Sept. 1858 tenue dans la Sacristie de la Cathédrale de N.Y. . . . An English draft of this report is in NYPA.

80 They had been selected at a meeting of the Mission consultors. NYPA, Acta consult., Aug. 30, 1858.

81 ArchRSJ, contains the copy of this statement sent to the General by Archbishop Hughes some time after the conference.

82 ArchRSJ, Legoüais, Procès-verbal.

83 NYPA, McElroy and Stonestreet to Beckx, Sept. 28, 1858.

84 ArchRSJ, McElroy to Beckx, Oct. 6, 1858.

85 ArchRSJ, Legoüais, 3e note sur les affaires de N.Y., Oct . 4, 1858.

86 ArchRSJ, Hus to Beckx, Sept. 29, 1858; Larkin to Beckx, Oct. 10, 1858.

87 ArchRSJ, Larkin to Beckx, Oct. 10, 1858.

88 Ibid.

89 ArchRSJ, Hus to Beckx, Sept. 29, 1858; Larkin to Beckx, Oct. 10, 1858.

90 ArchRSJ, Legoüais, 3e note sur les affaires de N.Y., Oct. 4, 1858.

91 Ibid. A study of the original contract in NYPA shows conclusively that the words "avec une maison" were part of the original text. By this assertion, the Archbishop, for all practical purposes, accused the Jesuits of tampering with documents, if not of forgery. The rather surprising thing is that the documents show that the Jesuit reaction to this charge was extremely mild possibly because the Fathers were accused of so many things, in their view baseless, that another charge could not disturb them.

92 ArchRSJ, Hus to Beckx, Sept. 29, 1858.

93 Ibid. The college had cost about $40,000—$29,000 for the land, $10,000 for re-modeling the buildings. Hus cites the letter of Hughes to Larkin, Oct. 8, 1845, in which the bishop said that of that sum he had paid $5-6,000 from money on hand, had collected $18-20,000 from the diocese, and had added sums from other sources, as subsidies of the Society of the Propagation of the Faith. Hus notes that the bishop, during the years 1840-1845, had received $48,000 from the French Society. Consequently, the bishop could have paid off every cent of the $40,000 before the Jesuits came to New York. There is independent evidence to show there is some justice in Hus' contention. In 1843, Bishop Hughes informed a Maryland Jesuit that the debts of the college were $19,000. ArchRSJ, Anthony Rey, S.J., to John Roothaan, Nov. 27, 1843. In the three subsequent years, according to the bishop's statement of profits the college would have cleared at least $30,000, wiping out the debt. John Hassard, *Life of the Most Rev. John Hughes*, (New York, Appleton, 1866), 204, notes, that of the $40,000 "A large part of the money was obtained in this way by voluntary subscription; a considerable sum was collected in Europe and the rest was finally raised by loans in small amounts . . ."

94 ArchRSJ, Hus to Rubillon, Oct. 6, 1858. He declares that the priest who had been the college treasurer during the years of Hughes' administration had informed the Jesuits that St. John's had lost money each year save one when its net profit was less than $1,000. Hus pointed out that, if the Archbishop's estimate of yearly profits were true, the Jesuits, in their dozen years at Fordham, would have cleared about $120,000; instead, they were able to reduce their debt only by $17,000.

95 Ibid. In 1843, the bishop had valued the college at only $70,000; ArchRSJ, Rey to Roothaan, Nov. 27, 1843.

96 ArchRSJ, Legoüais to Beckx, Oct. 13, 1858.

97 Hus had, in fact, introduced these problems at his first meetings with his consultors; NYPA, Acta consult., Dec. 20, 1855.

98 ArchRSJ, Hus to Rubillon, Oct. 22, 1858.

99 ArchRSJ, Boulanger to Rubillon (?), Oct. 20, 1858

100 ArchRSJ, Boulanger to Beckx, Nov. 5, 1858.

101 ArchRSJ, Hus to Rubillon, Oct. 22, 1858.

102 ArchRSJ, Legoüais to Beckx, Oct. 13, 1858; Tellier to Beckx, Oct. 26, 1858.

103 NYPA, Beckx to Hus, Nov. 2, 1858.

104 ArchRSJ, Tellier to Beckx, Oct. 26, 1858.

105 ArchRSJ, Hus to Beckx, Nov. 29, 1858.

106 ArchRSJ, Hus to Beckx, Dec. 1, 1858.

107 NYPA, Acta consult., Nov. 29, 1858.

108 ArchRSJ, Hus to Beckx, Dec. 1, 1858.

109 ArchRSJ, Hus to Rubillon, Dec. 9, 1858.

110 NYPA, Beckx to McElroy, Jan. 2, 1859.

111 NYPA, Beckx to Hughes, Jan. 4, 1859.

112 NYPA, Acta consult., Jan. 27, 1859.

113 ArchRSJ, Hus to Beckx, Feb. 10, 1859.

114 ArchRSJ, McElroy to Beckx, March 14, 1859.

115 NYPA, Acta consult., Feb. 23, 1859. ArchRSJ, Un extrait très ample de ces informations, traduit en Anglais par un des CC a été lu et remis sur sa demands au P. McElroy avant il a [sic] du faire sa 1ere démarche, Feb. 25, 1859.

116 NYPA, Acta consult., Feb. 26, 1859. McElroy to Beckx, March 14, 1859.

117 ArchRSJ, Hus to Beckx, March 3, 1859.

118 NYPA, Acta consult., Feb. 23, 1859, states that McElroy read the general's letter to Hus and the consultors.

119 ArchRSJ, Hus to Beckx, March 3, 1859.

120 ArchRSJ, McElroy to Beckx, March 14, 1859.

121 NYPA, Acta consult., Feb. 27, 1859; Apology made to Arch B.[ishop] Hughes by Father McElroy on behalf of the Fathers of New York, March 1, 1859.

122 Hus did not greet the Archbishop, nor appear at the dinner, which appeared to McElroy worthy of note; ArchRSJ, McElroy to Beckx, March 14, 1859. Hus explained his absence, declaring it his usual practice, due to his lack of English, to avoid such gatherings; ArchRSJ, Hus to Beckx, March 3, 1859.

123 ArchRSJ, Hus to Beckx, March 3, 1859. ArchRSJ, Legoüais(?), Actual State of Our Relations with the Archbishop, Nov. 27, 1859, states that Hus was informed of the meeting, and was told that he might attend but that he was not invited.

124 ArchRSJ, Legoüais (?), Actual State of Our Relations with the Archbishop, Nov. 27, 1859, has a report of this consultation.

125 ArchRSJ, Hus to Beckx, March 3, 1859.

126 ArchRSJ, Hus, "Protest and Appeal", March 3, 1859.

127 ArchRSJ, Hus to Beckx, Marcb 4, 1859.

128 ArchRSJ, McElroy to Beckx, March 14, 1859.

129 ArchRSJ, Hus to Beckx, March 4, 1859; Hus to Rubillon, March 6, March 7, March ?, 1859.

130 NYPA, Acta consult., April 23, 1859.

131 ArchRSJ, McElroy to Beckx, March 14, 1859.

132 NYPA, Hughes to McElroy, March 7, 1859.

133 NYPA, Beckx to McElroy, June 11, 1859.

134 ArchRSJ, Murphy to Beckx, March 22, 1859.

135 NYPA, Acta consult., April 23, 1859.

136 The news reached New York on May 7, 1859; NYPA, Acta consult., May 7, 1859.

137 Tellier's appointment dated from Nov. 7, 1859; *Catalogus Provinciae Franciae*, 1861, p. 86. Murphy was sent South for his health, whence he was recalled in 1861 to be vice-provincial of Missouri. Cf. Gilbert J. Garraghan, *The Jesuits of the Middle United States*, (3 vol. New York: America Press, 1938) I, 567.

138 ArchRSJ, Legoüais (?), Actual State of Our Relations with the Archbishop, Nov. 27, 1859.

139 ArchRSJ, Beckx to Sopranis, Sept. 20, 1859.

140 ArchRSJ, Notae circa missiones Provinciae Franciae, Sept. ?, 1859.

141 ArchRSJ, Benedict Sestini, Breve narrazione della visita di Maryland . . . , Aug. (?), 1860. For a time, Sestini acted as Sopranis' socius.

142 ArchRSJ, McElroy to Beckx, Dec. 16, 1859.

143 NYPA, Hughes to McElroy, Dec. 11, 1859.

144 ArchRSJ, Hughes to Beckx, Dec. 12, 1859.

145 ArchRSJ, McElroy to Beckx, Dec. 16, 1859.

146 ArchRSJ, Beckx to Sopranis, Jan. 21, 1860.

147 NYPA, Acta consult., July 7, 1856.

148 ArchRSJ, Sopranis to Beckx, March 31, 1860.

149 ArchRSJ, Beckx to Sopranis, April 27, 1860.

150 ArchRSJ, Sestini, Breve narrazione.

151 NYPA, Acta consult., April 17, 1860.

152 ArchRSJ, Hus to Michael Fessard, S.J., May ?, 1860. Fessard was provincial of the Province of France.

153 ArchRSJ, Beckx to Sopranis, June 9, 1860.

154 ArchRSJ, Beckx to Sopranis, May 19, 1860.

155 FUA, Minutes of Board, May 3, 1860.

156 NYPA, Tellier (?), Historical sketch of the transact. of the Sem., 1860.

157 FUA, Minutes of the Boards, June 29, 1860, authorized this transfer. At a meeting later in the year, Starrs, obviously under instructions of the Archbishop, moved that Augustus Thébaud, the new president of St. John's, consult with the Archbishop about the fancy-fence, still not erected by the railroad; ibid., Dec. 20, 1860. Thébaud did so, and reported that the railroad would at long last erect the fence in the Spring of 1862; ibid., Nov. 4, 1861.

158 ArchRSJ, Deed of sale of St. Joseph's Seminary, July 16,1860.

159 ArchRSJ, Beckx to Sopranis, Aug. 11, 1860.

160 ArchRSJ, Sopranis to Beckx, July 28, 1860.

161 ArchRSJ, Beckx to Sopranis, Aug. 28, 1860.

162 NYPA, Tellier, Statement, March 2, 1861. Tellier did destroy them. But first he made copies in a note-book still preserved in NYPA. A study of this note-book shows that, with the exception of the private deed confirming the ninth clause and signed in July 1845 by Boulanger, all the documents exist, in original or in copy in one or other Jesuit archive.

163 ArchRSJ, Beckx to Sopranis, Oct. 8, 1860.

164 ArchRSJ, Sopranis to Beckx, Oct. 21, 1860.

165 ArchRSJ, Beckx to Sopranis, Dec. 14, 1860.

166 NYPA, McElroy to Hughes, Aug. 24, 1861.

167 NYPA, Hughes to McElroy, Aug. 30, 1861.

168 ArchRSJ, Sopranis to Beckx, May 14, 1862.

169 ArchRSJ, Sopranis to Beckx, March 21, 1863.

170 ArchRSJ, Sopranis to Beckx, Dec. 2, 1863.

171 Woodstock Archives, McElroy to Angelo Paresce, S.J., Dec. 12, 1863. Paresce was provincial of the Maryland Province.

172 ArchRSJ, Joseph Loyzance, S.J., to Beckx, Dec. 19, 1864. Loyzance was Rector of Xavier. See the documents in John Cardinal Farley, *Life of John Cardinal McCloskey*, 248 ff.

173 ArchRSJ, Sopranis to Beckx, Jan. 4, 1864; Beckx to Sopranis, Jan. 17, 1864.

Chapter VIII

Towards
An Effective History
of The First Fordham Jesuits

By James R. Kelly

In reading the essays in this book, three words kept coming to my mind: community, memory and mission. I wanted to be sure not to use these words glibly. In this age of suspicion we are properly wary of any casual use of the precious term "community," as in a "community of nations" where national self-interest is sovereign. Or as in a "community of scholars," where too often careerism rules. The very urgency of our need for more solidarity among nations and more community among, in John Paul II's felicitous phrase, intellectual workers (*On Human Labor*, 1981) prompts our wariness. It seems to me that the best protection against trivialization is to show that, when they are authentic, the three terms belong together.

There are signs that tell us when we are in the presence of an aspiration towards community: when we can experience our daily labors as part of some larger and worthy goal. The aspiration towards community exists when we feel some significant connection with those who have gone before us, with our immediate colleagues, and with those who will take our place. The first of these three connections has passed into history and the third has yet to come. Only memory ties them together. A community without memory is a sociological contradiction in terms. The motive of memory is gratitude and the hope of memory is renewal of mission. Without community, idealism must wither. Although it is not much remarked on, intellectuals, since they must reject all false consolations, especially require community, for without its support idealism must wither and a sense of mission narrow to mere ambition.

It can be no surprise that, more than a century and a half after their arrival, we have this volume of essays written mostly by Jesuits about the first Fordham Jesuits. Gratitude is one of the defining characteristics of the Jesuit spiritual style. The culminating point of St. Ignatius' *Spiritual Exercises* is the fourth week where the director is advised to suggest for the retreatant's prayer four focal points — each dealing with the theme of gratitude: God's gifts to me; God's gift of himself to me; God's labors for me; God as Giver and Gift. The point of remembering (and we'll return to this crucial Ignatian theme) is the *present*: to better serve God's purposes in creation now. Only the grateful person can be motivated to serve purposes larger than his or her own interests. There is no surprise, then, in the appearance of this long overdue volume. The surprise — indeed, the shock — would be to have no Jesuit volume recalling the Fordham Jesuit founders.

Jesuit Memory and the Rest of Us

But the book is by contemporary Jesuits and about the first Fordham Jesuits. What about us non-Jesuits and Fordham's increasingly lay future? Is there something in this story — certainly fascinating in its own right — that can prompt something deeper than a civil acknowledgment that a Fordham history must begin with them?[1] Not all history is effective history. Do New York University professors, for example, remember who started NYU? Does it matter any more? Did the NYU founders have a particular "vision" and, if they did, what difference does it make for how contemporary NYU professors profess? Let's review some of the Fordham history seeing what can make it an effective history connected to our Fordham challenges. As a start, we should point out that the reader will find no myth making in this volume. Its authors seek only the complicated truth, which, right from the start, tells us something attractive about the Jesuit spirituality that animates their idealism.

Nearly Clueless in the New World

The first general impression one gets from this history is how seemingly haphazard, unplanned and even accidental Fordham's founding was. I take its "accidental" origin as an advantage for Fordham present. There is no originating Fordham golden era whose mythic security can distract it from confronting its own ambiguous present and challenging future. Fordham's history itself directs us bravely forward, not nostalgically backward. The point warrants a few particulars.

The intersecting historical accidents that finally conjoined to form Fordham University in the Bronx began in France. Only when the 1830 July Revolution closed down their colleges in France "leaving," in C. M. Buckley, S.J.'s cheeky phrase in Chapter III, "many talented men without jobs," did the French Jesuits accept an invitation to open a college in Kentucky. Fordham College owes its start to a religious downsizing in France.

Their history yields ample reasons for modesty. But also hope. Faith and hope, in fact, were their primary resources. When the first band of unemployed French Jesuits finally made their way to St. Mary's in Kentucky they discovered that their new college's main building was an abandoned moonshine distillery. Fr. Buckley does not say whether their distillery discovery dampened or deepened their enthusiasm but he highlights their dogged faith, "As Providence would have it, so modest a structure as an unused stillhouse was destined to be the embryo from which Fordham University has taken its present glorious shape."

The "so modest" above might even be a euphemism. There wasn't much Kentucky money around at the time and so the Jesuits discovered the *student* worker. Students could pay their college tuition in kind - including tobacco. And all students - even those from the better off families - were required to work at least one day a week on the Jesuit farm. Whether because of bad backs or bad breeding or bad booze, the Jesuit students were on occasion badly behaved. As in the rougher inner city schools of our day, rival groups of students fought over dormitory turf. It comes as a relief not to read that the Jesuits invented metal detectors. Fr. Buckley forgivingly observes, "You could take the stillhouse from the boys but it was another matter of taking boys from the stillhouse."

Chief among the reasons the Jesuits had for leaving their first college in Kentucky for a new one in what would become The Bronx was the fact that New York City Bishop John Hughes made them an offer they couldn't refuse: lots of land and not only a college but a seminary thrown in as well. The Rose Hill campus, besides, was close to many more (and more prosperous) Catholics. Jesuit sources note that the Kentucky bishops had not always recompensed them for their services and contributions.

But their first Fordham years were as tough as their last Kentucky years. And not merely economically tough. It was certainly no idyllic time of Jesuit-hierarchy harmony, as Francis X. Curran's decidedly non-hagiographic account of the first Fordham years makes clear. We might easily mistake his history of Jesuits' dealings with Archbishop Hughes for the minutes of a tortuous Wall Street merger between two suspicious corporations. Both sides ignored the Gospel injunction of reconciling with your brother before approaching the altar in favor of the American approach to conflicts of interest: hire the best lawyer. Hughes' style strikes the contemporary reader as abrupt. In Fordham's first five years there were four presidents and several acting presidents.

In terms of money, Catholic higher education never had a golden age. But even in a context of general penury, the early Fordham seems especially penurious. The first Jesuits had to make begging trips to Chile and Mexico. This was not a voluntary poverty, nor do the first Fordham Jesuits anticipate with any clarity the post-Second Vatican phrase, *option for the poor*. It was mostly, and probably inevitably, the sons of the middle and upper class Catholics who found their way to Fordham. But not exclusively. Jesuits sought to educate future leaders for the faith, not future apologists for wealth. We can take as a healthy sign of the continued presence of Jesuit educational ideals Fordham's recent announcement that freshmen from its surrounding boroughs who continue to live with their families will receive a substantial reduction in tuition.[2]

Fr. Hennessy's patient research on the first Fordham Jesuits informs us that they numbered 47 in the 1846 Fall semester. Twenty-five were faculty or staff and current faculty readers of this volume will be relieved to know that the remaining 22 were not administrators. (In fact, the Jesuit practice of that time was that administrators also taught.) The other Jesuits on campus were mostly seminarians or novices who also were engaged in pastoral work of various kinds including working with the poor, pertinently reminding us that the legacy of the first Fordham Jesuits includes outreach and community service.

So too was what we would now boastfully call *multiculturalism*. Indeed, if we speculate about what the first Fordham Jesuits might think about today's Fordham, among our certainties would be their approval of our new curriculum's encouragement of *global studies*. The first Jesuits embodied multiculturalism. The first 47 Jesuits came from 10 different nations — about two-fifths from France, one-fifth from Ireland and the rest from Germany, Canada, Spain, England, Czechoslovakia, Haiti and two from the United States. We read, for example, that Fr. Marinus Desjacques' (1824-1884) first assignment was at the seminary in 'Chang-Hai, China.

The Whole Being Much Larger than the Sum of Its Parts

But this reader must confess that he found a certain generic quality to these Jesuit biographical sketches. The first impression is how little of their individual emotional or spiritual lives comes through in the few lines that can be given to each. Limitations of space makes this a necessity. But it is also the case that their individual personas are absorbed in their communal calling. We can abstractly note this but in our more confessional, Oprhaettic era we are not prepared to instinctively admire it. We could use some more help. For example, in 1845 Fr. Clement Boulanger (1790-1868) was the official Visitor to the New York Mission from the Province of France. He played a key role in setting up the Jesuit-Archbishop Hughes' strained relationship. But he was more than a skilled administrator. We learn "His writings reflect his deep concern for the spiritual program of his fellow Jesuits and their studies." But we do not read any of his spiritual advice. We learn that Fr. Edward Doucet (1825-1890) was a friend of Edgar Allen Poe "who loved to wander about the college grounds and mingle with the Fathers." But we do not hear what they said to each other.

Occasionally, a detail by itself manages to suggest to the imagination a flesh and blood presence. My favorite comes in the sketch of Fr. John Aloysius Larkin, the first Jesuit college dean and the second Jesuit president who weighed more than 300 pounds and whose father was an Irish innkeeper. On the eve of Fr. Larkin's move from Louisville, Kentucky, to the Bronx we learn that "On a few days notice he delivered an eloquent address on 'Genius' before the Mercantile Library Association... supplying the place of ex-President John Quincy Adams who had been announced as the speaker." I think I have met this Jesuit. Or at least his spirit quite alive in some of his contemporary brothers.

At other times details would be superfluous. We can ourselves presume to supply the meaning of the act and understand the source of its motivation. About Fordham Fathers Driscol, Férard, Schiansky and Du Merle, I recall only that they "responded to a request for help from Jesuits in Montreal to assist them in their priestly ministry to Irish immigrants stricken with cholera." And for a community of memory, that's enough to know.

There might have been among these Jesuit pioneers spiritual "giants" and preternaturally gifted educators and even wise administrators, but from what we read we cannot say this with certainty. It is this very non-mythic quality of the first Fordham Jesuits and, as important, the complete disinterest in myth-making shown by their 20th century Jesuit historian brothers, that are important resources for thinking about the future of Jesuit educational ideals. For this larger context of Fordham and its future, a few general points made by Jesuit scholars about Jesuit education are pertinent.

Fordham Origins and the Larger Jesuit Picture

The First Jesuits by John W. O'Malley, S.J. is essential reading for anyone with even the slightest impulse towards memory and gratitude regarding things Jesuit.[3] O'Malley's book is about the first Jesuit years and, since Fordham was founded about three centuries after the founding of the first Jesuit College in Messina, Sicily, Fordham is absent from his history. But the early Jesuit history cannot be absent from Fordham's.

With an almost eerie parallelism, Fordham's history reads like the New York version of the larger Jesuit story in education. There was no Jesuit master plan for Jesuit education and O'Malley registers his amazement over "how easily the first Jesuits glided into a decision of this magnitude and how little account they seem to have taken of its manifold impact on them" (p. 200).[4] By 1773 (the date of the Order's suppression) the Jesuits were responsible for over 800 educational institutions (universities, seminaries and, mostly, secondary schools), comprising an international network never seen before. But the Jesuits followed no grand strategy except, as we saw in the case of Fordham, the preference for schools in the larger and more important cities. In retrospect, the Jesuit talent was in discernment and synthesis, not innovation, and they took for granted the humanist convictions of the time that learning and literacy were goods in themselves.[5]

It's pertinent for today's Fordham and its challenges to read that, counter to the stereotype, the first Jesuits showed no preoccupation with any counterreformation obsession[6] with orthodoxy, nor did they particularly link their schools with any of the more grandiose schemes for Church reform. Without defensiveness, the early Jesuits, intent on service, were attentive to the excellencies of mind and spirit of others and, with discrimination, carefully absorbed them into their own practices. We might even call this an adumbration of an ecumenical impulse that others can find intellectually attractive about Jesuit educational ideals. Discernment, it's worth repeating, is the ordinary kind of Jesuit creativity. It's important to realize that the intellectual values of discernment, discrimination and imaginative reconstruction were rooted in the spiritual experiences of the Jesuit founder, St. Ignatius, and in the legacy of spirituality he left in his Spiritual Exercises.

THE SPIRITUAL EXERCISES' ROLE IN EFFECTIVE HISTORY

Ignatius Loyola had elaborated a powerful method of spiritual introspection, dialogue with God,[7] to be more precise, to discern God's will. From the start, the spirit of the *Exercises*, the generous and free response to the movement of God's grace, infused the Jesuits' curriculum and their pedagogical methods. The point of the *Exercises* was greater service, and so, for example, the Jesuit techniques of frequent writing, oral exercises, theater-arts were all designed to make sure the student was actively involved in his education. Like other Fordham faculty, I have attended numerous curriculum discussions. In retrospect, their basic assumptions, what's taken for granted, have reflected the core premises of the *Exercises*, as I'll suggest with the most recent example.

At Fordham there is a constant tension, at its best, a creative tension, among the goals of research and publication, teaching and service. In what seems to me a "bottom line" fashion, undergraduate courses are "capped" at 35 students, making it more likely that each instructor can treat each student with the *familiaritas* urged by the first Jesuits. It is the Fordham expectation[8] that each student in each class be invited to become an active center of learning and integrity. With some regularity, departments think they have discovered a solution to this tension between research and teaching time and request permission for large "master" classes with a hundred or more students. This last happened during a Fall, 1997, Dean's meeting. The dean responded, "Not on my watch," as had all previous deans in my experience. Neither this dean nor any of his predecessors directly quoted from Fordham history, much less from the *Spiritual Exercises* of St. Ignatius. Rather, he simply reaffirmed a basic understanding held by this community of memory. He spoke confidently, as though he were simply reactivating a conviction held by most Fordham faculty. And the faculty reacted similarly. No one criticized the decision, not even the department whose request occasioned it. If these understandings are an effective part of a community of memory, will they remain so? And how?

228

Then and Now: Does Fordham Possess an Effective History

The editor suggested I address two questions in this chapter: "What have we learned about the pioneer Fordham Jesuits that might have pertinence today? Is there any lasting special impact of the French Province and French culture on the University? If not, why not?" I read the questions before I read the book and found myself muttering to myself, "Undoubtedly very little to the first, probably nothing to the second." I envisioned a very short chapter, but the book changed my mind. There is an effective history available at Fordham that isn't available, say, at New York University.[9]

As a group those first Jesuits were *extraordinary* not merely in their moral bravery but in their *intellectual* bravery in ways that warrant our close attention. They were the opposite of self-indulgent; they were not careerists; they did not whine. I now have longer answers to the editor's questions and to make them plausible I'll need three parts: the first, on changing times and the changing numbers of Jesuits at Fordham; the second, to consider Fordham's past; and the third, to look at Fordham's future in the context of the history of the secularization of Protestant higher education; in this third section I'll offer some examples of what seem to me creative efforts that offer some solid reasons for rejecting any hypothesis of an inevitable loss of Jesuit identity in Fordham's effective history.

PART I

Jesuit Numbers and Jesuit Ideals

Nineteen ninety-eight is a long time from 1846, not merely in time but in sensibility. America has changed from an agrarian nation of little world influence, either for good or for bad, to a superpower with nonpareil power for doing good or for doing bad. As I write this (February, 1998), the President just gave a speech telling the American people to prepare themselves for the bombing of Iraq.[10] And, as much (I think more) as any institutionalized presence in the modern world, Roman Catholicism has changed. In the words of the Second Vatican Council documents, the Catholic Church seeks a public presence not through political privilege but, with many lurches back and forth, by being Christ's sacrament as a servant church.

We have yet to absorb the full meaning of these changes. For example, both the Pope and the American Catholic bishops have said the Clinton plan to bomb Iraq to force compliance with United Nations inspection teams does not meet the criteria for a just war. These acts of public disagreement with an American President's judgments about national security would have been unthinkable before the Second Vatican Council. Finally, American Catholicism has changed as well, developing from a small and lowly presence to a relatively affluent, mainstream American denomination.

Of course, Fordham has changed as well. And will keep changing, as American society changes, as the world Church changes, as American Catholicism changes, and as higher education changes. Especially pertinent for Fordham are the changes in the Jesuit order, in self-conception, in mission, and in numbers.

Amidst these changes, the simplest fact to observe, the great decline in the number of Fordham Jesuits, is the most complicated to deal with. In 1846 Fordham College opened with 25 Jesuits and 5 lay faculty. We can be dramatic and say that the first Fordham Jesuits comprised 83% of the first Fordham faculty and now a mere 6%.[11] One hundred and fifty two years after its Jesuit founding Fordham actually had more Jesuit faculty (20 full time and 9 part-time; and 14 Jesuit administrators) than at its founding but now there were 508 full-time faculty. Numbers are not the same as "presence" but they are not unrelated. History will soon tell us just how interconnected they are.

Following Fr. Hennessy's lead we might ask ourselves what the first Fordham Jesuits might think of a Fordham where they would be the minority? In fact, they might not even qualify to join the Jesuit minority. Nowadays no one teaches at Fordham without a doctorate.[12] Perhaps the de facto most significant criterion in hiring and then in promotion is the faculty member's promise of contributing to his or her professional discipline. This was not the strongest motivation of the first Jesuits. O'Malley writes (1993: 214) "Under the influence of Quintillan and other theorists, the Jesuits looked more to formation of mind and character, to *Bildung*, than to the acquisition of ever more information or the advancement of the disciplines." No contemporary university can exist without approval of accreditation by numerous state and professional agencies. By the mid-1990s Fordham was, to varying degrees, accountable to over 25 of them.[13] There were none for the first Jesuits. They only had to convince the Governor or the legislature to grant them a charter.

The first Fordham Jesuits could expect something like a "captive" audience for their new college. If mid-19th century Catholic parents could afford a college education for their upwardly mobile sons, the college they picked would assuredly be Catholic. It was psychologically impossible, because sociologically unnecessary, to distinguish between their desire for social status and their desire for religious loyalty. In the nineteenth century there was little public (and so little introspective) differentiation among class, race, ethnicity, status and religion. Like all cultural others, Catholic identity became more explicit and more defensive the more Protestant America made them feel inferior and suspect; in those days this happened often.

Fordham's expansion was assured by its role (necessarily speaking broadly here) in a separatist and defensive American subculture of Roman Catholicism which, only a century later, was challenged religiously by the Second Vatican Council and demographically by the economic success and "Americanization" of Catholics. By the late 1960s, the income and education of American non-Hispanic Catholics surpassed Protestants and were exceeded only by Jews. The variables of religion, ethnicity, and class had become disentangled and so, by the late 1960s, the decision to attend Fordham as opposed to, say, a more prestigious Ivy college or a more economical state college, was no longer automatic. In mid-19th century religion was a "given," similar to ethnicity. By the mid-20th century religion was becoming a personal choice, similar to occupation.

And so to our obvious point. Questions of Fordham identity and its relationship to the Jesuits cannot be thought about apart from questions about the relationship between Catholicism and American Culture and about the fate of Protestant Colleges and Universities. How can we be succinct about such historically complex matters? Charles R. Morris' *American Catholic* (1997)[14] is a highly praised account of Catholicism in America. George M. Marsden's *The Soul of the American University From Protestant Establishment To Established Nonbelief* (1994)[15] is recognized as a major study of the secularization of initially Protestant colleges and universities. Together, Morris and Marsden can summarize for us Fordham's cultural and educational context.

PART II

FORDHAM'S PAST: IMAGES OF FORDHAM AND AMERICAN CATHOLICISM

As teachers like to remind freshmen, our sources give us no easy answers. If Marsden is right, and he doesn't want to be,[16] continuing secularization of higher education seems inevitable; if Morris is correct, Catholicism has unraveled, "stuck awkwardly in midtransition from one vision of Church and ministry to another, frightened of going forward but not quite able to go back" (1997: 373). Fordham is a topic in neither book but each author mentions Fordham in off-hand but revealing ways. It's the very "offhandedness" of these references by two highly praised authors that can serve us here. They unselfconsciously tell us how the cultural elite perceive Fordham. And the telling won't take long. In any substantive way[17] Morris mentions Fordham four times, Marsden twice.

Half of Morris' Fordham citations refer to events, and the remaining two use Fordham in an adjectival way to illustrate American Catholic culture. The two events cited by Morris will please Fordham boosters, while the two Fordham-as-adjective citations won't. Morris reports that Fordham Jesuits helped in the formation of the *American Catholic Trade Union* during the Depression years and that the first labor school opened at the downtown branch of Fordham, then at 302 Broadway, near City Hall. Next he reports that in June 1956 the festival of Puerto Rico's patron saint, John the Baptist, was held on the Rose Hill Fordham Campus.[18] Both citations are nice to read. Both show Fordham responding to what the Second Vatican Council would call "the signs of the time" and in ways that connected university and world, intellect and the common good.

But Fordham's appearance as Morris adjectives are not flattering. They inadvertently show Fordham's role in a defensive and insecure pre-Kennedy Catholicism. This era of Catholicism was marked by a *hyperpatriotism* adopted to show that, despite their "undemocratic, un-American" kind of religion, Catholics belonged here too. In his chapter about Catholicism during the Cold War and the McCarthy era, Morris cites Daniel Patrick Moynihan's much quoted comment, "To be Irish Catholic became prima facie evidence of loyalty. Harvard men were to be checked, *Fordham* men would do the checking" (p. 245; emphasis, of course, added).

What an ironic cultural switch! When Archbishop Hughes invited the first Jesuits to Fordham, Catholics were culturally suspect; a century latter, as Moynihan observed, Catholics were protecting America from its leftist enemies. This switch, of course, required no change of stereotype. Catholic practices and Catholic education made men loyal, first explicitly to Rome and then, through something like sheer habit, to civil authorities. A Catholic with a trained intellect was thought to be trustworthy and reliable, not often imaginative and never critical.

Morris briefly mentions Catholic colleges in the new age of Catholic acceptance and of Catholic affluence and wryly observes, "Bright college-bound Catholics could figure out that Fordham or Boston College did not open the same doors as Harvard" (277).

The Marsden citations echo Morris'. They show a Catholicism judged by cultural elites as ill equipped for responsible participation in a progressive America. The first (p. 10) reports the disdainful review written by Rev. Henry Sloan Coffin, a Yale Trustee, of William F. Buckley's *God and Man at Yale* (1951): "'Mr. Buckley's book is really a misrepresentation and distortion of his Roman Catholic point of view. Yale is a Puritan and Protestant institution by its heritage and he should have attended *Fordham* (emphasis added) or some similar institution." By simply referring to his Catholicism, Coffin thought he had answered Buckley's argument that Yale had de facto abandoned any substantive impact of Christianity on its intellectual life. Even more dismissively, the Yale historian Roland Bainton wondered aloud "whether Catholicism can be generally at home in any university other than a Catholic university" (p. 413).

The Marsden volume recounts how once Protestant universities drifted into secular institutions where *nonsectarian* gradually became defined as meaning "exclusively secular." Fordham's second and last appearance in Marsden's *The Soul Of The American University* is in footnote #19, page 443, which refers to Walter Gellhorn and R. Kent Greenawalt, *The Sectarian (sic) College and the Public Purse: Fordham — A Case Study*. Here Fordham is used to illustrate the more gradual secularization of American Catholic higher education.[19]

PART III

SOLID HOPES FOR KEEPING FAITH IN THE FUTURE

Protestant intellectuals did not intend that their colleges and universities would eventually define academic excellence as requiring their separation from their founding religious traditions. Marsden notes that as late as the 1950s there were impressive and well funded programs aimed at revitalizing religion on college and university campuses.[20] But in retrospect he finds them "superficial" in that they emphasized what in the Catholic tradition is called the "pastoral" and failed to link the life of faith precisely with the intellectual life. The Protestant effort to restore religious vitality to Colleges lacked an intellectual core and seemed to offer nothing more than the promotion of broad and generic ideals of service to humanity.

Catholicism, on the other hand, has energetically and without interruption sought to link religious belief and intellectual life, refusing to ground religion in a sentiment of the heart. Catholics instinctively support courses in philosophy as well as theology in their universities. Fordham, for example, has flourishing and large departments of philosophy and theology. The theology department currently reports 78 students in its Ph.D. program, 15 in its MA program, and 13 non-matriculating students.[21] In their first two years Fordham undergraduates are required to take at least two courses in philosophy and two in theology. Catholic intellectuals, even when they no longer use the phrase *natural law*, constantly seek to translate Catholic personal and social values into terms accessible, in the phrase of the Second Vatican Council, to "men and women of good will." The Ignatian absorption of the humanist movement of its day, and the careful attention to experience which is an essential part of the discernment sought in the *Spiritual Exercises*, strengthens the Catholic tradition's insistence that, as God is one, faith and reason, are mutually supportive.

History makes naiveté more difficult. Catholic administrators and Catholic faculty must now self-consciously think of their own colleges and universities precisely in terms of the history of Protestant higher education as ably recorded by Marsden. Mistakes in judgment are understandable, given the complexity of the aspirations of Catholic higher education; but not naiveté. A drift born in unreflective optimism is not likely to be a general characteristic of Catholic higher education. There are many examples of grass roots and administrative concerns about the future of Catholic education, and Fordham is part of many of them. It is important to note that, unlike the early Protestant efforts at revitalizing an originating Christian vision, the Catholic version seeks vitality by explicitly linking Catholicism and the intellectual life. The ways are varied and complex, but the integrative impulse is clear. Some examples, all involving Fordham, will secure the essential point that, in the Catholic tradition, and especially the Jesuit tradition, faith and reason are dialectically intertwined and, hence, must constantly be reintegrated within the university, among other places.

THE EXAMPLE OF COLLEGIUM

A good example of the Catholic instinct linking faith and reason for the health of both is *Collegium*, started in 1993 by Thomas M. Landry, then a Jesuit scholastic teaching at Fairfield University.[22] The program brings together graduate students and recent Ph.D.'s, faculty mentors and prominent Catholic scholars as a way of inviting promising young intellectuals to commit their lives of teaching, thinking, and researching to Catholic Colleges and Universities. In his remarks at the opening session of *Collegium* Landry evoked his undergraduate Fairfield experience of intellectual coherence, integration and religious commitment and wondered whether such an authentically liberating experience of integrity would be available for future generations. While still in his formative years, Landry obtained funding from the Lilly foundation and support from many Catholic intellectuals for what has become a successful summer institute on Catholic Faith and the Intellectual Life.[23] I was a mentor to a group of ten graduate students at the first *Collegium*. Each of them expressed the desire to make their scholarly and teaching lives a calling rather than a career. Each remarked how complicated and how increasingly difficult it was to keep an integrative ideal alive as they pursued their highly specialized graduate studies. Especially in terms of the long-run it is important to note that *Collegium* fostered a spirituality of the intellectual life. *Collegium* has a special day of retreat when participants can choose among three meditative workshops based on Ignatian, Benedictine and Franciscan spiritualities.[24]

I attended the workshop conducted by Virginia Sullivan Finn (she's from the Cambridge, Massachusetts Jesuit Weston School of Theology). The workshop was entitled "How Do I Experience God Within the Context of My Own Intellectual Commitment and Understanding of Faith?" She adapted Ignatian principles and encouraged us to imagine Christ's presence in our teaching and thinking and researching. Again, the connection between intellect and faith was stressed at the deepest level of one's person.[25] One of the descriptions of the

Collegium schedule read, "The discussion is not meant in any way to be comprehensive or conclusive but to be *compelling* (emphasis added). That is, to open participants' minds to see what might be naturally Catholic about the intellectual life." I liked that: an invitation to young scholars to see what might be "naturally" Catholic about the intellectual life. The intellect cannot be forced; faith cannot be forced. A life committed to faith and learning can only be invited.

Collegium provided an opportunity to think more deeply about what made for an authentic life of teaching and learning. This requires (forgive the cliché) some countercultural moments. I especially remember that at one of the *Collegium* sessions Notre Dame philosopher Alvin Plantinga (an Evangelical Protestant) remarked, "Princeton is in an important way a failed project. We can't take Princeton as a model; instead, we must try to learn from Princeton's mistakes." Later on a walk he told me he thought it was a "lingering inferiority complex" that kept Catholic academics still trying to prove to their betters that they belong, from challenging American intellectual life and culture using the powerful resources available to them in the Catholic tradition.

Especially as nurtured by the Ignatian (and Benedictine and Franciscan and Dominican) traditions, Catholic efforts like *Collegium* (and others I'll quickly get to) provide resources for a more effective resistance to secularization than Protestant academic life was able to muster. Besides, there are some non-assimilable characteristics of a Catholic intellectual life. The very internationality of the Catholic tradition, where nations are judged in terms of their contribution to the human family, makes any authentically renewed Catholic intellectual life less likely to be digested by narrowing national myths.

THE EVOLUTION OF JESUIT IDEALS AND JESUIT SELF-CONCEPTIONS

Remembering the first Fordham Jesuits is not a mechanical act. To discern is to deepen. The scholar considering Fordham University, or any Jesuit institution of higher learning, soon learns that the Jesuit mission stresses "social justice." This is not a theme prominent in the reflections of the first Fordham Jesuits nor is it as prominently central in other American institutions of higher learning (though on this issue I have not conducted an exhaustive survey). In a 1993 address entitled "Ignatian Pedagogy Today" the Jesuits' Superior General, Peter-Hans Kolvenbach, S.J., offered some searching questions about any authentic meaning of humanism for us at the end of the 20th century, remembering that the point of Jesuit education had always been characterized as "humanistic," the education for excellence of the student in his and her entire humanity:[26]

The root issue is this: what does faith in God mean in the face of Bosnia and Angola, Guatemala and Haiti, Auswitz and Hiroshima, the teeming streets of Calcutta and the broken bodies in Tiananmen Square? What is Christian humanism in the face of starving millions of men, women and children in Africa? What is Christian humanism as we view millions of people uprooted from their own countries by persecution and terror, and forced to seek a new life in foreign lands? What is Christian humanism when we see the homeless that roam our cities and the growing underclass who are reduced to permanent hopelessness? What is humanistic education in this context? A disciplined sensitivity to human misery and exploitation is not a single political doctrine or a system of economics. It is a humanism, a humane sensibility to be achieved anew within the demands of our own times and as a product of an education whose ideal continues to be motivated by the great commandments, love of God and love of neighbor.

The Jesuit Superior General calls this contemporary Christian humanism a social humanism, and it is important to note that, in the typical Jesuit way, he immediately adds that this ideal "shares much with the ideals of other faiths in bringing God's love to effective expression in building a just and peaceful kingdom of God on earth." It must or it could not contribute to a more just world. It's also important to note that he defines social humanism not as something "added" from the outside to education or something done after class by those interested in what is called "volunteer work." Jesuit scholars explicitly argue that a concern for justice is not merely *compatible* but is *required* by the critical tasks of the university (for example, see Hollenbach, 1996: 279).[27]

I think it's safe to say that all Jesuit commentators on Jesuit education now emphasize the promotion of justice. Decree 4 of the Documents of the Thirty-Second General Congregation of the Society of Jesus (1974-75) authoritatively teaches: "The mission of the Society of Jesus today is the service of faith, of which the promotion of justice is an absolute requirement." At the end of this century of massive destruction it takes considerable resources of faith to sustain a persistent "social humanism." The dead are already piled high and the century is not yet over. I recently read that "deaths from warfare in the first ninety years of the twentieth century would come to 107,800,000."[28] Against this background David Hollenbach, S.J.'s essay on Jesuit education "The Catholic University under the Sign of the Cross" seems soberly titled.[29] Hollenbach suggests that the Christian symbol of the Crucifixion can lead to a social humanism with the depth needed to anchor hope and will in our era of massive disintegration and disenchantment: "For the cross is the sign through which

Christians proclaim that the ultimate mystery that surrounds our lives embraces human suffering and shares human mystery" (1996: 293).

It's important to note that Hollenbach, in typical Jesuit fashion, understands that the particularistic Christian symbol of the cross must also be grasped as illuminating universally experienced needs and aspirations. For the intellect can only be freely attracted and tribal identities cannot motivate universal commitments. He cites the Hindu Gandhi and the secularist Rorty to show "that the cross can be a source of humanistic insight for believers and nonbelievers alike."[30] In "Is Tolerance Enough? The Catholic University and the Common Good" (*Conversations*, Spring, 1998), he shows that a nonjudgmental tolerance and the conception of the self as simply autonomous will not form students committed to lives of solidarity and justice. Dialogue, not avoidance, should be the authentic democratic response to the many disagreements about the human good in pluralistic societies. Ironically, a principled refusal to avoid sustained dialogue about the common good contributes to a downward spiral in which shared meaning, understanding, and community become even harder to achieve. Avoiding issues of good and bad might be good for the contentment of affluent people but it can't be good for the non-affluent. At any rate, accepting diversity will not by itself lead tolerant people to require of themselves tax policies and social changes that help poor people.

A multicultural society without awareness of its multiple class cleavages could conceivably be a victory for tolerance, but it cannot be a victory for justice. "The time is opportune," Hollenbach writes, "for an important contribution to the advancement of the common good of a deeply pluralistic world by education rooted in the Catholic tradition."[31]

In the context of the ecumenical and humanistic attractiveness of the social humanism now explicit in the Jesuit vision of education it is pertinent to recall that half of the founders of Fordham's contemporary *Peace and Justice Program* were not Catholic: Joseph Shapiro (Physics), Mark Naisson (Afro-American Studies) and long-term program director Martin Fergus. From their Jewish or Lutheran traditions, each found Fordham's Jesuit ideals supportive of their own deepest pedagogical aspirations.

A sociologist, we might suppose, will find such a social humanism immediately more pertinent than a philosopher who, in turn, will probably find a connection more quickly than a chemist. But an intellectual ideal, in analogous ways, must be able to inspire all intellectual endeavors. So it's encouraging to read in *Conversations* (Fall, 1997: 38-40) an account by two chemists[32] teaching at the University of Detroit-Mercy, describing their successful effort in introducing a service for justice component in their introduction to chemistry courses. They invite the freshmen in the class to themselves teach, after training, some of the very chemistry experiments they learned in their college class to 9th and 10th graders at a nearby high school. The chemistry faculty stress the "intrinsic" connection between the service and the learning component of their course. "The University of Detroit-Mercy students also commented (in their reports) that they had learned a great deal more from presenting demonstrations based on the principles than they would have by simply doing a research paper."[33]

THE HARD TOPIC OF HIRING FOR MISSION

The first Fordham Jesuits, and until very recently the Jesuits who followed, never gave explicit attention to Fordham's mission and how to ensure its continuance. Times have changed. Numbers have changed. There are relatively few Jesuits and, at least in the last legal analysis, an independent and largely lay board of trustees must make all decisive institutional decisions.[34] By the Fall of 1996, only 7 of the 28 Jesuit collegiate institutions had a Jesuit academic vice president and only six had Jesuit Deans" (Passon, Fall 1997). This is a difficult topic. Hiring by any criteria other than "merit" must be immediately suspect by all properly socialized American academics. What is most striking about the ways all the Jesuit institutions engage in *hiring for mission* is the largely "invitational" way they do it. Should we call this naiveté or confidence in Jesuit educational ideals?

An important issue of *Conversations On Jesuit Higher Education* (Fall, 1997)[35] is entitled "Hiring For Mission." It contains an overview by Richard H. Passon, Provost and Academic Vice President at the University of Scranton, based on his survey of the 28 American Jesuit colleges and universities. He observes that as recently as ten years ago "nobody was talking about hiring for mission" but now "all are engaged in some way in hiring for mission."[36]

I thought this issue of *Conversations On Jesuit Higher Education* on "Hiring for Mission" met anyone's high standards for integrity and realism. It could profitably be discussed at faculty fora, for it simplifies no issue and is keenly alert to any violation of academic integrity. It will promote dialogue. Indeed, each of the articles express serious misgivings about introducing mission statement concerns into the hiring interview.[37] The search committee of the St. Joseph University's English Department, for example, asked itself, "Will such hiring for mission lower the quality of the faculty? Will good candidates be scared away?[38] Will ecumenism or diversity be damaged? Are there legal implications? And how can mission friendly professors even be identified?" Besides being impressed with the honest misgivings expressed by each author, I was struck by the expressions of support offered by non-Catholic colleagues who discovered in their Jesuit institution's culture an important support of their own highest ideals.

One remarked that "a sense of mission informed the way things were done around here (St. Joseph's): students' embrace of service learning courses, the faculty commitment to education of the whole person." She found that "there was sometimes a gap between articulating the University mission and achieving it" and added "but the very fact that articulating that it mattered was impressive" (Fall, 1997: 22).

Another faculty member, identifying herself as "a non-Catholic with no previous experience of Jesuit or Catholic education," said her college's attention to mission and identity contributed to her own search for self-clarity and focus:

> This year, while writing a personal statement for my tenure file, I described the ways in which my teaching, research, and service supported the University of San Francisco's mission and how the mission supported my personal values and goals for my academic career. It was a valuable exercise in many ways, but the important outcome was the validation of my sense the USF was the right place for me to continue and ultimately complete my academic career, particularly as USF continues to move closer to its mission as a Catholic and Jesuit institution.[39]

Fordham's approach to hiring for mission must rank among the most low-keyed and overtly respectful of prevailing academic norms. Since the early 1990s, the Fordham College and the Fordham Graduate School Deans meet with each of the faculty finalists selected by department and division search committees for at least a 30-minute personal interview. With the additional time of writing and sharing reports about candidates, committee meetings, etc., the faculty interviews comprise a large part of the deans' calendar. For example, over the past three years the deans interviewed 95 prospective candidates.[40] College Dean Joseph McShane, S.J., told me he seeks in candidates some resonance with Fr. Peter-Hans Kolvenbach, S.J.'s explication of the goals of Jesuit education: "the formation of men and women for others, people of competence, conscience and compassionate commitment." He said he assures the candidate that while "there's no confessional answer" to his questions "It's important for this institution to retain its identity and mission." And so he asks, "How do you understand the mission of Fordham University? How do you feel about being a part of it?"

While I can only speak anecdotally,[41] it seems that a thoughtful, and thus respectful, effort to invitingly share Jesuit educational ideals with those from different traditions and backgrounds often succeeds and, indeed, often sparks some enthusiasm. Along with St. Peter's, LeMoyne and Canisius, Fordham recently participated in the first New York Province holding of the *Gatherings* program which had started a decade earlier in the Maryland Province. In its origins, structure and aspirations *Gatherings* clearly displays the confident, invitational tone characteristic of the Jesuit spirituality that animates Jesuit ideals of education. For this reason, it's worth sketching the origins of *Gatherings*.[42]

AS AN EXAMPLE OF JESUIT INVITATIONAL STYLE

The origins of *Gatherings* were spontaneous. At a conference at Loyola College, Baltimore, Joseph J. Feeney, S.J., said he had found many faculty, including lay, at his home campus, St. Joseph's University, "worried about the Jesuit dimensions of our colleges and universities, specifically in undergraduate education." When he left the podium, two professors, one from Georgetown, the other from Loyola, stopped and thanked him for giving public voice to their own concerns. They had coffee and talked and when they later announced an informal after-dinner discussion about the futures of Jesuit education, thirty others joined them. "In an hour," Feeney recalls, "*Gatherings* was launched." Its structure was that simple. Each of the five Jesuit collegiate institutions in the Maryland Province (Georgetown, Loyola, St. Joseph's, Scranton, Wheeling) would take turns inviting lay and Jesuit faculty and administrators to a once-a-semester, one-day discussion about some core element of the Jesuit character of their institution. The first was on October 23, 1993. A basic *Gatherings'* premise is that "given the declining number of Jesuits, the future of Jesuit education rests with lay professors" (1997: 42). The day-long structure of *Gatherings* is designed for conversation. I liked Feeney's modestly confident tone: "Our methodology is equally forthright. Since the professors and administrators who come are already experts, we can reflect on our own experience without outside help and, on going home, we can work to change our institutions" (*Conversations*, Spring, 1997: 44). A *Gathering* takes place on a Saturday, begins at 10:00 and ends at 4:30. It starts with a short keynote, followed by small group discussions, with faculty mixed from the participating institutions, who then reconvene for small group reports and a general discussion. The day concludes with a small group discussion among colleagues about what they might do when they return to their home college.

Each *Gathering* has its own theme and new participants. For example, the theme of Maryland Province's *Gathering* #8, held on March 22, 1997, was "Jesuit education in service of the poor." Earlier *Gathering* themes dealt with such core themes as teaching, faculty development and faculty hiring.[43] Like all Jesuits who comment on Jesuit educational values, Feeney writes that *Gatherings* seeks an invitational, dialogic approach that all faculty of good will can find attractive. He reports (*Conversations*, Spring, 1997: 44) "a felt colleagueship among lay professors and Jesuits, professors and administrators, and women and men of varied religious traditions: Jewish, Islamic, Lutheran, Episcopalian, Zen Buddhist, Agnostic and Catholic."

On October 4, 1997 in Syracuse, Fordham participated in the first New York Province *Gathering*, along with St. Peter's, Canisius and host college LeMoyne. The keynote address by John B. Breslin, S.J., was entitled "Reflection, Gratitude and Service: Three Virtues for Jesuit Graduates." Like other Jesuit commentators on Jesuit education, Breslin eventually brought up the topic of justice and the intellectual virtues. "How does what I'm doing, how does what we're doing promote greater justice in the world and thereby serve to make faith in God more possible for men and women of our time and place? Jesuit colleges are not exempted from such self-examinations wherever they happen to be." As a way of being concrete, Breslin suggested that we look at student volunteer programs as a partial test of the Jesuit "culture" of our institutions. "Without this involvement toward active involvement in the world," he said, "the previous habits become suspect as mere mental gymnastics and emotional self-indulgence."

A CONCRETE TEST OF FORDHAM'S JESUIT CULTURE

I thought the first Fordham Jesuits, who left the familiarity of country and culture to come to teach in America, would approve of taking as a specific measure of the depth of Fordham's Jesuit culture the level of student volunteer service activities. By definition, a missionary belongs more to a world community than to a particular nation or state. How much of this originating universalism, exemplified by the College's Jesuit founders, can be seen and felt and experienced on the Fordham campus?

It seems to have developed slowly. The important factors in its evolution include the enormous shift in Catholic consciousness achieved at the Second Vatican Council and mediated by a corresponding evolution or deepening of Jesuit collective consciousness. It is far from the *hyperpatriotism* that prompted Moynihan's remark about Fordham men checking the loyalty of Harvard men.

A decade before the opening of the Second Vatican Council in 1962 Fordham did have a volunteer program, called the "Mexico Project," which obviously embodied a moral concern that clearly transcended national self interest. But the "Mexico Project" was solitary and sporadic, and in some years Fordham sent no students to help the volunteer doctors and nurses who were contributing their services to the health needs of various Mexican villages. This changed after the Second Vatican Council.[44]

It will be recalled that Pope John XXII called the Second Vatican Council to open a dialogue between the Church and the World. Significantly, the Council's first public message, released on October 20, 1962, nine days after its opening, was entitled "Message to Humanity" and they addressed it to all persons and to all nations. Abbott (1962: 3) pertinently notes that "For the first time in the history of ecumenical councils, a council addresses itself to all men, not just members of the Catholic Church."[45]

Very soon after the Council, Fordham's campus ministry added two more outreach programs to Peru and to Appalachia. And then they doubled again, following Decree Four passed at the Jesuits' thirty second General Congregation (1975) which taught that "The mission of the Society of Jesus is the service of faith, of which the promotion of justice is an absolute requirement."[46] By the mid-1990s Fordham's institutional culture, paralleling that of the Church and of the Jesuit Order, explicitly included a global justice dimension in its curriculum and its student life. The College's once sporadic and inconstant outreach was now institutionalized and formally known as *Global Outreach*.

Global Outreach comprises 10 projects, including the originating ones to Mexico and Peru: Guatemala, the Dominican Republic, Haiti, Ecuador, Jamaica, the Glenmary Appalachian projects in Mississippi and Kentucky, New York City's Harlem and New York State's Mohawk Nation.

The present *Global Outreach* director, Frank Rizzo, told me that between 350-400 students from each college cohort (4 years) participate in a *Global Outreach* project, making it the largest campus activity. Indeed, he receives three times as many applicants as he can place in programs. In *Global Outreach*, service and spirituality are consciously linked, as it was for the first Fordham Jesuits. Besides campus training in cultural sensitivity, participants attend a weekend retreat, often led by peers who have been trained in the Fordham campus ministry Retreat Training program. A typical student reflection reads, "Our days begin at 5:00 AM with Mass and ends around midnight."[47] Students must raise their own travel and upkeep expenses, usually by begging for alms at their home parish or church. They are also expected to beg for something extra as a contribution that Fordham, as a sign of gratitude, can leave for the people with whom they have lived and worked.

Closer to Home: Fordham Community Service

Fordham students don't have to go far from campus to make some connection with people marginalized by global economic forces. While the South Bronx has done some heavy metaphoric duty for inner city despair, for a considerable number of Fordham students the South Bronx is specific neighborhoods where they can help a little. The Community Service Office began in the mid-1980s, institutionalizing the community service work previously dependent on very informal networks of mostly unconnected groups of students. The present Community Services director, Pat Logan, told me that more than one-quarter of all Fordham students have volunteered for such neighborhood services as mentoring and tutoring, soup kitchen help, delivering meals to home bound AIDS victims, as "Catholic big-brothers" and "sisters", and for Bronx River clean up and restoration projects, and others.

Both directors report an enthusiasm that would have pleased the first Fordham Jesuits. "Way more applicants than we can place," Rizzo said. "Unbelievable response," Logan told me.

FINAL REFLECTIONS BACK TO THE BEGINNING

Fr. Hennessy's unvarnished volume about the first Fordham Jesuits inspires honesty. So we should avoid any naiveté in our conclusions. We can expect that Fordham students mostly choose Fordham because they think that what will happen here will best train them for the increasingly competitive upper middle class futures they anxiously imagine for themselves. Likewise, Fordham faculty, for the most part, chose Fordham in terms of a similar rational calculation about their career aspirations defined in largely departmental and disciplinary terms. It should cause no surprise whatsoever that the *Fordham Fact Book*, for example, includes but the briefest reference to Fordham's service and volunteer work and *only* after a far lengthier account of the economic and professional success achieved by Fordham graduates.[48] But it's what happens to men and women of good will after they come to Fordham that should especially interest us. Education is supposed to transform.

This unembellished history of the first Fordham Jesuits can help us sustain a non-utopian idealism. After all, the story about the first Fordham Jesuits shows a very human mix of circumstance, rational self-interest, mixed motives, tough bargaining and, of course, high ideals. They sought no escape from reality. "Contemplatives in action," Ignatius described them. The first Fordham Jesuits needed no romantic fictions, no illusions. Their formative influence, the *Spiritual Exercises*, structures the search for the achievement of the inner liberty necessary for the pursuit of truth.

The first paragraph of a contemporary translation of Ignatius' introduction to the *Spiritual Exercises* reads: "The structure of these exercises has the purpose of leading a person to a true spiritual freedom. We attain the goal of gradually bringing an order of values into our lives so that we make no choice because we have been influenced by some disordered attachment or love."[49]

It would be a mistake to regard these remarks about the *Spiritual Exercises* and Fordham as pietistic or as lacking in pertinence. That robust and secular student of language, Roland Barthes, correctly points out that Ignatian 'discernment' clothes Aristotelian phronesis with imaginative resources so that the judgment can work at its highest level.[50] Discernment is an affective intelligence at work. There's much to discern.

Catholicism is in a period of great transition. Morris (1997: 431) entitles his last chapter "Crisis" and asks "whether, after all the turmoil of the past thirty years, the era of the Vatican II is ending or is just beginning." Fordham is in transition as well, most notably from its role as a "custodial" institution in a mostly defensive American Roman Catholicism to a role increasingly judged by Jesuits and others in terms of its scholarly contributions to a global dialogue seeking a global justice. It might not be wrong to think that the contemporary mission of Fordham is even more challenging, and even more precarious, than that faced by its first Jesuits. Catholic intellect is no longer primarily attached to Catholic institutional self-interest, as it tended to be in their day. Serving a self-interest, even an exalted one, simplifies mission. In my judgment, the obstacles to this renewed sense of intellectual mission religiously challenged to dialogue for the sake of justice is more likely to be impeded by the internal dynamics of American higher education than by Catholic authorities. The fragmentation of American higher education, the intense, almost vocational, specialization in most disciplines, the natural drift towards "careerism," all powerfully impede the social humanism that now justifies the name Jesuit education.

Jesuits have more resources to deal with such daunting challenges than the rest of us. Consider, for example, the reflections on the Passon survey made by Joseph A. Panuska, S.J., the outgoing president of Scranton University, as reported in "Hiring For Mission" (*Conversations*, Fall, 1997: 11):

> With so many new faces and with fewer Jesuits, formerly and erroneously seen as the embodiment of Ignatian identity, institutions could no longer take for granted that everyone understood and embraced the mission or that mission was the responsibility of Jesuits alone. These pressures are not altogether unhealthy. They are forcing us to regroup and follow the pattern of the Spiritual Exercises by beginning to ask ourselves who we are and what we want to be (emphasis added).

The Jesuit Order existed before Jesuit colleges existed and the Jesuits can exist after their colleges. In the long run this would be far more a loss to higher education than to them. But this loss is not likely, however difficult and painful the present era of transition continues to be. A culture of "social humanism," which everyone in their most alert moments knows is desperately needed, is neither easily formulated nor institutionalized. The experiences of *Collegium*, of *Gatherings*, of the response of students to any vital experience of Jesuit educational ideals can each give modest confidence to anyone who seeks it.

The first Fordham Jesuits, crossing an ocean, settling first in the farmlands of Kentucky and then in the largest metropolis of the country, required great and courageous faith. The act of courageous faith in our time is that scholar-teachers, when invited, will embrace the Ignatian vision of the education of the whole person for service as a completion of their own deepest aspirations.

NOTES

1 Besides, as several papers in this volume show, the Jesuits weren't even the first educators on the Fordham campus.

2 David Hollenbach, S.J., has raised the difficult question about the Jesuit embrace of justice as a constitutive part of faith and education and the upper middle class population some of its institutions almost exclusively recruit from. He writes that the cost of attending one year at Boston College, where he teaches, was "Only a bit below 50 percent of the total income of half the families in the country." In 1997, Fordham charged $16,800 in tuition (and $8,000 in room and board). In the spirit of the Jesuit ideal of education each Jesuit institution should, as a community, scrutinize its financial aid practices and the effort it makes to enroll those from poorer backgrounds. From personal experience, I know there is strong Fordham support for our *Higher Education Opportunity Act* program. See David Hollenbach, S.J., "The Catholic University Under the Sign of the Cross," in Michael J. Himes and Stephen J. Pope, *Finding God In All Things*, Crossroad, NY, 1996: 287.

3 Fordham administrators might consider giving each faculty applicant a copy of this insightful history which itself exemplifies the high ideals of a Jesuit inspired scholarship: graceful intellect, spiritual maturity, persuasive integrity, and concern for a more just future.

4 The *Formula of the Institute* was written to explain to the pope the basic elements of the new association Ignatius and his companions wished to form. There were two versions, the first in 1540 and a second in 1550. Neither refers to education although, when interpreted in the light of experience, both can certainly lead there. In light of the complexity and balance of the Jesuit ideals in education, it might be interesting for the reader to quickly read the basic elements as found in the 1550 *Formula* (O'Malley, p. 5): *public preaching, lectures, and any other ministrations whatsoever of the Word of God, and further by means of the 'Spiritual Exercises,' the education of children and unlettered persons in Christianity, and the spiritual consolation of Christ's faithful through hearing confessions and administering the other sacraments. Moreover, the Society should show itself no less useful in reconciling the estranged, in holily assisting and serving those who are found in prisons and hospitals, and indeed in performing any other work of charity, according to what will seem expedient for the glory of God and the common good.* This list is certainly a good foundation for the inclusion of "social solidarity" experiences for students and faculty at Jesuit institutions.

5 "In other words," O'Malley writes, "despite the Jesuits' great faith in education, they did not elaborate a philosophy of education in the ordinary sense of that term, probably because the humanists had already done it for them" (p. 214).

6 Showing the falsity of this stereotype, O'Malley also gives, in my judgment, a superior insight into the Jesuit style of spirituality: "They in fact tended to understand the Reformation as primarily a pastoral problem. They saw its fundamental cause and cures as related not so much to doctrinal issues as to the spiritual conditions of the person concerned" (p. 16).

7 Despite his many convolutions and idiosyncrasies, Roland Barthes in his *SADE/ FOURIER/ LOYOLA* (tr. by Richard Miller, The Johns Hopkins University Press, 1976: 45-46) perceptively identifies the heart of the *Exercises* and, indeed, characterizes Ignatius as a logothete, a founder of a new language: "The language Ignatius is trying to constitute is a language of interrogation. Whereas in natural idioms, the elementary structure of the

sentence, articulated in subjects and predicate, is assertive in order, the articulation current here is that of a question and an answer. This interrogative structure gives the *Exercises* its historical originality; hitherto, a commentator remarks, the preoccupation was more with carrying out God's will; Ignatius wants rather to discover this will. (What is it? Where is it? Toward what does it tend?) ..."

8 As we say in sociology, this is the "norm" which is not to be automatically equated with the empirical reality. But norms count - they set standards; departures from norms must be explained, not least to oneself.

9 Maybe it's unfair to use NYU as a contrast. I've done no systematic research into NYU and its internal resources for renewal. But from my discussions with family members who went there and some faculty I know, there's no impulse toward any pertinent *retrieval* of values and motivation that one finds at Fordham. I'm prepared to apologize. I certainly desire no invidious comparisons here. On the point of what's different about Jesuit education and what does it matter I agree with Buckley's point that "Even when objectives coincide, motivations can be very different. School policies combat racism and sexual harassment, for example, not because a 'rights'-based culture frowns on such conduct or deems it politically incorrect, but because such behavior denies central Christian values" Thomas E. Buckley, S.J., "Academic Excellence Is Not Enough: The Moral Formation of Our Students," *Conversations*, Spring, 1997: 26). Specific motivations matter even when external actions seem similar. Consider, for example, opposing war for tactical reasons and opposing war because of the Christian understanding of non-violence.

10 Because the United Nations Secretary General Kofi Annan said he had secured Saddam Hassein's compliance with United States requirement for weapons inspection, President Clinton said there would be no bombing. But Mr. Clinton warned that if ambiguities remained, or the accord was not kept, the United States would bomb "at a time, place and manner of our choosing." Michael R. Gordon and Elaine Sciolino, "Fingerprints on Iraqi Accord Belong to Albright," *The New York Times*, February 25, 1998: A10.

11 I've included part-time Jesuit faculty in the numerator but only full-time faculty in the denominator. Data come from the *Fordham Fact Book* 1995-1996 collected by the Office of Institutional Research. Hennessy included no data on the first Fordham lay faculty. Which reminds us to note that while there were no women faculty in 1846, 152 years later 31 percent of the full-time faculty were women. Further, 12 percent of the 1996 faculty were, in the words of the data book, "members of racial minorities."

12 More precisely, according to the *Fordham Fact Book* (1995-1996: 10), "Among the full-time faculty, 98 percent hold the Ph.D. or other terminal degree from major institutions throughout the United States and abroad."

13 They are listed on page 109 of the *Fact Book*. The first is the American Council on Education; the last is the American Psychological Association. There are about two dozen in between.

14 Charles R. Morris, *American Catholic, New York*, Random House, 1997.

15 George M. Marsden, *The Soul of the American University From Protestant Establishment To Established Nonbelief*, New York, Oxford: 1994.

16 In his "Concluding Unscientific Postscript" Marsden writes that the relegation of religion to the periphery of American universities was justified by the Enlightenment judgment that religion was "both unscientific and socially disruptive" and that a universal science, embracing the social sciences, would direct and unify society. This Enlightenment judgment corresponded with the confident self-conceptions of liberal Protestantism and, initially, served their cultural self-interests. Marsden writes (1994: 429): "The Liberal Protestant establishment endorsed this ideal, which had the added attraction of effectively excluding from the front ranks of American education its two most numerous religious rivals, Catholics and more traditional Protestants." We should immediately include the point

that there was a positive congruence between the Enlightenment judgment about progress and liberal Protestant's sense of mission: "Liberal Protestants justified these exclusions not only on the negative grounds that traditional Christian beliefs were unscientific, but also by the positive rationale that cultural development advanced the Kingdom of God." A more discriminating attitude about the overlaps between what is taken to be progress and what is understood to be the theology of the Kingdom of God would be, "sometimes they might, sometimes they don't;" in any case, vigilance is required.

17 Six times in total, but in very loose and peripheral connection with other topics, such as the Fordham choir performing at a New York meeting of the Catholic Theological Society.

18 Both of these Fordham events involved Joseph Fitzpatrick, S.J., who, as a scholastic, ran the Xavier Labor School and then as a priest, and after his Harvard degree in sociology, became the first scholar of (and advisor to) the Puerto Rican migration.

19 In Tilton v. Richardson (1971) the Supreme Court permitted aid for specific facilities at Catholic colleges if they would not be used for religious purposes and the applying colleges were "characterized by an atmosphere of academic freedom rather than religious indoctrination."

20 "In addition to active campus ministries and opportunities for student worship and service, there was funding to encourage students to study for the ministry, increased interest in building religion departments and strengthening divinity schools, and an immense literature on how to promote religion on campus. Particularly there was widespread concern that higher education promote higher values that would reflect the best in the Judeo-Christian and American heritages" (p. 409).

21 Department secretary, February 15, 1998.

22 After completing theology, Landry did not advance to ordination and has since been laicized. He is presently studying for a Ph.D. in sociology at Northeastern University.

23 I've been at two, including the first on which I report in "Collegium and the Futures of Catholic Higher Education," in *America*, Sept. 11, 1993: 15-17. Participants included 33 (seven of whom were women) "faculty fellows" who had recently begun teaching at Catholic institutions; 28 (10 women) "graduate fellows" who were either completing their Ph.D.'s or doing postdoctoral study, most in the natural and social sciences and humanities (5 in philosophy and theology) and only six from Catholic institutions. There were 8 mentors, representing 8 disciplines. The four plenary addresses were given by:

Georgetown theologian Monika Hellwig (now director of the National Catholic Educational Association), *The Church As A Learning Church: The Church's Need for Intellectual Reflection*;

Boston College theologian Michael Himes, *A Sacramental World View*;

Brian E. Daley, S.J., then of Weston School of Theology, now of Notre Dame, *Christ and the Catholic University*;

J. Brian Hehir, now at Harvard Divinity School, *Gaudium et Spes: The Church in the Modern World*.

In their own polished way, each characterized Catholic intellectual life as Christocentric, sacramental, communitarian, critical.

24 A fourth workshop offered Christian feminist spiritualities. I'm sure that when Dominican colleges send representatives, there will be a Dominican spiritual workshop.

25 Speaking personally, the experience both solidified and deepened my growing sense that social science must ask the larger questions about justice and community that bring us into the company of theologians and philosophers. When challenged in writing or teaching to think harder, I found myself explicitly and unashamedly using the resources of the rich tradition of Catholic social thought, not as a matter of apologetics or piety but simply

"to get to the bottom of things," to think more deeply about society and culture. Increasingly I encouraged students and myself to test our integrity by our practices of concern for others, especially those marginalized by the increasingly single-minded pursuit of Western affluence. Far from something "added on," priorities, directions and conceptual resources of Catholic social thought increasingly seem intrinsic to any sociology seriously concerned with grasping social realities.

26 Peter-Hans Kolvenbach, S.J., "Ignatian Pedagogy Today," *Education SJ*, the International Center for Jesuit Education, 1993, No. 2: 5-8).

27 Hollenbach, in Himes and Pope (eds.), op. cit.

28 Donald W. Shriver, Jr. *An Ethic For Enemies: Forgiveness In Politics*, NY. Oxford, 1995:65.

29 Op. cit.

30 Gandhi said his experience of the Christian story of Christ's crucifixion helped him to reread the Hindu *Bhagavad Gita* as a parable of nonviolence; Richard Rorty has recently acknowledged that the story of Jesus, far more than any philosophy or ideology, motivated the revolution of 1989 that ended the Russian empire. (1996: 294-295).

31 David Hollenbach, S.J., "Is Tolerance Enough? The Catholic University and the Common Good," *Conversations*, Spring, 1998: 5- 15. Hollenbach suggests the term "personalist communitarianism" to characterize the Catholic tradition's solidaristic vision of interdependence. He suggests that in effect Pope John Paul II has added *social solidarity* to the classical list of cardinal virtues. He adds *intellectual solidarity* which "is similar to tolerance in that it recognizes and respects these differences. It does not seek to eliminate pluralism through coercion. But it differs radically from pure tolerance by seeking positive engagement with the other through both listening and speaking. It is rooted in a hope that understanding might replace incomprehension and that perhaps even agreement could result. Where such engaged conversation about the good life begins and develops, a community of freedom begins to exist" (p. 13).

32 Mark A. Benvenuto and Collen Kaminski (with Catherine Gammage of Melvin Dale High School), "A Service Learning Project in General Chemistry."

33 Their teachers describe as "interlocking purposes" the class goals of learning more chemistry by becoming student teachers and providing a community service. "We required that the students' final report include, not just a simple recitation of the chemical principles they presented, but also a reflection on what the project taught them" about chemistry and about community service.

34 Or at least not veto them.

35 Which title is itself an indication of the "invitational" tone I found and describe below. A "conversation" is less threatening than a dialogue which is itself the most civil of terms. *Conversations* began in the early 1980s following *Assembly*, which was held in St. Louis to commemorate 450 years of Jesuit higher education, as a way to stimulate among faculty and administrators discussion about Jesuit education.

36 Passon provides the following low-keyed, minimalist definition of the term "hiring for mission": Hiring for Mission "means that in some way (emphasis added) a university informs faculty candidates (and *perhaps* [emphasis added] staff and administrators as well) about the institution's mission, and then makes commitment to the mission one of the relevant issues in the hiring process".

37 Including a literate critique of any incorporation of a "mission statement" in the hiring process. See John J. Pauly's subversive "Mission Talk and the Bugaboo of Modernity," *Conversations*, Fall, 1997: 24-29.

38 This worry, at any rate, proved groundless. Over 750 applicants answered the advertisement which identified St. Joseph's as "an institution in the Jesuit, Catholic tradition." Jo-

seph J. Feeney, S.J., Owen W. Gilman, Jr. and Jo Alyson Parker, "Hiring Faculty for Mission: A Case Study of a Department's Search," *Conversations*, Fall, 1997: 20-23.

39 She approvingly referred to the formulation of the Jesuit educational values which was made by Robert Mitchell, S.J. We cite that formulation here as representative of many others: "A passion for quality and excellence; the study of the humanities and sciences, no matter the specialization; a preoccupation with questions of ethics and values for both the professional and personal lives of students; the importance of the religious experience, for both Catholic and non-Catholic students; and the importance of and attendance to the individual needs of each student." See Kathleen Kane, "Value-Oriented Hiring and Promotion and the University of San Francisco's Vision 20005," *Conversations*, Fall, 1997: 30-37.

40 Personal communication, Dean Joseph McShane, S.J.' Feb. 21, 1998.

41 I note, however, that in his survey of Jesuit colleges and universities Passon found that "a good number of my colleagues around the country who have responsibility for faculty hiring, while they do not downplay the difficulties, report positive experiences both in terms of the real interest in mission questions by departments and in terms of the ways in which good faculty candidates are attracted to institutions that are clear about their identity" (*Conversations*, Fall, 1997: 9).

42 I rely on Joseph J. Feeney, S.J.'s account "What are the Gatherings and how did they start?" in *Conversations*, Spring, 1997: 42-44 and my own experience at the first NY Province Gathering held at LeMoyne College on October 4, 1997.

43 The titles are lively and pertinent: "The Pivotal Role of Lay Professors;" "Spirituality in the Classroom: The Teacher and the Student;" "Faculty Development for Jesuit Education;" "Do Professors Really Change Students?"; "Faculty Hiring and Development."

44 Historical causality, of course, is a complicated matter. Other influences played their part. For example, I remember teaching in 1966 and welcoming a representative of the Peace Corps to talk to my class. Even earlier the Maryland-New York province received the Philippines as its "mission" and the college's relief drives, including "mite box" contributions, certainly introduced at least a minimum sense of cultural awareness among the college students. More formal and more universal in scope were seminars, institutes and writings by anthropologist Rev. J. Franklin Ewing, S.J., who had been interned in a camp in the Philippines during World War II. In the years following that war he urged the need for inculturation by those who work abroad. We might also note that Fordham's president, Rev. Joseph A. O'Hare, S.J., as well as economics professor, Rev. Edward Dowling, S.J. and theology professor Alfred Hennelly, S.J., taught in the Philippines; Rev. Joseph A. Currie, S.J., director of campus ministry, spent many years in India.

But it seems clear that a primary influence is the impact, as mediated by Jesuit and some lay faculty, of the extraordinary challenge of the Second Vatican Council for Catholics to participate in the clarification and promotion of the human aspiration towards a world community.

45 Reading all "men" here reminds us that all appropriations of core values is to some degree time-bound and thus partially limiting even as it challenges. One year after the Council opened, Pope John XXIII added, for the first time in papal history, to his encyclical *Pacem In Terris* the salutation "and to men of good will." See Walter Abbott, S.J., (editor) *The Documents of Vatican II*, NY.: The America Press, 1966: 3

46 During this period of rapid growth, Rev. Paul Brant, S.J., and David Phillipson of campus ministry played important roles.

47 *Global Outreach Newsletter*, Vol. I, No. 1, Spring 1998.

48 "Approximately 75 percent of all public accounting majors receive job offers from 'Big 6' accounting firms. More than 91 percent of Fordham's premed students who graduate with a 3.4 grade-point average or better go on to attend American medical schools. Among pre-law students, 87 percent are accepted into law school each year. Since 1983,

100 percent of Fordham's predental students have been admitted to dental schools. In a recent Standard & Poor's survey that assessed the number of degrees awarded to senior business executives, Fordham ranked in the top 8 percent for undergraduate degrees and the top 5 percent for graduate degrees in the United States. Fordham has consistently ranked number one in the S&P survey among all Jesuit institutions." Next comes a description of Fordham's internship program, "one of the nation's largest," and only then is information about opportunities to serve given (and very briefly). Moreover, it appears in the same sentence as intramural sports: "Students also enjoy the offerings of more than 150 student clubs and organizations, intramurals, club sports, campus ministries, numerous outreach programs including the P.O.T.S (Part of the Solution) soup kitchen in the Bronx and summer service programs in Mexico and Peru, and a host of other activities." *Fact Book* 1995-1996, Office of Institutional Research: 10.

49 David C. Fleming, S.J., *Modern Spiritual Exercises*, NY, Doubleday, 1983: 21.

50 Barthes , op. cit., 52-53.

A GLOSSARY OF JESUIT TERMS

Some terms and concepts used in this book that may be unfamiliar to some readers. We explain here several of the terms which are used frequently in the previous pages.

Governance in the Society of Jesus is hierarchical. The *Father General* in Rome is at the top; he is elected for life. During the first years of Fordham there were two Fathers General: Jan Roothan (1829-1853), a Dutchman , and Pieter Beckx (1853-1887), a Belgian.

The Father General appoints *Provincials* and *Mission Superiors* (such superiors as Clément Boulanger were also called *Superior General of the Mission* or *Regional Superior of the Mission*) who in turn assign individuals to various tasks and residences. The Father General also at times appoints an official *Visitor* to make on-site decisions in his name; for a specific time the Visitor supersedes other local authorities.

Rectors and *Superiors* administer the activities of a college or house. In colleges and universities until recently the Rector was also the President of the institution.

The *vow of obedience* to one's superior is important to Jesuit living; equally important is the right of individuals to appeal a decision of a local superior to a superior at a higher level.

Socius (literally from the Latin, companion) is an executive assistant who is appointed to work with a Provincial or other high level Jesuit administrators.

Minister, or *Father Minister*, is an administrator who is in charge of the temporal affairs of the house and performs other duties as the delegate of the Rector or Superior.

Novice is a beginner or initiate in any specialized activity. In the Jesuits this is a two year period during which the novice learns of Jesuit "ways of proceeding" and is exercised in various Christian virtues like humility.

Prefect (with no modifier) is an assignment that typically required close supervision of students in dormitories, study halls, dining rooms, etc.

Prefect of Studies would mean in today's language the Dean (in a college) or the Principal (in secondary education).

A *Scholastic* is a Jesuit who has completed his novitiate and is engaged in the study of literature, philosophy, theology or other assigned tasks, such as teaching students and or prefecting. Generally, he is referred to this way until ordination to the priesthood.

ABOUT THE CONTRIBUTORS

Cornelius Michael Buckley, S.J.

Professor of History and lecturer in the St. Ignatius Institute, University of San Francisco, he is the author of a number of articles and books on nineteenth-century French Jesuits in the United States, among which are *A Frenchman, A Chaplain, A Rebel: The War Letters of Louis-Hippolyte Gache, S.J.* (1981) and *Nicolas Point, S.J.: His Life and Northwest Indian Chronicles* (1989).

Francis X. Curran, S.J. (1914-1991)

Late Professor of Church History at Fordham University and archivist for the New York Province of the Society of Jesus. His research and writings centered around the nineteenth century Jesuits of the New York and Maryland provinces. Among his writings his *The Return of the Jesuits: Chapters in the History of the Society of Jesus in Nineteenth-century America* (1966) offers excellent background reading for students of the early Fordham years.

Allan S. Gilbert

Associate Professor of Anthropology at Fordham University, he is Archaeological Director of the Rose Hill manor excavations, New York City's longest continuous excavation. He began his academic career in ancient Near Eastern studies and maintains active research and publication in this area as well as the historical archaeology of the northeastern U.S. His forthcoming *Archaeology in the Bronx* will be published by the Bronx County Historical Society.

James Hennesey, S.J.

Among other appointments he was Rector of the Fordham Jesuit community at a critical time. Well known as a distinguished historian of American Catholic culture and Jesuit history, his books, *The First Council of the Vatican: The American Experience* (1963), and *American Catholics: A History of the Roman Catholic Community in the United States* (1981), were widely praised. The Fall 1996 issue of the *U.S. Catholic Historian* honored him "for his singular contribution to American Catholic studies."

Thomas C. Hennessy, S.J.

Professor Emeritus, Fordham University Graduate School of Education, he taught and counseled in many schools of the university, wrote many articles in educational journals and edited several books that pertain to counseling and values.

James R. Kelly

Professor of Sociology, Fordham University, he has written widely on Catholic social thought, issues of public policy and the sociology of religion. He is the 1998 president of the Association for the Sociology of Religion. He has served as secretary to the Cardinal Bernardin Catholic Common Ground Initiative. Besides writing for sociology journals, he is a frequent contributor to *America* and *Commonweal*, and wrote the essay on American Roman Catholicism for the *Encyclopedia of Religion and Society* (1998).

John W. Padberg, S.J.

Director and general editor of the Institute of Jesuit Sources, chair of the National Seminar on Jesuit Higher Education, professor of theology, St. Louis University. In addition to writing and editing numerous other publications connected with Jesuit life and history, he wrote *Colleges in Controversy: the Jesuit Schools in France from Revival to Suppression, 1815-1880* (1969).

Thomas J. Shelley

A priest of the Archdiocese of New York, he is Associate Professor of Historical Theology, Fordham University. A contributor to numerous journals that specialize in church history, he wrote the *History of St. Joseph's Seminary* (1993), and is coeditor of the *Encyclopedia of American Catholic Church History* (1997).

Roger Wines

Professor of History at Fordham University, he teaches European and New York history and is Historical Director of the Rose Hill manor excavations. His publications include *Leopold van Ranke: The Secret of World History* (1981) and various articles on New York history.

Index

119, 209
Careys 55
Carleton, Guy 151
Carlow 103
Carrell, George 127
Carrigan, Andrew 174
Carroll, Bishop John 27, 31, 72
Carroll Hall 62, 69
Cassé, Josephte 118
Casserly, Eugene A. 68
Catalogus defunctorum Societatis Jesu 133
Catholic Association 62
Catholic Encyclopedia 104
Catholic Quarterly Review 89
Catholic Trade Union Association 232
Catholic World 89
Chabrat, Bishop Guy 3, 47, 48
Chang-Hai, China 114
Charles X 17, 22, 27
Charleston 103, 127
Chazelle, Pierre 2, 31, 32, 33, 35, 39, 80, 97, 105
Chesebrough Mfg. Co. 166
Chesebrough, Robert 166
City the Falls 83
Civil War 137
Clancy, Thomas 136
Clinton, Henry 172
Clorivière, Pierre 11, 19, 28
Co. Cork 133
Co. Durham 83
Cohen, David S. 170
Collegium 234, 235, 244, 247
Colmar 119
Columbia College 73
Commissioners of Forfeiture 152
Comte d'Artois 17
Connolly, Gerard 172
Connolly, John 58
Connors, Edward M. 74
Conroy, John 64
Constance, Peter 91
Continental Army 150
Conyngham, David 137
Corby, William 122, 137
Cormican, Patrick J. 148, 170
Corne, Philip 11, 31, 32, 35, 36, 37, 40, 91
Cornell, Thomas C. 101, 134
Cornucopias 49
Corrigan, Archbishop 121

Corriveau, Josephte 110
Corsa, Andrew 173
Corsa, Benjamin Fletcher 150, 151, 172, 173
Corsa family 172
Corsa, Isaac 150, 173
Council of Baltimore 103
Crary, Catherine S. 173
Croton Falls 124
Crowe, Patrick 44, 107
Cubi, Geoffrey 9
Curran, Francis X. 10, 81, 177, 249

D

Daley, Brian E. 247
Dansette, Adrien 28
Daubresse, Isidore 51, 91, 127, 182, 211
Davenport, William 149
De Béranger, Pierre-Jean 14
Dealy Hall 163
Dealy, Patrick Francis, 9, 112, 146
DeCice, Adelaide 11
De la Barre, Victoire-Marine Le Mau 105
DeLamennais, Félicité 24, 25, 29
Delancey family 141
Delancey, Col. James 151

Delancey, Warren 174
DeLande, Marianne 11
DeLimoëlan, Joseph Picot 11
DeLuynes, Charles Hippolyte 6, 44, 79, 100-102, 127
DeLuynes, Laurent 102
DeMaistre Joseph 24
DeNeckere, Bishop Leo 32
Denis, General Burke 123
DeNoyelles, Daniel 175
DePeyster, John Watts 173
Desjacques, Marinus 114, 226
DeSmet, Peter 81, 214
DeTournely, Francois-Eleonor 12
Diaries 133
Dillon, James 123
Dirvin, Joseph I. 176
Dobbs Ferry 101
Dolan, Jay P. 74
Donnelly, Terence 179, 182
Donovan, William 108
Doucet, Edward 51, 93, 226
Doughty, Elias 172

Dowling, Edward 249
Doyle, Bishop James ("JKL") 103
Driscol, Michael 44, 94, 127, 217, 227
Dubois, Bishop John 53 55, 58, 64
DuBourg, Bishop Louis 27
Duc de Polignac 17
DuMerle, Henri 6, 49, 91, 227
Dunn, Edward 172
Dutch Reformed Church 149

E

Eccleston, Samuel 56
Edwards Parade 144
Elliott, Marianne 135
Emmitsburg 55, 64, 67
England, John 72
Ennis (Co. Clare) 94
Ernst, Robert 173

F

Fathers of the Faith 105
Feeney, Joseph J. 249
Fenwick, Benedict 127
Férard, Martin 96, 227
Fessard, Michael 221
Fickett, Samuel 174
Fighting 69th 122
Fike, Richard E. 176
Fitzpatrick, Joseph 247
Flaget, Bishop Benedict Joseph 25, 31,
    32, 33, 34, 41, 45, 47, 48, 95, 103
Fleming, David C. 250
Flood, Mary 137
Florissant 25
Fordham 139, 223, 224, 225, 226, 227,
    228, 229, 230, 231, 232, 233, 234,
    235, 237, 238, 239, 241, 242, 243,
    244, 245, 246, 247, 249, 250, 251,
    252, 253
Fordham Manor 149, 172
Fordham Monthly 113, 130, 144
Fordham Prep viii, 147
Fort Hill, N.Y. 136
Fortis, Luigi 18, 24
Fort William 96
Fouché, Simon 36, 97
Frederick, MD 91
Fredericksburgh 122
Freeman Hall 146

Freeman, Thomas 146
Freeman's Journal 68, 86
French, Alvah P. 172
Frias, L. 100, 135
Fribourg 23

G

Gabriels, Henry 170
Gache, Louis-Hipollyte 137
Gache, Louis-Hippolyte 125
Gagnon, Angélique 123
Gandhi 237
Gannon, Elizabeth 117
Gannon, Robert I. 9, 113, 148, 171
Garden River 123
Garraghan, Gilbert J. 133, 220
Garvey, Jeremiah 44, 49, 79
Gatherings 239, 240, 244, 249
Gellhorn, Walter 233
General Congregation XXXII 236
Georgetown 5, 66, 89, 155
Georgian Bay 119
Gesu Parish, Montreal 123
Gettysburg, Battle of 123
Gilbert, Allan S. 171, 175
Gilles, Guy 35, 112
Gilles, Nicholas 43
Gillow, Joseph 133
Gilman, Owen W. 249
Gilmary, John Shea 104, 135
Global Outreach 242
Glover, Thomas James 179, 180,
    181, 184, 186, 217
Gockelen, Bernard 115
Gockeln, William Frederick 3, 44,
    107, 115, 187
Godden, Geoffrey A. 176
Godinot, Nicolas 25
Golding, Stuart D. 173
Grand Act 134
Grand Coteau 40
Graves, James Madison 44, 116
Graves, Jesse 116
Greenawalt, Kent 233
Grist mill 106
Guadalajara 103
Guelph 121, 123
Guiana 8, 45
Guth, Francis 57

H

I

J

K

L

Smith, William Pelletreau 173
Smithsonian Institute 77
Snuff mill 148
Society of the Sacred Heart 13
Somervogel 84, 115, 133
Sonderbund 23
Sopranis, Felix 92,
    210, 211, 212, 213, 214, 220, 221
Southern Boulevard 113
Spalding, Bishop John L. 50
Spalding, Archbishop Martin 37, 38
Spencer, John 62
Spiritual Exercises 127, 131, 223, 228,
    233, 243, 244, 245, 246, 250
Spring Hill College 112, 117
Spuyten Duyvil 140
St. Acheul 16,
    18, 20, 22, 29, 80, 85, 91, 119
St. Boniface College (Calgary) 119
St. Charles Parish 48
St. Francis Xavier Parish and College 5, 7,
    76, 82, 84, 89, 95, 100, 101, 105, 113,
    118, 179, 191, 200, 206, 213, 221
St. Ignatius Literary Institution 65, 78, 83,
    109
St. John's College 5, 8, 53, 55, 59, 63, 65,
    71, 77, 139, 157, 166, 171, 174, 178,
    188, 201, 212
St. John's College Collection 129
St. Joseph's Seminary 100, 158
St. Lawrence O'Toole Church 5, 113, 121
St. Louis University 86
St. Mary's College, Kentucky 9, 50, 78,
    81, 224
St. Mary's College, Montreal 118
St. Mary's, Yonkers 101
St. Vincent of Paul Seminary 57
Staffordshire pottery 161
Stained glass 146
Starrs, William 75, 179, 190
Statham, Thomas 149, 172
Steenwyck, Cornelius 149
Stock, Leo F. 10
Stone, William L. 70
Stonestreet, Charles 8, 193, 197, 201
Stryker-Rodda, Harriet Mott 173
Stuart, Charles 74
Suarez, Francisco 100
Sue, Eugène 17
Sullivan, Virginia Finn 234

T

Taaffe, Thomas Gaffney 74, 133, 148, 170
Taylor, Clifton James 173
Tellier, Remigius 8,
    158, 180182, 186, 205, 209, 217, 220
The Catholic Advocate 103
Thébaud August 8, 77, 80, 86, 88,
    90, 142, 144, 148, 155, 171, 175
Thébaud, Louis Clément 88
Throg's Point 75
Tilton v. Richardson 247
Timon, Bishop John 67
Tissot, Peter 51, 93, 124, 148
Tone, Theobald Wolfe 102
Toronto 127
Trois Riviéres 93
Troy 5, 89, 121
Truth Teller 67

U

United Irishmen 102, 135

V

Vachette, Adrien Maximillian 168
Vachon, Augustin 111
Vachon, Francis 111
Valentine, Alan 174
Van de Velde, Bishop James 127
Vandreuil 110
Vannes 117
Varela, Felix 60
Varin, Joseph 12
Vatican II 229, 241, 249
Vilanis, Felix 60
Vincennes, Ind. 127
Vincentians 67
Vivier, Alexander 29
Volney, Count Constantin 4
Voltaire 11, 15

W

Watson, Alexander 174
Watts, John Jr. 151
Watts, Ridley 173
Watts, Robert 150-153, 158, 173
Webb, Benjamin J. 133
Weiss, Arthur 10
Weiss, Norman R. 171
Welfare Island 124